MW01504100

Rural Education Research in the United States

Gwen C. Nugent · Gina M. Kunz
Susan M. Sheridan · Todd A. Glover
Lisa L. Knoche
Editors

Rural Education Research in the United States

State of the Science and Emerging Directions

 Springer

Editors
Gwen C. Nugent
National Center for Research on Rural
  Education
University of Nebraska-Lincoln
Lincoln, NE
USA

Gina M. Kunz
National Center for Research on Rural
  Education
University of Nebraska-Lincoln
Lincoln, NE
USA

Susan M. Sheridan
National Center for Research on Rural
  Education
University of Nebraska-Lincoln
Lincoln, NE
USA

Todd A. Glover
Rutgers University
Piscataway, NJ
USA

Lisa L. Knoche
National Center for Research on Rural
  Education
University of Nebraska-Lincoln
Lincoln, NE
USA

ISBN 978-3-319-42938-0 ISBN 978-3-319-42940-3 (eBook)
DOI 10.1007/978-3-319-42940-3

Library of Congress Control Number: 2016946942

Printed on acid-free paper

This Springer imprint is published by Springer Nature
The registered company is Springer International Publishing AG Switzerland

Contents

Introduction: Current State of the Science in Rural Education Research

Louis F. Cicchinelli and Andrea D. Beesley

Abstract Public education in the United States must meet the needs of nearly ten million children attending schools in rural communities across the country. This comprises about 20 % of the nation's student population and over 23 % of state expenditures on education. Since the 1990s there has been an increasing emphasis on examining rural education—policy, practice, and student outcomes—in research and in the programs of the U.S. Department of Education. In this chapter we describe the most frequent rural education issues addressed in recent research literature, and propose a research agenda for the next generation of work on rural issues. This book grew out of the 2013 Connect-Inform-Advance rural conference hosted by the National Center for Research Rural Education that was intended to take stock of what is known about rural education, how we have come to know it, and what will be important to learn more about in the coming years. The chapters of this book represent a natural extension of the conference discussion themes of defining and describing rural context and culture in research, examining influences on student outcomes, the use of interdisciplinary research partnerships, and future directions for conducting and disseminating rural education research results.

Keywords Rural education · Education research · Federal role in rural education · Literature review of rural research

L.F. Cicchinelli (✉)
Cicchinelli Consulting Ltd., Parker, CO, USA
e-mail: Louis.cicchinelli@gmail.com

A.D. Beesley
IMPAQ International, Columbia, MD, USA
e-mail: abeesley@impaqint.com

© Springer International Publishing Switzerland 2017
G.C. Nugent et al. (eds.), *Rural Education Research in the United States*,
DOI 10.1007/978-3-319-42940-3_1

1 So You're from a Rural Area

When a new acquaintance tells you they are from a rural area, you probably conjure up a vision of a quaint community, with one or two paved streets and maybe a few dirt roads as well. Certainly a church or two, a school, market, hardware store, diner, and even a gas station and garage. Depending on what part of the country your new friend is from (assuming they are from the United States) you might add in some cows and farms, cattle and ranches, or mines and mountains. Almost certainly the community is small and everyone knows one another and there is a real sense of community, helpfulness, and mutual concern. The nearest larger city is at least a few miles away—too far to travel for work and services on a daily basis.

You may or may not be correct in every case, but what is certain is that you didn't use one of the following three urban-centric definitions to conjure up your vision of rural:

- *Rural fringe*—5 miles or less to an urbanized area,[1] or 2.5 miles or less from an urban cluster.[2]
- *Rural distant*—more than 5 but 25 miles or less from an urbanized area, or more than 2.5 but 10 miles or less from an urban cluster.
- *Rural remote*—more than 25 miles from an urbanized area, and also more than 10 miles from an urban cluster (National Center for Education Statistics 2006).

These are the definitions of rural locations offered by the National Center for Education Statistics (NCES), and they are the ones that education researchers typically use to demonstrate that their study is about rural education and related issues. Even though these descriptions offer clear and widely accepted definitions of rural in the United States, there continues to be considerable debate about whether these urban-based definitions capture the most important characteristics of rural communities and their education systems. Some argue that it may be more informative to include the operational aspects of a community when deciding what is rural and what is not. Characteristics of communities such as population density, availability of services and goods, the condition of basic infrastructure, access to transportation networks, the type of work that residents do, the ways in which residents spend leisure time, and the nature of the tax base may more aptly define what is rural. When it comes to education, factors such as internet connectivity, access to technology, the condition of facilities, the composition of the student population, and stability of the local population may be more closely tied to the quality and effectiveness of rural education systems than overall geographic or population characteristics reflective of place.

---

[1]An urbanized area is defined by NCES as an area that has a central core and adjacent densely settled territory containing at least 50,000 people.

[2]An urban cluster is defined by NCES as an area that has a central core and adjacent densely settled territory containing at between 2500 and 49,000 people.

Rural places do not necessarily remain the same over time. In some locations, the boom-bust cycles associated with the rise and fall of oil, gas, and mineral prices on the world market may quickly and dramatically change the face of a rural community. In others, long-term trends in agribusiness may lead to more gradual population expansion and contraction, or to changing demographics due to an influx of immigrants.

Some scholars and policymakers have argued that the perceived strengths of rural contexts offer unique opportunities to deliver high-quality education for every child; others have argued that the perceived challenges to life posed by rural settings make it difficult to offer a quality education.

2 Why Rural Education Matters

The numbers alone argue for giving rural education a substantial position in the public education dialogue. About 50 % of all school districts are classified as rural and they account for 33 % of the public schools in which over 9.7 million (about 20 %) of this nation's students are educated. Over 23 % of state education expenditures are allocated to rural districts. In fact, in 16 states over one-third of the students are enrolled in rural school districts. The analysis of rural student characteristics also shows that nearly 47 % of these students are living in poverty, 27 % are minority, and nearly 13 % require special education services. These recent statistics indicate a shift in the rural student population toward more students, more diversity, more poverty, and more students with special needs (Johnson et al. 2014). Without question, these changing student demographics together with increased job mobility/transportability and more readily accessible educational resources are likely to change the face of rural education forever. It would seem that the success of rural education has much to do with the long term success of this nation's political and economic future.

3 An Evolving Literature

Historically, education researchers and evaluators have not built their careers on studying the workings of rural education systems and the performance of rural students. Even a cursory overview of the rural education literature reveals a passion among rural educators and researchers for rural communities and the lifestyle they seem to promise. They believe in the opportunities and benefits afforded to families and children in rural America and they have set out to share their beliefs, document the validity of their assertions, and encourage their preservation and replication in communities across the nation.

Although the public education of children in rural communities has been a topic of some discussion in the literature for well over 150 years, DeYoung (1987) pointed out that the focus of education scholarship in the 19th and 20th centuries was predominately on urban environments. He went on to credit Sher's (1977) edited collection, titled *Education in Rural America: A Reassessment of Conventional Wisdom*, with calling attention to the fact that policymakers and researchers had been overlooking rural schools and actually knew very little about what works in rural education. In the early 1980s a number of studies began to establish a benchmark for rural education knowledge and policy and the future direction of research. In general, these efforts sought to establish a rural research agenda by examining the feedback provided by rural educators to surveys and polls. Staff development and support, teacher recruitment and retention, leveraging the strengths of rural schools, financing education in rural communities, and effective practices and programs all emerged as leading contenders for research (Dunne and Carlsen 1982; Helge 1985; Hubel and Barker 1986).

Khattri et al. (1997) reviewed education research literature that examined the extent to which poverty placed rural students at risk for educational failure. While they found the literature to be lacking in general, they also reported that the lack of rigorous research designs using comparison or control groups further limited the conclusions that could be drawn about the relationship between poverty and rural student outcomes. Recognizing the limitations of the formal research literature in addressing rural education issues, Harmon et al. (1996) analyzed nearly 200 doctoral dissertations in view of the topics in the rural agenda developed by the Federal Interagency Committee on Education (FICE Subcommittee) and the U.S. Department of Education. They found that "overall school effectiveness" was the topic most often addressed by dissertations and the use of technology in rural schools was the topic least often studied. Just a few years later, Sherwood (2000) noted that the education literature addressing rural issues was still very limited and that federal support for such investigations had been traditionally minimal. As a result, few scholars were studying rural education issues and that situation was unlikely to change without a shift in federal support for rural research.

Upon reviewing nearly 500 rural education research studies conducted between 1991 and 2003, Arnold et al. (2005) found that about two-thirds of the studies conducted during that period were "rural specific;" that is, they actually focused on examining rural education issues. To illustrate, a study that attempted to answer the question "how does the percentage of teaching assignments filled by highly qualified teachers vary in rural districts across New York State?" constitutes a rural research study, whereas a study that attempts to answer the question "what are the greatest challenges impeding effective education of English Language Learners across the state?" may include data from rural sites but is not rural specific since it addresses an issue relevant to both rural and non-rural jurisdictions. Arnold et al. (2005) also found that 21 % of the studies reviewed used comparative designs, although the quality of even these studies varied considerably. And finally, although the over 100 study topics initially identified were consolidated into a set of 40 topics, this relatively large number of topics still indicated that the rural literature reviewed was diverse in its focus, and rarely offered a substantial, cohesive body of knowledge on any single rural education issue.

As a follow-up to the Arnold et al. (2005) study, Cicchinelli and Barley (2010) reviewed the literature published between 2005 and 2010 to determine if there were changes in the design of rural education research studies or shifts in the topical focus of the rural education literature in response to the various research agendas proposed since the turn of the century. A total of 62 articles were reviewed; again only a subset of the studies focused on uniquely rural issues when the definitions of rural research developed by Coladarci's (2007) were applied. That is, 27 (44 %) of the studies examined were conducted in rural context but did not address a uniquely rural issue, only 4 of the 16 (26 %) of the studies that made rural–non-rural comparisons included rural questions as part of the comparison, and 19 (31 %) of the studies using a non-comparative design had a rural specific. Thus, 23 (37 %) of the 62 studies that surfaced in the search for rural education research addressed rural education issues.

Table 1 provides an overview of the top ten rural education issues addressed in the literature between 1991 and 2010 as identified by Arnold et al. (2005) and Cicchinelli and Barley (2010). While there is considerable overlap in the leading issues addressed in the literature over the two time periods reviewed, there is a definite shift toward research on student academic achievement and teacher preparation and behaviors in literature published from 2005 to 2010.[3]

The previous focus on *students with special needs*, *school safety*, and *instruction* identified by Arnold et al. (2005) was not reflected in the set of studies review by Cicchinelli and Barley (2010). Most certainly the addition of the *curriculum* topic to the top issues studies in the Cicchinelli and Barley (2010) review reflects the growing emphasis on content standards in the United States. The inclusion of the *characteristics of rural schools* and *school-community relationships* topics may be a reflection of the U.S. Department of Education's increased attention to the challenges of rural education, whereas the emerging focus on *teacher and staff characteristics* is likely related to an ongoing need to understand who is attracted to rural setting and characteristics that distinguish effective teachers from non-effective teachers.

The rural research agenda initially introduced by Arnold (2004) was developed in part based on input from a regional Rural Advisory Committee comprised of policymakers, practitioners and researchers. This agenda was subsequently reexamined by Arnold et al. (2005) in view of the more structured literature review conducted, the challenges schools encountered when implementing the provisions of the No Child Left Behind legislation, and the ongoing concerns of rural schools.

---

[3]It is important to note that a single primary focus of the studies review by Arnold et al. (2005) was coded since only the study abstracts were reviewed. In contrast, the full articles were reviewed by Cicchinelli and Barley (2010) and a primary topic as well as secondary topics of focus were coded for each of the 23 articles identified as rural specific. Therefore, it is not possible to merge the two sets of studies reviewed into a single set of rural studies. It is still possible, however, to observe any shifts in the emphasis of the rural literature reviewed during the two time periods reviewed.

Table 1 Overview of the most frequently addressed rural education issues in the 1991–2010 literature

Priority rural research topics				Description of topic	Primary subtopics included
#[a]	Arnold et al. (2005)	#	Cicchinelli and Barley (2010)		
1	Programs and strategies for special needs students			Education services for special needs students in rural schools	Students with disabilities Gifted and talented students At risk students
2	Instruction			The delivery of instruction in core content areas and the use of technology to deliver it in rural settings	Technology based instruction Math Science Reading
3	School safety and discipline			Violence in rural schools and the effectiveness of violence prevention programs	Violence in schools Violence prevention Student discipline
4	Student life and work planning	4	Student life and work planning	Rural student aspirations and the pursuit of post-secondary education and the knowledge and skills students need to succeed in the workplace	Student aspirations Post-secondary education Career education and development
5	Factors influencing academic performance	1	Factors influences academic performance	Comparison of rural and non-rural student performance and the influence of small school size on performance	School locale School size
6	Student attitudes and behaviors			Rural students' views of specific course content areas	Student views about curriculum Student views about instruction
7	Leadership	7	Leadership	Characteristics and responsibilities of rural school administrators	Administrator behavior and characteristics Leadership roles and responsibilities
8	Staff recruitment and retention	10	Staff recruitment and retention	Examination of the circumstances and reasons educators chose to work in rural schools, stay in rural settings, or leave rural environment	Factors influencing retention Educator stress and burnout
9	Teacher preparation and development	2	Teacher preparation and development	Examination of the continuum of teacher training from teacher preparation to in-service	Influence of professional development on practice

(continued)

Table 1 (continued)

Priority rural research topics				Description of topic	Primary subtopics included
#[a]	Arnold et al. (2005)	#	Cicchinelli and Barley (2010)		
10	Teachers' beliefs and practices	8	Teachers' beliefs and practices	Comparisons of rural and non-rural teacher beliefs about classroom practices	Classroom techniques and practices Reading programs and strategies
		3	Characteristics of rural schools	Descriptive or comparative analysis of the attributes of rural schools	School size Grade configuration Course scheduling Multiage grouping
		5	Curriculum	Descriptive or comparative analyses of rural curricula	Reading programs Advanced Placement programs Physical education Agricultural education Locally relevant curriculum
		6	Teacher and staff characteristics	Descriptive or comparative analysis of rural teacher and staff characteristics and practices	Teacher experience Classroom practices Characteristics of support staff
		9	Schools and community relationships	Examination of the communication and interactions between rural schools and local communities	Patterns of parent and family engagement School-community educational partnerships

[a]#s reflect the level of priority for each topic as determined by authors of the two review articles

This study confirmed that the original research agenda could serve as viable guide for future research. In fact, the list of nine priority topics outlined bears a remarkable similarity to agendas cited nearly 20 years earlier (e.g., Helge 1985), and continues to be aligned with the priority rural research topics identified in the literature (see Table 1). In order to provide a single comprehensive agenda to guide future rural research that also reflects the priority areas identified in the literature reviewed from 1991 through 2010, we have organized the agenda originally put forth by Arnold (2004) into the seven agenda items shown in Table 2. While some of these items have been studied frequently in the rural research literature, they remain on the list because the quality of the rural research published to date has received mixed reviews.

Table 2 Proposed rural research agenda

Agenda item	Description of item	Sample research questions
Opportunity to learn	Policy and practice investigations about how rural schools and districts assure all students have equal access to a quality education	To what extent and under what circumstances are advanced courses available to all rural students? Do advanced courses affect the overall achievement of rural students?
School size and student achievement	Analyses of the relationship between rural school size and organization and student performance	In what ways, if any, does school size affect student outcomes? Do small classroom size and low student-teacher ratios improve student performance? What is the impact of consolidating small rural schools on opportunity to learn and student outcomes?
Assuring and maintaining teacher and administrator quality	Analyses of the effectiveness of rural school policy and practice related to developing, recruiting, and retaining high-quality teachers and administrators	What teacher and staff retention strategies are most effective in rural schools? To what extent does technology increase access to professional development opportunities? What strategies strengthen the pipeline of new teachers to rural areas? What state and local policies help attract and keep teachers in rural places?
School and district capacity to function effectively	Examination of the ways rural schools and districts develop or access the capacity to create/adapt and implement curriculum and benchmark assessments, and assess their overall effectiveness	How do rural schools develop a K-12 curriculum? How are student assessments selected and administered? How are educational programs and classroom practices assessed in rural schools? How can rural schools and districts build the capacity to use their data effectively?
School finance	Examination of school budgets and the allocation of funds to various essential functions	How can rural schools increase efficiency without a negative impact on student performance? How do rural schools finance special needs educational programs and staff expenses?
Local control and school choice	What governance and decision making structures are in place and how effective they are in	What types of local control are exhibited in rural communities, and how do they relate to student outcomes?

(continued)

Table 2 (continued)

Agenda item	Description of item	Sample research questions
	providing a quality education in rural settings	What options for providing school choice exist in rural communities?
Community and parent expectations	Examination of community and parent expectations of rural schools and parent and student aspirations for the future	How do parents and community leaders think about factors influencing student achievement? How can schools support community development?

Source Adapted from Arnold (2004) and Arnold et al. (2005)

Overall, the nature of rural research and literature over the last few decades can be characterized as a sparse body of strong rural research studies in which only about 20 % of the studies employ comparative designs and two-thirds of the studies actually address rural specific issues. The entire set of literature includes only a handful of review and synthesis papers.

4 Challenges of Conducting Rural Research

Given the relatively small size of schools in rural communities, it is often difficult to maintain the confidentiality of individual participants' perceptions or achievement levels, since the performance or views of some individuals are often easily identifiable by community members. Investigations in rural settings that attempt to target specific segments of the student or teacher population, or a specific ethnic group, are especially susceptible to this challenge to confidentiality due to the relatively small number of participants available for inclusion in these subgroups. And when these small study samples are distributed across a number of grade levels, subject areas, or classrooms, the result is often very small cell sizes. Finally, an issue related to the small cell sizes often generated in rural studies is the increased impact of incomplete or missing data and inadequate levels of statistical power in the study design which restricts researchers' ability to attain conclusive findings.

The existence of control or comparison groups are often non-existent, leaving researchers with only the option of conducting descriptive studies, which are considered to be less rigorous and definitive in the conclusions that can be drawn.

The geographic isolation of rural schools and districts is certainly a factor to be considered in designing rural research studies. Access to these often remote locations consumes both time and money at an alarming rate. Further, the commitment of time from local staff is often difficult to obtain and maintain given the multiple roles a single rural administrator or teacher is likely to fulfill.

5 Federal Support for Education Reform

The limited local financial resources available for rural education and rural research often restrict the scale and scope of the services that can be provided, the complexity of the research questions that can be examined, and methodologies that can be used. The level of state funding directed toward the rural education sector is typically only a small portion of the available local funding. Given that local and state funding targeting the needs of rural schools is generally inadequate to support rural research initiatives, it is not surprising that local jurisdictions have turned to the federal government, and the U.S. Department of Education in particular, for additional financial support for rural education and rural research as a focus of federal education initiatives.

Although the first National Research Center on Rural Education Support was funded in 2004, federal attention to rural education issues has increased considerably since then. Secretary Duncan directed considerable effort toward learning more about the successes and shortcomings of educating this nation's children, especially who live in rural communities. During his tenure, Secretary Duncan visited numerous rural schools and classrooms across the nation, including those on the American Indian reservations in the nation's western plains states. A Deputy Assistant Secretary for Rural Outreach was also appointed for the first time during Duncan's tenure. The charge to this position has been to foster improvement in rural education through the identification and dissemination of exemplary interventions that might be made more visible and applied in other rural jurisdictions. This focus on disseminating exemplary interventions throughout rural schools increased the demand for rigorous research and evaluation studies that can help practitioners select the most appropriate and effective programs for implementation in their schools and districts. In a further show of support for rural America, in 2011 President Obama established the White House Rural Council to assist with job creation and economic development in rural communities by increasing the flow of capital to these areas (Obama 2011). The Council, comprised of the executive branch department heads and chaired by the Secretary of Agriculture, was charged with coordinating federal engagement with rural stakeholders to strengthen rural communities. In recent years, the Chief State School Officers from rural states such as Alabama, Alaska, Montana, South Dakota, North Dakota, and Vermont have convened annually, in collaboration with federal representative of the U.S. Department of Education, to discuss common rural education concerns, and to share policy and practice solutions that have been successfully (and unsuccessfully) implemented. Research and evaluation should be at the core of this group's deliberations about which programs are successful in which contexts and under what circumstances.

While the increased attention on rural education in America has brought attention of the general public, the education community, and researchers alike to the challenges of education the nation's children in rural settings, it does not directly influence the level of funding available for rural research, and therefore the quality and amount of rural education research conducted.

In support of the reauthorization of the Elementary and Secondary Education Act (ESEA) in 2010, the Obama administration outlined a blueprint for education reform, complete with specified funding streams (Office of Planning, Evaluation and Policy Development, March 2010a). President Barack Obama declared that "by 2020, America will once again have the highest proportion of college graduates in the world" (Obama 2009). The ESEA Blueprint for Reform includes six reform priorities: ensuring that all students are college- and career-ready; developing a workforce of effective teachers and leaders and ensuring the equitable distribution of great teachers and great leaders across the nation; meeting the needs of diverse learners and historically underserved groups (including rural students); making available to all students a complete, well-rounded education; promoting the success, safety, and health of students; and fostering innovation and excellence throughout the education enterprise. While this Blueprint did chart a course of education reform and therefore an agenda for future research in priority areas that are reflected in research program announcements and the requirements of the various centers and laboratories funded by the U.S. Department of Education, it still did not clearly target the education needs of rural communities, students, and educators.

It was a few months after the release of the Blueprint for Reform that the renewed commitment to public education was accompanied by an explicit proposal for supporting rural schools. Secretary Duncan stated that "rural schools have unique challenges and benefits, and we value the input of rural school leaders as we work together to improve education for all children" (Office of Planning, Evaluation and Policy Development, July 2010b). Dedicated formula funding was continued through the Rural Education Achievement Program to ensure that rural districts received additional funds to support their schools and other formula programs that serve disadvantaged student groups (e.g., students with disabilities, English learners, American Indian students). Funds were allocated to improving the teaching corps in rural and other high needs schools, and policy changes made it possible for rural teachers to teach multiple subjects. More choice was given to underperforming rural schools regarding the selection of research-based interventions and turnaround options. And finally, the Blueprint for Reform encouraged the use of technology for improving instruction and delivering content in rural settings; the development of school and community collaborations to foster student success, safety, and health; and adoption of more autonomous, innovative rural school models.

6   The Impetus for This Book

The 2013 Connect-Inform-Advance rural conference hosted by the National Center for Research on Rural Education, with its numerous content-rich presentations and thought-provoking roundtable discussions among educators, researchers and policymakers provided the motivation to write this book. Its purpose is to articulate essential directions for research in order to enhance the rural educational experience and maximize achievement for rural students. The overall goals of compiling this book are to (1) enhance empirical and scientific understandings of variables' and contexts that influence rural student academic success; (2) advance a rural research agenda; and (3) explore needs, opportunities, and realities associated with connecting rural research with practice and policy. The book features the presentations from the conference, supplemented with chapters that focus on the themes that emerged from the small group discussion groups. Two major topics are addressed in the pages that follow. First, the process of conducting research in rural areas and methodological issues are examined. Second, the current research on teacher, family and community influences on rural student academic achievements is presented and supported by new research by leading rural scholars.

In Chapter "Multidisciplinary Perspectives to Advance Rural Education Research", Nugent, Kunz, Sheridan, Hellwege, and O'Connor highlight the four discussion themes that emerged during the *Connect-Inform-Advance Conference* sponsored by the National Center for Research in Rural Education which sets the stage for this book. The themes of defining and describing rural context and culture in research, examining influences on student outcomes, the use of interdisciplinary research partnerships, future directions for conducting and disseminating rural education research results. These themes are the natural extension of ongoing conversations in the rural research literature and support observation that new ways of defining rural and conducting quality rural research that focuses on outcomes for students.

The authors charged with exploring the process of conducting research on rural education have chosen a particular research issue to discuss. In Chapter "Defining and Communicating Rural", Hawley, Koziol, and Bovaird focus on the persistent challenge of defining rural in ways that recognize the uniqueness of rural communities and their residents. In Chapter "Partnership-Based Approaches in Rural Education Research", Kunz, Buffington, Green, Mahaffey, and Widner discuss the value of and challenges associated with involving a multidisciplinary set of partners in rural research initiatives. In Chapter "Recruiting Rural Schools for Education Research: Challenges and Strategies", Autio and Deussen provide insights and examples of successful recruitment of rural schools in prior research projects. Without effectively addressing this thorny issue it is likely that rural schools will continue to be underrepresented in education research. In Chapter "Methodology Challenges and Cutting Edge Designs for Rural Education Research", Bovaird discusses how rural researchers need to overcome the limitations present in rural settings (e.g., small sample sizes, challenges to confidentiality, lack of statistical power) to rigorous research design through the use of statistically modeling, quasi-experimental designs, and efficient measurement paradigms.

Authors charged with discussing teacher and school influences on rural student academic achievement discuss a unique instructional strategy or program that has been shown to have promise of success in rural settings with rural students. In Chapter "The Effectiveness of E-Coaching in Rural Science Classrooms", Nugent, Kunz, Houston, Kalutskaya and Pedersen discuss the results of delivering the professional development for Coaching Science Inquiry to rural science teachers using both a face to face training institute in combination with e-coaching. In Chapter "Accelerating the Mathematical Development of Young Navajo Children", Sorensen and Price present the results of their initiate to enhance mathematical development in preschool Navajo students. The initiative relied on a long-term collaborative relationship between practice and research to realize positive student outcomes. In Chapter "Investigating Teacher Professional Development with Distance Coaching to Promote" Glover, Ihlo, and Wu discuss the use of distance coaching to assist teachers in adapting Response to Intervention concepts in the implementation of an early readers program in rural schools. In Chapter "Rural Language and Literacy Connections: An Integrated Approach to Supporting Low-Income Preschool Children's Language and Literacy Development", Knoche and Davis also focus on language and literacy development in preschool children and discuss the outcomes of the program on classrooms, teachers, and children.

Each author charged with discussing family and community influences on rural student academic achievement focuses their attention a unique engagement strategy or program that has promise for successfully affecting outcomes to rural students. In Chapter "Rural Parenting: Cumulative Risk and Parenting Process", Mokrova, Vernon-Feagans, and Garrett-Peters explore the relationship between family stress, parenting interactions and child outcomes in impoverished rural communities. In Chapter "The Effects of Rurality on Parents' Engagement in Children's Early Literacy", Clarke, Koziol, and Sheridan discuss the findings of a study of the effects of rurality on parent engagement and children's literacy in rural communities. In Chapter "Improving Education Outcomes for American Indian Children: Community and Family Influences on Rural Student Academic Success", Gebhardt and Pfannenstiel describe a use of home visiting model as a strategy for helping American Indian families influence educational outcomes at the earliest possible stages of child development. In Chapter "Family-School Partnerships in Rural Communities: Benefits, Exemplars, and Future Research", Sheridan, Kunz, Holmes, and Witte examine the utility and impact of the implementing the *Teachers and Parents as Partners* program in rural communities.

Many of the chapter authors have suggested future directions and agendas that will advance the field of rural research. In the final chapter, Sheridan and Beesley draw on the individual chapters to provide an integrated and coherent view of the guidance provided by each author, and highlight the essential elements of a path forward for rural researchers, policymakers, and practitioners.

We trust that idea, innovations, and outcomes for rural education and students presented the following pages will stimulate and advance your thinking about rural education and rural research, as well as reinvigorate your passion for the continued improvement of rural education and success of rural students.

References

Arnold, M. L. (2004). *Guiding rural schools and districts: A research agenda*. Aurora, CO: Mid-continent Research for Education and Learning.

Arnold, M. L., Newman, J. H., Gaddy, B. B., & Dean, C. G. (2005). A look at the condition of rural education research: Setting a direction for future research. *Journal of Research in Rural Education, 20*(6). Retrieved from http://www.umaine.edu/jrre/20-6.pdf.

Cicchinelli, L. F., & Barley, Z. A. (2010). *A review of current rural education research: Are we making progress?* Paper presented at the American Educational Research Association annual conference, Denver, CO.

Coladarci, T. (2007). Improving the yield of rural education research: An editor's swan song. *Journal of Research in Rural Education, 22*(3), 1–9.

DeYoung, A. J. (1987). The status of American rural education research: An integrated review and commentary. *Review of Educational Research, 57*, 123–148.

Dunne, F., & Carlsen, W. (1982). *Small rural schools in the United States: A statistical profile*. Washington, DC: The National Rural Center.

Harmon, H. L., Howley, C. B., & Sanders, J. R. (1996). Doctoral research in rural education and the rural R&D menu. *Journal of Research in Rural Education, 12*, 68–75.

Helge, D. (1985). *Establishing a national rural education research agenda*. Bellingham, WA: National Rural Development Institute.

Hubel, K., & Barker, B. (1986). *Rural education association research agenda report*. Fort Collins, CO: Colorado State University.

Johnson, J., Showalter, D., Klein, R., & Lester, C. (2014). *Why rural matters 2013–2014: The condition of rural education in the 50 states*. Washington, DC: Rural School and Community Trust.

Khattri, N., Riley, K. W., & Kane, M. B. (1997). Students at risk in poor, rural areas: A review of research. *Journal of Research in Rural Education, 13*(2), 79–100.

National Center for Education Statistics. (2006). *The condition of education*. Washington, DC: U. S. Department of Education.

Obama, B. (2009). *Address by the President to the joint session of congress*. Washington, DC: The White House, Office of the Press Secretary.

Obama, B. (2011). *Executive order: Establishment of the White House Rural Council*. Washington, DC: The White House, Office of the Press Secretary.

Office of Planning, Evaluation and Policy Development. (2010a). *A blueprint for reform: The reauthorization of the elementary and secondary education act*. Washington, DC: U.S. Department of Education.

Office of Planning, Evaluation and Policy Development. (2010b). *Supporting rural education: The reauthorization of the elementary and secondary education act*. Washington, DC: U.S. Department of Education.

Sher, J. (Ed.). (1977). *Education in rural America: A reassessment of conventional wisdom*. Boulder, CO: Westview.

Sherwood, T. (2000). Where has all the "rural" gone? Rural education research and current federal reform. *Journal of Research in Rural Education, 16*(3), 159–167.

Multidisciplinary Perspectives to Advance Rural Education Research

Gwen C. Nugent, Gina M. Kunz, Susan M. Sheridan, Mary Hellwege and Maureen O'Connor

Abstract This chapter focuses on perspectives and recommendations of rural education researchers, practitioners, and policy makers about the critical role of research in rural education, the current condition of rural education research, and future directions. These perspectives were obtained from focused discussions of participants attending *Connect-Inform-Advance*, a National Conference on Rural Education Research held in April 2013 and sponsored by the National Center for Research on Rural Education. In order to capture the depth of these discussions, extensive notes were taken and analyzed qualitatively to glean insight into key considerations for future rural education research agendas. Results from the analysis resulted in four major themes: (a) defining and accounting for the rural context and culture, (b) identifying rural influences on student outcomes, (c) engaging in interdisciplinary and multidirectional research partnerships, and (d) disseminating rural research results and determining future targets.

Keywords Rural context · Rural partnerships · Rural research dissemination · Rural definitions · Rural student academic outcomes

Approximately 50 % of school districts in the United States are classified as rural (Johnson et al. 2014). As the demography of rural communities continues to change, research on this segment of our educational landscape must take into consideration its unique characteristics and pivotal concerns. There have been a series of syntheses of rural education research, each with recommendations for

G.C. Nugent · G.M. Kunz · S.M. Sheridan · M. Hellwege
National Center for Research on Rural Education, Nebraska Center for Research on Children, Youth, Families and Schools, University of Nebraska—Lincoln, Lincoln, NE, USA

G.C. Nugent (✉) · G.M. Kunz · S.M. Sheridan
Nebraska Center for Research on Children, Youth, Families and Schools, University of Nebraska—Lincoln, 216 Mabel Lee Hall, Lincoln, NE 68588-0235, USA
e-mail: gnugent@unl.edu

M. O'Connor
John Hopkins University School of Medicine, Baltimore, MD, USA

© Springer International Publishing Switzerland 2017   15
G.C. Nugent et al. (eds.), *Rural Education Research in the United States*,
DOI 10.1007/978-3-319-42940-3_2

future research directions (Arnold et al. 2005; Cicchinelli 2011). Arnold et al. concluded that there was no topical area appearing in the rural education literature that had a sufficient body of research for policy makers and practitioners to make informed decisions about the success of any given intervention. He also cited earlier research (Arnold 2004) which showed that the top three research topics for rural school improvement were opportunity to learn, school size and school achievement, and teacher quality. Cicchinelli's work suggested that future research should use longitudinal state and national data sets to better define pressing needs and policy. He also emphasized the importance of research that would (a) promote better quality teachers and instruction and (b) study the effectiveness of school and district leadership. Additional perspective comes from Coladarci's (2007) paper written upon leaving his position as editor of the *Journal of Research in Rural Education.* His comments focused on methodological and substantive shortcomings of rural education research. Also addressed were future directions for overcoming such limitations, including a challenge to rural researchers to explicitly establish the relevance of rural to their research questions.

These early reviews are presented from a *researcher* perspective; however, it is clear that the perspectives of practitioners and policy makers must be considered in setting research agendas. Their recommendations about current and future needs in rural education research are essential to represent a broader perspective. Such a perspective was reinforced during discussions of participants attending *Connect-Inform-Advance,* the National Conference on Rural Education Research (National Center for Research on Rural Education, April, 2013). By engaging national *researchers, practitioners, and policy makers* in focused discussion about current and future needs in rural education research, the conference provided a platform for exploring the critical role of research in rural education, the current condition of rural education research, and future directions.

The purposes of the conference included engaging national researchers, practitioners, policy makers, trainers, and leaders in constructive dialogue about current and future rural education research, communicating current rural education research findings, and exploring methods by which research findings can be translated and transmitted to rural practice and policy. In order to capture the depth of the discussions at the conference, notes taken during these guided discussions were analyzed to glean insight into key considerations for future rural education research agendas, including how to more effectively translate research into practice and policy.

The conference included presentations organized around three sources that influence rural student academic success: teachers, communities and families, and school context. Teacher influences explored the impact of targeted professional development experiences as well as the differences in professional development experiences for teachers in rural, urban, and suburban areas. Community and family influences explored the impact that community resources and parent involvement can make in rural student academic success. Specific presentations focused on the utility and efficacy of parent-teacher partnerships in rural settings, the mediating effects of parent engagement on the relationship between rurality and young children's reading development, and community and family influences on American

Indian children's school readiness. The third source, school and contextual influences, included a presentation about combining empirically validated curricula with an innovative cultural approach to rural education, a descriptive study of differences in academic performance based on location and access to certain resources, and a discussion of methodological considerations that impact rural education research. After each set of influences were explored, conference participants took part in facilitated discussions. Discussion questions were designed to spur fruitful dialogue of current work in rural education research related to the conference themes and future directions for rural education research (see "Appendix" for a full list of questions). Analysis of the facilitated discussions offers insight into the current perceptions of rural education research by practitioners, policy makers, and researchers and provides future directions for the rural education research agenda based on this broad, multidisciplinary perspective.

1 Method

1.1 Participants

Participants included 156 conference attendees from 19 states throughout the U.S. Participants represented a diverse range of professional perspectives related to rural education (see Fig. 1).

1.2 Data Collection and Analysis

The conference was organized around the three themes of interrelated influences and their impacts on rural school performance: (a) teaching, (b) family/community, and (c) school context. Research presentations addressing these three topic areas laid the foundations for the breakout roundtable discussions that were led by designated facilitators who had been invited prior to the conference to lead the

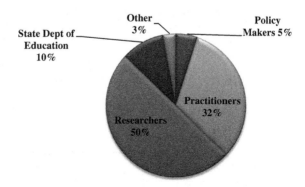

Fig. 1 Percent of conference participants representing different professional perspectives

discussions. The facilitators were conference participants who represented various perspectives and who could stimulate productive conversations. The discussions for each topic area centered on the guiding questions prepared in advance and distributed to table discussion facilitators (see "Appendix"). Extensive notes of the discussions at each table were taken by either graduate research assistants or volunteer conference attendees. In all, 28 discussions were held across the three topic areas, and 46 pages of single-spaced notes were generated to capture these discussions. Notes from discussions contained mostly bulleted summaries of information but also included some participant quotes. These notes formed the basis of the qualitative content analysis.

We chose a general, inductive qualitative approach for educational research to understand the participants' perspectives related to the conference themes (Creswell 2012; Hatch 2002). Data analysis was conducted using qualitative research software MAXQDA to help codify and organize the roundtable discussion notes into major themes and ideas. Specifically, two graduate research assistants used inductive reasoning to independently identify code labels that captured the meaning of the recorded statements. Through research team meetings, a shared code list of eight overarching categories was developed by refining the initial code labels. These eight overarching categories were: connection of policy to practice, connection of research to practice, context, organizational structure, partnership, research, student outcomes and training. After these categories were identified, the research team looked for interrelationships and overlapping ideas among the categories to synthesize the data into major themes, as suggested by Bazeley (2013) and Saldana (2013).

2 Results

Analysis revealed four major themes in conference discussions: (a) defining and accounting for the rural context and culture in research, (b) identifying rural influences on student outcomes, (c) engaging in interdisciplinary and multidirectional research partnerships, and (d) disseminating rural research results and determining future targets. These themes emerged over the course of the 2-day conference and across the conference topic areas (i.e., teacher, family/community, and school context influences on rural student academic success).

2.1 Defining and Accounting for the Rural Context and Culture

The lack of a consistent definition of "rural" was a recurring theme throughout discussions. Specifically, participants commented that it can be difficult to capture a unified definition of rurality. Since the rural context is considered a defining variable in conducting research in rural communities, the need for meaningful, relevant criteria for the rural designation is critical.

Beyond specific rural definitional criteria, however, there is also the need to more carefully identify contextual variables that could influence educational experiences in rural settings. As one participant stated, "Rural communities have special contexts, and research needs to be done to highlight the contexts so we can bring light to them." Another urged, "What we are saying is look deeply at our place. We are not saying this is exactly going to be what your place is. But after looking at your place deeply, we might compare and see some commonality." Participants acknowledged that there are contextual factors that define rural schools/communities outside of those typically reported (i.e., free and reduced lunch, etc.) that can help with understanding rural communities and the differences among them. These factors—such as cultural diversity, distance traveled to school, increase in commuter residents, access to technology, and economic affluence and stability—may have a unique impact on the educational experience of students attending rural schools. Consolidation was also mentioned as a critical factor, as it impacts the role of community in the school and can lead to a loss of identity and culture. For example, the distance traveled by students to attend school, and thus the distance parents must travel in order to participate in conferences or other school activities can influence the "connection" between families and school. Participants acknowledged that identifying and defining these factors can be difficult. As such, they suggested that it is important to determine which factors are context relevant and should be accounted for in research and which are context independent. Participants also suggested that identifying and understanding these contextual influences will help researchers understand the local culture, which is important to gaining trust, accessibility, and sustainability for researchers.

Some participants stated it is important to consider the commonalities that exist among rural communities and between urban and rural communities. By focusing on common characteristics of rural schools, researchers could explore broader research objectives so that they can focus on similar issues that can then be translated to the local context. Participants also commented that presentation of contextual variables in research reports would help practitioners and policy makers assess the relevance for their local situation.

2.2 Identifying Rural Influences on Student Outcomes

Participants identified several factors that are important to consider when examining rural student outcomes. First, an overarching concern was a lack of a unified definition of and methods for measuring student success. Participants pointed out that the differences in rural student outcomes may not be captured because we may not be measuring "right" things or measuring them in ways that make sense. Several participants suggested that standardized testing is insufficient for capturing the breadth of student success. As one participant mentioned, "What we consider success is probably broader than achievement." Others mentioned that having a broader meaning of the important outcomes may shed light on different ways to solve problems. For example, it was suggested to consider outcomes such as critical thinking and engagement.

Second, participants wondered what factors influence these outcomes and how they can be captured in research. Suggestions were made to more deeply explore the nature of achievement outcomes by looking at mediators and moderators that are affecting the outcomes. Participants discussed that there are a myriad of influences (e.g., student engagement in the classroom, community support, parent involvement, and educational experiences) on rural student success that are not traditionally considered in research but need to be examined in future studies. Described as "inner relationships," these factors were recognized as complex and potentially interacting in their influence.

Third, participants discussed the role distance education can have in rural education. Some felt that distance education provided opportunities to advance student achievement and provide unique opportunities, but others felt it could provide a threat to some schools. One participant asserted, "If someone would come in and open up an online school, our enrollment would be halved." Also mentioned was the isolation of online classes, asserting that online classes are "pretty lonely" with limited sharing and meeting with classmates. The conclusion was that a completely online program might not work because of the lack of interpersonal communication and the opportunity to develop in-person social skills.

Lastly, although professional development opportunities for rural teachers were seen as pivotal to rural student success, many barriers to participation in such training were cited, including cost, distance to be traveled, or technology required to attend virtually. One participant commented that college teacher training should also be examined: "In higher education, we complain about the quality of the students coming into college. We don't realize that we are part of the problem because we train the teachers who taught them, so in a sense we train those students." The need for follow-up to research interventions and rural teacher professional development was also brought up as key to improving student success. Coaching was mentioned as a promising strategy to ensure that the knowledge gained is applied to their teaching, sustained over time, and used to improve student outcomes. Another suggestion to improve rural student performance was training teachers on how to use data to make instructional decisions.

2.3 Engaging Interdisciplinary and Multidirectional Research Partnerships

Overall, participants identified that multidirectional partnership among research, practice, and policy will help accomplish a translational agenda that comes from a meaningful, ongoing dialogue among multiple stakeholders. Participants noted that "Researchers need to be available to help those who would like to implement the research." Others discouraged "parachute" research where data are gathered and researchers are not heard from again. They suggested that building partnerships would promote more acceptance and investment in the research process by the community. Furthermore, it was mentioned that building a bi-directional relationship could also help reduce the fear that research results would present a negative picture of educational quality.

One group of participants summarized, "The foundation of rural research is building relationships, building capacities, and creating meaningful opportunities." Collaborations and partnerships need to be developed among various educational stakeholders such as local educational agencies, educational service units, state agencies, higher education, local school boards, families, communities, researchers, and policy makers. Participants also indicated that funding agencies could benefit by participating in these partnerships.

Research partnerships were viewed as providing a platform for more informed decision-making for policies and educational interventions. One participant noted that "It is important to get input about what needs to be studied; stakeholders should drive the topics of research." Another stated that researchers should "get schools to invest in research prior to beginning projects in order to design projects that schools want." Also discussed was the need for research to inform policy makers so that they make informed decisions about educational policy while assessing past initiatives. Furthermore, participants mentioned that school boards can use data from research not only to make decisions but also to engage in data-driven strategic planning.

Participants expressed a desire to advance the research agenda through continuing the dialogue that was started at the conference and to build "more authentic partnerships" among educational stakeholders. They recommended that systems of communication should be developed to promote a continuous dialogue among the different stakeholders. This ongoing dialogue and relationship was seen as key to "marry research and practice so that they understand each other." Developing ways to effectively maintain communication and insure sustainability was seen as a critical, but challenging, step. Participants suggested that responsibilities to each other should be defined. Ultimately, these partnerships were seen as a way to "elevate the status of research in the community" in such a way as to promote the application of research to educational practice and policy.

2.4 Disseminating Rural Research Results and Determining Future Targets

Participants consistently commented that rural education research must identify efficient and effective means for ensuring that rural practitioners and other consumers responsible for implementing educational programs have access to research findings. One discussion group noted, "Teachers are incredibly hungry for what works." Participants commented that it can be frustrating if results are hard to find or delayed in their publication: "The results don't come out until years later. We want the results now, not after the kids are gone." They suggested that after research is concluded, the researchers should communicate the results to the participating schools so they can know the impact of the programs on student outcomes.

Participants noted that research results should be communicated in a user-friendly and easily consumable format (e.g., video/modeling examples, focus on outcomes) that emphasizes how the research is effective so that results can be translated into meaningful, understandable discussions that practitioners can apply to their local situations. In addition to sharing results, participants also commented that they needed to have an idea of the resources necessary to support and implement the researched interventions so that they can be effective in their implementation. As one group suggested, "You have to empower the schools with the knowledge and data to make decisions." Technology was mentioned as a powerful platform to help share the results given its searchable online websites or databases. Newsletters to teachers were also seen as a viable option.

Participants addressed the need for a comprehensive research agenda using multiple rigorous methodologies to advance the field of rural education research. According to one participant, rural education researchers need to "develop methodologies that will allow us to capture the unique factors of rural communities instead of excluding them from designs/research projects."

Throughout the discussions, specific suggestions for future rural education research were provided. Participants urged that research critically evaluate existing issues in rural education, such as staff turnover and how rural teachers need to allocate their time to fulfill multiple roles. Participants also suggested targeted evaluation of the *sustained* impact of teacher professional development experiences. Longitudinal research was suggested to explore the long-term impact of educational interventions. Participants stressed the need to move away from a deficit model to build upon existing strengths. Community-related variables, such as service-learning opportunities, social services availability, generational influences, family involvement and the "big picture of community" were discussed as pivotal considerations for future research. Overall, participants echoed what one of the panelists shared, "Research validates the good things we're already doing. It's important to remind folks that there are a lot of things we already know how to do and do well. Confirmatory research is really helpful as opposed to big city researchers coming in and saying 'that's all wrong, this is how to do it.'"

3   Discussion

The results of this study shed light on future approaches to rural education research and extend and complement earlier comprehensive reviews provided by rural researchers. As did earlier authors Arnold et al. (2005) and Cicchinelli (2011), this study provides recommendations of priority areas for future research. For example, this research supports previously identified areas such as teacher professional development and community influences. This study also focused on key methodological considerations, addressing some of the concerns raised by Coladarci (2007) regarding the lack of rigor in existing rural research. For example, this research identified the need for longitudinal research to focus on sustainability and long-term effects on teachers and students, as well as the use of multiple rigorous methodologies.

One key theme from the conference discussions was the importance of capturing and accounting for the rural context and culture and the lack of a consistent definition of "rural"—a shortcoming that has been noted by others. Coladarci (2007) argued, for example, that without a consistent definition, it is imperative that researchers describe the context of their research in detail. One panelist during the conference urged researchers to clearly identify contextual variables arising from their research that could provide direction for future explorations. These variables may not have been an initial research focus but arise out of the researchers' direct experience with the target audience and setting. While this reporting may be at the qualitative and descriptive level, it provides a starting point for rural education research to document meaningful contextual variables—variables that go beyond traditional population figures, geographic location, and locale codes. These unique rural characteristics can form the basis for urban-rural comparisons, but also comparisons *between* rural populations. By providing a clear definition and categorization of these contextual factors, research could also aid in providing comparison and contrast points between rural contexts. Such comparisons can, for example, lead to better understanding of why one instructional or organizational approach (e.g. coaching or family-school partnerships) is more suited to a particular rural context than to another. It is only through such documentation that we can begin to understand the nuances of rural education and its unique characteristics and underlying mechanisms that mediate and moderate outcomes. Such understanding can also facilitate researcher-school partnerships. Conference participants suggested that understanding rural culture is important for gaining access, trust, and sustainability.

Conference participants also identified the importance of defining rural student academic success broadly—going beyond a focus on achievement and standardized tests. This result is consistent with those found in earlier studies (Arnold et al. 2005), showing that instruction was a recurring topic in rural education research, as was student life and work planning. The Arnold study went on to identify student achievement, and organizational structures of rural schools that could support achievement, as a priority area for future research. Cicchinelli's (2011) update of the Arnold et al. study suggested that rural research has shifted from an emphasis on instructional programs to an outcome focus, examining factors influencing student achievement, attitudes and behavior. Teacher professional development, another topic of prominence in the conference, was seen as a critical influence.

The National Conference on Rural Education Research, *Connect-Inform-Advance,* was organized to include representatives from educational research, policy and practice in discussions about rural education research, and conference participants emphasized the need for interdisciplinary partnerships among these three constituencies. This theme, not explicitly articulated in previous research reviews, was seen as providing a critical foundation to achieve a translational research agenda. Partnership discussions were far reaching and touched upon elements of rural context, student outcomes, and future directions. Conference attendees emphasized the need for input from stakeholders (e.g., policy makers, practitioners, families, communities) in determining research agendas and defining research questions. This multi-directional dialogue was seen as the ideal way to develop a meaningful research agenda and better insure that research findings get infused into practice. These collaborative relationships may help to address some of the definitional issues identified by participants. Working together, all parties can determine how to define student outcomes and rurality, as well as account for the unique context of rural communities. These partnerships can help insure follow-up to ensure lasting improvement for teacher practice and student success outcomes, as well as needed funding priorities. These partnerships could also provide a built-in opportunity for dissemination and input on how to communicate findings so that they are easily transferable to practice and can empower schools to improve teacher quality and student outcomes.

This need to get research results into the hands of practitioners more quickly and in a user-friendly format was a common topic running throughout the discussion. One rural practitioner provided a clear example of the issue. She commented that she could not understand the research document provided to her prior to the conference because the terms and acronyms were unfamiliar. Communicating the results in ways that the various stakeholders can understand is a critical step in the dissemination process. The field needs to consider how this process can best be accomplished, considering such factors as new and existing delivery methods (web, social media, print), target audiences and their go-to information sources, and utility (timeliness and readability).

In conclusion, future rural education research needs to honor the unique characteristics of the rural context and culture while looking for common factors among different types of communities. Research questions need to better address the needs and characteristics of rural education to better serve students, teachers, and administrators in rural communities. These ideas, as well as the four major findings that emerged from the analysis of conference discussions are reflected in specific chapters that follow. Defining and accounting for the rural context will be specifically discussed in a chapter focusing on defining and communicating rural (Chapter "Defining and Communicating Rural"). Rural education research partnerships will be explored in a chapter on multi-disciplinary approaches to rural education research

(Chapter "Partnership-Based Approaches in Rural Education Research"). Rural student outcomes are examined in a series of chapters dealing with interventions in the areas of mathematics, science, and language and literacy (Chapters "The Effectiveness of E-Coaching in Rural Science Classrooms", "Accelerating the Mathematical Development of Young Navajo Children", "Investigating Teacher Professional Development with Distance Coaching to Promote Students' Response to Reading Interventions in Rural Schools" and "Rural Language and Literacy Connections: An Integrated Approach to Supporting Low-Income Preschool Children's Language and Literacy Development"). Family and community influences are discussed in Chapters "Rural Parenting: Cumulative Risk and Parenting Process", "The Effects of Rurality on Parents' Engagement in Children's Early Literacy", "Improving Education Outcomes for American Indian Children: Community and Family Influences on Rural Student Academic Success" and "Family-School Partnerships in Rural Communities: Benefits, Exemplars, and Future Research". Future directions are explored in all chapters, as authors report on next steps to advance research related to their respective area. The final chapter synthesizes material from individual chapters and summarizes future directions for rural education research. Our hope is that the overarching themes emanating from the multiple (research, practice, policy) perspectives and related research agendas specified in the chapters that follow will collectively and systematically provide fruitful directions for the next generation of research in rural education.

Acknowledgments We thank our colleague Michelle Howell Smith for her critical review and suggestions for this manuscript.

Appendix: Guiding Questions for Roundtable Discussions

Questions Addressed at Each Roundtable:

1. What have we learned from research that can inform practice and policy related to (a) teacher, (b) family and community/school and (c) contextual influences* on rural student achievement?
2. What can we learn from future research that can inform practice and policy related to (a) teacher, (b) family and (c) community/school and contextual influences* on rural student achievement?
3. What are the challenges associated with conducting research related to (a) teacher, (b) family and (c) community/school and contextual influences* on rural student achievement and how can we meet these challenges?
4. What is needed at this point to move this rural education research agenda forward?
5. What are the ongoing supports needed in this interplay among research, practice, and policy to make this a meaningful and progressive process that leads to

improved outcomes for rural students? For example, how do we maintain collaborative partnerships so that the dialogue leads to meaningful research and application?

6. Thinking ahead to translation of research to classroom, what should we bear in mind when conducting research that we hope will lead to acceptable and meaningful outcomes for rural students?

7. How can researchers, practitioners and policy makers best incorporate feedback from teachers, parents and caregivers regarding intervention acceptability and utility?

Questions Dealing with Teacher Influences on Rural Academic Success:

1. How can schools, districts, states and universities use research to inform professional development opportunities for rural teachers?

2. How can practitioners' experiences with current professional development practices, including coaching, inform future rural education research?

3. Based on the research and your experiences, what are your perceptions of the role of distance technology research in influencing rural education practice and policy?

4. What are the next immediate steps for rural education research, practice and policy related to teacher influences on rural students' success?

Questions Dealing with Community and Family Influences on Rural Student Academic Success:

1. How can schools, districts, states and universities use research to inform family-school partnership approaches/programs implemented in rural communities?

2. How can families' and practitioners' experiences with family-school partnership approaches/programs inform future rural education research?

3. What are the next immediate steps for rural education research, practice and policy related to community and family influences on rural students' success?

Questions Dealing with School and Contextual Influences on rural Student Academic Success:

1. Based on the research and your experiences, what do you believe schools, districts, states and universities have begun to learn about school and contextual factors that influence student outcomes in rural communities?

2. How are changes in rural education environments—including demographic factors, school consolidation, and the growth of charter schools—influencing rural education research?

3. What are the next immediate steps for rural education research, practice and policy related to school and contextual influences on rural students' success?

*Discussions focused on just one of these three influences.

References

Arnold, M. (2004). *Guiding rural schools and districts: A research agenda.* Aurora, CO: McREL.

Arnold, M. L., Newman, J. H., Gaddy, B. B., & Dean, C. B. (2005). A look at the condition of rural education research: Setting a direction for future research. *Journal of Research in Rural Education, 20*(6), 1–25.

Bazeley, P. (2013). *Qualitative data analysis: Practical strategies.* Thousand Oaks, CA: Sage.

Cicchinelli, L. (2011). *Rural schooling: Necessity is the mother of innovation.* Invited presentation, Advances in Rural Education Research Speaker Series at the National Center for Research on Rural Education, Lincoln, NE.

Coladarci, T. (2007). Improving the yield of rural education research: An editor's swan song. *Journal of Research in Rural Education, 22*(3), 1–9.

Creswell, J. W. (2012). *Qualitative inquiry and research design: Choosing among five approaches.* Thousand Oaks, CA: Sage.

Hatch, J. A. (2002). *Doing qualitative research in education settings.* Albany, NY: State University of New York Press.

Johnson, J., Showalter, D., Klein, R., & Lester, C. (2014). *Why rural matters 2013–2014.* Washington, DC: Rural School and Community Trust.

Saldana, J. (2013). *The coding manual for qualitative researchers.* Thousand Oaks, CA: Sage.

Part I
Methodological Approaches to Rural Education Research

Defining and Communicating Rural

Leslie R. Hawley, Natalie A. Koziol and James A. Bovaird

Abstract Developing an operational definition of rural is a crucial component of rural education research. Although researchers have discussed the challenges of defining rural (e.g., Coladarci in J Res Rural Educ 22(3), 2007; Cromartie and Bucholtz in Amber Waves 6:28–34, 2008; Hart et al. in Am J Public Health 95:1149–1155, 2005; Howley et al. in J Res Rural Educ 20(18), 2005; Isserman in Int Reg Sci Rev 28:465–499, 2005), these discussions have generally been presented at a theoretical level or do not consider issues that occur once a definition has been chosen. Examples of existing definitions and suggested guidelines are needed to ensure researchers understand the importance of aligning their operational definition of rural with the context and goals of their study, as this alignment influences the generalizability of their findings. The purpose of this chapter is threefold. First, we aim to inform rural researchers of the variety of definitions used within policy and research by providing a description of the most common definitions available to education policy makers and researchers. Next, we provide empirical examples of the impact of the choice of rural definition on statistical results and substantive inferences. Finally, we discuss practices advocated by Koziol et al. (J Res Rural Educ 30(4), 2015) that outline how to identify a suitable definition of rural, and communicate the findings given the chosen definition. We conclude by providing recommendations for future research.

Keywords Rural research · Rural policy · Rural definitions · Operational definition · Validity · Generalizability · Communicating rural

L.R. Hawley · N.A. Koziol · J.A. Bovaird
National Center for Research on Rural Education (R2Ed), The Nebraska Center for Research on Children, Youth, Families and Schools (CYFS), Nebraska Academy for Methodology, Analytics and Psychometrics (MAP), University of Nebraska—Lincoln, Lincoln, NE, USA

L.R. Hawley (✉) · N.A. Koziol · J.A. Bovaird
CYFS, University of Nebraska—Lincoln, 216 Mabel Lee Hall, Lincoln, NE 68588-0345, USA
e-mail: lhawley2@unl.edu

© Springer International Publishing Switzerland 2017
G.C. Nugent et al. (eds.), *Rural Education Research in the United States*,
DOI 10.1007/978-3-319-42940-3_3

Rural research ideally preserves and features the uniqueness of the rural setting; however, researchers generally agree that no one definition of rural fully describes the unique aspects inherent to rural contexts (e.g., Coburn et al. 2007; Coladarci 2007; Cromartie and Bucholtz 2008; Hart et al. 2005; Howley et al. 2005; The Rural School and Community Trust 2013). The lack of a standardized definition is problematic from a measurement and validity perspective. The heterogeneity in rural contexts, and the corresponding heterogeneity in coding schemes used to operationalize these contexts, makes it difficult to compare, interpret, and generalize results across rural education research studies.

Context is a key consideration when conducting research in rural areas. The choice of an operational definition of 'rural'—the primary grouping or selection variable in a rural evaluation—has important implications for study design and inference. Specifically, operationalization and measurement of rurality influences the sampling design (including the determination of a proper comparison group), statistical analysis plan, and validity and generalizability of inferences. This applies to any number of research and evaluation applications in rural education, such as randomized control trials (RCTs), quasi-experimental designs (QED), and observational evaluations.

Different rural definitions are often treated as exchangeable, but depending on the study context, certain rural definitions may be more relevant than others. Although we do not claim superiority of one definition over another, we provide guidance to help researchers identify a rural definition that is appropriate for a given study context and communicate findings based on their chosen definition. While our examples and discussion are primarily designed for researchers conducting quantitative research, our general recommendations apply to both quantitative and qualitative research. In both instances, researchers need to clearly define 'rural' in order to best communicate what rural constitutes for their intended audience.

1 Defining Rural

A first step in determining an appropriate operational definition of rural is to examine the classification systems that are currently in use in the United States. There are numerous rural classification systems that are used, to varying degrees, by federal agencies, policy-makers, and researchers in the educational, behavioral, and social sciences and health fields. In order to identify the most commonly used rural definitions, we collected evidence from several sources. For instance, we reviewed recent editions of the *Journal of Rural Health*, *Journal of Rural Sociology*, *Journal of Research in Rural Education*, *Rural Special Education Quarterly*, and *The Rural Educator*. We also conducted Internet searches and evaluated previous literature summarizing rural coding schemes (Arnold et al. 2007; Davis and Lohse 2011; Hart 2012; Hart et al. 2005).

Based on the results of our searches, we established that most coding schemes used within rural research fall under one of three broad categories based on the geographic unit (e.g., census tracts, counties, school districts) to which the coding scheme is applied. The three broad categories include: (a) county level systems; (b) sub-county systems; and (c) educational jurisdiction systems. A fourth category, researcher developed systems, also warrants attention. Each of these categories is discussed below with examples provided of the most commonly used rural definitions within each of these broader systems. For each definition, we provide information on key components such as the level of classification (i.e., county or census tract), basis for the classification, and strengths and limitations of the classification. Tables 1, 2, and 3 include brief summary information for the more commonly used county, sub-county, and educational jurisdiction classification systems.

It is important for educational researchers to understand how different rural/urban definitions fit within each of these broad systems, because the chosen classification system has direct implications for the generalizability of research findings. As explained in more detail later in this chapter, research inferences and generalizations only extend to the specific indicators and geographic units represented in a particular rural definition. Thus, it is imperative education researchers understand the details, benefits, and limitations of the commonly used definitions provided below. The choice of rural definition requires careful thought and consideration, because every subsequent interpretation rests on this decision.

1.1 County Level Systems

Economic information and other demographic characteristics are often summarized at the county level, so it is generally convenient to choose a county level rural taxonomy. However, such a gross level of classification can be problematic, as counties often contain a diverse collection of communities within the same boundary lines. Isserman (2005) refers to this problem as the "county trap" because rural communities may be misclassified due to heterogeneity within the county. As an example, Isserman points out that the Grand Canyon is located within an area designated as metropolitan because a large city is located within the same county. Other researchers have described this phenomenon as overbounding—where rural areas are classified as metropolitan due to county level boundaries (Morrill et al. 1999). The reverse occurs as well, where underbounding may lead to county level classifications that overestimate the degree of rurality within a county. Both phenomena highlight the tendency for county level classification systems to be less sensitive to the heterogeneity of communities that lie within county lines.

Although county level systems have their disadvantages, they may be particularly useful for investigating longitudinal trends in education. For instance, Jordan et al. (2012) relied on a county level system to examine changes in high school dropout rates across a two-decade span. Unlike zip code areas, county level

Table 1 Commonly used county level classification systems

Code	Unit	Coding terminology and description	Rural research considerations	Literature examples
Metropolitan and micropolitan statistical areas	County	*Metropolitan statistical areas* —urbanized area with a population of at least 50,000 persons, plus adjacent territory with commuting ties	The OMB's county level coding scheme may be less sensitive to heterogeneity within rural communities, but it does take into account commuting ties between adjacent areas and tends to be more stable across time. The goal of this coding scheme was to evaluate areas for federal statistics, not classify rural areas (OMB 2013)	Erickson et al. (2012) and Hardré and Hennessey (2010)
		Micropolitan statistical areas —urban cluster with a population of 10,000 but less than 50,000 persons, plus adjacent territory with commuting ties		
		Outside core areas—counties with less than 10,000 persons		
Rural-urban continuum codes (RUCC; Beale codes)	County	*Metropolitan (3 codes)*—counties are divided into three categories based on population (1 million or more; between 250,000 and 1 million; less than 250,000)	This county level classification system is based on the OMB's metropolitan/micropolitan coding scheme, but the additional codes within the metropolitan/nonmetropolitan (micropolitan) categories provide more detailed information regarding population size. Adjacency information may be relevant to researchers who want to understand impact of access to metropolitan area resources	Crosby et al. (2011), Jordan et al. (2012), Murphy and Ruble (2012) and Murphy et al. (2013)
		Nonmetropolitan (6 codes)— counties are divided into three categories based on population (urban population of 19,999 or more; 2500–20,000; less than 2500 persons) and then by adjacency to metro areas		

(continued)

Table 1 (continued)

Code	Unit	Coding terminology and description	Rural research considerations	Literature examples
Urban influence codes (UIC)	County	*Metropolitan (2 codes)*—counties are divided based on population size (large is more than 1 million; small is less than 1 million) *Nonmetropolitan (9 codes)*—counties classified as OMB's micropolitan and noncore areas are delineated by population and distance from a large urban area	This county level classification system is based on the OMB's coding scheme, but the additional codes provide more detailed information regarding population size. Compared to RUCCs, there are three additional UIC nonmetropolitan codes that provide greater detail as to the type of metro area (small/large) a county is adjacent to. The detailed adjacency information may be relevant to understand whether the type of metro (small/large) impacts access to resources	Befort et al. (2012), Parker and Ghelfi (2004), Pitts and Reeves (1999) and Uva et al. (2012)

boundaries tend to be relatively stable over time (Coburn et al. 2007). Such stability reduces the possibility that differences across time are due to confounding explanations like varying geographical boundaries.

1.1.1 Office of Management and Budget (OMB)

The county level OMB classification system determines eligibility and funding for several federal programs, such as the Department of Education's Race to the Top initiative (Hart et al. 2005; OMB 2012). The OMB system uses the terms *metropolitan, micropolitan,* and *non-core based statistical areas* to delineate among counties. Metropolitan and micropolitan areas are considered core based statistical areas (CBSAs). At a minimum, CBSAs are defined as units having a population of 10,000 or more individuals. Metropolitan areas are located in urbanized areas and have a population of at least 50,000, while micropolitan areas are located within an urban cluster having a population of at least 10,000 but no more than 50,000 persons (OMB 2010). Adjacent counties with a strong degree of integration from commuting ties can also qualify as core based areas (Brown and Kandel 2006; DOC n.d.-b).

Table 2 Commonly used sub-county classification systems

Code	Unit	Coding terminology and description	Rural research considerations	Literature examples
Urban and rural classification	Census tracts and/or blocks	*Urbanized areas*—urban area with a population of 50,000 or more people	The Census Bureau's urban/rural classification scheme is more sensitive to heterogeneity within rural communities because tract/block level data are subdivisions of a county that do not cross county boundaries. However, Census classifications do not take into account commuting patterns or adjacency to metro areas	Curtis et al. (2011), Stufft and Brogadir (2010) and Wenger et al. (2012)
		Urban clusters—urban area with a population of at least 2500 but less than 50,000 people		
		Rural—territory located outside of urbanized areas and urban clusters		
Rural-urban commuting area codes (RUCA)	Census tract or zip code	*RUCA codes (33 categories)*—codes are based on the OMB's metropolitan/micropolitan terminology but applied to census tracts/zip codes; codes account for urbanization and commuting ties	RUCA codes utilize the Census Bureau's population density classifications as well as the degree of economic integration (urbanization and commuting patterns) within a Census tract. These codes provide researchers with many possibilities for a more detailed understanding of rurality and impact of adjacency to metro areas. Compared to county level	Abrams et al. (2010), Bigbee et al. (2011), Maher et al. (2008) and Miller and Votruba-Drzal (2013)

(continued)

Table 2 (continued)

Code	Unit	Coding terminology and description	Rural research considerations	Literature examples
			classifications, census tract and ZIP codes facilitate generalizations at multiple levels	

The OMB classifications were developed to measure the degree of integration between urban cores and surrounding areas, not to delineate between urban and rural communities (Isserman 2005; OMB 2010). In particular, the OMB notes that the three classification areas have the potential to contain both urban and rural populations (OMB 2010). Nevertheless, there is a tendency for agencies and researchers to use the OMB classification system to make urban/rural distinctions. This tendency may be due to previous OMB definitions grouping micropolitan and the outside core based statistical areas together as *nonmetropolitan*, where the term nonmetropolitan became associated with rural (Brown and Kandel 2006; Isserman 2005). This limitation of the OMB system is important because several other classification systems, such as those within the Economic Research Service of the United States Department of Agriculture (ERS USDA) are based on the OMB's system.

The OMB classification system is not as widely used in education research as some of the other coding schemes, but examples of its use do exist. For instance, Erickson et al. (2012) compared the effects of an online professional development program on rural and non-rural special education teachers' competency, where rural was defined according to the OMB's designation of non-core based statistical areas. Other education researchers have used the OMB system in conjunction with, or to corroborate, the classifications of alternative coding schemes (e.g., Hardré 2011; Hardré and Hennessey 2013).

1.1.2 ERS USDA: Rural-Urban Continuum Codes (RUCC)

The current RUCCs, also referred to as Beale codes, are based on the most recent version (February, 2013) of OMB's county level metro (metropolitan) and non-metro (nonmetropolitan) classification system (ERS USDA, n.d.-b). A total of nine codes differentiate among counties, with three codes differentiating among metro counties and six codes differentiating among nonmetro counties. Metro areas are categorized by population size, whereas nonmetro areas are defined by population size and degree of adjacency to a larger metro area (ERS USDA, n.d.-b). Codes are intended to provide a more detailed classification scheme for users working with county level data. Nonmetro counties are first divided into categories based on

Table 3 Commonly used educational jurisdiction classification systems

Code	Unit	Coding terminology and description	Rural research considerations	Literature examples
Metro-centric locale codes	Schools and school districts	*City (4 codes)*—schools and districts classified based on population size and proximity to metropolitan statistical area (MSA)	This coding scheme is no longer used by NCES, but it still serves as an inclusion measure for the Rural Education Achievement Program (REAP). Many education researchers use school districts' REAP qualification as a proxy for rural	Berry (2012), Berry et al. (2011), Demi et al. (2010), Coomber et al. (2011), Farmer et al. (2006) and Miller (2012)
		Town (2 codes)—schools and districts classified based on population size and location outside of a MSA		
		Rural (2 codes)—schools and districts classified based on based on proximity to MSA; locations must be census-defined rural territory		
Urban-centric locale codes	Schools and school districts	*City (large, midsize, small)*—schools and districts must be inside an urbanized area inside a principal city; codes are delineated based on population size	Researchers who wish to make inferences at the school level should consider either the urban-centric or metro-centric locale codes. Compared to the metro-centric, these codes provide more precise geocoding information for determining school/school district location. Metro-centric codes are unable to distinguish remotely isolated rural schools from rural schools closer to urban cores.	Barley and Wegner (2010), Byun et al. (2012), Isernhagen (2010), Sheridan et al. (2014), Tekniepe (2015) and Wilcox et al. (2014)
		Suburb (large, midsize, small)—schools and districts must be outside a principal city and inside an urbanized area; codes are delineated based on population size		
		Town (fringe, distant, remote)—schools and districts must be inside an urban cluster; codes		

(continued)

Table 3 (continued)

Code	Unit	Coding terminology and description	Rural research considerations	Literature examples
		are delineated based on population size	Urban-centric locale codes are readily available in secondary datasets from NCES-sponsored studies	
		Rural (fringe, distant, remote)— schools and districts must be census-defined rural territory; codes are delineated based on population size		

urban population and then further divided according to adjacency to one or more metro areas. Counties are considered adjacent if at least 2 % of the labor force commutes to a central metro county, and the county physically adjoins to one or more metro areas (ERS USDA, n.d.-b).

The major strength of the RUCCs is the degree of data available at the county level and the general stability of county level boundaries compared to less stable boundaries like ZIP codes. As mentioned above, the primary limitation of using county level information is the increased propensity of falling into the "county trap" (Hart et al. 2005; Isserman 2005).

Of the county level classifications, the RUCCs appear to be one of the most commonly used within education research. For example, prior to 2006, the RUCCs were one of the three primary rural/urban classification systems used by the National Center for Education Statistics (NCES, n.d.-a). More recent examples of their use in education research also exist. Murphy and Ruble (2012) used the codes to examine differences in rural and urban parents' satisfaction with services made available to their children with autism spectrum disorder, and Murphy et al. (2013) used the codes to compare transitional practices of rural and urban preschool teachers. Jordan et al. (2012) provide an extended justification for their use of the RUCCs (Beale Codes) in investigating high school dropout rates:

> Beale Codes were used here because they were designed specifically to examine the continuum between urban and rural areas. They were developed for the analysis of trends in non-metro areas that are related to population density and metropolitan influence. Beale Codes allow a more detailed analysis of the survey data than the more common urban-suburban-rural classification systems (p. 4).

1.1.3 ERS USDA: Urban Influence Codes (UIC)

The ERS USDA coding system, referred to as the urban influence codes (UIC), is based on the OMB's county level classification system (ERS USDA, n.d.-c). Although UICs are based on the OMB categories, they provide a more informed county level classification than the three general OMB categories. UICs separate counties based on their OMB status as well as their population density and metropolitan influence.

The UICs are grouped into two main categories: *metropolitan* and *non-metropolitan*. Metropolitan areas containing at least 1 million residents are considered large metro counties, whereas areas with populations less than 1 million but at least 50,000 are considered small metro counties (ERS USDA, n.d.-c). Nonmetropolitan counties include counties that are classified by the OMB as micropolitan or noncore statistical areas. Nonmetropolitan counties are further classified into one of ten categories based on OMB classification (micropolitan or noncore) and distance from an urban area. The more populated areas qualifying as micropolitan counties are divided into three groups based on their adjacency to a metropolitan area (adjacent to a large metro area, adjacent to a small metro area, or not adjacent to a metro area) and the size of the metropolitan area. Counties are considered adjacent if they border a larger urbanized area and a minimum of 2 % of the workforce commutes to the larger core area. Noncore counties are classified based on their adjacency to a metropolitan or micropolitan area and whether a minimum of 2500 persons reside within the county (ERS USDA, n.d.-c).

Because the UICs are based on the OMB's taxonomy, they have similar benefits and limitations. While there is potential for classifications to suffer from the "county trap," the use of commuting patterns and adjacency information gives UICs an advantage over the OMB system. UICs provide a level of detail that can inform more nuanced funding decisions than the OMB taxonomy.

The UICs are not as widely used in education research as the RUCCs, but they are not completely absent from the literature. For instance, the UICs have been used to describe differences in educational attainment across rural and urban counties (Parker and Ghelfi 2004), and to examine the influence of geographic context on the educational accountability scores of Kentucky school districts (Pitts and Reeves 1999).

1.2 Sub-county Systems

Some rural/urban classification systems are based on sub-county level aspects such as census tracts, census blocks, and/or ZIP codes. Census tracts are statistical subdivisions of a county that usually include between 2500 and 8000 persons. Tracts are the smallest geographical units to which urban/rural definitions are applied (Coburn et al. 2007; Department of Commerce, Bureau of the Census (DOC), n.d.-a). The size of the tract depends on the density of the area, but tracts do not cross county boundaries. Because census tracts are smaller, census tract-level classifications have fewer problems related to the "county trap" (Hart et al. 2005; Isserman 2005). Yet, some drawbacks of the DOC's tract-level system are the degree of instability in tracts over time, the complexity of the data (e.g., multiple tracts within counties and/or ZIP codes), as well as the limited number of government agencies that use census tract-level information (Coburn et al. 2007; Hart et al. 2005; Ponce 2013).

For education researchers, sub-county systems may be the only feasible option, or the easiest to implement option, when relying on secondary data. For instance, due to confidentiality concerns, the public- and restricted-use datasets of large-scale federally funded studies do not provide exact addresses of participants, so researchers must rely on whatever geographic identifiers are available. The availability of geographic identifiers in turn determines the availability of the various geographic classification systems, as the process of merging codes with the dataset assumes a common identifying variable.

1.2.1 Department of Commerce (DOC), Bureau of the Census

The DOC defines an urban area as an area containing a densely populated core (density of 1000 persons per square mile or 500 persons per square mile for adjoining territory) and surrounding residential, commercial, and nonresidential territory that links with that core (DOC 2011; ERS USDA, n.d.-a). Based on the DOC's taxonomy, there are two types of urban areas: a) urbanized areas (50,000 or more people) and b) urban clusters (at least 2500 but less than 50,000 people). Urbanized areas are not required to include a city as long as the population thresholds are met. The DOC defines all urban areas first, and once these areas have been classified, remaining areas are classified as rural (DOC 2011). Thus, rural areas under the DOC's system are defined as areas that are not urban rather than defined by particular features unique to rural locations.

1.2.2 Rural-Urban Commuting Area (RUCA) Codes

RUCA codes were developed by the University of Washington's WWAMI[1] Rural Health Research Center and the ERS USDA, and have been adopted by agencies such as the Centers for Medicare and Medicaid services (Hart et al. 2005). Codes can be applied at the census tract or ZIP code level. At the census tract level, the coding system includes 33 categories of rural and urban tracts (Coburn et al. 2007). Codes are based on the OMB's metropolitan and micropolitan categorizations and modified to reflect economic ties between areas. In order to identify economically integrated areas, codes consider aspects such as population density, urbanization, and commuting patterns (ERS USDA, n.d.-d). Density and urbanization are defined according to the Census Bureau's classifications for size and population density (Hart et al. 2005).

---

[1]WWAMI stands for the University of Washington School of Medicine and the states of Washington, Wyoming, Alaska, Montana and Idaho.

RUCAs can be quite complex and some data may not be available at the tract level. As such, crosswalk files are often available to link ZIP codes to census tracts. A caution with using ZIP code-level information is the potential for units to change if ZIP codes are altered over time (West et al. 2010). Despite these potential limitations, RUCA codes have several strengths, such as their sensitivity to demographic change, and their facilitation of generalizations at multiple levels (i.e., tract and ZIP code levels) (Hart et al. 2005).

In education research, the RUCA codes have been used to compare characteristics of child care settings (Maher et al. 2008) and children's academic readiness (Miller and Votruba-Drzal 2013) across rural and urban locations. Maher et al. (2008) justify their use of the RUCAs by noting that, "While the RUCA codes' census tract designations are based on the same theoretical constructs of metropolitan and micropolitan used to classify counties, making these designations at the census tract level is a more geographically precise categorization system enabling application to zip codes" (p. 4).

1.3 Educational Jurisdictions

Local education agencies (LEAs; school districts) and schools are classified using coding schemes developed by NCES. Educational jurisdiction coding systems permit policy decisions and/or research conclusions to be made at the school and school district level. The most recent codes were developed in 2006 with the help of the Census Bureau. Key features of this new system are the use of geocoding information (i.e., longitude and latitude information), supplemental ZIP code locales, and explicit distance measures to identify town and rural subtypes (NCES, n.d.-a).

As discussed later in this chapter, it is important to select a classification system that can be applied to the geographic units most conceptually relevant to the research context at hand. Classification systems at the school district and school level are particularly useful for education researchers who are naturally interested in school-related issues. It is no surprise, then, that school-based classification systems are commonly used by rural education researchers.

1.3.1 National Center for Education Statistics (NCES)

Prior to 2006, NCES used a coding system referred to as metro-centric locale codes or simply locale codes (NCES, n.d.-b). Metro-centric locale codes were used from the 1980s until 2006, and although this coding scheme is no longer used by NCES, it still serves as an inclusion measure for one of the main federal programs for rural schools—the Rural Education Achievement Program (REAP) (Apling and Kuenzi 2008; Department of Education [DOE], n.d.-a to -c; Strange et al. 2012).

Consequently, some education researchers use school districts' REAP qualification as a means for defining rural (e.g., Berry 2012; Berry et al. 2011; Farmer et al. 2006).

NCES, in conjunction with the Census Bureau, released a new coding system for LEAs (school districts) in 2006, referred to as urban-centric locale codes. Urban-centric locale codes classify schools and LEAs into four main categories (i.e., city, suburban, town, and rural), and within each of the main categories, further classify locations into three subcategories. Classifications between- and within-categories are based on the population size and/or the location's distance from an urbanized area. Census tract-level information regarding a location's designation as an urban area is used to determine the appropriate code for each school and school district. It is possible for schools and their district to receive different codes, but when the majority of students in a district attend schools with the same code, the same code is applied at the district-level (Strange et al. 2012). If there is a great deal of heterogeneity within a district and no single locale code accounts for the majority of students, then a combination of procedures is used to determine the district-level locale code. The locale code for the largest percentage of students determines the broad locale (i.e., city, suburban, town, or rural), and the locale code assigned to the district is the most remote or smallest subcategory within the broad locale (NCES, n.d.-a).

A central feature of the urban-centric locale system is the use of geocoding information to determine the precise location of schools and school districts. Geocoding is particularly helpful for differentiating school districts located just outside an urban area from those located in more distant or remote areas (Apling and Kuenzi 2008). For instance, the previous metro-centric locale codes were not able to distinguish remotely isolated rural schools from rural schools closer to urban cores (NCES, n.d.-b).

There are numerous examples of the urban-centric locale codes being used in education research, for instance, to study the impact of social capital on rural children's educational aspirations (Byun et al. 2012), and evaluate the effects of geographic context on parents' affective behaviors and children's social and behavioral functioning (Sheridan et al. 2014). Rural education researchers who utilize secondary data from NCES-sponsored studies, such as the High School Longitudinal Study of 2009 and Early Childhood Longitudinal Study, are particularly apt to use the urban-centric locale codes, as these are the codes that are readily available in the secondary datasets.

1.4 Researcher Developed Systems

Several researchers have attempted to address some of the limitations with existing urban/rural classification systems by developing their own measures of rurality. The purpose of discussing these measures is to highlight the fact that education researchers are not limited to the established definitions described above. While it is not possible to include all possible researcher developed measures, two measures are highlighted below that take into account the heterogeneity of communities within geographic boundaries. One of the highlighted measures is categorical, whereas the other is a first attempt at putting rurality on a continuous scale.

1.4.1 Rural-Urban Density Typology

Andrew Isserman introduced a categorical Rural-Urban Density Typology in 2005 that combines elements of the Census Bureau and OMB definitions. The four categories of the rural-urban density typology include: (1) urban county; (2) rural county; (3) mixed urban county; and (4) mixed rural county. Categories are assigned based on the percentage of urban residents, total number of urban residents, population density, and population of largest urban area within the county (Waldorf 2006a). A mixed rural county is defined as one which does not meet the urban or rural county criteria and the population density is less than 320 persons per square mile. Mixed urban counties follow the same criteria except the population density is at least 320 people per square mile.

The Rural-Urban Density Typology was developed in order to address problems related to the "country trap." The country trap occurs when there is a failure to recognize heterogeneity among settings within counties that leads to rural areas not qualifying for rural-based federal funding because the corresponding county boundaries include urban areas. Although this coding scheme takes into account the fact that counties may contain a heterogeneous mix of urban and rural communities, its categorical nature may limit its effectiveness to distinguish among mixed counties. In particular, Waldorf (2006a) criticizes the use of what she perceives as arbitrary thresholds for creating the categories.

1.4.2 Index of Relative Rurality (IRR)

Waldorf (2006b) introduced a continuous measure of rurality, called the index of relative rurality (IRR), that aggregates four indicators: (a) population size; (b) population density; (c) percentage of the population that is urban; and (d) distance from metropolitan areas (remoteness). This measure was developed in order to address some of the shortcomings of current urban/rural classification schemes that depend on thresholds for determining classification. Waldorf (2006a) contends that using arbitrary thresholds creates artificial separations and similarities within rural classifications. As opposed to using thresholds to determine rural/urban classifications, the IRR evaluates the *degree* to which a county is rural. The index measures the degree of rurality on a scale from 0 to 1, where 0 indicates low rurality and 1 indicates high rurality. The IRR index is a comparative rather than an absolute measure of rurality, where rurality is measured relative to all of the spatial units considered during the index creation.

Although the IRR is not widely used, it has several benefits. For instance, the use of a continuous measure over traditional categorical taxonomies permits researchers to examine changes in the degree of rurality over time, and to evaluate interactions between these changes and variables such as poverty rate or educational attainment (Waldorf 2006b). Nevertheless, the IRR has its limitations. Hart (2012) urges caution in using the IRR because of its lack of a theoretical basis for equal weighting of the four indicators, and potential for generating misleading results due to inadequate sample sizes and variability within different geographical and aggregate units. Another potential limitation with this measure is its assumption that geographical context is a unidimensional construct, as some researchers may argue that rural is multidimensional.

2   Impact of Rural Definition

Several articles provide information regarding the possible ramifications of using a particular rural definition over another. For instance, classifications based on the Census Bureau and the OMB result in different proportions of the population being classified as rural (Coburn et al. 2007; Hart et al. 2005; Jordan and Hargrove 1987; Miller 2010). Hart et al. (2005) found that the percentage of the population classified as rural based on 2000 Census data varied from 10 to 28 % depending on the use of Census Bureau or OMB taxonomies. In another study, Miller (2010) evaluated the rates of 'rural poverty' across Census Bureau and OMB classifications and found that rates were higher when using the OMB's nonmetropolitan classification compared to the Census Bureau's rural classification.

Additional work has examined the impact of different rural definitions in terms of the percentage of the sampled population that is classified consistently across different taxonomies (Jordan and Hargrove 1987; West et al. 2010). Jordan and Hargrove (1987) applied eight urban/rural definitions to 93 counties within Nebraska and found that the majority (54 %) of the counties were defined as rural by seven of the eight taxonomies. Jordan and Hargrove also used cluster analysis techniques to statistically derive four clusters of potential sub-counties within nonmetropolitan counties. The authors note the cluster analyses were especially sensitive to the specific indicators used to operationalize rural, such that different clusters were obtained depending on which indicators were included in the model.

West et al. (2010) compared the overlap in the Veterans Health Administration (VHA) health care enrollees across OMB, RUCA, and VHA[2] rural taxonomies. Their evaluation revealed that the highly rural VHA classification included far fewer veterans (1.5 % of veterans) than the isolated rural (RUCA) and noncore (OMB) classifications (which were more than four and six times larger,

---

[2]The VHA's coding scheme has three classification levels (urban, rural, and highly rural) that are derived from a combination of census tract, county, and geocoding data.

respectively). The VHA's rural classification included three to five times as many veterans as similar OMB and RUCA classifications. More than a third of veterans classified as rural using the VHA taxonomy were classified as urban (RUCA) or metropolitan (OMB), depending on the coding scheme. In general, the authors found that the VHA taxonomy tended to include more veterans in the rural category than in the urban and highly rural categories. Based on their findings, West et al. suggest using a combination of rural classification systems rather than relying on a single taxonomy.

In terms of educational jurisdictions, the rural definition used to classify LEAs can lead to as few as 11 % to more than 60 % of all LEAs being classified as rural (Apling and Kuenzi 2008). Likewise, the definition used to classify schools can lead to as few as 2 % to as many as 25 % of all public schools being classified as rural (Apling and Kuenzi 2008). These numbers are particularly important if an LEA is applying for grant money earmarked for rural schools/students. According to a Congressional Research Service Report (Apling and Kuenzi 2008), approximately 4000 LEAs received aid from the REAP initiatives of the Elementary and Secondary Education Act [ESEA; DOE, n.d.-c and -d]. REAP initiatives such as the Small, Rural School Grant program, and the Rural and Low-Income School program, are one method that Congress uses to target funding for rural schools (Apling and Kuenzi 2008; DOE, n.d.-a to n.d.-c; Strange et al. 2012). Inclusion in REAP programs requires that all schools served by the LEA meet the requirements for being classified as rural based on the NCES metro-centric coding scheme (i.e., locale codes 6, 7, or 8). Yet, NCES has altered its coding scheme to the current urban-centric locale codes, and within this system, LEAs are classified based on the majority or plurality of schools. Apling and Kuenzi (2008) found that about 8 % of schools classified as rural under the metro-centric locale codes would not be classified as rural based on the current urban-centric system. In total, they estimated that 386 fewer LEAs would receive REAP grants using the updated urban-centric locale coding system.

Finally, a study by Koziol et al. (2015) used the Early Childhood Longitudinal Study, Kindergarten Class of 1998–1999 (ECLS-K; developed by the NCES, n. d.-d) to demonstrate how the effect of geographic context (rural vs. urban) on students' science test scores differed as a function of the rural definition applied. The three coding schemes used in their study included: (a) county level OMB designations, (b) school-level Metro-Centric Locale Codes, and (c) census-tract-level RUCAs. Results indicated that urban children had significantly higher science scores than rural children when using the OMB classification, rural children had significantly higher science scores than urban children when using the Metro-Centric Locale Codes, and urban and rural children had statistically equivalent science scores when using the RUCAs. This work highlights the fact that the chosen rural definition may critically impact study inferences.

These examples demonstrate the practical implications of choosing among the various urban/rural definitions. Although primarily descriptive in nature, research has demonstrated that different definitions lead to differences in the numbers of individuals assigned to each rural classification. While research is not available regarding the potential impact of using different rural definitions in the context of a randomized control trial (RCT) or quasi-experimental design (QED), the existing literature suggests the potential for drawing discrepant conclusions. Discrepant conclusions may occur when one definition is chosen over another, leading to different populations of rural individuals that may not be comparable. In particular, even if random assignment is conducted within communities defined as rural by one definition, inferences may not generalize to other communities defined as rural by another definition.

Overall, there is evidence that the choice of rural definition leads to different sampled populations, thereby influencing the inferences and generalizability of rural research findings. While no one rural definition is appropriate for all contexts, certain definitions may be more suitable for particular contexts. We stress that individuals conducting research in rural contexts need to be cognizant of their program's goals and the intended analyses when choosing a coding scheme.

3   Identifying and Communicating Rural

The number of available definitions of rural can make it difficult to identify an appropriate definition. In this section we summarize the practices advocated by Koziol et al. (2015) for identifying the most appropriate definition of rural. We also provide suggestions for communicating this information in terms of the intended inferences. Interested readers should refer to Koziol et al. for a more in-depth review and detailed application.

When choosing a definition of rural, education researchers need to consider the purpose for which a particular rural system was developed. For instance, the OMB metropolitan and nonmetropolitan system was never intended to classify rural areas or to be used for funding allocation or program eligibility; rather, the goal of the taxonomy was to evaluate areas for federal statistics (OMB 2013). Choosing among the various rural definitions requires that researchers carefully consider the benefits and limitations of each definition in conjunction with the goals of their research.

Education researchers also need to consider the type(s) of indicators used to operationalize rurality within a particular coding system. As discussed in the preceding section, different indicators of rurality can produce divergent results. Depending on the research context, certain indicators of rurality (e.g., population size, geographic isolation) and conceptual definitions will be more relevant than others. For example, the Census Bureau distinguishes between urban and rural areas primarily by population size and density (DOC, n.d.-c), whereas the OMB and RUCA systems use both population characteristics and measures of commuting patterns (OMB 2010; WWAMI RHRC, n.d.-b). The additional commuting information embedded in the OMB and RUCA definitions may be more relevant to researchers who want to understand the impact of access to metropolitan area resources (e.g., libraries, museums) on educational outcomes. Along this line, researchers who want to understand how geographic remoteness influences child outcomes may prefer to use the Urban-Centric Locale Codes because the geocoding methods used to create these codes may be more precise than the information provided by the RUCAs (NCES, n.d.-a).

Another aspect requiring consideration is the geographic unit (e.g., schools, school districts, ZIP code areas, census tracts, counties) to which rurality indicator(s) are applied. These units are important in determining the most appropriate definition because the geographic unit represents the experimental unit for the rural/urban predictor—the smallest unit to which the "treatment" is applied (Milliken and Johnson 2009). Any inferences a researcher intends to make about rural phenomena exist at the level of the experimental unit (e.g., the county when using a county level definition), which is not always the same as the lowest-level sampling unit (e.g., the child). Thus, researchers should use a geographic unit that matches their target unit. For instance, researchers who intend to make inferences about conditions between rural and urban counties should consider county level systems such as the RUCCs or UICs. Education researchers intending to make inferences regarding the efficacy of a reading intervention in rural versus urban schools or school districts should consider the Urban-Centric Locale Codes.

Once researchers have carefully considered an appropriate definition of rural given the context and goals of their study, they must appropriately communicate and provide rationale for their chosen definition. At a minimum, researchers should specify the specific indicators and geographic unit they used to operationalize rural. Together, this information communicates to the reader how rural has been conceptualized and the extent to which inferences may (or may not) generalize to other contexts. Researchers need to be clear that inferences extend only to the specific indicators and geographic units represented by the rural definition used in the study. Clearly, the choice in definition is one that requires careful thought.

4 Recommendations for Future Research

As discussed throughout this chapter, there is a lack of consensus in both research and policy as to what constitutes a rural setting, and as a result, numerous definitions have been developed across and within disciplines. In choosing among well-established definitions or creating a new coding scheme, researchers should keep in mind the guidelines of Hart et al. (2005). Hart et al. (2005) advise that rural definitions need to "(1) measure something explicit and meaningful; (2) be replicable; (3) be derived from available, high-quality data; (4) be quantifiable and not subjective, and (5) have on-the-ground validity" (p. 1150).

Coladarci (2007) advocates the need for researchers to provide a description of the rural context. With this in mind, we recommend researchers both define and describe the rural context in order to operationalize rurality for their audience. For instance, when only a few locales are compared or a single locale is evaluated (as is the case with most qualitative studies), researchers have the opportunity to incorporate detailed descriptions about each location. Quantitative measures such as one of the definitions discussed in the previous sections and/or information on the total population, population density, number of students in the school district, and median income can also be included with the narrative descriptive to provide a better understanding of the setting. Although standardized classification systems are unlikely to be incorporated as explicit variables in studies with a small number of locales, it is beneficial for researchers to list how the locale(s) are classified in at least one major classification system in order to facilitate comparisons with other studies. When researchers examine a large number of locations, we recommend choosing an existing classification system and listing its defining indicators and geographic units, or fully detailing any locally-developed definition of rurality. Whether researchers are evaluating a small or large number of locales, providing detailed information regarding the rural context facilitates the ability to make comparisons across research studies.

We also support the recommendation of West et al. (2010) who advocate the use of a combination of rural classification systems rather than relying upon a single taxonomy. In their research, West et al. found that the particular type of definition used to classify rurality lead to different study conclusions. Thus, they cautioned against overreliance on a single coding scheme, particularly when different definitions may be used for policy and funding decisions by government entities. In general, comparing results across multiple classification systems and finding consistent patterns provides more evidence for the presence of a particular phenomenon whereas finding contradictory evidence could reveal potential areas of instability and concern. This type of approach is especially advantageous when inferences from a particular study may be used for high-stakes decision-making.

5 Summary

When conducting research in rural settings, researchers are faced with a difficult task of operationalizing rural. Throughout this chapter, our objective was not to recommend one coding or classification scheme over another; rather, our goal was to highlight the need to provide accurate and meaningful information about the rural context. The most appropriate rural definition depends on the alignment between the goals of a particular research project and the foundations of the rural definition (e.g., the geographic indicators comprising the definition and the geographic unit to which the definition is applied). Once researchers have determined the most appropriate definition for their particular study, it is their responsibility to provide transparent information regarding the rationale for choosing that definition. It is our hope that adherence to these recommendations will increase the utility of rural education research by allowing for more direct comparisons and generalizations across studies.

Acknowledgments Preparation of this manuscript was supported by a grant awarded to Susan M. Sheridan and colleagues (IES #R305C090022) by the Institute of Education Sciences. The opinions expressed herein are those of the authors and should not be considered reflective of the funding agency.

References

Abrams, T. E., Vaughan-Sarrazin, M., & Kaboli, P. J. (2010). Mortality and revascularization following admission for acute myocardial infarction: Implication for rural veterans. *Journal of Rural Health, 26*, 310–317.

Apling, R. N., & Kuenzi, J. J. (2008). Rural education and the Rural Education Achievement Program (REAP) overview and policy issues. Congressional Research Service (CRS) report for Congress (Order code: RL33804). Retrieved at http://nationalaglawcenter.org/assets/crs/RL33804.pdf

Arnold, M. L., Biscoe, B., Farmer, T. W., Robertson, D. L., & Shapley, K. L. (2007). *How the government defines rural has implications for education policies and practices* (Issues & Answers Report, REL 2007–No. 010). Washington, DC: U.S. Department of Education, Institute of Education Sciences, National Center for Education Evaluation and Regional Assistance, Regional Educational Laboratory Southwest. Retrieved from http://ies.ed.gov/ncee/edlabs/regions/southwest/pdf/REL_2007010.pdf

Barley, Z. A., & Wegner, S. (2010). An examination of the provision of supplemental educational services in nine rural schools. *Journal of Research in Rural Education, 25*(4). Retrieved from http://www.jrre.psu.edu/articles/25.5.pdf

Befort, C. A., Nazir, N., & Perri, M. G. (2012). Prevalence of obesity among adults from rural and urban areas of the United States: Findings from NHANES (2005–2008). *Journal of Rural Health, 28*, 392–397.

Berry, A. B. (2012). The relationship of perceived support to satisfaction and commitment for special education teachers in rural areas. *Rural Special Education Quarterly, 31*, 3–14.

Berry, A. B., Petrin, R. A., Gravelle, M. L., & Farmer, T. W. (2011). Issues in special education teacher recruitment, retention, and professional development: Considerations in supporting rural teachers. *Rural Special Education Quarterly, 30*, 3–11.

Bigbee, J. L., Musil, C., & Kinski, D. (2011). The health of caregiving grandmothers: A rural-urban comparison. *Journal of Rural Health, 27*, 289–296.

Brown, D. L., & Kandel, W. A. (2006). Rural America through a demographic lens. In W. A. Kandel & D. L. Brown (Eds.), *Population change and rural society* (pp. 3–23). Dordrecht: Springer.

Byun, S.-Y., Meece, J. L., Irvin, M. J., & Hutchins, B. C. (2012). The role of social capital in educational aspirations of rural youth. *Rural Sociology, 77*, 355–379.

Coburn, A. F., MacKinney, A. C., McBride, T. D., Mueller, K. J., Slifkin, R. T., & Wakefield, M. K. (2007). *Choosing rural definitions: Implications for health policy* (Issue Brief No. 2). Columbia, MO: Rural Policy Research Institute Health Panel. Retrieved from http://www.rupri.org/Forms/RuralDefinitionsBrief.pdf

Coladarci, T. (2007). Improving the yield of rural education research: An editor's swan song. *Journal of Research in Rural Education, 22*(3). Retrieved from http://jrre.psu.edu/articles/22-3.pdf

Coomber, K., Toumbourou, J. W., Miller, P., Staiger, P. K., Hemphill, S. A., & Catalano, R. F. (2011). Rural adolescent alcohol, tobacco, and illicit drug use: A comparison of students in Victoria, Australia, and Washington State, United States. *Journal of Rural Health, 27*, 409–415.

Cromartie, J., & Bucholtz, S. (2008). Defining the "rural" in rural America. *Amber Waves, 6*, 28–34. Retrieved from http://www.ers.usda.gov/amber-waves/2008-june/defining-the-%E2%80%9Crural%E2%80%9D-in-rural-america.aspx#.VL_TeGTF_3o

Crosby, R. A., Casey, B. R., Vanderpool, R., Collins, T., & Moore, G. R. (2011). Uptake of free HPV vaccination among young women: A comparison of rural versus urban rates. *Journal of Rural Health, 27*, 380–384.

Curtis, A. C., Waters, C. M., & Brindis, C. (2011). Rural adolescent health: The importance of prevention services in the rural community. *Journal of Rural Health, 27*, 60–71.

Davis, J., & Lohse, C. (2011). *Understanding the gradients of "rural": A guide to the various definitions of "rural" and their implications for states.* Presentation by developed by the research, development and dissemination service of the chief council of state school officers for the council of chief state school officers' annual rural chiefs meeting. Retrieved June 8, from http://opi.mt.gov/PUb/PDF/Superintendent/RuralityReport.pdf

Demi, M., Coleman-Jensen, A., & Snyder, A. (2010). The rural context and post-secondary school enrollment: An ecological systems approach. *Journal of Research in Rural Education, 25*(4). Retrieved from http://jrre.psu.edu/articles/25-7.pdf

Department of Commerce, Bureau of the Census (DOC, 2011). Urban Area criteria for the 2010 Census. Federal Register (Vol. 76, No. 164). Retrieved from https://www.census.gov/geo/reference/pdfs/fedreg/fedregv76n164.pdf

Department of Commerce, Bureau of the Census (DOC, n.d.-a). Census tract and block numbering areas. Retrieved from http://www.census.gov/geo/www/cen_tract.html

Department of Commerce, Bureau of the Census (DOC, n.d.-b). Metropolitan and micropolitan statistical areas main. Retrieved from http://www.census.gov/population/metro/

Department of Commerce, Bureau of the Census (DOC, n.d.-c). 2010 Census urban and rural classification and urban area criteria. Retrieved from http://www.census.gov/geo/reference/ua/urban-rural-2010.html

Erickson, A. S. G., Noonan, P. M., & McCall, Z. (2012). Effectiveness of online professional development for rural special educators. *Rural Special Education Quarterly, 31*, 22–32.

Farmer, T. W., Leung, M.-C., Banks, J., Schaefer, V., Andrews, B., & Murray, R. A. (2006). Adequate yearly progress in small rural schools and rural low-income schools. *The Rural Educator, 27*(3). Retrieved from http://www.ruraleducator.net/archive/27-3/27-3_Farmer.pdf

Hardré, P. L. (2011). Motivation for math in rural schools: Student and teacher perspectives. *Mathematics Education Research Journal, 23*, 213–233.

Hardré, P. & Hennessey, M. (2010). Two rural worlds: Differences of rural high school students' motivational profiles in Indiana and Colorado. *Journal of Research in Rural Education, 25*. Retrieved from http://jrre.psu.edu/articles/25-8.pdf

Hardré, P. L., & Hennessey, M. N. (2013). What they think, what they know, what they do: Rural secondary teachers' motivational beliefs and strategies. *Learning Environments Research, 16*(8), 411–436.

Hart, L. G. (2012). *Frontier/remote, island, and rural literature review* (Version 2.99). Grand Forks, ND: The University of North Dakota, School of Medicine & Health Sciences, Center for Rural Health. Retrieved from http://ruralhealth.und.edu/pdf/frontierreview.pdf

Hart, L. G., Larson, E. H., & Lishner, D. M. (2005). Rural definitions for health policy and research. *American Journal of Public Health, 95*, 1149–1155.

Howley, C. B., Theobald, P., & Howley, A. (2005). What rural education research is of most worth? A reply to Arnold, Newman, Gaddy, and Dean. *Journal of Research in Rural Education, 20*(18). Retrieved from http://www.jrre.psu.edu/articles/20-18.pdf

Isernhagen, J. C. (2010). TeamMates: Providing emotional and academic support in rural schools. *The Rural Educator, 32*, 29–36.

Isserman, A. M. (2005). In the national interest: Defining rural and urban correctly in research and public policy. *International Regional Science Review, 28*, 465–499.

Jordan, S. A., & Hargrove, D. S. (1987). Implications of an empirical application of categorical definitions of rural. *Journal of Rural Community Psychology, 8*, 14–29.

Jordan, J. L., Kostandini, G., & Mykerezi, E. (2012). Rural and urban high school dropout rates: Are they different? *Journal of Research in Rural Education, 27*(12). Retrieved from http://www.jrre.psu.edu/articles/27-12.pdf

Koziol, N. A., Arthur, A., Hawley, L. R., Bovaird, J. A., Bash, K. L., McCormick, C., et al. (2015). Identifying, analyzing, and communicating rural: A quantitative perspective. *Journal of Research in Rural Education, 30*(4). Retrieved from http://www.jrre.psu.edu/articles/30-4.pdf

Maher, E. J., Frestedt, B., & Grace, C. (2008). Differences in child care quality in rural and non-rural areas. *Journal of Research in Rural Education, 23*(4). Retrieved from http://www.jrre.psu.edu/articles/23-4.pdf

Miller, P., & Votruba-Drzal, E. (2013). Early academic skills and childhood experiences across the urban-rural continuum. *Early Childhood Research Quarterly, 28*, 234–248.

Milliken, G. A., & Johnson, D. E. (2009). *Analysis of messy data: Designed experiments* (2nd ed., Vol. 1). Boca Raton, FL: CRC Press.

Miller, L. C. (2012). Situating the rural teacher labor market in the broader context: A descriptive analysis of the market dynamics in New York State. *Journal of Research in Rural Education, 27*, 1–31.

Miller, K. (2010). Why definitions matter: Rural definitions and state poverty rankings. Rural Policy Research Institute: Data Brief. Retrieved from http://www.rupri.org/Forms/Poverty%20and%20Definition%20of%20Rural.pdf

Morrill, R., Cromartie, J., & Hart, G. (1999). Metropolitan, urban, and rural commuting areas: Toward a better depictions of the United States settlement system. *Urban Geography, 20*, 727–748.

Murphy, M. A., McCormick, K. M., & Rous, B. S. (2013). Rural influence on the use of transition practices by preschool teachers. *Rural Special Education Quarterly, 32*, 29–37.

Murphy, M. A., & Ruble, L. A. (2012). Comparative study of rurality and urbanicity on access to and satisfaction with services for children with Autism Spectrum disorders. *Rural Special Education Quarterly, 31*, 3–11.

Parker, T., & Ghelfi, L. M. (2004). Using the 2003 urban influence codes to understand rural America. *Amber Waves*. Retrieved from http://www.ers.usda.gov/amber-waves/2004-april/using-the-2003-urban-influence-codes-to-understand-rural-america.aspx#.VRhKki42XsA

Pitts, T. C., & Reeves, E. B. (1999). *A spatial analysis of contextual effects on educational accountability in Kentucky* (Occasional Research Paper No. 3). Morehead, KY: Center for Educational Research and Leadership. Retrieved from http://irapp.moreheadstate.edu/cerl/orp

Ponce, N. A. (2013). Measuring neighborhood effects and the use of geo-coded variables. Presentation for the CTSI Clinical Research Development Seminar. Retrieved from http://www.ctsi.ucla.edu/education/files/view/training/docs/Ponce_Neigborhood_Data_Sources_012213.pdf

Sheridan, S. M., Koziol, N. A., Clarke, B. L., Rispoli, K. M., & Coutts, M. J. (2014). The influence of rurality and parental affect on kindergarten children's social and behavioral functioning. *Early Education and Development, 25*, 1057–1082.

Strange, M., Johnson, J., Showalter, D., & Klein, R. (2012). Why rural matters 2011–2012: The condition of rural education in the 50 states. A report of the Rural School and Community Trust Policy Program. Retrieved from http://www.aplusala.org/uploadedFiles/File/WRM2011-12.pdf

Stufft, D. L., & Brogadir, R. (2010). Educating the culturally and linguistically diverse non-urban population: Three cost-effective strategies. *The Rural Educator, 31*, 21–26.

Tekniepe, R. J. (2015). Identifying the factors that contribute to involuntary departures of school superintendents in rural America. *Journal of Research in Rural Education, 30*, 1–13.

The Rural School and Community Trust. (2013). It's complicated… Why what's rural matters. *Rural Policy Matters, 15*(7). Retrieved from http://www.ruraledu.org/user_uploads/file/rpm/RPM15_07.pdf

U.S. Department of Agriculture, Economic Research Service (ERS USDA, n.d.-a). What is rural? Retrieved from http://www.ers.usda.gov/topics/rural-economy-population/rural-classifications/what-is-rural.aspx#.U3paza1dVqs

U.S. Department of Agriculture, Economic Research Service (ERS USDA, n.d.-b). Rural-Urban Continuum Codes: Documentation. Retrieved from http://www.ers.usda.gov/data-products/urban-influence-codes/documentation.aspx#.Uv5QSvldV1k

U.S. Department of Agriculture, Economic Research Service (ERS USDA, n.d.-c). Urban influence codes: Documentation. Retrieved from http://www.ers.usda.gov/data-products/urban-influence-codes/documentation.aspx

U.S. Department of Agriculture, Economic Research Service (ERS USDA, n.d.-d). 2010 Rural-urban commuting area codes: Documentation. Retrieved from http://www.ers.usda.gov/data-products/rural-urban-commuting-area-codes/documentation.aspx

U.S. Department of Education (DOE, n.d.-a). Rural and Low-Income School Program: Eligibility. Retrieved from http://www2.ed.gov/programs/reaprlisp/eligibility.html

U.S. Department of Education (DOE, n.d.-b). Small, Rural School Achievement Program: Eligibility. Retrieved from http://www2.ed.gov/programs/reapsrsa/eligibility.html

U.S. Department of Education (DOE, n.d.-c). Flexibility and Waivers. Retrieved from http://www2.ed.gov/nclb/freedom/local/flexibility/index.html

U.S. Department of Education (DOE, n.d.-d). Rural Education and Achievement Program. Retrieved from http://www2.ed.gov/nclb/freedom/local/reap.html

U.S. Department of Education, Institute of Education Sciences, National Center for Education Statistics (NCES, n.d.-a). Common Core of Data: Identification of Rural Locales. Retrieved from http://nces.ed.gov/surveys/ruraled/definitions.asp

U.S. Department of Education, Institute of Education Sciences, National Center for Education Statistics (NCES, n.d.-b). Rural education in America: Prior Urban/Rural Classification Systems. Retrieved from http://nces.ed.gov/ccd/rural_locales.asp

U.S. Department of Education, Institute of Education Sciences, National Center for Education Statistics. (NCES, n.d.-c). Kindergarten class of 1998–99 (ECLS-K). Retrieved from http://nces.ed.gov/ecls/Kindergarten.asp

U.S. Department of Education, Institute of Education Sciences, National Center for Education Statistics. (n.d.-d). Frequently asked questions: Data file information. Retrieved from http://nces.ed.gov/ecls/kinderfaq.asp?faq=5

U.S. Office of Management and Budget. (OMB, February 28, 2013). *Revised delineations of metropolitan statistical areas, micropolitan statistical areas, and combined statistical areas, and guidance on uses of the delineations of these areas* (OMB Bulletin No. 13-01). Washington, DC: Author. Retrieved from http://www.whitehouse.gov/sites/default/files/omb/bulletins/2013/b-13-01.pdf

U.S. Office of Management and Budget. (OMB, February 13, 2012). Fiscal Year 2013 Budget of the U.S. Government. Retrieved from http://www.whitehouse.gov/sites/default/files/omb/budget/fy2013/assets/budget.pdf

U.S. Office of Management and Budget. (OMB, June 28, 2010). 2010 Standards for delineating metropolitan and micropolitan statistical areas; Notice. *Federal Register, 75*(123). Retrieved from http://www.whitehouse.gov/sites/default/files/omb/assets/fedreg_2010/06282010_metro_standards-Complete.pdf

Uva, J. L., Wagner, V. L., & Gesten, F. C. (2012). Emergency department reliance among rural children in medicaid in New York State. *Journal of Rural Health, 28*, 152–161.

Waldorf, B. S. (2006a). *A continuous multi-dimensional measure of rurality: Moving beyond threshold measures.* Paper presented at the Annual Meetings of the Association of Agricultural Economics, Long Beach, CA, July 2006. Retrieved from http://ageconsearch.umn.edu/bitstream/21383/1/sp06wa02.pdf

Waldorf, B. S. (2006b). *What is rural and what is urban in Indiana.* Working Paper, Purdue Center for Regional Development. Retrieved from http://www.pcrd.purdue.edu/documents/publications/What_is_Rural_and_What_is_Urban_in_Indiana.pdf

Washington, Wyoming, Alaska, Montana, and Idaho Rural Health Research Center. (n.d.-a). Rural-Urban Commuting Area Codes (RUCAs). Retrieved from http://depts.washington.edu/uwruca/index.php

Wenger, K. J., Dinsmore, J., & Villagómez, A. (2012). Teacher identity in a multicultural rural school: Lessons learned at Vista Charter. *Journal of Research in Rural Education, 27*. Retrieved from http://www.jrre.psu.edu/articles/27-5.pdf

West, A. N., Lee, R. E., Shambaugh-Miller, M. D., Bair, B. D., Mueller, K. J., Lilly, R. S., et al. (2010). Defining "rural" for veterans' health care planning. *The Journal of Rural Health, 26*, 301–309.

Wilcox, K. C., Angelis, J. I., Baker, L., & Lawson, H. A. (2014). The value of people, place and possibilities: A multiple case study of rural high school completion. *Journal of Research in Rural Education, 29*, 1–18.

Partnership-Based Approaches in Rural Education Research

Gina M. Kunz, Pamela Buffington, Charles P. Schroeder,
Ronnie Green, Robert Mahaffey, Jennifer Widner,
Michelle Howell Smith and Mary Hellwege

Abstract This chapter represents multiple perspectives of collaboration suggested by conference participants of the *Connect-Inform-Advance: 2013 Conference on Rural Education Research (C-I-A)*, sponsored by the National Center for Research on Rural Education at the University of Nebraska-Lincoln. Conference participants endorsed effective partnership-based approaches in rural education research including multiple perspectives of rural education research, practice, policy and community. The consensus from C-I-A conference participants was that partnership-based approaches provide a unique and valuable approach to conducting the complete cycle of rural education research (e.g., development, conduction and dissemination). Participant-authors of this chapter represent key stakeholder groups identified by conference participants of rural education research, practice, policy and community. A primary data source included participant-authors' shared experiences

G.M. Kunz (✉) · M.H. Smith · M. Hellwege
National Center for Research on Rural Education, Nebraska Center for Research on Children, Youth, Families and Schools, University of Nebraska—Lincoln, 216 Mabel Lee Hall, Lincoln, NE 68588-0235, USA
e-mail: gkunz2@unl.edu

P. Buffington
Education Development Center, Inc., Gardiner, USA

C.P. Schroeder
Rural Futures Institute, University of Nebraska, Lincoln, USA

R. Green
University of Nebraska—Lincoln, Lincoln, USA

R. Mahaffey
The Rural School and Community Trust Organizations Concerned about Education, Washington, D.C., USA

J. Widner
O'Neill Elementary School, O'Neill, USA

J. Widner
Wayne State College, Wayne, NE, USA

© Springer International Publishing Switzerland 2017
G.C. Nugent et al. (eds.), *Rural Education Research in the United States*,
DOI 10.1007/978-3-319-42940-3_4

in rural education research, perspectives on developing, maintaining partnerships, and suggestions for future directions. Another source comes from findings related to multiple perspective partnerships in rural educational research emerging from a qualitative analysis of participant responses in the roundtable discussions conducted during the C-I-A conference (findings presented in Chapter "Multidisciplinary Perspectives to Advance Rural Education Research" of this book). A third source is literature relevant to partnership-based approaches to rural education research. Participant-authors' perspectives, conference participants' consensus and relevant literature were triangulated in identifying the themes presented in this chapter.

Keywords Rural education research partnerships · Rural education partnerships · Rural partnerships · Research and practice · Rural research and practice partnerships · Research and practice partnerships · Rural education research · Rural research

1   Introduction to Rural Education Research Partnership-Based Approaches

Partnerships are critical to conducting, implementing and sustaining meaningful and impactful rural education research (Alber and Nelson 2002; Bauch 2001; Coburn et al. 2013; Davis et al. 2014; Tseng 2011). Unfortunately, there is no agreed upon definition of research partnerships or a guide for how to develop and sustain meaningful partnerships in rural education research. This discrepancy begs the questions of "What constitutes partnerships in rural education research? How can such partnerships be formed and sustained? What roles and perspectives are important to have involved in partnerships?" We grapple with these questions in this chapter.

To inform our discussion, we have turned to representative voices of rural education research, practice, policy, and community; findings from the *Connect-Inform-Advance: 2013 Conference on Rural Education Research* (C-I-A; see Chapter "Multidisciplinary Perspectives to Advance Rural Education Research" of this book) related specifically to partnerships in rural education research; and literature on research partnerships. This chapter does not pretend to determine exactly what partnerships in rural education research are, nor does it promise to provide a step-by-step "how to" instruction manual for developing and sustaining such partnerships. Rather, this chapter attempts to highlight various perspectives on partnerships in rural education research. This chapter is unique in that the multiple perspectives presented have been interwoven to provide shared and unique perspectives on rural education research partnerships based on decades of practical experiences. Drawing from the literature, C-I-A conference findings and the participant-authors' experiences, this chapter provides suggestions for how to establish and maintain partnerships, suggestions for overcoming challenges to partnerships, and ways to communicate successful strategies to others in the field.

2 Methodology

This chapter represents the triangulation of three sources of data: literature on partnership-based approaches relevant to rural education research, findings from the 2013 Connect-Inform-Advance National Conference on Rural Education Research, and input from participant-authors.

2.1 Literature

In 2005, Minner and Hiles summarized the literature on rural school-community partnerships within the context of the National Science Foundation Rural Systemic Initiative. They found literature based on case studies, focus groups, and anecdotal information, but no empirical studies specific to rural school-community partnerships. A decade later, we had similar results. Our initial review of the literature exclusively on partnership-based approaches in rural education research resulted in a limited number of articles. Therefore, we expanded the review to include literature in the areas of rural and non-rural partnerships in education research as well as health-related research. We identified 20 articles that offered some insight into the common practices and challenges related to rural education research partnerships.

2.2 Conference Findings

A primary purpose of the C-I-A conference was to provide a platform for interactive discussion among participants related to research that focused on factors that influence rural student educational outcomes. Conference participants represented multiple stakeholders, including rural education researchers, practitioners and policy-makers. Conference attendees actively participated in roundtable discussions that followed research presentations. The discussions were designed to engage participants in meaningful conversations to address critical issues of how to advance rural education research. Data from the conference round-table discussions were qualitatively analyzed, and findings revealed that developing authentic partnerships among multiple voices—including research, practice, policy and community—in rural education research were critical in advancing a meaningful and timely research agenda for rural education (see Chapter "Multidisciplinary Perspectives to Advance Rural Education Research" of this book). Discussions of what was needed in order to accomplish these types of research partnerships in rural education resulted in the identification of several key recommendations which are fully discussed in Chapter "Multidisciplinary Perspectives to Advance Rural Education Research" of this book. These recommendations were used as an additional source of data for this chapter.

2.3 Participant Authors

The lead author used a purposive sampling in selecting participant authors to collaboratively develop this chapter because of their (a) representation of multiple voices of rural education research, practice, policy and community experience and (b) participation in the 2013 Connect-Inform-Advance National Conference. All participant authors except Chuck Schroeder actively participated in the National Conference, and all participant-authors have vast experience with research partnerships in rural education.

Several months after the conference, the lead author contacted these co-authors and invited them to participate in collaboratively contributing their knowledge and expertise to the development of this chapter on partnerships in rural education research; all enthusiastically accepted the invitation. True to an authentic partnership approach, the participant-authors met in person (some joined by phone) to discuss the approach to the chapter, overarching content to include, and main messages they wanted the chapter to convey. Participant-authors decided that the best way to communicate their knowledge and experience on this topic was by having the lead author email a list of guiding questions based on the content of their conversation at that meeting (see Table 1 for a list of the guiding questions). Then, the lead author, with assistance from two non-participant co-authors, would conduct

Table 1 Guiding questions and other item prompts to stimulate author responses	1. What is your *definition* of a partnership, especially as it relates to a partnership in rural education research?
	2. How do you *conceptualize* partnerships in rural education research, especially as it relates to your perspective given your role (e.g., research, educational practice, policy, community)?
	3. What contributes to a successful partnership in rural education research?
	4. What are some of the challenges to a successful rural education research partnership?
	5. How are successful partnerships related to rural education research established and maintained in the rural context?
	6. What are unique aspects of partnerships in the rural context?
	7. Please share a summary of your experiences OR one representative experience related to your role in partnerships in rural education research
	8. How do you define "community" as it relates to partnerships in rural education research? What characteristics are markedly unique to the rural context?
	9. Please provide recommendations for future directions to advance rural education research

a qualitative analysis of the type-written responses to identify themes related to partnerships in rural education research. The participant-authors agreed to provide any further information or clarification needed through written or verbal communication with the lead author. Participant authors were sent respective descriptions of personal information and a summary of the primary themes identified and asked to provide fact checks and clarifications.

What follows is a summary of the "rural story" of the participant authors, organized by the respective voices and roles they represent: rural education researcher, practitioner, community perspective, and policy maker. Their backgrounds and experiences in the rural education research arena collectively demonstrate their seasoned ability to serve as representatives for these perspectives.

2.3.1 Rural Education Researchers

Gina M. Kunz, PhD, first became involved with rural education when she provided behavioral health services to students and their families in rural communities in the Deep South as well as the Midwest. She has engaged in numerous research-based rural education partnerships primarily involving K-12 teachers, administrators, and families. Dr. Kunz has extensive experience establishing research-practice partnerships, maintaining those partnerships, and re-establishing partnerships in some communities after administrative turnover. She believes that what contributed to the success of those partnerships was the honesty and transparency with which the proposed project was presented. She believes it was critical that she presented the potential benefits to partnering schools. She has found that acknowledging the potential partner's critical role and expressing much appreciation for their consideration has gone a long way in the initial stages of partnership development. Interacting with teacher research participants as professional colleagues has also been crucial to establishing and maintaining partnerships in rural communities. Follow-through has been critical. One example was that at the end of a year-long project, a principal of one partner school told her that he was so pleased, and quite surprised, that their research team members "did everything they said they would do – and more!" Unfortunately, according to the principal, that school had been involved in several research projects, and rarely had team members even come somewhat close to delivering what they had promised and that often the team members just disappeared over time. He also shared that in previous experiences, the research team came in, gathered the data they needed, and left. They did not even share findings with the school. Unlike previous experiences he was convinced that their school was better off because of their participation in the project. Dr. Kunz is a Research Associate Professor in the Nebraska Center for Research on Children, Youth, Families and Schools, housed in the College of Education and Human Sciences at the University of Nebraska-Lincoln.

Pamela Buffington, PhD, grew up in a rural setting, attended rural schools, and currently lives in a rural community. She engages in multiple projects within rural schools and communities across the Northeast. She is co-principal investigator of a National Science Foundation funded project, the Research and Practice Collaboratory, which has an overarching goal to decrease the gap between research and practice. In this project she has engaged in partnership among researchers, content experts, district leaders, teachers, and other education stakeholders to collectively identify a persistent problem of practice and design and test appropriate interventions. This type of collaborative research partnership has helped to surface ways of working between and among research and practice that can be leveraged in rural schools. She views her role across multiple projects as engaging in *praxis*, the bridging of theory and practice. She is able to leverage her deep knowledge of the rural context to surface issues relevant to both researchers and practitioners as she and her colleagues design and engage in research in rural schools and communities. She also is able to act as translator between and among participants as they bridge the vernacular of research and practice. Dr. Buffington is the Regional Educational Laboratory Northeast and Islands (REL-NEI) Co-Facilitator of the Northeast Rural Districts Research Alliance (NRDRA) and the State Liaison for Maine, New Hampshire, and Vermont. This alliance includes rural practitioners, rural researchers, policy makers from rural states in the Northeast, and additional researchers from REL-NEI. This alliance represents a successful, on-going effort to co-develop and conduct a rural education research agenda that is meaningful to all partners. They have met approximately monthly over the last four years through face-to-face and online conferencing meetings. They have established a multi-year, multi-project research agenda; organized and run multiple webinars around critical rural issues and topics; presented collaboratively at national rural education conferences; organized and conducted a rural research symposium; and shared research and rural initiatives among and between members (http://www.relnei.org/research-alliances/northeast-rural-districts-alliance.html). The Core Planning Group members of NRDRA assume leadership roles during events, bring issues to the group to keep both researcher and practitioner members abreast of emerging rural issues, serve as advisors during NRDRA research studies and projects, act as ambassadors to rural serving organizations and networks, and engage in activities that increase the capacity of all involved to engage in rural research in more informed and authentic ways.

2.3.2 Rural Educational Practitioner

Jennifer Widner, MS, shared that her best representative experience with a rural education research-based partnership occurred in 2011 when she and the superintendent of the school district for which she was principal attended a session on rural research opportunities at the Nebraska School Boards Convention in Omaha. The presenters described a project in which a team approach with teacher and parent support would be used to address behavioral needs of students. This project matched concerns that had been expressed by several teachers in their school building. Upon invitation from Ms. Widner, the UNL research representative spoke with their staff and discussed the benefits for students. The required number of teachers agreed to participate. The research team began quickly to organize the project. They met with teachers and parents. They randomly assigned a control group and an experimental group. Team meetings were held with teachers, parents and research project-based consultants to establish behavioral plans for students. During the data collection period, teachers and parents received guidance and support to help their students make behavioral changes. Each student that was supported by a unified team made progress toward their goal. The majority of teachers and parents participating learned new strategies for helping children successfully manage their behavior. Ms. Widner commented that the support provided to the teachers and the parents by the research staff was wonderful, and this research project provided a great opportunity for their elementary school. Ms. Widner is a Retired Principal from an elementary school in rural Nebraska and Adjunct Faculty at Wayne State College.

2.3.3 Rural Education Community Perspective Representatives

Charles (Chuck) P. Schroeder, BS, spent the first thirty years of his life living in a rural Nebraska community where the school was the hub of area activity. Members of his family were involved in bringing outside resources to the school to enhance learning opportunities, broadening exposure to perspectives beyond the local realm, and celebrating the value of the community. Through five careers since leaving that community, he has been in leadership positions with the Nebraska Department of Agriculture, the University of Nebraska Foundation, the National Cattlemen's Beef Association (NCBA), and the National Cowboy & Western Heritage Museum, and now the Rural Futures Institute. He shared that in each of those enterprises, he has had the opportunity to connect research and educational resources at state, regional and national levels with local schools in order to strengthen educational opportunities. During his tenure with the Nebraska Department of Agriculture, the "Ag in the Classroom" program connected government agencies at the federal and state levels, as well as state and national farm organizations, directly with teachers across the K-12 spectrum to provide effective curriculum focused on America's food production system. While at NCBA, the research and education team, along with leading nutritionists from a variety of organizations and institutions, provided strong research-based education materials on the role of red meat in the human diet, particularly for women, to middle and high school teachers across the country. At the National Cowboy & Western Heritage Museum, their education team assembled and provided "trunk shows" for elementary schools in Oklahoma and regionally, partnering with teachers in local schools to help students learn about the diverse heritage of the American West with hands-on educational materials. They also worked with other museums in several states exploring effective distance learning techniques that would allow teachers, even in very rural locations, to access top quality instructors in various aspects of Western art, history and cultures. Mr. Schroder firmly believes that creative educational practitioners in rural schools, with the means to connect their students to appropriate resources via innovative partnerships, can build exceptional opportunities for learning across disciplines. Mr. Schroeder is Executive Director for the Rural Futures Institute at the University of Nebraska.

Ronnie Green, PhD, was raised on a mixed beef, dairy, and cropping farm in rural southwestern Virginia, where he learned to appreciate the value of hard work and the important role rural communities play in our nation's food production system. These early experiences led Dr. Green to pursue a career in animal science to research more effective an efficient ways to raise cattle. Dr. Green's passion for helping agriculturally-based rural communities has led him to key national leadership positions including the national program leader for animal production research for the USDA's Agricultural Research Service and executive secretary of the White House's interagency working group on animal genomics within the National Science and Technology Council. Throughout his vast experiences in collaborations in rural communities, Dr. Green has learned the important role that community champions play when conducting research in rural areas. It matters less what position the champion holds in the community and more that the person has a passion for the project and is willing to encourage others in the community to be supportive and even get involved. Dr. Green is the former Harlan Vice Chancellor of the Institute of Agriculture and Natural Resources at the University of Nebraska-Lincoln and recently became Chancellor of UNL.

2.3.4   Rural Educational Policy Maker

Robert Mahaffey, MS, firmly believes that collaboration among multiple voices in rural education research partnerships is critical. Further, he asserts that holding to all high standards for research excellence will lead the way to broadening rural education research opportunities. He views the bottom line as more investment must be made in rural education research that is timely, practical, and designed to attract multiple partners that value and want to improve learning opportunities for all rural students where they live and go to school. This is close to home for Mr. Mahaffey as he serves as a substitute teacher in his home state of West Virginia. Mr. Mahaffey is Director of Marketing and Communications at the Rural School and Community Trust, and he is President for the Organizations Concerned about Rural Education. Since 1998, the Rural School and Community Trust has issued the biennial research report *Why Rural Matters*. In his role as a policymaker, this work stands out because it is grounded in rural context exclusively, has secured the interest of researchers, policymakers, community members and funders, and has had funding support for more than a decade. He believes that *Why Rural Matters* has and will continue to overcome several key realities of high quality rural education research. Namely, it is grounded authentically in rural context, it is committed to providing rural practitioner-relevant findings, and it involves and promotes building partnerships dedicated to delivering a body of knowledge that is uniquely rural. He believes the key to the success and value of *Why Rural Matters* is that each edition has a focus area designed to be of interest to rural education practitioners, community voices, researchers and funders.

2.4   Data Analysis

We used a two-phase process to analyze data from the three sources: literature reviews, C-I-A conference findings, and participant-authors. For the first coding cycle, we used a provisional coding approach (Saldaña 2013; Miles et al. 2014). This deductive approach was based on key ideas that emerged from the literature review and the findings from the C-I-A conference. This became a "start list" of codes that seemed reasonable to appear in the texts provided by the participant-authors, and additional codes were added to reflect new ideas and concepts as they emerged from the data. This phase was followed by a second cycle of analysis across all three sources of data using an inductive pattern coding approach (Saldaña 2013; Miles et al. 2014). This phase of analysis involved the development of themes related to rural education research partnerships and identification of relationships among those themes. By condensing data into more meaningful units of analysis, we were able to identify the overarching themes presented in the findings.

3   Findings

We begin with a discussion about the how educational research partnerships are defined and conceptualized within rural communities. This discussion frames a context for the themes and related key ideas that emerged from the two-phase analysis.

3.1   Defining and Approaching Partnerships in Rural Education Research

There are several methodological traditions that use a partnership approach when conducting research that can inform our understanding of partnerships in rural education research. A few examples include "community-based participatory research," "action research," and "participatory action research" (Israel et al. 1998; Kennedy et al. 2011; Spoth 2007). Community-based participatory research is frequently used in health-related studies as a way to involve community members in the process of building capacity to address health disparities and inequities (Minkler and Wallerstein 2008). Action research involves practitioners in a cyclical process to address a real problem within a local setting (Plano Clark and Creswell 2014). Participatory action research blends elements of both approaches by including practitioners in the research process to address a specific social justice issue or inequity (Plano Clark and Creswell 2014). While these approaches offer some examples of partnering in research, they may not always be appropriate for rural education research. Sometimes opportunities to partner on a rural education research project evolve from an existing relationship. Other times, researchers seek to form a partnership only after a grant proposal is funded to conduct a specific research study. Research conducted as a result of the latter circumstance has the potential to be just as mutually beneficial for rural education outcomes as research that emerges from collaboratively-set research agendas. In some cases, having the funding already secured can help facilitate the partnership-building process by relieving the partnership of the burden of identifying, applying for, and securing funding.

Given the limited research partnership literature available specific to the rural educational context, it is not surprising that there is not one agreed-upon definition of "partnerships" in rural education research, and that the meaning of the available definitions can differ contextually (Bauch 2001; Coburn et al. 2013; Spoth 2007). Coburn et al. (2013) offered a definition of partnerships in rural education that includes many key elements identified in the literature: long-term collaborations between educational practitioners and researchers that are mutually beneficial and are organized for a specific purpose—to explore practice challenges and identify solutions that will improve outcomes. Other definitions build on these basic descriptors by including policy-makers as key stakeholders in addition to practitioners and researchers or by expanding the scope of the partnership to include every iterative stage of the research process from concept formation to conduction to dissemination of findings and to application (Barton et al. 2014; Israel et al. 1998).

Regardless of the way the partnership is formed or the specific term used to describe it, the conceptualization seems to be consistent. These research partnerships bring together stakeholders from multiple perspectives with diverse knowledge, expertise and skills for a common purpose of actively co-developing and/or conducting research that addresses complex and relevant issues unique to the setting in which the research is situated. There is a mutual expectation from the outset among partners that results from the research will be applied in order to advance pre-identified, desired outcomes. Perhaps the definition that most closely aligns with the purpose and perspectives of this chapter was provided by Barton et al. (2014): "Research partnerships bring practitioners, policymakers, and researchers together to develop questions, share data, conduct analyses, and use results. Across the country, diverse partnerships are working together to solve problems and bridge the worlds of practice, policy, and research" (p. 1).

3.2 Themes and Related Key Ideas Concerning Rural Education Research Partnerships

As we considered the three sources of data, three themes emerged. Each theme, noted in Table 2, will be described, with relevant evidence across all data sources provided. These ideas emerged as important and inter-related. Thus, these are not

Table 2 Themes and key ideas of authentic partnerships in rural education research

Theme 1	Authentic partnerships in rural education research include all stakeholders as valued, equal partners in research planning and coordination, conducting the study and applying and communicating the findings Key Idea 1: Authentic partnerships are inclusive, mutual, equitable and multi-directional with clearly defined goals and roles Key Idea 2: Authentic partnerships are genuine and ongoing Key Idea 3: Authentic partnerships proactively address differences
Theme 2	Authentic partnerships in rural education research focus on improving and sustaining educational outcomes within the community Key Idea 1: Authentic partnerships focus on improving educational outcomes (e.g., students, teachers, parents as educators or contributors to student outcomes) Key Idea 2: Authentic partnerships are committed to sustained service delivery Key Idea 3: Authentic partnerships apply and disseminate findings
Theme 3	Authentic partnerships in rural education research reflect the values and address the challenges of the rural context Key Idea 1: Authentic partnerships value the rural context Key Idea 2: Authentic partnerships overcome challenges to partnerships in the rural context

written from a "check-list" approach, but rather from the perspective of what constitutes authentic and productive partnerships. In brief, authentic partnerships hinge on meaningful, active, frequent, and on-going communication among partners that are multi-directional, mutual and respectful.

Theme 1: Authentic partnerships in rural education research include all stakeholders as valued, equal partners in research planning and coordination, conducting the study and applying and communicating the findings.

Inclusive Authentic partnerships are inclusive of relevant stakeholders. Examples from the literature tend to focus on practitioners, researchers, and policy-makers as the key stakeholders in research partnerships (Barton et al. 2014; Israel et al. 1998). Participant authors resoundingly agreed that practitioners, researchers, and policy makers all bring unique perspectives when conducting educational research in a rural setting that are critical to the successful implementation of the research study, dissemination of the results, and the application of the findings. Participant authors also advocated for involvement from the community in rural educational research partnerships. Although members of rural communities may be geographically linked, they have diverse social, economic, and/or political interests and views. Despite these differences, they often have a deep commitment to place and a vested interest in the success of the schools.

Community champions "Community champions" are influential and well-respected people in the community who have a passion for the project, can encourage others in the community to be supportive, and even can get involved. Strong leadership from school and community champions was also noted as a key component to the success of school-community partnerships in a case study of five rural Australian communities (Kilpatrick et al. 2002). While it is not always necessary or appropriate to have all possible stakeholder roles represented in the research partnership, it is important to consider all potential representatives when deciding who should comprise the partnership and be open to adding new partners as the goals and the needs of the project evolve.

Multi-directional Having an inclusive partnership is not, in and of itself, sufficient for a successful rural educational research partnership. Conference participants identified the need for multi-directional partnerships that establish meaningful and on-going dialogues regarding critical aspects of research, practice and policy related to rural education from the initial phases of research through dissemination and application. Unidirectional approaches that flow from research-to-practice can actually impede the translation of research findings by minimizing the contributions of practitioners in the research development process. Several articles noted that by taking a multidirectional approach to the research partnership, the research conducted is more relevant and meaningful to educational practice (Alber and Nelson 2002; Bauch 2001; Coburn et al. 2013; Davis et al. 2014; Tseng 2011). University extension programs, whose research programs are typically developed around needs identified within the communities they serve, are uniquely situated to facilitate multi-directional research partnerships because of the direct roles that extension faculty members serve with community organizations and citizens (Brown et al. 2013; Kennedy et al. 2011; Spoth 2007).

Collaborative Participant authors collectively viewed successful partnerships as those that had clearly identified goals that were developed collaboratively. Successful partnerships consist of ongoing dialogues about key factors related to each stage of research, including collaboratively interpreting and applying results and strategizing dissemination of gained knowledge. The notion that the needs, goals and purposes were clearly identified and that shared decision-making was characteristic of successful partnerships was also noted in the literature (Bauch 2001; Israel et al. 1998). Having partners develop research topics and questions together and developing a written partnership agreement that specifies responsibilities were key opportunities for collaboration (Alber and Nelson 2002; Barton et al. 2014; Ebersöhn et al. 2015). Co-development of research could be a viable alternative to traditional professional development experiences which can be difficult for rural teachers to access and translate into the classroom (Alber and Nelson 2002). Participant authors reflected that a shared understanding of and commitment to the research objective creates a partnership with purpose that can persist even in the absence of immediate projects. They also noted that shared planning and leading of meetings keeps them focused and productive for all partners.

Equal value Creating a successful research partnership requires an investment of time and energy from all stakeholders in order to establish trust and mutual respect, key ingredients identified in the literature (e.g., Bauch 2001; Brown et al. 2012; Ferman and Hill 2004; Israel et al. 1998; Kennedy et al. 2011; Minner and Hiles 2005; Tseng 2011, 2012a, b). Valuing each stakeholder's voice equally was a defining characteristic of successful partnerships from the literature (Bauch 2001; Israel et al. 1998). Participant authors concurred that successful partnerships require mutual respect for each other as professionals and equal value for everyone's unique contributions. Perceptions and realities of equal value in contributions can be a challenge, especially when researchers are typically compensated for their time spent conducting research while teachers and administrators typically add the work onto their existing responsibilities. Each partner needs an equitable voice which requires constant diligence and mindfulness not to privilege one voice, role, or perspective over another. The educational practitioner emphasized that each stakeholder in the partnership wants to be an informed participant which requires open and on-going communication. Examples from the literature of how the value of all partners' contributions was demonstrated included ensuring that credit is shared among all partners and that all partners' efforts are recognized in ways that are relevant to their careers and including all partners in dissemination efforts (e.g., publications, conference presentations, and presentations to educational practice colleagues) (Alber and Nelson 2002; Barton et al. 2014; Ebersöhn et al. 2015; Tseng 2012b).

Genuine Conference participants indicated that development and maintenance of genuine multi-disciplinary partnerships provides a sustainable process for rural education research that can lead to meaningful, valid and translational research needed to advance the rural educational research agenda. Participant authors agreed that it is especially important that partners from outside the community (e.g., university researchers) take a personal interest in the other partners as unique individuals and in the community. They suggested that strategically establishing relationships through face-to-face interaction and then follow-up with technology-assisted interaction can facilitate a genuine connection. This will help to address the isolation that many rural school administrators feel and establish a foundation upon which the relationship can build. Occasional opportunities for "one-on-one connecting and/or follow-up" will help to nurture the individual relationships and overall partnership over time, resulting in increased capacity of all stakeholders. The literature recommends social interaction among partners during their conversations rather than a strictly professional focus (Bauch 2001; Israel et al. 1998). A key indicator of genuine relationships among partners is maintaining close connections after the research is completed to support the sustained implementation of the findings in educational practice settings (Alber and Nelson 2002; Barton et al. 2014; Ebersöhn et al. 2015; Tseng 2012b).

Proactively address differences Participant authors acknowledged that in order to develop and maintain effective rural education research partnerships, it is important to be upfront about potential differences, actively and openly discuss them early on, and work toward resolutions and compromises to minimize likely negative effects. Potential challenges identified in the literature included misaligned agendas among partners, competing demands on time, effort and resources, and differences in incentive systems and structures in the various settings, especially in academic settings for researchers and practice settings for educational practitioners (Coburn et al. 2013; Downey et al. 2011; Ebersöhn et al. 2015; Israel et al. 1998; Spoth 2007). For example, while researchers' jobs include expectations of conducting research, teachers' jobs do not. These types of differences can lead to very different expectations from the partnership and the research process itself. Participant authors suggested that researchers and practitioners need to develop a shared language to talk about the context and phenomena being investigated in order to overcome specialized and often segregated ways researchers and practitioners talk about their work. Unfortunately, when differences and challenges are not recognized and resolved, partnerships can be destroyed despite well-intentioned partners from different perspectives. However, positive experiences that include researchers, practitioners, policy-makers and community stakeholders provide encouragement and strengthen the multi-disciplinary partnerships.

Theme 2: Authentic partnerships in rural education research focus on improving and sustaining educational outcomes within the community.

Focus on student outcomes No matter the role or perspective of the partners involved, the participant authors were clear that partnerships in rural education research are focused on improving educational outcomes for the students as well as teachers and, when appropriate, parents in rural communities. Community representatives expressed the importance of connecting the academic, social, emotional and physical elements of the school environment and leveraging shared resources and knowledge to discover new ways to help students. The literature also acknowledged the focus of research-based partnerships is on exploring challenges in educational practice and identifying solutions that will improve outcomes (Coburn et al. 2013), thus bridging the gap between educational research and practice (Alber and Nelson 2002).

Putting findings to work While findings from research partnerships have applications beyond the communities in which the research was conducted (e.g., implications for practice, policy, and future research), participant authors acknowledged that it is the immediate, local, and internal dissemination of research findings to the partnership members and educational consumers that is critical to the research partnership relationship. Because research takes a long time to conduct and publishing results takes additional time, there can be a delay in having the research study results available to impact practice and policy. Communication needs to be on-going in order to keep all partners informed in a meaningful way about findings throughout the research process. On-going communication in turn provides an opportunity for K-12 practitioners to not only inform the application of the findings but also shape the future direction of the research.

Sustained delivery Informing partners of the findings is only the first step in translating them into practice. Participant authors agreed that researchers need to make themselves available to educational practice settings outside the specified parameters of an individual research project. Researchers need to form long-term partnerships rather than coming into the schools, collecting data and leaving.

Partnerships that result from relationships that are built and refined over time, result in increased capacity of all stakeholders and in sustaining the benefits of the research for educational outcomes. A case study of research partnerships from the community perspective revealed frustration when services provided by the research team (e.g., undergraduate or graduate students) were withdrawn from the community following the conclusion of the academic semester or the research study (Ferman and Hill 2004). From the community perspective, the critical on-going supports and capacity-building were missing and they were no better off when the research team left than when they entered.

Theme 3: Authentic partnerships in rural education research reflect the values and address the challenges of the rural context.

Reserved An overarching frame for "rural" education research partnerships was clear: partnerships are grounded in the rural context. Many rural communities operate under an agricultural economy, typically with fewer specialized educational support services available. These factors, together with a poor economy, can lead to struggling families and schools. Isolation can lead to less access to research results and instructional methods. The K-12 rural school culture is still sometimes hesitant to embrace innovative research-to-practice findings, particularly when they have not been tested in rural settings. As a result, rural communities may be wary of outsiders who challenge an educational system that they may see as adequate.

Time and distance One challenge to building research partnerships that is uniquely rural is the additional time required to build relationships as a result of the geographic isolation of many rural communities from each other and the distance from researchers (Ebersöhn et al. 2015; Kennedy et al. 2011; Kilpatrick et al. 2002; Minner and Hiles 2005). Participant authors noted that travel time can exceed 3 h to meet face-to-face, challenging recruitment, relationship building and ongoing collaboration. Although technology helps maintain relationships, face-to-face interaction is essential even though it can be difficult.

Limits on methodology The remote location and small size of rural communities can limit the kinds of research methodologies that can be used. Research methods used in urban and suburban communities may not be appropriate due to smaller student enrollments, smaller number of faculty, or other factors (e.g., one school building for all grades K-12) within these schools and districts. Research studies using large scale experimental designs will likely require more participants than can be found in one rural district, or even among neighboring districts, in order to satisfy the statistical requirements necessary to detect meaningful effects. As a result, rural education research partnerships either need to span numerous communities or implement research designs that would have more limitations to consider when generalizing the results. Qualitative and mixed methods studies can also be impacted by the geographic isolation, with increased time and resources required to travel for on-site data collection.

Prior experiences It is important for researchers to be aware that they may need to repair relationships with rural communities that have had prior negative experiences working with other researchers. Frustrations that developed from poor communication, lack of follow-through, or other adverse occurrences can discourage or completely curtail researcher-initiated efforts to partner with those districts. Even when a rural community had a good experience with a research partnership, the high turnover rate of personnel in rural schools can also pose challenges in having to "start over" in efforts to establish relationships and shared agendas.

Know the culture Participant authors emphasized the importance of listening to the collaborative voices of all partners to develop an awareness of and an appreciation for the rural context in which the research takes place. In fact, a shared understanding of the rural context prior to the design of the research was seen as essential. Partners need to engage with the varying contexts of rural schools and communities so that the (a) particular realties of the schools and communities involved can be considered, explored and addressed in the research, (b) commonalities can be identified, and (c) the unique, and often complicated, context of the rural community can be respected. This idea was supported in the literature. Placing value for the culture of the community among the partners was noted as an important aspect of partnerships involving schools and communities in the rural context (Minner and Hiles 2005).

Rural communities are engaged Successful partnerships in rural education research are grounded in the rural community that includes families, businesses and town residents. From the rural community perspective, the concept of "community" is the entire school district from farms and ranches to the care center for the elderly and the families with children. Stakeholders include students, parents, educators, school boards, and taxpayers who are all active in rural school decision making. In rural communities, political and personal are intertwined (e.g., how tax dollars will be spent, school-based challenges that are experienced by key community leaders, etc.). Thus, these realities need to be explored and understood when engaging in collaborative efforts. This broad stakeholder involvement in school decision making is more prolific than in non-rural communities. Unlike urban and suburban areas, community members in rural areas who are uninvolved in the research can be well aware of its existence because rural communities are often small and close knit. Therefore, explicit attention needs to be paid to the community outside of the schools, as the community's support or lack thereof can affect the conduction of the research project at hand and future projects.

Champions Community members and organizations in the rural context can provide "champions" for research that can advance the rural education research agenda in a meaningful way. While champions for research are not exclusive in the rural context, they were viewed as critical in rural settings. Community champions can not only help identify school and community priorities which results in rural education research agendas that are more relevant and meaningful and can have sustainable impacts but also help strategize the best ways to approach the research process (e.g., community buy-in, participant recruitment, etc.).

Benefits Another uniquely positive rural consideration for research is the reduced bureaucracy when collaboratively designing and conducting research in smaller rural schools and districts. Minimized bureaucracy can facilitate faster, more responsive research. In addition, the smaller size can speed up gathering of appropriate consent necessary after the formal review board process is complete.

4 Discussion and Recommendations for Future Directions to Advance Partnership-Based Approaches in Rural Education Research

Recently, increased attention has been given to partnership-based approaches to research in rural education. While various terms and definitions for partnerships have been identified in the literature, there is currently no agreed upon definition for partnerships in rural education research. General consensus from the participant authors, results from the C-I-A conference and through the literature, is that partnerships in rural education research should include relevant stakeholders representing research, practice, policy and community in order to advance a rural education research agenda that is relevant, meaningful, sustainable and timely. Based on the literature, the predominant approach to rural education research partnerships has been that partnerships are practiced after the research has been developed by the researcher. Yet, having researchers and practitioners co-develop the research agenda or individual studies together and then have the researchers "go off and do" also seems *not* to be what is most needed. What appears to be missing is the blending of both aspects—co-developing the research agenda and then co-conducting the research. This practice can lead to a stronger connection of implementation between research and practice and increase the likelihood of changing policy.

Relationships In this chapter, we identified suggestions for establishing and maintaining rural education research partnerships. While many suggestions could apply to non-rural contexts, some were seen as particularly relevant and critical in the rural context to advance a rural education research agenda related to partnership-based approaches. One resounding message was that in order to truly advance the rural educational research agenda, multiple perspectives (i.e., rural educational research, practice, policy and community) partnership-based approaches were absolutely critical. Establishing and maintaining trust and mutual respect for all partners was also viewed as foundational for successful partnerships. Another important characteristic of successful partnerships that was identified in the literature and recognized by the participant authors was that elements of social interaction among partners need to be present rather than maintaining a strictly professionally focused conversation. While the literature did not limit this characteristic to the rural context, the collective perspectives of the participant authors supported this element as being especially relevant to partnerships in the rural context. Another critical component was that goals and purposes for the research and research partnership, as well as partner roles and responsibilities, were clearly identified from the outset. Finally, maintaining frequent and on-going communication throughout the process and following completion of the research was viewed as necessary for establishing as well as maintaining successful partnerships.

Overcoming challenges A second set of suggestions involved overcoming challenges to partnerships. First, potential barriers to the partnership should be explored at the outset and addressed as soon as possible. Examples of potential barriers were seen routinely in misaligned agendas, competing contingencies among partners, and differences in the incentive systems practiced in the various settings. A second suggestion for overcoming potential barriers was ensuring that contributions are viewed as equally important among all partners. Relatedly, recognition and credit should be shared among participants. Finally, it was pointed out that establishing and maintaining partnerships in rural areas often requires more time than in non-rural areas (Ebersöhn et al. 2015; Minner and Hiles 2005); thus, it was suggested to budget the time needed in order to establish a solid partnership with all the key representatives included.

Communicating findings A third set of suggestions relates to ways to communicate and disseminate effective strategies for establishing and maintaining successful rural education research partnerships. There is a profound need to establish and maintain effective and frequent methods of multi-directional communication among partners. Results from research partnerships should be presented in local rural communities through local newspapers, school board meetings, and in-services for school administrators and teachers. In addition to traditional outlets, social media (e.g., Facebook, Twitter, a website dedicated to communication among the partners, etc.) could be used to share potential projects, provide a platform to generate project ideas, and share project updates and results.

Communicating among partners There is also a need to identify or create intentional opportunities for multiple disciplines of research, practice, policy and community for large-scale discussions about critical issues surrounding partnerships and to develop strategic agendas to advance research on rural education (e.g., see Chapter "Multidisciplinary Perspectives to Advance Rural Education Research" of this book highlighting the C-I-A conference). By the conclusion of the C-I-A conference, it became evident through direct and implied statements that the conference was viewed as the opportunity to start these conversations addressing partnership-based approaches to rural education research. There was a well-articulated desire expressed by participants to continue these types of conversations in order to maximize the benefits of rural education research, in general, and in particular to develop successful rural education research partnerships involving research, practice, policy and community.

Policy Through the development of this chapter content, it became apparent that of all the stakeholders, policy is the voice least integrated into the partnerships in rural education research. Our policy-maker participant author shared that policy-makers need to become aware of prominent researchers in rural educational research and purposefully interact with them, for example, by attending rural education conferences. Policy-makers want to use the information from research and from demonstrations of effectiveness in practice in order to inform policy and policy changes needed, but that information is not always available. Sometimes, the policies come first and then practitioners are expected to implement based on the policy without the benefit of research evidence or having been able to test it out in practice. When meaningful, interactive partnerships are in place, access to the research process and the outcomes are increased for all partners involved. The implications are that practice and policy can be affected in more timely and meaningful ways based on evidence from research.

Lack of empirical studies Not much research has focused specifically on the process of partnerships in rural education research. While multiple-perspective partnerships have been acknowledged in previous literature, what is known about partnerships comes from focus groups, observations, case studies and anecdotal information; thus, there is a need for research studies that take a systematic approach, using more rigorous methodologies in studying partnerships in rural education research (Minner and Hiles 2005). The process is important. Research should include what accounts for successful partnerships and the process and conductions under which successful partnerships are developed and maintained. We need to establish empirical support for effective models of partnership development, productivity and sustainability, and we need opportunities to communicate findings about the process of effective partnerships.

Several gaps and recommendations have been identified in the literature on partnership-based approaches to rural education research. Recommendations have been made for further research on the process, the outcomes and the long-term effectiveness of partnerships-based approaches to research in rural education, as well as a careful study of contextual factors (Ferman and Hill 2004; Israel et al. 1998). Suggestions were made that future research studies are needed to examine and identify specifically what factors contribute to rural research partnerships between researchers and communities (Ferman and Hill; Spoth 2007) and that there is a great need for research to determine how to align incentives and to examine the long-term effectiveness of these research partnerships (Ferman and Hill). Studies should specifically examine variations in partnerships among diverse rural community cultural contexts to determine the similarities and differences among them that account for successful partnerships (Minner and Hiles 2005). Bauch (2001) stated the importance of local communities as a resource for rural schools, even though he acknowledged that research on this topic was scarce and that future research should examine important questions such as "how" and "how many" rural communities access their local communities as resources in models of school renewal. Another gap identified was that many published articles addressing partnership-based approaches in educational research, including rural and non-rural settings, were written from the perspective of the academic researchers; however, it is equally important to learn best approaches to partnerships from educational practice and community partners (Downey et al. 2011; Ferman and Hill 2004).

Disseminating research on research In order to truly advance the field of partnership-based approaches in rural education research, having well-articulated definitions are critical for conducting high-quality, meaningful research studies with "partnerships" as a primary variable of interest. Attention needs to be given to a variety of high-quality research approaches to studying partnerships in rural education research. In particular, increased consideration should be given to mixed methods approaches that involve schools and communities in order to avoid missing the aspect of context that is so important to rural education. The findings from studies focusing on successful partnerships and lessons learned need to be published (e.g., see Chapter "Recruiting Rural Schools for Education Research: Challenges and Strategies" of this book which discusses successful strategies for recruiting participants in rural education research; Minner and Hiles 2005) as well as presented at national conferences at which researchers, practitioners and policy-makers regularly attend (e.g., National Rural Education Association annual conference).

Partnership-based approaches to research are critical in order to advance conditions for using empirical findings to support practice and policy (Tseng 2012a). One author posed the following challenge for multidisciplinary research partnerships that seems to be a direct call for future research on how to conduct research partnerships:

> The challenge ahead for connecting research, policy, and practice is not just promoting the production and use of rigorous research, but creating the conditions that enable productive integration of multiple types of evidence. It will require building policymakers' and practitioners' capacities to evaluate different types of evidence and weigh their potential contributions to (and limitations for) solving specific problems (Tseng 2012a, p. 21).

The literature-base would benefit from future studies that provide an overview and the components addressed in the process of developing partnerships for conducting rural education research, with identification of challenges encountered in rural populations and settings. In this manner, integrative voices representing the various roles can be acknowledged and examined in future studies on effective partnership-based approaches in rural education research. Finally, there is a critical need to identify through systematic research effective partnership-based practices to meet the challenges in rural education research.

We issue a call to action to researchers, educators, and policy-makers that we all have a responsibility to develop authentic research partnerships in rural education research. We all need to take the initiative to seek opportunities to collaborate as well as accept invitations for collaborative, authentic partnerships. We are calling for a paradigm shift from traditional unidirectional approaches of "research to practice" or "research to policy" to partnerships that are multi-directional, reciprocal and include stakeholders from rural education research, practice, policy and community. Once this new way of doing business becomes the norm, then the full benefit of advancing the agenda for partnership-based approaches in rural education research can be realized.

Acknowledgments We thank Dr. Jeanne Surface, a professional colleague at the University of Nebraska at Omaha, for her collaborative contributions to the community aspect of partnership-based approaches articulated in this manuscript. Production of this manuscript was supported by the U.S. Department of Education's Institute of Education Sciences (Grant #: R305C090022).

References

Alber, S. R., & Nelson, J. S. (2002). Putting research in the collaborative hands of teachers and researchers: An alternative to traditional staff development. *Rural Special Education Quarterly, 21*, 24–30.

Barton, R., Nelsestuen, K., & Mazzeo, C. (2014). Addressing the challenges of building and maintaining effective research partnerships. *Lessons Learned, 4*(1), 1–6. Retrieved from http://wtgrantfoundation.org/FocusAreas#research-practice-partnerships

Bauch, P. A. (2001). Reexamining relations and a sense of place between schools and their constituents. *Peabody Journal of Education, 76*, 204–221.

Brown, L. D., Alter, T. R., Brown, L. G., Corbin, M. A., Flaherty-Craig, C., McPhail, L. G., et al. (2013). Rural Embedded Assistants for Community Health (REACH) network: First-person accounts in a community-university partnership. *American Journal of Community Psychology, 51*, 206–216.

Coburn, C. E., Penuel, W. R., & Geil, K. E. (2013). *Research-practice partnerships at the district level: A strategy for leveraging research for educational improvement in school districts.* New York, NY: William T. Grant Foundation. Retrieved from http://wtgrantfoundation.org/FocusAreas#research-practice-partnerships

Davis, M. M., Aromaa, S., McGinnis, P. B., Ramsey, K., Rollins, N., Smith, J., et al. (2014). Engaging the underserved: A process model to mobilize rural community health coalitions as partners in translational research. *Clinical and Translational Science, 7*, 300–306.

Downey, L. H., Castellanos, D. G., Yadrick, K., Avis-Williams, A., Graham-Kresge, S., & Bogle, M. (2011). Perceptions of community-based participatory research in the Delta Nutrition Intervention Research Initiative: An academic perspective. *Health Promotion Practice, 12*, 744–752.

Ebersöhn, L., Loots, T., Eloff, I., & Ferreira, R. (2015). Taking note of obstacles research partners negotiate in long-term higher education community engagement partnerships. *Teaching and Teacher Education, 45*, 59–72.

Ferman, B., & Hill, T. L. (2004). The challenges of agenda conflict in higher-education-community research partnerships: Views from the community side. *Journal of Urban Affairs, 26*, 241–257.

Israel, B. A., Schulz, A. J., Parker, E. A., & Becker, A. B. (1998). Review of community-based research: Assessing partnership approaches to improve public health. *Annual Review of Public Health, 19*, 173–202.

Kennedy, B. M., Prewitt, T. E., McCabe-Sellers, B., Strickland, E., Yadrick, K., Threadgill, P., et al. (2011). Academic partnerships and key leaders emerging from communities in the Lower

Mississippi Delta (LMD): A community-based participatory research model. *Journal of Cultural Diversity, 18*, 90–94.

Kilpatrick, S., Johns, S., Mulford, B., Falk, I., & Prescott, L. (2002). More than an education: Leadership for rural school–community partnerships (RIRDC Publication No. 02/055). Retrieved from http://pandora.nla.gov.au/pan/36440/20030717-0000/www.rirdc.gov.au/reports/HCC/02-055.pdf

Miles, M. B., Huberman, A. M., & Saldaña, J. (2014). *Qualitative data analysis: A methods sourcebook* (3rd ed.). Thousand Oaks, CA: SAGE Publications Inc.

Minkler, M., & Wallerstein, N. (Eds.). (2008). *Community-based participatory research for health: From process to outcomes* (2nd ed.). San Francisco, CA: Jossey-Bass.

Minner, D. D., & Hiles, E. (2005). Rural school–community partnerships: The case of science education. *Issues in Teacher Education, 14*, 81–94.

Plano Clark, V. L., & Creswell, J. W. (Eds.). (2014). *Understanding research: A consumer's guide* (2nd ed.). Upper Saddle River, NJ: Pearson.

Saldaña, J. (2013). *The coding manual for qualitative researchers* (2nd ed.). Thousand Oaks, CA: SAGE Publications Inc.

Spoth, R. (2007). Opportunities to meet challenges in rural prevention research: Findings from an evolving community-university partnership model. *The Journal of Rural Health, 23*(s1), 42–54.

Tseng, V. (2011). Forging common ground. In *2012 Annual Report* (pp. 18–25). William T. Grant Foundation.

Tseng, V. (2012a). *Improving the connections between research and practice*. New York, NY: William T. Grant Foundation. Retrieved from http://wtgrantfoundation.org/FocusAreas#research-practice-partnerships

Tseng, V. (2012b). *Partnerships: Shifting the dynamics between research and practice*. New York, NY: William T. Grant Foundation.

Recruiting Rural Schools for Education Research: Challenges and Strategies

Elizabeth Autio and Theresa Deussen

Abstract One third of all schools in the United States are located in rural areas, sharing characteristics that affect the way education is delivered. These include smaller average class sizes, geographic isolation, and reduced access to professional development for teachers. Despite their numbers, rural schools have historically been underrepresented in education research, particularly in rigorous studies. This chapter examines the recruitment of rural schools for education research, including an approach used to recruit Idaho schools for a cluster randomized trial. The authors describe how their approach addressed many of the unique features of rural schools. The focus on understanding local context, establishing personal connections, and offering high-quality professional development aligned with regional needs allowed the study team to recruit a sample that reflected the proportion of rural schools in the state. This proved to be an effective approach, although more expensive and time-consuming than recruitment efforts in urban and suburban settings. The authors conclude by discussing some considerations for researchers, as well as for funding agencies that wish to include rural school perspectives in future education research.

Keywords Rural schools · Randomized trial · Research design · Recruitment · Retention · Education research funding

E. Autio (✉)
7248 SE Grant Street, Portland, OR 97215, USA
e-mail: elizabethautio@gmail.com

E. Autio · T. Deussen
Education Northwest, 101 SW Main Street, Ste 500, Portland, OR 97204, USA
e-mail: theresa.deussen@educationnorthwest.org

© Springer International Publishing Switzerland 2017
G.C. Nugent et al. (eds.), *Rural Education Research in the United States*,
DOI 10.1007/978-3-319-42940-3_5

1   Introduction

One third (33 %) of all schools in the United States are located in rural areas; together, these schools serve a quarter (25 %) of the nation's students (U.S. Department of Education, National Center for Education Statistics 2013). Although rural schools share many similarities with schools in other geographic settings, they also have unique characteristics that may affect the implementation and impact of educational programs and interventions.

Rural schools have historically been underrepresented in educational research, particularly in high-quality experimental or quasi-experimental studies (Arnold et al. 2005). For example, about 6 % of all grants and contracts awarded by the U.S. Department of Education Institute of Education Sciences (IES) between 2002 and 2014 included the keyword "rural," versus 21 % with the keywords "urban" or "suburban" (U.S. Department of Education, Institute of Education Sciences 2015). This pattern appears to be slowly changing; a new group of rigorous studies, such as those conducted by the co-authors of this book, are examining program implementation and outcomes in the rural context. Still, there is a paucity of rigorous, extant studies to inform instructional practice and policy in rural schools.

As educators increasingly are called on to use high-quality evidence to make decisions about the programs they adopt for their schools, including rural schools in education research becomes more important. If, in fact, the differences between rural and urban/suburban schools translate into differences in impact, rural schools and districts need to know whether programs and interventions will work in their own settings.

Recruitment of willing participants is among the first steps in any research study and can be especially challenging in designs that include random assignment. Failure to successfully recruit an adequate sample can reduce a study's statistical power or even lead to the termination of a study before it begins. Poor or haphazard recruitment can introduce bias or set the stage for high attrition, invalidating the study's findings.

Recruiting rural participants may require modified strategies, compared to those used in urban and suburban locales. The existing literature on recruitment for educational research, however, is fairly thin and fails to addresses rural communities. In an attempt to fill this gap, we first examine the unique challenges and advantages of recruiting schools from rural settings for education research. We then describe how we successfully recruited teachers from rural areas of Idaho to participate in a two-year cluster randomized trial.

2 Characteristics of Rural Schools That Potentially Affect Recruitment

Although there is a lack of literature on recruitment for educational research, there is documentation of the characteristics of rural areas and schools, some of which might impact recruitment for participation in research studies. A number of these attributes may present challenges, while others may be advantageous in recruiting.

2.1 Small Size

Rural schools and districts are comparatively small and, on average, have smaller class sizes than schools in other settings (Jimerson 2005; Khattri et al. 1997; Monk 2007). From a research perspective, this can pose several challenges. First, it becomes more difficult to recruit a large enough sample of students, teachers, and/or schools to power an experimental design or to create an adequate control group for a quasi-experimental design. Second, because rural school districts are small, with fewer schools in a single district, a rigorous study will inevitably require the participation of multiple districts. Reaching out to multiple districts takes an investment of time and budget that goes far beyond what is necessary in urban or suburban settings.

Small school and class sizes also might mean that there are fewer students eligible for an intervention that is targeted to a specific segment of the school population. Researchers might encounter more multigrade classrooms, in which students of two or more grade levels are taught in the same room by the same teacher. This arrangement is one way that rural schools manage low student populations, but it can pose challenges for studies of interventions that are grade-specific.

2.2 Isolation and Self-Reliance

The geographic isolation of many rural schools, and the large distances between them, makes travel more costly and time-consuming, as well as presenting challenges for communication (Jimerson 2005; Khattri et al. 1997; Monk 2007). Therefore, travel budgets for recruitment in rural areas are important and usually must be larger than for the same activity in large urban or suburban districts.

For people who live far from services and from one another, the values of independence and self-reliance can be a matter of survival and a core part of rural culture (Slama 2004; Wagenfeld 2003). This insularity might contribute to an initial wariness of outsiders (Wagenfeld 2003), which poses a challenge to recruiters and researchers who are not already connected to and accepted by the community. It also may be one reason why rural communities often have strong traditions of local control and decision-making (Khattri et al. 1997). Randomized studies, on the other hand, require a high degree of control by the research team over the assignment of condition, implementation, and data collection (Roschelle et al. 2014); this might lead to a conflict in rural schools if not thoughtfully handled.

2.3 Technology Access and Use

Technology can be a valuable tool in connecting rural educators with the research team. While Internet access in rural communities has expanded greatly (Howley et al. 2011), there continues to be limited bandwidth in some areas that hampers practices such as distance education, videoconferencing, and use of streaming video (Hannum et al. 2009; Howley et al. 2011). Technology use in schools also depends on the ability of the local education agency to install, maintain, and support advanced technology, which is not always possible in rural districts (Howley et al. 2011). Consequently, it is not necessarily feasible to use distance technology as a reliable tool for recruiting and as a substitute for face-to-face communication.

2.4 Reduced Access to Professional Development and Research Study Participation

The combination of remote geography with strained district education budgets means that rural teachers have a difficult time accessing resources in general, including professional development (Jimerson 2005; Khattri et al. 1997; Gándara et al. 2005). Rural teachers in some areas are also far less likely to have been tapped for prior research studies than their urban counterparts, perhaps in part because there are fewer research institution in rural areas. This can pose a challenge for recruitment, as teachers could require additional explanation about the research process and purpose than those who have been study subjects before. On the other hand, it can also be an advantage to researchers; since there are fewer initiatives competing for teachers' time, they may be enthusiastic for professional development that meets an area of need, and they have not experienced "research fatigue."

2.5 Cultural Norms

Rural communities tend to be tight-knit with many longtime residents and families. Coupled with low population density, this means that people who live in the area are more likely to know each other. They are aware that others are interested in them and what they do, and that this information is shared with others in the community (Slama 2004).

The resulting lack of anonymity in rural areas might be alien to researchers who hail from bigger, more populous environments. Researchers venturing into a rural community for the first time may be blissfully unaware that their activities and behavior are observed and discussed among residents (including those who are and are not part of the school). For this reason, it becomes all the more important to be aware of local social and cultural norms, especially those that differ from their own locale.

3 Situating a Randomized Trial in Rural Idaho

3.1 The Intervention

Over the past 20 years, the proportion of students in U.S. schools who are not fully proficient in English has increased notably. Between 1994–1995 and 2009–2010, English learner (EL) enrollment grew from 3.18 to 5.21 million, a gain of 64 % (National Clearinghouse for English Language Acquisition 2011). Some growth has occurred in settings that have not historically served many ELs, such as rural communities (Jimerson 2005; Monk 2007). Much of this change is attributable to the employment of seasonal and migrant workers in the agriculture industry (Monk 2007). Many teachers in such locations have only recently started educating ELs for the first time, and often lack the background and training necessary to do so (Jimerson 2005), and states vary substantially in what they require teachers to know about teaching ELs (Ballantyne et al. 2008).

While recent demographic shifts have greatly increased the number of schools that serve ELs (Capps et al. 2005; National Clearinghouse for English Language Acquisition 2014), many serve comparatively small numbers of these students (Capps et al. 2005; Passel and Zimmerman 2001; Terrazas 2011). In these situations, ELs tend to be educated in mainstream classrooms alongside their non-EL peers. One popular way that districts attempt to address the needs of ELs is through "sheltered instruction," which uses specialized strategies and techniques to make the regular curriculum accessible to ELs in classrooms that also serve non-ELs (Echevarria et al. 2006). For example, sheltered instructional approaches often provide students with non-linguistic supports for understanding content, such as photographs, drawings or models to depict concepts. They also promote cooperative learning and small group conversation, which give students more opportunities to practice using oral language. Our study examined one variant of sheltered instruction that is widely used on the West Coast of the United States but had not previously been the subject of a rigorous impact study: Project GLAD (Guided Language Acquisition Design).

Project GLAD is a K–12 instructional approach initially developed in southern California in the late 1980s by teachers who wanted to better serve the growing numbers of ELs in their classrooms (Brechtel 2001). In Project GLAD, teachers use a set of discrete, specific instructional strategies to teach their state or district standards using the locally adopted curriculum. Thus, Project GLAD specifies not *what* is taught, but rather *how* it is taught.

Project GLAD provides intensive professional development to teachers following a highly structured 7-day training sequence. Teachers begin by attending a 2-day introductory workshop, which presents the strategies and addresses language acquisition, cultural influences in learning, and differentiation. The 2-day introduction is followed by a 5-day classroom demonstration. For five consecutive mornings, teachers observe a consultant trainer teach a thematic unit in a classroom at their own school using Project GLAD strategies. In the afternoons of the demonstration days, consultants support teachers in planning lessons that are connected to standards. Following the 5-day demonstration, trainers provide ongoing, onsite coaching. The amount of coaching varies and is negotiated between the district and trainers. For our study, we provided teachers with 3 days of coaching per school, per year, for 2 years: an amount that seemed feasible for districts to actually purchase.

3.2 Study Design

Our study examined the efficacy of Project GLAD on fifth-grade academic achievement through a 2-year cluster randomized trial, funded by the U.S. Department of Education's IES Research Grant Program. Schools were randomly assigned to treatment or control conditions. In treatment schools, fifth-grade teachers received standard Project GLAD professional development and follow-up coaching to learn how to implement the instructional model. In control schools, fifth-grade teachers continued to deliver business as usual. Control teachers received Project GLAD professional development in the third year, after data collection was completed, in a delayed treatment design.

Our research questions were:

1. To what extent do teachers implement the teaching strategies promoted by Project GLAD during the training year and the following school year?
2. What is the impact of Project GLAD teacher training on the reading, writing, and science achievement of fifth-grade students in the treatment classrooms during the initial training year, compared to a "business as usual" control group?
3. What is the impact of Project GLAD teacher training on the reading, writing, and science achievement of fifth-grade students in the treatment classrooms during the year following the initial training year, compared to a "business as usual" control group?
4. Is the impact of Project GLAD different for fifth-grade ELs and non-ELs?

We chose to focus on fifth grade for two reasons. First, since we were interested in literacy outcomes, the upper elementary grades were preferable, as students at this level are able to produce more complex writing samples than those in earlier grades. Second, we knew that Idaho had a statewide science assessment at the fifth grade level, which we would be able to use as one of our outcome measures for content area learning without adding the burden of administering another assessment to teachers.

Since our research questions asked whether the impact of Project GLAD was different for ELs and non-ELs, we needed to ensure that there was an adequate number of ELs for the study. Therefore, eligibility was determined by a school's EL enrollment in grade 5. Using Bloom's (2006) formula under several different assumptions about the number and distribution of ELs across schools and classrooms helped us set a target for a minimum number of EL students. Of the 355 Idaho elementary and middle schools that serve fifth grade, 85 met the minimum necessary number of EL students.

We collected data on student outcomes in reading comprehension, vocabulary, writing, and science. For teachers in the treatment condition, we captured implementation through classroom observations, conducted three times per year, and surveys, administered online once a month. To document the counterfactual, we conducted classroom observations in control classrooms twice a year and administered an annual paper and pencil survey to control teachers. Finally, to probe more deeply into specific areas of interest, we interviewed principals and teachers once or twice a year.

3.3 Location

When we first designed our study, we did not specifically target rural schools; rather, we used two key criteria in selecting a location. First, we sought a growing EL population and teacher demand for instructional practices to work with these students. We reasoned that if the study provided a skill or set of strategies that were perceived as desirable or worthwhile, it would make participation more attractive. This, in turn, could lead to easier recruitment, higher buy in, and lower attrition. Second, to minimize contamination of the control group, we sought a sample of teachers who had not previously been overly saturated with professional development in Project GLAD.

With our knowledge of the Pacific Northwest, where we conduct most of our work, we decided to locate the study in the state of Idaho. Idaho is a sparsely populated state in which 48 % of schools were classified as rural at the time of our study (U.S. Department of Education, National Center for Education Statistics 2011). Idaho also met both of the above criteria. A recent influx of migrant workers and refugees sharply increased the EL population: from 2007 to 2011, the proportion of foreign-born residents grew by 6 % and the proportion of people speaking a language other than English at home increased by 10 % (U.S. Department of Commerce 2013). By 2012, 5.9 % of Idaho's students were ELs and 13.2 % of all children lived in immigrant families (Migration Policy Institute 2012).

Accordingly, as these students were different from those that Idaho teachers had taught in the past, we heard from both teachers and administrators that there was a growing demand for instructional strategies designed to meet ELs' needs.

4 Recruitment Approach

Over an 11-month period, we created and implemented a plan to recruit a minimum of 28 schools from an eligibility pool of 85 rural, urban, and suburban schools. Almost half of the schools in the pool were located in rural areas. Given the small number of schools in the pool, we knew that we had to be highly successful in our recruitment efforts. Many aspects of our approach were recruitment practices that could be used regardless of locale. However, we were continually thinking about the rural context and the experience of teachers within it; thus, we did our best to address characteristics specific to rural schools.

4.1 Small Size

Sample size is crucial to ensuring sufficient statistical power for an experimental study (i.e., the ability to detect an effect that actually exists). Power is determined primarily by the number of units that will be randomly assigned to the treatment or control condition. Originally, we intended to recruit about 80–90 teachers who would be individually and randomly assigned to the treatment and control groups; with this design, we had no major concerns about sufficient power. Later, however, at teachers' insistence, we moved to a design that would assign entire schools to treatment or control groups. We neither had the funds to support 80 or more schools in the study, nor could we imagine that nearly all eligible schools in the state would participate. Therefore, we shifted to a target of recruiting at least 28 schools with an average of three teachers per school.

In a large urban setting, it might be possible to recruit 28 or more schools in a single district. When including the rural context, however, achieving this goal meant reaching out to many different districts. To recruit an adequate number of schools to power our study, we approached 42 districts, of which 21 agreed to participate. At each of the 42 districts, we spent time speaking with district administrators and sharing information about the study. Repeating this task 42 times, rather than once or twice, necessitated a larger recruitment budget than typical for other settings.

We utilized several strategies to maximize the cost-effectiveness of our recruitment efforts. First, our outreach began with the state department of education. Once funded, we held a daylong meeting with state staff to share information about the intervention and study. This included showing actual examples of Project GLAD strategies that participating teachers would learn and discussing evidence of their impact to date (which in this case was limited). Further, we invited state staff to attend an upcoming Project GLAD training to see, in person, the professional development approach and content. This meeting built a partnership between the researchers and state agency staff members, who said they considered it "an honor" to have the study conducted in Idaho. In turn, we learned about the local context in eligible districts and advice about how to approach them. We also obtained valuable introductions to district leadership, including a presentation slot at an upcoming state-convened conference where several districts would be in attendance.

As we moved forward, we continued to follow the chain of command—first approaching districts, then principals, and eventually teachers—which is always important, but becomes more complicated when there are multiple districts geographically spread out. Traveling in person to all 42 districts, only to wait for later meetings with their schools, would have quickly consumed our travel budget. Instead, we reached out to as many districts as possible through presentations at state meetings that district leaders were already attending. We approached the remaining districts via email and telephone, and then explained the study in greater detail through webinars and conference calls. Interested district staff introduced us to building principals, who arranged times for us to visit teachers in person.

Managing communications with 42 different districts, their principals, and their teachers quickly translated into a Herculean task. To track contacts, we created a relational database (as recommended in Redwood et al. 2011). This prevented confusion and also enabled different research team members to pick up threads of conversation as necessary. By the end of our recruitment period, our database contained 1773 communications with 314 different contacts.

Once we obtained entry to a school, we needed to consider the smaller class sizes and numbers of students typical of rural schools. For our study, we were interested in ensuring not only recruitment of a sufficient number of schools, but also a sufficient number of ELs in fifth-grade classrooms.

Even when we identified interested schools and teachers who taught ELs, we were not always able to include them in the study. This applied particularly to multigrade, or combination, classrooms. Because our study design involved following teachers for two consecutive years with two cohorts of fifth-grade students, we had to disallow several teachers who taught 4/5 combination classrooms. Including them would have meant that some students in our study might have 2 years of exposure to Project GLAD, while most would have only 1 year.

4.2   Isolation and Self-Reliance

Despite the geographic isolation of many of our eligible schools and the distances between them, we recruited every teacher who joined the study at a face-to-face meeting at his or her school. Within our limited recruitment budget, making initial personal contacts with teachers was where we chose to concentrate our travel dollars. Besides aiding in recruitment, these meetings created a relationship between the researchers and school staff, giving the study a "face" for potential participants.

Following the chain of command was one way in which we showed respect for local control and decision-making. Another way was allowing potential participants at each step to make the choice about joining or declining the study. We wanted teachers in particular to feel a sense of autonomy, as distinguished from a top-down approach in which the district or building leadership would mandate their participation. After visiting their schools, we left teachers with an unsigned memorandum of understanding (MOU) outlining what the study entailed, what they were responsible for, and what they would receive in turn, along with a postage-paid return envelope. We encouraged them to take time to think about their participation before returning, or not returning, the MOU.

Once teachers agreed to participate in the study, we continued to build our relationships with them through a range of personalized and friendly communications strategies. For example, as soon as we received a signed MOU, we sent a personally signed thank-you note along with a photocopy of the agreement. The research team member who had visited the school for recruitment remained the contact for teachers and other school staff until we conducted random assignment. We communicated the results of random assignment in personal phone calls and letters to district and building leaders, and then to teachers via email. At that point, communications were transferred to one of six "site liaisons": study team members who worked with three to five schools for the duration of the 2-year study, including conducting site visits and ensuring completion of data collection activities. We tried to reach as many teachers as possible through webinars and email, but we also used "old-fashioned" methods such as hand-written cards and phone calls, which added a more personalized touch.

As we met with teachers, concerns arose that were specific to the geographic isolation of their rural sites. The first had to do with the distances among participating schools, which were spread out over a 330-mile area. Rather than holding the 7 days of Project GLAD professional development in one central location, we held trainings at three locations with each accessible to a cluster of participating teachers. We covered the transportation and lodging costs for the few teachers who still had to travel more than 50 miles to the nearest training site.

A second concern had to do with our level of random assignment. We originally planned to randomly assign teachers to treatment or control conditions, meaning that within a given school, some teachers would receive professional development while others would be conducting business as usual. However, we found that many teachers balked at this idea. They felt it would be impossible for treatment teachers to keep the intervention strategies a "secret" from their colleagues, and the idea that they should do so made them not want to join the study.

The importance of teacher teams holds true across most schools, regardless of their location, but we found that teacher teams were all the more important in rural environments due to the small number of teachers on each team (typically 1–4); the lack of other nearby collaborators; and the strength of long-term relationships. We therefore revised our original plan and switched to random assignment at the school level. This lowered our power but was a necessary recalculation for working in the rural context.

4.3 Technology Access and Use

During recruitment, we did turn to some forms of technology to reach potential participants, particularly when contacting districts and principals. When presenting the study to district staff, we arranged for webinars when possible to show visual information such as timelines and examples of the intervention.

We also created a study website with information pertinent to recruitment. This included an overview of the intervention, the study design, the research team, map of schools that had signed up, and links to MOUs and other materials. We have continued to use the website for the duration of the study, sharing links to surveys, training materials, calendars, and, once data collection was concluded, findings.

We found, however, that using technology felt artificial when meeting new people with whom we did not have established relationships. Moreover, technology was not always available or reliable, particularly in smaller districts and schools; as well, some teachers were not regular users. After the study commenced, we made more frequent use of technology in the form of webinars explaining what it meant to be in the treatment or control group and updating schools on what to expect over the next few months of the study. These were sparsely attended.

For these reasons, in hindsight we believe we made the right decision to visit teachers in person for recruitment purposes. Each school presentation was led by one of two researchers who traveled to the school site after arranging a time with the principal (typically before or after school, sometimes during lunch or a planning period). The meetings lasted 45–60 min, including ample time for questions. After an introduction, the researcher explained the study and showed examples of the intervention without sharing any strategies that would be easily replicable by teachers who would be assigned to the control condition. A great deal of time was spent talking through a graphic representation of random assignment, data collection, incentives for participants, and the project timeline. To ensure that teachers fully understood what participation would mean, question and answer periods typically lasted for 20 min or more. Teachers were given a two-page summary of the study, which included names, photographs, and contact information for the study team.

Although traveling to rural areas to conduct these presentations took time and money, we believe that this ultimately led to higher teacher buy-in to the intervention and lower attrition. We also found that it was easier to answer questions in this setting, rather than through distance technology, which helped ensure that every teacher heard the same message about the study.

4.4   Reduced Access to Professional Development and Research Study Participation

As suggested by the literature, we found that teachers in rural Idaho had reduced access to professional development. This was partially attributable to some schools' geographic isolation; it was also due to statewide patterns in education spending and budget shortfalls. Idaho ranks 50th nationwide in per pupil spending and was undergoing additional cuts to its education budget at the time of our study (Dixon 2013). This translated into fewer and fewer training opportunities for its teachers, an unfortunate condition that turned out to be advantageous for our recruitment.

By selecting Idaho, we had already chosen a location where the intervention being studied (i.e., instructional strategies that work with EL and non-EL students in the same classroom) attempted to address local needs (i.e., a growing EL population). In our outreach to districts and principals, we deliberately emphasized the "opportunity for high-quality professional development" paid for by the study. This was very appealing to administrative staff, and teachers themselves were eager to learn techniques to work with their growing EL populations.

The goal of making participation attractive—and meaningful—also influenced our decision to use a delayed treatment design, in which teachers in the control group receive the intervention after official data collection for the experiment has been completed. With very few exceptions, teachers in the study had not previously been part of research. It felt unfair to ask teachers to commit to the study with only a 50 % chance that they would be able to receive the professional development that came with it, particularly when their other opportunities for training were so limited. Therefore, we assured teachers that those assigned to the control group could receive Project GLAD training in the final year of the study.

In addition to offering professional development in an area of need and interest, we wanted teachers to feel that we appreciated the extra time they took out of their day to engage in a fairly extensive array of data collection activities. We offered several incentives—in the form of cash cards and credits for classroom materials—to recognize the effort involved in administering assessments, completing surveys, sitting for interviews, and arranging classroom observations. Furthermore, we incentivized participation by providing teacher stipends for the summer workshop and substitutes for the demonstration and coaching time.

Finally, many teachers and administrators found the idea of being part of a research study attractive. We discovered an openness and interest we might not have encountered in an urban setting, as teachers were not fatigued from being asked to participate in multiple studies. Rather, they reported that they viewed the invitation as "exciting" and "an honor." With the national emphasis on using research to inform instruction, they were happy to take part in something that was part of the "bigger picture" in education and would help other educators.

4.5   Cultural Norms

For most of the study's participants, this was their first time being a part of a research endeavor. We therefore were particularly interested in leaving them with positive feelings about the experience. An essential, but often overlooked, component of this involves showing respect for local context by observing the community's cultural norms. In our situation, Idaho—with the exception of the capital city Boise—is politically conservative, and religion plays a large role for many residents. Eastern Idaho in particular has a local culture that reflects its large Mormon population. In contrast, our study team hails from a liberal, urban environment.

Through conversations with Idahoans and our own observations, we took the time to learn and respect local cultural norms, particularly regarding dress and personal conduct. (For example, in our particular locale we learned that in some parts of the state it would be inappropriate for a woman to go running in shorts; men should not wear sandals; school staff typically refers to each other as "Mr." or "Mrs.") Our training for research staff conducting school visits included a discussion of these norms and expectations. Due to the interconnectedness of rural schools and their communities, we also emphasized the importance for research team members to conduct themselves professionally at all times, not just while onsite, and to refrain from any public discussion (e.g., over dinner at a local restaurant) that would reflect negatively on what they had seen that day at the local school.

5   How Well Did Our Approach Work?

In many ways, our recruitment approach was successful. We recruited 30 schools, meeting the high end of our target. Our sample was adequately representative of rural Idaho schools: 50 % of schools in our sample were rural, which is very close to the 48 % of all Idaho schools.

We also had fairly high buy-in to the study: 80 % of participating teachers said they were pleased that their school was participating. Teachers were also extremely responsive to our data collection efforts: survey response rates were well over 90 % and participation in interviews and classroom observations was almost 100 %. This likely contributed to our low levels of teacher attrition. Among teachers who left the study between the beginning of the first year and end of the second, most moved, retired, or lost their job; a few were assigned to a different grade level.

While the recruitment process took more time than we anticipated when designing the study, we succeeded in completing recruitment within our specified time frame. Including planning time, the process took 11 months, with 2 planning months and 9 months for active recruitment (i.e., from our first presentation to random assignment). This is aligned with what others have found to be typical of recruitment timelines—namely, up to a year—in urban and suburban settings (Roschelle et al. 2014). Recruitment, however, was expensive: it cost five times what we originally estimated and required 0.7 FTE of researcher staff time over that 11-month period, plus some additional support staff time (for arranging travel and handling paperwork). Ultimately, we felt that this was a worthwhile investment in laying the foundation of the project, as it built relationships and understanding of the scope and timeline among participants, almost all of whom had not been part of a research study before.

In other ways, our recruitment efforts did not fully meet all our needs. While we were sufficiently powered to address our first three research questions, we were somewhat underpowered to answer our fourth question about how Project GLAD might impact ELs and non-ELs differently. There were multiple reasons for this, including a decline in the EL enrollment between the time we first ran our power estimates and when we began data collection.[1] In the end, however, we were able to pool data for ELs across 2 years, thereby increasing our statistical power.

6 Discussion and Implications

The continued inclusion of rural schools in high-quality experimental and quasi-experimental studies is essential, as "what works" for schools may vary contextually. In the case of interventions designed to serve ELs, for example, much of the guidance on how to support this population assumes contexts with trained staff and relevant resources and does not address the challenges faced in small rural districts (Lowenhaupt and Camburn 2011). The same may be true for special education or other interventions that are most often tested in well-resourced environments.

Rural schools also offer unique benefits to a research study. Educators in these locations tend to have less access to high-quality professional development than their peers. Therefore, they may be more eager to participate in the intervention than those who already have a plethora of professional development opportunities and existing initiatives. Moreover, contamination risks may be reduced, as educators in a control group are less likely to have been exposed to the intervention or similar programs in the past and, due to distance, are less likely to interact with members of the treatment group.

At the same time, there are considerations for working with rural schools. A central concern is sample size and power. In our study, we had a limited pool of schools from which to recruit. Although we met our recruitment target, we later lost power due to a change from teacher- to school-level random assignment and were

---

[1]We also experienced a particular situation in which Bloom's (2006) hypothesis that moderator analyses often have more statistical power does not hold true: that is, when the interclass correlation of the subgroup is very low.

underpowered for our subgroup analyses due to an unforeseen decline in EL enrollment. We would recommend that researchers designing future studies in rural schools use the worst-case assumptions and take the most conservative power estimates. This would help to ensure sufficient power for subgroup analyses for fluctuating populations such as ELs or students in special education.

Also, we had not anticipated rural teachers' reluctance to be assigned to a different group from their colleagues; future research designs should take this into consideration. While, as researchers, we might tolerate the possible contamination that could occur with control and treatment teachers in the same school (Rhoads 2011), this was highly disagreeable for teachers in our study, particularly those who had only one or two grade-level collaborators.

We also found that recruiting rural schools required additional time, effort, and budget. This can be attributed to travel distances, the number of districts involved, and the importance of developing personal relationships with participants. Our recruitment process took 11 months and could have taken longer, had we not been able to leverage prior working relationships and state support that facilitated access to eligible districts and schools.

It is important that future educational research continues to include rural schools. Not including the perspective of this important segment of our nation's schools in the research base may translate into inappropriately applying interventions that are successful in other settings without considering whether they are less effective or require modification for rural contexts. Funding streams that require study recruitment to be underway or completed by the time of grant application may inadvertently discourage researchers from conducting research in rural settings. While all research grant applications require an investment of time and effort, the cost and level of effort involved in recruiting 30 schools from 21 districts prior to applying for a grant is not feasible for most research institutions. If research focuses on urban and suburban settings, it risks not meeting student needs in rural settings. It further could alienate rural educators from the idea that their practices should be research based, since the research is not steeped in their context.

Therefore, we encourage funders interested in promoting the use of evidence-based programs to consider funding allocations and time allotments that permit the inclusion of rural sites in rigorous research. Funders might consider allowing researchers to budget for recruitment of rural schools in their grant applications, as a first-year planning activity, and making subsequent years of funding conditional on effective recruitment. Meanwhile, as researchers, we can share information about the costs of working in rural areas, as well as strategies for recruitment and data collection that fit the rural context. Most importantly, we must continue to advocate for the inclusion of rural schools and design studies that do so.

Acknowledgments The research reported here was supported by the Institute of Education Sciences, U.S. Department of Education, through Grant R305A100583 to Education Northwest. The opinions expressed are those of the authors and do not represent views of the Institute or the U.S. Department of Education.

References

Arnold, M. L., Newman, J. H., Gaddy, B. B., & Dean, C. B. (2005). A look at the condition of rural education research: Setting a difference for future research. *Journal of Research in Rural Education, 20*(6). Retrieved from http://www.jrre.psu.edu/articles/20-6.pdf

Ballantyne, K. G., Sanderman, A. R., & Levy, J. (2008). *Educating English language learners: Building teacher capacity*. Washington, DC: National Clearinghouse for English Language Acquisition. Retrieved from http://www.ncela.us/files/uploads/3/EducatingELLsBuildingTeacherCapacityVol1.pdf

Bloom, H. S. (2006). Randomizing groups to evaluate place-based programs. In H. S. Bloom (Ed.), *Learning more from social experiments: Evolving analytical approaches* (pp. 115–172). New York, NY: Russell Sage Foundation.

Brechtel, M. (2001). *Bringing it all together: Language and literacy in the multilingual classroom* (Rev ed.). Carlsbad, CA: Dominie Press.

Capps, R., Fix, M., Murray, J., Ost, J., Passel, J. S., & Herwantoro, S. (2005). *The new demography of America's schools: Immigration and the No Child Left Behind Act*. Washington DC: Urban Institute.

Dixon, M. (2013). *Public education finances: 2011 (G11-ASPEF)*. Retrieved from U.S. Department of Commerce, U.S. Census Bureau website: http://www2.census.gov/govs/school/11f33pub.pdf

Echevarria, J., Short, D., & Powers, K. (2006). School reform and standards-based education: A model for English-language learners. *Journal of Educational Research, 99*(4), 195–211.

Gándara, P., Maxwell-Jolly, J., & Driscoll, A. (2005). *Listening to teachers of English language learners: A survey of California teachers' challenges, experiences, and professional development needs*. Retrieved from ERIC database (ED491701).

Hannum, W. H., Irvin, M. J., Banks, J. B., & Farmer, T. W. (2009). Distance education use in rural schools. *Journal of Research in Rural Education, 24*(3), 1–15.

Howley, A., Wood, L., & Hough, B. (2011). Rural elementary school teachers' technology integration. *Journal of Research in Rural Education, 26*(9). Retrieved from http://jrre.vmhost.psu.edu/wp-content/uploads/2014/02/26-9.pdf

Jimerson, L. (2005). Special challenges for the "No Child Left Behind" act for rural schools and districts. *Rural Educator, 26*(3), 1–4. Retrieved from ERIC database (EJ783827).

Khattri, N., Riley, K. W., & Kane, M. B. (1997). Students at risk in poor, rural areas: A review of the research. *Journal of Research in Rural Education, 13*(2), 79–100. Retrieved from http://jrre.vmhost.psu.edu/wp-content/uploads/2014/02/26-9.pdf

Lowenhaupt, R., & Camburn, E. (2011). *Changing demographics in the schools: Wisconsin's New Latino Diaspora* (WCER Working Paper No. 2011-4). Madison, WI: University of Wisconsin-Madison, Wisconsin Center for Education Research.

Migration Policy Institute. (2012). *Number and share of English language learners by state: 2010–11*. Retrieved February 1, 2015, from http://www.migrationpolicy.org/programs/data-hub/charts/number-and-share-english-language-learners-state?width=1000&height=850&iframe=true

Monk, D. H. (2007). Recruiting and retaining high-quality teachers in rural areas. *Future of Children, 17*(1), 155–174.

National Clearinghouse for English Language Acquisition. (2011). *The growing numbers of English learner students: 2009/10*. Retrieved from http://www.ncela.us/files/uploads/9/growing_EL_0910.pdf

National Clearinghouse for English Language Acquisition. (2014). *NCELA Title III state profiles*. Retrieved from http://www.ncela.us/t3sis

Passel, J. S., & Zimmerman, W. (2001). *Are immigrants leaving California? Settlement patterns of immigrants in the late 1990s*. Washington, DC: Urban Institute.

Redwood, D., Leston, J., Asay, E., Ferucci, E., Etzel, R., & Lanier, A. P. (2011). Strategies for successful retention of Alaska Native and American Indian study participants. *Journal of Primary Prevention, 32*(1), 43–52.

Rhoads, C. H. (2011). The implications of "contamination" for experimental design in education. *Journal of Educational and Behavioral Statistics, 36*(1), 76–104.

Roschelle, J., Feng, M., Gallagher, H., Murphy, R., Harris, C., Kamdar, D., et al. (2014). *Recruiting participants for large-scale random assignment experiments in school settings.* Menlo Park, CA: SRI International.

Slama, K. (2004, January). Rural culture is a diversity issue. *Minnesota Psychologist*, 9–11, 13. Retrieved from http://www.apa.org/practice/programs/rural/rural-culture.pdf

Terrazas, A. (2011). *Immigrants in new-destination states.* Retrieved from Migration Policy Institute website: http://www.migrationpolicy.org/article/immigrants-new-destination-states

U.S. Department of Commerce, U.S. Census Bureau. (2013). "*State & County QuickFacts: Idaho,*" 2011. Retrieved January 10, 2013 from http://quickfacts.census.gov/qfd/states/16000.html

U.S. Department of Education, Institute of Education Sciences. (2015). "*Funded research grants and contracts*", 2002–2014. Retrieved January 8, 2015 from http://ies.ed.gov/funding/grantsearch/

U.S. Department of Education, National Center for Education Statistics. (2011). Common core of data. *Public elementary/secondary school universe survey*", 2008–09 (v. 1b). Retrieved January 2, 2014, from http://nces.ed.gov/ccd/pubschuniv.asp

U.S. Department of Education, National Center for Education Statistics. (2013). Common core of data. *Public elementary/secondary school universe survey,*" 2011–12 (v. 1a). Retrieved January 2, 2014, from http://nces.ed.gov/ccd/pubschuniv.asp

Wagenfeld, M. O. (2003). A snapshot of rural and frontier America. In B. H. Stamm (Ed.), *Rural behavioral health care: An interdisciplinary guide* (pp. 33–40). Washington, DC: American Psychological Association.

Methodology Challenges and Cutting Edge Designs for Rural Education Research

James A. Bovaird and Kirstie L. Bash

Abstract The unique contexts and features of rural education systems lead to the need for unique and innovative solutions. In particular, rural research is commonly perceived to face major logistical research hurdles such as small populations, low densities, poor access, and geographic isolation. These limitations make the rural setting a challenging context within which to conduct education research. This chapter presents considerations for overcoming such challenges while still striving towards employing rigorous methodologies, achieving desired generalizability, and reaching causal inferences when relevant. To accomplish this, a number of inter-disciplinary statistical and design-based solutions can be translated to rural edu-cation research. In particular, this chapter discusses: (a) using advanced statistical modeling to preserve and feature the uniqueness of rural settings, (b) alternatives to traditional simple random assignment, (c) measurement paradigms to reduce the amount of data required, and (d) innovations for working with small samples and complex models. Most of these topics and approaches can be combined to accommodate the complexities and realities of conducting rural research. The fundamental message is that all research contexts present their own unique chal-lenges, but as researchers, we can look outside of our disciplines to find solutions that can help us pursue our necessary research agendas.

Keywords Ecological systems · Multilevel modeling · Causal inference · Cluster randomized trials · Quasi-experimental design · Planned missing data · Small sample inference · Finite samples

J.A. Bovaird · K.L. Bash
National Center for Research on Rural Education (R²Ed), The Nebraska
Center for Research on Children, Youth, Families & Schools (CYFS),
University of Nebraska–Lincoln, Lincoln, USA

J.A. Bovaird (✉)
University of Nebraska–Lincoln, 114 Teachers College Hall, Lincoln
NE 68588-0345, USA
e-mail: jbovaird2@unl.edu

© Springer International Publishing Switzerland 2017   95
G.C. Nugent et al. (eds.), *Rural Education Research in the United States*,
DOI 10.1007/978-3-319-42940-3_6

Rural education research is no different from general education research in that most endeavors can be classified as exploration, development, evaluation, or measurement. In particular, it is important to make the distinction between research in general and evaluation. Research can be considered a systematic investigation and/or study of sources of evidence to establish facts and reach new conclusions, whereas evaluation more specifically involves making a systematic judgment regarding something's worth or significance where the judgment is guided by a set of standards-driven criteria and based on evidence. However, regardless of the type of research, the strongest degree of rigor possible is necessary to ensure the generalizability of the findings to the target populations. Despite this clear need, teacher education and development research in rural contexts has been criticized for its lack of methodological rigor (Harmon et al. 2003; Oliver 2007). Unfortunately, methodologically rigorous research with a strong scientific basis is limited in rural education settings (see Coladarci 2007, for a commentary). Experimental control is broadly considered the ideal mechanism for establishing strong evaluative evidence of causal mechanisms; however, field evaluations of education programs, practices, and policies are often difficult due to the commonly perceived lack of experimental control possible over the surrounding environment. Consequently, comprehensive literature reviews disclose limited examples of true experimentation, especially in the form of randomized field trials evaluating effectiveness of education programs in rural settings (Arnold et al. 2005). Evaluations conducted in rural settings can be additionally complex, given characteristics such as population size and density, and spatial disparities for allocating resources. It is further complicated by the fact that not all types of rural education research are evaluation in nature, but instead rely on less rigorous methodologies in exchange for producing results faster. Therefore, there is an increased need for leadership and resources to address the lack of scientifically-based research on rural education and in rural settings, especially in designing and implementing focused research programs that employ rigorous empirical methodologies with sound theoretical underpinnings.

Despite obvious comparisons between the development of research methodologies and statistics through agricultural experiments and similar applications in educational research, the unique contexts and features of *rural* education systems lead to the need for unique and innovative solutions. In particular, rural research is commonly perceived to face major hurdles such as small population sizes and low population densities leading to poor access to adequate research samples, and geographic isolation leading to increased heterogeneity between contexts and perhaps increased homogeneity within rural contexts. Combining such hurdles with a strong sense of community makes the rural setting a truly unique context within which to conduct education research. In the rural research community, these challenges are viewed as inherent to the very context being studied rather than as nuisances that need to be controlled or eliminated. While agricultural experimentation has contributed heavily to the development of statistics applicable to overcoming such hurdles, some of the more relevant analytic tools available for non-experimental research come from fields outside of agriculture. This chapter will present some considerations for how rural education research can continue to overcome perceived limitations to true experimentation, yet still approximate the level of knowledge available through random assignment and explicit environmental control necessary for evaluation work. This chapter will also discuss several rigorous design and analysis decisions that can assist those researchers conducting important non-evaluation research in rural settings.

Researchers who take an interdisciplinary approach to problem solving may be better equipped with creative solutions when challenges arise within their own unique research context. Through perseverance and ingenuity, researchers can confidently pursue the appropriate design and analytic approach based on their particular question of interest. A central hypothesis guiding this discussion is that educational policy must be utilitarian; consequently, research impacting educational policy in rural settings must focus on systems-level applications evaluated through rigorous quantitative data. Many viable statistical and design-based solutions exist in other disciplines and can be translated to rural education research. In particular, this chapter will discuss: (a) preserving and featuring the uniqueness of rural settings in systems level investigations through advanced statistical modeling, (b) alternatives to traditional simple random assignment for rural settings, (c) efficiency of measurement paradigms to reduce the amount of data necessary for valid inferences, and (d) innovations in small sample inferential testing. The innovative approaches to be addressed in this chapter provide strong evidence that will advance the next generation of education research in rural settings.

1 Modeling the Rural Context

Clearly, observation of behavior and development cannot occur in isolation, but rather must occur in the context of the environment (Steele and Aylward 2010). Without understanding influences at the multiple levels representing the ecology of behavioral phenomenon, we are unable to develop or evaluate programs that are responsive to key ecological factors. The environment is known to affect individual behavior, and numerous micro- and macro-level environmental influences can be identified in virtually all research settings. Developmentalists have long recognized the need to look at the "ecosystem" in which humans learn and develop. As an example of one such ecological modeling framework, Bronfenbrenner (1979, 1986) conceptualized an ecological model that identifies four nested levels: the *microsystem* level consisting of the individual's immediate social settings that directly affect the individual's life, the *mesosystem* level that connects the various microsystems together, the *exosystem* made up of neighborhood and community structures that affect the functioning of micro- and meso- systems, and the overarching *macrosystem* of cultural, political, and economic patterns that influence the lower levels. The framework was later extended to include the *chronosystem* to reflect the impact of time (Bronfenbrenner 1988). Research using the ecological perspective assumes that such aspects of the natural environment are a major source of developmental influence, yet those potential sources are often overlooked or ignored. Ecological theorists do not try to study the effects of environmental influences in the lab, maintaining that true understanding must be obtained in a natural setting. The complexity of the nested-levels theoretical perspective and the additional intricacies that result from non-laboratory research and data collection methods necessarily pose unique difficulties in terms of data analysis.

Context is an important consideration in rigorous research, and especially evaluation, settings, and the heterogeneity of the rural context is a critical consideration for rural researchers. A critical concern is to preserve and feature the uniqueness of rural settings. A common criticism of quantitative approaches to rural research is that quantitative approaches tend to minimize the uniqueness of individual rural settings. However, modern methods are available to (a) measure what makes contexts unique, (b) select or control for salient contextual features, and (c) incorporate contextual knowledge into the study design. A full discussion of all of these topics is beyond the scope of this chapter, but there are numerous sources for more information for the interested reader. Hawley, Koziol, and Bovaird (Chapter "Defining and Communicating Rural" of this volume) discuss the operational definitions of what constitutes *rural* and the implications of such definitional decisions on inferences and generalizability. The various operational definitions of rurality discussed by Hawley et al. reflect differences in the critical contextual features. The third advancement by modern methods—incorporating context into study designs—can be easily addressed by using a complex yet intuitive modeling approach generally referred to as multilevel modeling. For example, a randomized control trial (RCT) with organizational units such as rural communities assigned to condition could be designed as a *cluster* RCT, where characteristics of each community beyond just being distinct and rural can be assessed, controlled for, and statistically modeled to allow researchers to consider the similarities between rural contexts while preserving context differences.

Cook and Campbell (1979) make the distinction between generalizing across subpopulations versus to a population. For example, an evaluation may show evidence of program efficacy in a rural school district in a highly populated state like California; however, it may be irresponsible to infer that the same program works in any rural setting across the United States. Instead, a common argument in rural research circles is that such research conclusions should be made through strong tests of whether that program's effect is moderated by context. Although there can be clear similarities across rural contexts around the United States (e.g., access to participants, limited resources, prohibitive distances, low incomes, infrastructure challenges, etc.), there are potentially different impacts of these contextual characteristics across different rural as well as urban and suburban communities (see Coladarci 2007).

Great strides have been made over the last few decades in developing models appropriate for Bronfenbrenner-type ecological models. Considering each ecological level as a system, it is necessary to understand that no single part of the system operates in isolation with each individual influencing the other system components as much as the system influences the individual. Microsystems, especially, are truly dynamic systems in which each person influences and is influenced by the other persons present. Larger more sophisticated models of the dynamic change relations can now be specified and have emerged as a powerful technique for complex inter-relations in developmental data measured at many short intervals (Boker and Laurenceau 2008; Grimm and McArdle 2007). As many Bronfenbrenner-type microsystemic relationships can be conceptualized as dyadic relationships, advancements in the use of dyads as units of analysis (e.g., parent-child, teacher-student, coach-player) should also be brought to the attention of the researcher (see Bolger and Shrout 2007; Wendorf 2002, for examples). Accounting for dyadic interactions in rural education research further takes into consideration the unique rural context and the reciprocal relationship of the context and individuals.

Despite calls for consideration of systemic influences in rural education research, often research efforts are hindered by a lack of sophisticated methodologies that would enable consideration of ecological models. Such calls have been mirrored in other developmental disciplines as well. For instance, Kazak et al. (2003), Nelson et al. (2008), and Power et al. (2003) have specifically called for advanced statistical techniques that would allow testing of multi-systemic social and ecological models in pediatric research. A 2004 conference, "Modeling Longitudinal Processes in an Ecological Context," funded by the National Science Foundation, the Society for Multivariate Experimental Psychology, and the Merrill Center for Advanced Studies at the University of Kansas was convened specifically to address the lack of quantitative methodologies appropriate for considering ecological models of development, resulting in the edited volume, *Modeling Contextual Effects in Longitudinal Studies* (Little et al. 2007).

1.1 Multilevel Modeling

Using a general definition, multilevel modeling involves incorporating variables that apply to two or more sampling levels (Bovaird 2007). Children in the same environmental context tend to be more similar than children in other contexts, and both the children and their contexts have distinguishing characteristics that may be of substantive interest. Such an ecological system can be conceptualized as containing multiple levels, nested within one another. Multiple levels (i.e., more than 2) of contextual influence can be considered through the multilevel modeling (MLM; Snijders and Bosker 2012) framework, also referred to as hierarchical linear modeling (HLM, Raudenbush and Bryk 2002). The complexity of the nested-levels theoretical perspective and the additional intricacies that result from such complex sampling necessarily pose unique difficulties in terms of data analysis, thus the need to consider multilevel modeling as a means of data analysis. Not coincidentally, multilevel modeling is sometimes referred to as contextual modeling (Kreft and de Leeuw 1998).

The ubiquitous example of a multilevel system in education is the case of sampling classrooms within schools and then sampling children from those sampled classrooms. The sampled children are said to be *nested* within their respective classrooms, and the sampled classrooms are *nested* within their respective schools. The example could be carried further to allow for multiple schools to be nested within their rural communities, etc. If the analytic model, conceptual model, or theory of change involves aspects of the higher-level grouping units such as the community, school, or classroom environment along with student characteristics and/or performance, a multilevel model is necessary. Multilevel modeling, the appropriate procedure when accounting for non-independence due to the complex sampling process, also incorporates sample sizes at all levels. This integration allows the researcher to make simultaneous inferences at all levels of the hierarchy. Multilevel models attempt to represent the dynamic nature of complex sampling as a "mixed" combination of fixed and random coefficients or effects, hence the term *linear mixed model* that is sometimes used to describe this type of analysis (Stroup 2013). In the mixed model, using the example of children nested within classrooms, the basic components for a sample of classrooms are (a) the *fixed* average intercept, or level of the outcome; (b) the *fixed* average slope, or typical effect of a predictor across all classrooms; (c) the *random* variability between classrooms around the average slope; and (d) the *random* variability between classrooms around the average effect of a predictor. If we make the key assumption that the sample is homogeneous with regard to the effect of a predictor across classrooms, then we assume that the data follow a 2-level hierarchy (children within classrooms) and there is not a higher level of sampling present in the data (i.e., a "level 3," say perhaps schools). As a 2-level multilevel model, the analysis framework can be specified by two sets of equations. The micro-level regression equation is

$$y_{ij} = \beta_{0j} + \beta_{1j}X_{ij} + e_{ij} \qquad (1)$$

where y_{ij} is the outcome variable score (e.g., math score) at for child i in class j, X_{ij} is a predictor (e.g., reading ability) that varies across children within a classroom j, β_{0j} represents the overall average outcome when the predictor equals zero (intercept), β_{1j} represents the average effect of the predictor, and e_{ij} is a within-classroom residual. Conceptually, the micro-level model above defines a separate regression equation for each of the j classrooms, such that across classrooms, there is a typical intercept and typical slope, but the effect of the predictor within an individual classroom is allowed to deviate. These individual-classroom differences in effect are modeled by the macro-level regression equations:

$$\begin{aligned} \beta_{0j} &= \gamma_{00} + u_{0j} \\ \beta_{1j} &= \gamma_{10} + u_{1j} \end{aligned} \qquad (2)$$

where γ_{00} is the mean intercept, γ_{10} is the mean slope, and the u's are classroom-level residuals. By substituting the macro-level equations into the micro-level equation, γ_{00} and γ_{10} become the traditional fixed effects as would be seen in a GLM approach, but the single GLM random effect (i.e., the error term) has been divided into three random separate sources of variance.

$$y_{ij} = \gamma_{00} + X_{ij}\gamma_{10} + u_{0j} + X_{ij}u_{1j} + e_{ij} \tag{3}$$

The multilevel model becomes a contextual model by expanding Eqs. 1 and 2 to include additional context-level predictors or covariates by adding additional β or γ parameters, respectively. Additional characteristics, predictors, covariates, etc. that pertain to the child would be added to Eq. 1 while similar variables pertaining to the classroom context would be added to Eq. 2.

A strength of multilevel modeling is that the framework allows researchers to maintain the context-specific uniquenesses to model heterogeneity across rural contexts, yet simultaneously model the degree to which there is a common effect across contexts. A simplistic approach to modeling multilevel data would be to pose a separate model at each level of the hierarchy, as is done in 'slopes-as-outcomes' analyses (Burstein et al. 1978). The slopes-as-outcomes analysis would be akin to developing a model for every school or community in the current example. However, it is essential that the model employ a statistical integration of all levels of the hierarchy which can be accomplished by extending the general linear model to include random sources of variance in addition to fixed sources. Goldstein (1986), Laird and Ware (1982), and Longford (1987), among others, can be credited with providing some of the seminal work in extending the general linear model to allow for complex nested data structures.

Student readiness for kindergarten. Applying multilevel modeling to rural education research, Bovaird et al. (2006) presented a cross-sectional contextual (county) model of (student) school readiness as part of the Kansas Kindergarten Readiness Project (Fig. 1). This large-scale study involved 154 school districts across 95 of the 105 Kansas counties. The goal of the project was to describe the relationship between county-level contextual characteristics and kindergarten preparedness, controlling for student-level characteristics. The primary outcome was the *Kansas School Entry Assessment*, a teacher-completed measure of kindergarten preparedness consisting of 41 items in 6 areas of school readiness. Six student-level predictors—age, body-mass index, gender, language status, eligibility for free or reduced lunch, and special education status—were used to account for individual-student differences. The focal predictors were 21 contextual variables supplied by state agencies, measured at the county level, and grouped into three goal areas: children live in safe and stable families that support learning; children live in safe and stable communities that support learning, health, and family services; and children attend schools that support learning.

As would be expected, the multilevel model developed by Bovaird et al. (2006) found that students vary in their degree of readiness within a county. Counties also

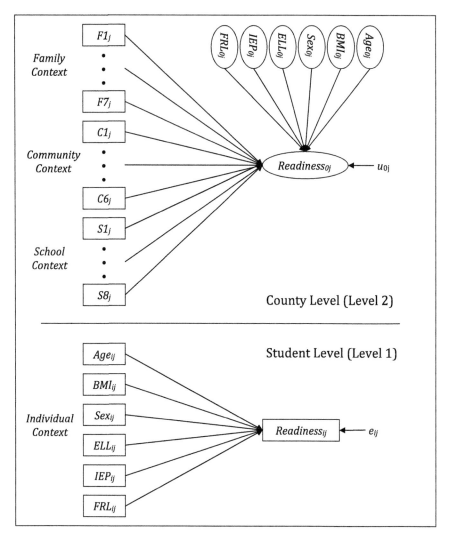

Fig. 1 Multilevel structural equation model of kindergarten readiness based on the model tested in Bovaird et al. (2006). *Note* Variables labeled *F1–F7*, *C1–C6*, and *S1–S8* represent contextual variables measured at the county level. Subscripts and general notations were chosen to reflect the same notations presented in Eqs. 1–3. Elements that appear in both *rectangles* and *ovals* reflect fixed and random effects, respectively

varied in terms of the average degree of readiness for students within the county. In general, all six student level covariates accounted for a significant proportion of variance in readiness: older native English-speaking female children with lower BMI, higher socioeconomic status, and who do not have an IEP, tended to be significantly more ready for kindergarten across all facets of readiness. Bovaird et al. also found that the county context matters. Counties that reported significantly fewer child abuse claims, fewer child care enforcement citations, higher crime rates per capita, lower student-teacher ratios, and lower community usage of school buildings also tended to have children with higher average levels of school readiness as well. Bovaird et al. (2011) further investigated the degree to which rurality impacted kindergarten readiness by studying several competing operational definitions of rurality (see Hawley et al., in Chapter "Defining and Communicating Rural" of this volume, for more information on differences in rural definitions). Again using multilevel modeling, the Kansas study found that there were significant differences in the between-county variability in readiness between rural and urban counties, indicating that while urban counties were fairly consistent in the degree of kindergarten readiness, rural counties showed considerable variability. The study further found that rurality did indeed moderate the impact of child protective services, child care capacity, instructional environment, community school building usage, and presence of early childhood licensed teachers on average kindergarten readiness. In particular, child protective services, child care capacity, instructional environment, and community school building usage were significant predictors in rural counties (and not urban counties) while only presence of early childhood licensed teachers was a significant predictor in urban counties (and not rural).

2 Experimental Designs with Strong Causal Inferences

Experimentation is generally considered ideal for establishing a strong causal inference. However, field evaluations of education programs, practices, and policies are often difficult due to the commonly perceived lack of experimental control possible over the surrounding environment, regardless of whether the evaluation is conducted in rural or urban settings. The fundamental principals of random assignment and true experimentation are well known, so this chapter will not belabor the point. Instead, interested readers are referred to some of the many excellent sources on experimental design of field studies, including but not limited to Shadish et al. (2002). Rather, this section will focus on four alternatives to traditional experimental designs involving simple random assignment of participants to condition that may be applicable in rural settings.

2.1 Two Variations on a Randomized Design

Cluster randomized control trials. First, building off the principles of multilevel modeling, a cluster randomized control trial (CRCT) is a type of true experimental design where "clusters" or organizational units such as neighborhoods, communities, or districts are randomly assigned to a study condition instead of individuals within those units. This type of design is often used in school-based evaluation when there is perceived to be a need to protect against participants in one study condition influencing participants in another condition, or *contamination*. In this context, sophisticated analytic methods such as multilevel modeling are required for data analysis due to the hierarchical nesting of units within groups (i.e., members of a community).

An additional consideration in cluster randomized trials is that the *unit of analysis* and *unit of assignment* (randomization) may be different, depending on the level of inference. For example, the evaluation may seek to find evidence that a reading intervention improves student test scores by randomly assigning rural classrooms to a condition while measuring outcomes at the student level, where classrooms are the unit of assignment and students are the unit of analysis. Alternatively, both units of assignment and analysis would be one and the same in a coaching trial that evaluates whether a professional development curriculum increases the fidelity of teachers' implementation of the program with the target of the intervention explicitly defined as the teacher intervention implementation fidelity (see Glover, this volume).

The Conjoint Behavioral Consultation (CBC) in Rural Communities project (IES #R324A100115), conducted by the National Center for Research on Rural Education is an example of a CRCT evaluating the efficacy of CBC for addressing significant behavioral challenges among 250 students in Kindergarten through Grade 3, in 45 rural Nebraska elementary schools. See Sheridan et al. (2014) for more information on the Rural CBC project. The CBC in Rural Communities project illustrates the flexibility in alternative experimental designs by integrating the CRCT design and the multiple baseline design (MBD discussed below).

Stepped-wedge designs. A typical experimental design where the panel of recruited participants is assigned to two or more groups that participate in the evaluation and are evaluated concurrently can be referred to as a *parallel design*. Alternatively, participants in a *stepped wedge design* (SWD; e.g., Hussey and Hughes 2007) participate in the evaluation condition sequentially. Cook and Campbell (1979) referred to the SWD as an *experimentally staged introduction*, Brown and Lilford (2006) termed the design a *phased introduction or implementation*, and the wait-list control design is considered a special case of the SWD.

As might be inferred by its association with the waitlist control design, the SWD is useful for situations in which a program cannot be delivered concurrently to all participating units. This design is essentially a cross-over design with all assigned units serving as their own control and eventually participating in the program to be evaluated. Participating units—individuals or groups (i.e., a cluster randomized SWD)—are randomly assigned to 2 or more groups, and groups are randomly assigned to crossover from control to program at different times. Unlike a true cross-over design, the SWD is unidirectional—all units transition from control to program and never the reverse. Thus groups vary in when they transition from one condition to the other. The SWD may be considered preferable over a parallel design for logistical, practical, or financial reasons such as when it is impossible to deliver the intervention in parallel. This is particularly true for studies that require the use of cohorts. Noted advantages (Brown and Lilford 2006; Hussey and Hughes 2007; Woertman et al. 2013) include (a) requiring smaller sample sizes than a parallel design by using multiple participating units (i.e., between-groups information) who receive both control and intervention conditions to produce within-groups information rather than two groups of participants who participate in either the control or intervention condition, (b) the treatment effect can be disentangled from the effects of natural growth and cohorts, (c) all units receive the program which is beneficial from both an ethical and recruitment perspective, (d) the threat of carryover effect bias in two-way crossover designs is avoided, and (e) the program can be administered over several cohorts which can aid in logistics. The sequential nature of the SWD allows researchers to facilitate evaluation in rural communities through this use of cohorts (or clustering of participating units), such that the distance or geographical isolation dictates the availability of cohorts, and therefore, the cohorts that can be used within the evaluation.

"CSI: Coaching Science Inquiry in Rural Schools" project (Kunz et al. 2013), one of the efficacy studies conducted by the National Center for Research on Rural Education (IES #R305AC090022) is a CRCT to evaluate the effects of instructional coaching focused on guided scientific inquiry among middle and high school teachers across rural schools in Nebraska and surrounding states. The CSI project utilizes a wait-list control design, as a special case of the SWD, where all participating schools are initially randomly assigned to one of two conditions: an untreated comparison group and an active intervention group. Those schools in the untreated comparison group all then received the CSI intervention in the second year of the study. This variation of the SWD follows the same sequential process, but provides the researcher greater flexibility by reducing the financial burden in requiring fewer participants and enabling more efficient intervention administration since trained project personnel can be retained for consecutive years rather than hiring additional 1-year personnel.

2.2 Two Strong Quasi-Experimental Designs

Multiple baseline designs. The multiple baseline design (MBD) is a special case of the SWD that focuses on intra-individual change instead of inter-individual differences. Like the SWD, all participants serve as their own controls, but unlike the SWD, each group is of size $n = 1$ (i.e., a set of single-subject designs). The MBD provides strong protection against many threats to the internal validity, and if well designed may be considered to "Meet Evidence Standards" and result in a causal inference (U.S. Department of Education, Institute of Education Sciences, What Works Clearinghouse 2013). Like any experimental design, stronger inferences are obtained when a strong protocol is strictly followed. As with the SWD, a MBD is most commonly implemented as a set of groups, which happen to be single-subject, with staggered phase changes (Baer et al. 1968), where all single-subject groups eventually transition from a baseline or control phase into a treatment or intervention phase. The key feature is the staggered implementation of the program or treatment condition across individuals (Christ 2007). The staggered transition points control for confounding factors so that observed differences in control versus intervention performance can be attributed to the program rather than chance. This type of design can vary on the degree and structure of overlap between the single-subject participants (concurrent or nonconcurrent) and the number of probes used (i.e., multiple parallel outcomes). Concurrent MBDs, where participants vary only in when they shift one phase to the other (Barlow and Hersen 1984) particularly moderates the history threat to internal validity and serves to minimize the overall evaluation time. Nonconcurrent designs (Watson and Workman 1981) partial or non-overlap between subjects and provide greater recruiting flexibility but can have weakened inference due to weaker control of threats to internal validity. Like any experimental design, a priori protocol specification eliminates experimenter bias regardless of whether the MBD is concurrent or nonconcurrent. Multiple parallel outcomes help identify potential confounding variables and minimize construct explication bias.

Within the "Conjoint Behavioral Consultation (CBC) in Rural Communities" project (IES #R324A100115), conducted in collaboration with the National Center for Research on Rural Education (R^2Ed, IES #R305AC090022), all 250 students and 146 teachers from 45 rural Nebraska elementary schools participated in a nonconcurrent MBD to evaluate the efficacy of CBC in these rural schools. Small groups averaging 1.7 identified students per classroom were created and randomly assigned as a group to participate in the larger randomized control trial. Participants whose small groups are assigned to the intervention condition were observed in the classroom for 3 weeks during the baseline phase prior to introduction of the CBC intervention. Once the intervention had been introduced, they were observed for an additional five occasions during the intervention phase for a total of eight observations. Small groups began the intervention as the schools and classrooms were recruited, screened, and groups formed, which created the nonconcurrent MBD.[1] The MBD is a viable alternative to traditional experimental designs for rural research, because MBD provides the flexibility of staggering the intervention across individuals as to avoid complications such as geographical isolation which can make simultaneous introduction to the intervention across cohorts impractical. See Sheridan et al. (see Chapter "Improving Education Outcomes for American Indian Children: Community and Family Influences on Rural Student Academic Success" in this book) for more information on the Rural CBC project.

Regression discontinuity designs. Inferences from a regression discontinuity design (RDD) have been found to have comparable *internal validity* to conclusions from randomized designs (Campbell 1969). The defining characteristics of a RDD is assignment to condition based on a pre-determined cut-off score rather than random assignment. The RDD typically is presented as a two-group pretest-posttest design where only one group is administered a program to be evaluated. A relevant measure is given as a pretest on all participants. Given a pre-determined cut-score, participants

---

[1]Participants in the control condition are also observed on a total of eight occasions, with no phase shift, creating a counterfactual condition for the larger RCT.

are divided into two groups based on their score relative to the cut-score. After assignment, only one group receives the program followed by a post-program assessment for all participants. For example, participants who meet the criteria for inclusion (i.e., scores higher than the cut-score) are assigned to the intervention group and participants who did not meet the criteria (i.e., scores at or below the cut-score) do not receive the intervention. The pre-program measure must be quantitative and continuous so that a *regression-based* analysis can be used where the post-program outcome is simply regressed upon the pre-test score, the program indicator, and their interaction. Because of this analytic framework, the pre- and post-program measures may be different. Again, the defining feature is the cut-off score which can be based on any number of factors (i.e., program resources, ethical considerations, or substantive grounds). For instance, funding and/or staffing may only be available to intervene with 10 schools, so it might be the case that the ten lowest-performing schools on a state accountability measure may be selected to receive a program, where school is both the unit of assignment and the unit of intervention. Alternatively, using ethical considerations, it might be the case that all rural school districts with a median income below the federal poverty designation are offered increment school funding, as they represent the districts with the greatest need.

The Reading First Impact Study was designed as a RDD to determine the effects of the federal Reading First program on classroom instruction and student reading achievement (Gamse et al. 2008). Data were collected from students and teachers residing in 125 Reading First schools and 123 non-Reading First schools, where schools were located in 18 geographically diverse sites (ranging from large cities to rural areas) that spanned 13 states. Schools eligible for funding were ranked according to a relevant quantitative measure of poverty, a cut-point was identified, and all schools above the cut-point were awarded funding. The two-group comparison was then those schools that received funding (intervention) versus those schools which were not eligible and did not receive funding (control). While the report showed general support for positive outcomes such as reading instructional time, professional development in scientifically-based reading instruction, and supports for struggling readers, there was no statistical support for increased student reading comprehension and only minimal support for improving decoding skills among first graders only. Secondary analyses suggested that these results did not vary across the geographically diverse sites, including those from rural areas. See Gamse et al. (2008) for more information on this study.

3 More Efficient Measurement: Planned Missing Data Designs

Graham et al. (2006) describe a set of designs they refer to as *efficiency-of-measurement designs*. Such designs are intended to minimize the amount of information needed to generate a valid and strong inference by systematically reducing the number of measurements administered to participants. In doing so, access to potentially limited samples of participants in rural contexts can be accommodated by making data collection more efficient while ensuring strong generalizability and statistical precision. Simple random sampling is the most common example of this type of strategy, but other approaches are also within this methodological class. For example, optimal designs (see Allison et al. 1997) attempt to balance cost with statistical power; and fractional factorial designs (see Box et al. 2005) utilize a carefully chosen subset of cells from a factorial design to focus "information" on the most important conditions while minimizing the resources necessary to do so. Beyond these "classic" approaches are more modern perspectives based on intentionally collecting some, but not all, potentially available data. In the following sections, the distinction is made between designs that measure some information on all participants and designs that intentionally do not collect data from all available participants but get maximal information from those that are assessed. This perspective is sometimes referred to more generally as a *planned missing data design*.

3.1 Measurement Models

One class of planned missing data designs involves variations on fundamental measurement using multiple items or indicators of a construct (i.e., items on a test, or multiple questions on a non-cognitive assessment). This class of procedures is based on the idea of splitting the total item pool into subsets of items and administering those subsets to different participants. Examples include, but are not limited to, simple matrix sampling (Shoemaker 1973), fractional block designs (McArdle 1994), balanced incomplete blocks (spiral) designs (Johnson 1992), the split questionnaire survey design (Raghunathan and Grizzle 1995), and the three-form design (e.g., Graham et al. 1994). While simple matrix sampling does not contain any overlap among subsets, these other example designs all have some degree of overlap between subsets enabling a broader set of testable hypotheses to be tested.

Graham et al. (2006) proposed a two-method measurement approach which balances psychometric precision with logistical efficiency. In two-method measurement, a large sample is administered a relatively cheap yet relatively noisy measure (i.e., one that yields total scores with lower reliability such as many self-report instruments). A subset of the overall sample is then administered a more expensive or difficult to administer, yet more psychometrically reliable measure (i.e., biological markers) in addition to the cheaper measure. In this type of design, the higher-reliability measure anchors the overall psychometric properties of construct estimates.

3.1.1 Accelerated Longitudinal Designs

The accelerated longitudinal design (Tonry et al. 1991)—sometimes referred to as a convergence design (Bell 1953), cross-sequential design (Schaie 1965), or cohort-sequential design (Nesselroade and Baltes 1979)—is a special type of planned missing data design that may be used when measuring the *change* in a construct over time. Similar to a fractional block design, spiral design, or three-form design in structure (as discussed in previous section), an accelerated longitudinal design utilizes a set of cohorts of participants that overlap in terms of *when* they are assessed over time in a repeated measures design. In this application, a cohort is a group of participants that begin a study at a common age or grade in school and are then tracked for a limited number of measurement occasions. The groups are linked at their overlapping time points to approximate the true longitudinal curve or trajectory over the entire developmental span. The accelerated longitudinal design has many advantages to measuring change over time compared to non-accelerated designs, including allowing for assessment of intra-individual change, taking less time than a purely longitudinal design, and minimizing participant attrition and cumulative testing effects. These designs are commonly used in virtually all longitudinal or developmental research settings. They are especially prevalent in gerontology and aging research. For rural research, the accelerated longitudinal design promotes evaluation in rural settings by requiring only a limited number of measurements while minimizing concerns about unplanned missing data.

3.2 Sequentially Designed Experiments

Instead of collecting partial information on all participants recruited into a study, often called a panel, another approach is to only collect data on the participants necessary to make a reliable and valid inference. Traditional study designs in the educational, social, and behavioral sciences are characterized by sample sizes and compositions (e.g., who and how many participants are assigned to which conditions) that are determined prior to conducting the experiment. This type of approach is commonly referred to as a fixed design. In contrast, a sequential design treats the sample size as a random variable where the final sample may be substantially less than what was initially recruited into the study.

Sequential designs (Armitage 1975; Chernoff 1959; Wald 1945) allow periodic interim analyses and decision-making based on cumulative data and previous design decisions while maintaining both appropriate Type I (α) and Type II (β) error rates. These designs require at least one interim analysis, called a stage, at a pre-specified interim stage scheduled to occur prior to formal completion of the experiment. An a priori protocol is developed to guide the statistical details, including the number of interim stages, the sample size at each stage, and the desired nominal α and β levels. Critical values (boundary values—similar to the ± 1.96 used in a z-test—that help to determine whether or not the experiment advances to the next stage in the sequential design) are computed for each interim stage, and all available data is analyzed (i.e., data from that stage plus all previous stages). The appropriate test statistic is then computed and compared with critical boundary values determined a priori to maintain appropriate nominal experiment-wise Type I and Type II error rates given the occurrence of multiple statistical tests at interim stages. If the test statistic falls within a decision region, the experiment stops; otherwise, the experiment continues to the next stage or until the entire panel has been evaluated. Sequential designs can be of three general types: fully sequential designs updated after every observation or after every participant completes the study; group sequential designs where boundary values are computed for a predetermined number of equally spaced stages rather than after each participant; and flexible sequential designs which can be viewed as a compromise between fully sequential and group sequential designs. Sequential designs have the benefit of potential early termination which can lead to financial savings, and limiting unnecessary exposure or withholding administration. The trade-off is an increase in the design complexity and computational burdens.

Using a group-sequential experimental design, Bovaird et al. (2009) and Bovaird (2010) re-analyzed data from the CBC in the Early Grades study (Sheridan et al. 2012, a predecessor to CBC in Rural Communities referenced earlier). Parallel to the CBC in Rural Communities project,[2] the CBC in the Early Grades project was conceptualized as a four-cohort fixed-design cluster randomized trial to evaluate the effectiveness of a school-based consultation (CBC) approach for students with challenging classroom behaviors. The CBC in the Early Grades project involved 22 schools, 90 classrooms/teachers, and 270 K-3rd grade students and parents. Small, 2–3 parents/children dyads were randomly assigned as small groups to either a business-as-usual control condition or an experimental CBC condition. Bovaird and colleagues implemented a post hoc application of a sequential design and analysis strategy on four cohorts of participants. Assuming that the eventual "known" fixed design conclusions were true, this study determined that six of the reported eight primary outcomes could have been concluded after the second cohort and only two measures needed to have been carried out to the end of the fourth cohort. In any research context that faces adverse logistical conditions—restricted resources, limited access to participants, time demands, etc.—and in this case rural education research, it is important for the researcher to select an experimental design that will efficiently maximize their resources. In this context, consideration of a sequential design versus a fixed design places the emphasis on the quality of measurements as opposed to the quantity of measurements.

4 Approaches to Complex Modeling with Small Samples

There are two pervasive issues in analysis of data from rural settings when the amount of data or the sample size is limited. First, most analytic approaches appropriate for testing intervention effects in complex sampling settings or for

---

[2]The CBC in Rural Communities project was still undergoing final data analysis at the time that this chapter was written, preventing its use as an example in this chapter.

evaluating the role of mediators and moderators are considered asymptotic which means that large samples are required for accurate estimation. Second, statistical power is always a consideration when sample sizes become limited. This section will present two approaches that can be used to ameliorate these challenges.

4.1 Complex Modeling and Modeling Complex Samples

In partial response to heightened expectations from federal agencies for funded research to consider the causal mechanisms underlying effective programs (i.e., mediators) and/or the contexts or conditions under which a program may impact student outcomes (i.e., moderators) in addition to direct evaluations of a program's efficacy or effectiveness, current trends in educational research require scientists to investigate increasingly complex phenomena. These additional layers of exploration and understanding lead to increasingly elaborate hypotheses, and require advanced statistical techniques, especially those available through latent variable and simultaneous equation approaches, like structural equation modeling (SEM; see Kline 2010). Analysis of traditional efficacy data from interventions in school settings also requires advanced statistical techniques such as the previously discussed multilevel modeling due to the hierarchical organization and dependent nature of the data system.

SEM can be considered an "umbrella" concept; much like the general linear model (GLM) is to traditional analysis of variance and regression where each is a special case of the broader general linear model. SEM encompasses not only the GLM family, but also the broader class of multivariate methods such as the multivariate analysis of variance (MANOVA), factor analysis, and many multilevel modeling approaches. This means that SEM can be used to model and statistically evaluate traditional intervention effects as well as the impact of mediators and moderators, even in a multilevel setting such as a cluster RCT. Multilevel modeling can also be considered an extension of the general linear model to include what are referred to as *random* effects in addition to traditional *fixed* effects. As discussed in a previous section, consideration of random effects becomes necessary anytime there are hierarchically organized data as is typically the case in school-based research (i.e., kids nested within classrooms, classrooms nested within school, etc.). Many random effects can also be operationalized as latent variables, or unobservable constructs that cannot be directly measured, thus multilevel modeling can be implemented within the SEM paradigm as well.

Applied researchers are often faced with an inferential dilemma caused by a mismatch between their research hypotheses and the available sample size. The use of small samples tends to increase the chance of a researcher capitalizing on sample-specific variability, or sampling error. This often occurs when the research question, under ideal sample size conditions, would require a complex statistical procedure such as SEM for proper inference. Such a need for SEM would arise from research scenarios involving multiple latent variables with multiple indicators (observed variables for indirectly measuring latent variables), multiple structural effects (regression parameters relating variables to each other in an implied causal or predictive manner) that should be tested simultaneously, or when multiple causal links lead to issues of direct and indirect effects (i.e., mediation). Traditionally, SEM requires the use of maximum likelihood (ML) estimation. Due to its reliance on this type of estimation, SEM is considered a large-sample procedure. Unfortunately, a number of studies have concluded that properties of statistics from ML-based SEM are not robust to small sample sizes (see Lei and Wu 2012). For education researchers in general, large samples are often difficult and even impossible to obtain, and this is especially true for rural research.

Faced with the need for large samples to test hypotheses through SEM, researchers are often told to find a way to increase the sample size. However, they are often limited by available resources, population size, or population accessibility as is the case with many types of rural research. Two undesirable alternatives would be to use an approach that is not as good a fit to the research question but is appropriate for small samples or re-orient the research so that the questions can be addressed by small sample techniques. Both approaches allow the data to guide the research question when it should be the other way around. Instead, researchers should choose an analytic strategy that offers complexity and flexibility without requiring large samples for inference.

Increased focus on individual contexts, often manifested as context- or group-specific models and frequently referred to as simply sub-group analyses, can lead to further segmentation of the sample which further reduces sample sizes available for complex analyses. Fortunately, a number of emerging estimation alternatives to maximum likelihood have been developed and their applicability to rural intervention studies will be discussed in this section. These include partial least squares (PLS; Wold 1975, 1982) and generalized structured component analysis (GSCA; Hwang and Takane 2004) from the information sciences and marketing literatures, and Bayesian estimation through Markov Chain Monte Carlo (MCMC; Kaplan 2014) techniques. The modeling frameworks presented in the following sections offer rural researchers with statistical alternatives for dealing with small sample sizes in rural research. These models provide researchers with opportunities for selecting the most appropriate model based on the theory and data of rural education research.

Partial least squares. As an alternative to ML, partial least squares (PLS) places minimal demands on measurement scales and residual distributions, and is considered to be distribution-free and appropriate for relatively small sample sizes (Chin 1998). Similar to SEM, PLS can be used to evaluate SEM-like models. Within the PLS framework, the relationship between a set of observed variables and their hypothesized constructs, or latent variables, are assessed. These "outer model" estimates are expressed as loadings or weights for each indicator, and specify how well each indicator relates to the latent construct. The inner model (i.e., associations among latent variables) is then obtained by regression coefficients that simultaneously describe the linear relationships between the constructs. PLS avoids improper solutions, which are common in small samples, by replacing factors with linear composites of observed variables like in principal components analysis and does not rely on distributional assumptions. PLS, however, does not have a single criterion that is consistently minimized or maximized to determine model parameter estimates (i.e., the fit function in SEM). Consequently, it is difficult to evaluate the quality of a PLS analysis due to the lack of available model fit information. Due to its reliance on principal components, the focus of PLS is on maximizing variance accounted for rather than confirmation of a specific model. Several programs with accessible graphical-user interfaces have been made available recently to conduct PLS analyses, including PLS-Graph (Chin 2001), SmartPLS (Ringle et al. 2005), and Visual PLS (Fu 2006). These programs offer rural researchers sophisticated statistical techniques for analyzing rural data where small sample sizes may otherwise be problematic.

Generalized structured component analysis. Generalized Structured Component Analysis (GSCA; Hwang and Takane 2004) is a "cousin" to SEM which, similar to PLS, also substitutes components for factors and requires less restricted distributional assumptions. Like PLS and SEM, GSCA can also flexibly test higher order constructs, multiple groups, etc. However, GSCA improves upon the PLS framework to offer a global optimization criteria for evaluating the fit of the model to the data. GSCA has been demonstrated to reproduce population parameters to an acceptable degree with sample sizes as low as $n = 10$ (Hwang and Takane 2004). Interested readers should refer to Hwang and Takane (2004) for a thorough examination of GSCA.

Markov Chain Monte Carlo. Recent advances with Bayesian methods (see Kaplan 2014; Lee and Song 2004) have shown that informative priors (i.e., the statistical concept that allows the researcher to incorporate prior "informed" knowledge into an analysis) can lead to more accurate estimates of parameters of interest, because the researcher utilizes known information about the substantive problem based on prior data. In contrast to SEM, since sampling-based Bayesian methods (i.e., Markov Chain Monte Carlo; MCMC) do not rely on asymptotic theory (the theory that large samples are required), they have been shown to be useful for smaller samples. Lee and Song (2004) found that for data that are normally distributed, the Bayesian approach can be used with small sample sizes while ML cannot—even when the sample size is only two to three times the number of parameters.

4.2 Working with Small and Countable Samples

Finally, computation of traditional inferential statistics used in evaluating rigorous research designs assumes that the obtained sample is constructed through random sampling with replacement from an infinitely large or a practically infinite, yet finite (or countable), population. However, most sampling is conducted without replacement from finite populations. In some sampling applications in education, especially in rural contexts, it is possible to obtain proportionally large samples or near-census sampling when the size of the population, while small, is finite. Under such circumstances, experimental units can be "catalogued" to the extent that the members of the population are explicitly defined and countable as is the case when experimental units are operationalized by geographical locations such as school buildings, school districts, counties, states, or even countries. In each of these examples, a researcher could reasonably create a list of all possible units which could potentially participate. Prominent examples of this research context are statewide educational assessments conducted in accordance with the federal *No Child Left Behind Act* (NCLB), nationwide assessments such as the National Assessment of Educational Progress (NAEP), and international efforts such as the OECD Programme for International Student Assessment (PISA). However, typical hypothesis testing in these contexts utilize traditional standard errors based on infinite populations which may overestimate the true degree of sampling error and reduce statistical power.

While the correction for using finite populations, the *fpc*, has been discussed in survey sampling texts for over 30 years (see Cochran 1977), there have been very few applications in educational contexts, until recently. In one notable exception, Chromy (1998) reported on the use of the fpc in the context of NAEP. In the first of two models, Chromy applied the fpc at the school level, while ignoring the proportion of the population sampled at the student level. It was noted that this approach may be more relevant to analysis of assessment data as well as consistent with concepts of stratification in research design. In the second model, the fpc was applied at both the student and school levels. Overall, Chromy concluded that when applying the fpc to estimation of effect sizes at the student and school levels, neither effect size estimation is reduced very much. However, this conclusion may be somewhat misguided in that the fpc is intended to reduce estimates of the *sampling* variability used in inference rather than the *sample* variability as used in computation of effect sizes.

The primary question to answer is how realistic, or meaningful, are finite samples? Bovaird et al. (2008) argue that they are *very realistic* for investigations dealing with experimental units that are higher-level organizational units, or where randomization occurs at a higher organizational level. Obvious examples could involve school districts when assessing progress under NCLB guidelines, early childhood educational opportunities by county tracked by state education departments, and assessment of state-level accountability or educational progress as in both NAEP and NCLB. The existence of finite samples may be *moderately realistic* for cross-cultural studies when assessing country-level variables and *potentially realistic* for small, clinical, under-represented, or geographically isolatable populations, especially studies involving immigrants, migrant workers, and Native Americans.

5 Conclusions

Rural education research often struggles with the limited use of both methodological rigor and a strong scientific basis. The unique context that rural communities offer provides researchers with ample opportunities to utilize innovative solutions for the challenges involved in conducting rural research, such as small population sizes, low population densities, and geographical isolation. This chapter has discussed a number of statistical and research design alternatives that may be applicable to rural research. Four general topics were discussed and alternatives provided that may assist rural researchers overcome many real or merely perceived impediments to conducting rigorous quantitative research in rural contexts. Topics discussed included (a) preserving and featuring the uniqueness of rural settings in systems level investigations through advanced statistical modeling, (b) alternatives to traditional random assignment, (c) efficiency of measurement paradigms to reduce the amount of data necessary for valid inferences, and (d) innovations in small sample inferential testing. Many of the discussed topics and approaches can be combined given the complexity of the problem at hand. Virtually all analytic models can be presented as special cases of SEM, enabling small sample estimation of complex analytic systems through alternative estimators like partial least squares, generalized structured component analysis, or Markov Chain Monte Carlo. If the research calls for the use of a regression discontinuity design with archival policy data that encompasses the entire or large percentage of a population, perhaps the correction for using finite populations can be used to improve statistical power. Planned missing data designs utilize analytic methods to address missing data, and while missing data estimation was not discussed in this chapter (see Enders 2010, as an excellent reference on modern missing data techniques), use of planned missingness can be implemented to reduce the data burden in any design or with any analytic procedure discussed in this chapter. The fundamental message is that all research contexts present their own unique challenges, but as researchers, we can look outside of our disciplines to find solutions that can help us pursue our necessary research agendas. Sometimes, all it takes is a little creativity and perseverance to pursue the appropriate design and analytic approach given the question we really want to answer rather than shaping the question to match what is perceived to be the only available course of action.

Acknowledgments Preparation of this manuscript was supported by a grant awarded to Susan M. Sheridan and colleagues (IES #R305C090022) by the Institute of Education Sciences. The opinions expressed herein are those of the author and should not be considered reflective of the funding agency.

References

Allison, D. B., Allison, R. L., Faith, M. S., Paultre, F., & Pi-Sunyer, F. X. (1997). Power and money: Designing statistically powerful studies while minimizing financial costs. *Psychological Methods, 2*, 20–33.

Armitage, P. (1975). *Sequential medical trials* (2nd ed.). New York: Wiley.

Arnold, M., Newman, J., Gaddy, B., & Dean, C. (2005). A look at the condition of rural education research: Setting a direction for future research. *Journal of Research in Rural Education, 20*, 1–25.

Baer, D. M., Wolf, M. M., & Risley, T. R. (1968). Some current dimensions of applied behavior analysis. *Journal of Applied Behavior Analysis, 1*, 91–97.

Barlow, D. H., & Hersen, M. (1984). *Single case experimental designs: Strategies for studying behavior change* (2nd ed.). New York: Pergamon Press.

Bell, R. Q. (1953). Convergence: An accelerated longitudinal approach. *Child Development, 24* (2), 145–152.

Boker, S. M., & Laurenceau, J. (2008). Coupled dynamics and mutually adaptive context. In T. D. Little, J. A. Bovaird, & N. A. Card (Eds.), *Modeling contextual effects in longitudinal studies* (pp. 299–324). Mahwah, NJ: Erlbaum.

Bolger, N., & Shrout, P. E. (2007). Accounting for statistical dependency in longitudinal data on dyads). In T. D. Little, J. A. Bovaird, & N. A. Card (Eds.), *Modeling contextual effects in longitudinal studies* (pp. 285–298). Mahwah, NJ: Erlbaum.

Bovaird, J. A. (2007). Multilevel structural equation models for contextual factors. In T. D. Little, J. A. Bovaird, & N. A. Card (Eds.), *Modeling contextual effects in longitudinal studies*. Mahwah, NJ: Erlbaum.

Bovaird, J. A. (2010, August). *Exploring sequential design of cluster randomized trials.* Paper presented at the American Psychological Association annual meeting. San Diego, CA.

Bovaird, J. A., Chumney, F., & Wu, C. (2008, June). *On the finite population correction in multilevel modeling: Implications for nesting within geographic region.* Paper presented at the International Meeting of the Psychometric Society. Durham, NH.

Bovaird, J. A., Koziol, N. A., & Chumney, F. (2011, October). *An ecological model of school readiness: A methodological investigation into the role of rurality.* Paper presented at the Building Solutions to Poverty: Methods and Metrics for Identifying Success Conference. Columbus, OH.

Bovaird, J. A., Martinez, S., & Stuber, G. (2006, August). *Multilevel structural equation modeling of kindergarten readiness with finite samples.* Paper presented at the American Psychological Association annual meeting. New Orleans, LA.

Bovaird, J. A., Sheridan, S. M., Glover, T. A., & Garbacz, S. A. (2009, June). *Fixed vs. sequential experimental designs: implications for cluster randomized trials in education.* Paper presented at the Institute for Education Science Research Conference. Washington, DC.

Box, G. E., Hunter, J. S., & Hunter, W. G. (2005). *Statistics for experimenters: Design, innovation, and discovery.* Hoboken, NJ: Wiley.

Bronfenbrenner, U. (1979). *The ecology of human development: Experiments by nature.* Cambridge, MA: Harvard University Press.

Bronfenbrenner, U. (1986). Ecology of the family as a context for human development: Research perspectives. *Developmental Psychology, 22*, 723–742.

Bronfenbrenner, U. (1988). Interacting systems in human development. Research paradigms: Present and future. In N. Bolger, A. Caspi, G. Downey, & M. Moorehouse (Eds.), *Persons in context: Developmental processes* (pp. 25–49). New York: Cambridge University Press.

Brown, C. A., & Lilford, R. J. (2006). The stepped wedge trial design: A systematic review. *BMC Medical Research Methodology, 6*, 1–9.

Burstein, L., Linn, R. L., & Cappel, F. J. (1978). Analyzing multilevel data in the presence of heterogeneous within-class regression. *Journal of Educational Statistics, 3*, 347–383.

Campbell, D. T. (1969). Reforms as experiments. *American psychologist, 24*(4), 409–429. Retrieved from http://www.cem.org/attachments/publications/CEMWeb027%20Reforms%20 As%20Experiments.pdf

Chernoff, H. (1959). Sequential design of experiments. *The Annals of Mathematical Statistics, 30*, 755–770.

Chin, W. W. (1998). The partial least squares approach to structural equation modeling. In G. A. Marcoulides (Ed.), *Modern methods for business research* (pp. 295–336). Mahwah, NJ: Lawrence Erlbaum Associates Inc.

Chin, W. W. (2001). *PLS-Graph user's guide version 3.0.* Houston, TX: C.T. Bauer College of Business, University of Houston.

Christ, T. J. (2007). Experimental control and threats to internal validity of concurrent and nonconcurrent multiple baseline designs. *Psychology in the Schools, 44*, 451–459.

Chromy, J. R. (1998). *The effects of finite sampling corrections on state assessment sample requirements.* Palo Alto, CA: NAEP Validity Studies, American Institutes for Research.

Cochran, W. G. (1977). *Sampling techniques* (3rd ed.). New York: Wiley.

Coladarci, T. (2007). Improving the yield of rural education research: An editor's swan song. *Journal of Research in Rural Education, 22*(3). Retrieved from http://jrre.psu.edu/articles/22-3. pdf

Cook, T. D., & Campbell, D. T. (1979). *Quasi-experimentation: Design and analysis issues for field settings.* Boston, MA: Houghton Mifflin.

Enders, C. K. (2010). *Applied missing data analysis.* New York: Guilford Press.

Fu, J. R. (2006). *VisualPLS—Partial least square (PLS) regression—An enhanced GUI for lvpls (PLS 1.8 PC) version 1.04.* Taiwan, ROC: National Kaohsiung University of Applied Sciences.

Gamse, B. C., Jacob, R. T., Horst, M., Boulay, B., & Unlu, F. (2008). *Reading first impact study final report (NCEE 2009-4038).* Washington, DC: National Center for Education Evaluation and Regional Assistance, Institute of Education Sciences, U.S. Department of Education.

Goldstein, H. I. (1986). Multilevel mixed linear model analysis using iterative general least squares. *Biometrika, 73*, 43–56.

Graham, J. W., Hofer, S. M., & Piccinin, A. M. (1994). Analysis with missing data in drug prevention research. In L. M. Collins & L. Seitz (Eds.), *Advances in data analysis for prevention intervention research: National Institute on Drug Abuse Research monograph series* (Vol. 142, pp. 13–63). Washington, DC: National Institute on Drug Abuse.

Graham, J. W., Taylor, B. J., Olchowski, A. E., & Cumsille, P. E. (2006). Planned missing data designs in psychological research. *Psychological Methods, 11*, 323–343. doi:10.1037/1082-989X.11.4.323

Grimm, K. J., & McArdle, J. J. (2007). A dynamic structural analysis of the impacts of context on shifts in lifespan cognitive development. In T. D. Little, J. A. Bovaird, & N. A. Card (Eds.), *Modeling contextual effects in longitudinal studies* (pp. 363–368). Mahwah, NJ: Erlbaum.

Harmon, H., Henderson, S., & Royster, W. (2003). A research agenda for improving science and mathematics education in rural schools. *Journal of Research in Rural Education, 18*, 52–58.

Hawley, L., Koziol, N., & Bovaird, J. A. (this volume). Defining and communicating rural: An overview and empirical illustration. In G. C. Nugent, G. M. Kunz, S. M. Sheridan, T. A. Glover, & L. L. Knoche (Eds.) *Rural education research: State of the Science and emerging directions.* New York: Springer.

Hussey, M. A., & Hughes, J. P. (2007). Design and analysis of stepped wedge cluster randomized trials. *Contemporary Clinical Trials, 28*, 182–191.

Hwang, H., & Takane, Y. (2004). Generalized structured component analysis. *Psychometrika, 69*(1), 81–99.

Johnson, E. G. (1992). The design of the national assessment of educational progress. *Journal of Educational Measurement, 29*, 95–110.

Kaplan, D. (2014). *Bayesian statistics for the social sciences.* New York: Guilford Press.

Kazak, A. E., Rourke, M. T., & Crump, T. A. (2003). Families and other systems in pediatric psychology. In M. C. Roberts (Ed.), *Handbook of pediatric psychology* (3rd ed., pp. 159–175). New York: Guilford.

Kline, R. B. (2010). *Principles and practice of structural equation modeling* (3rd ed.). New York: Guilford.

Kreft, I. G. G., & de Leeuw, J. (1998). *Introduction to multilevel modeling*. London: Sage.

Kunz, G. M., Nugent, G. C., Pedersen, J. E., DeChenne, S. E., & Houston, J. (2013). Meeting rural science teachers' needs: Professional development with on-going technology-delivered instructional coaching (R^2Ed Working Paper No. 2013-8). Retrieved from the National Center for Research on Rural Education: http:\\r2ed.unl.edu

Laird, N. M., & Ware, J. H. (1982). Random effects models for longitudinal data. *Biometrics, 38*, 963–974.

Lee, S., & Song, X. (2004). Evaluation of the Bayesian and maximum likelihood approaches in analyzing structural equation models with small sample sizes. *Multivariate Behavioral Research, 39*, 653–686.

Lei, P. W., & Wu, Q. (2012). Estimation in structural equation modeling. In R. H. Hoyle (Ed.), *Handbook of structural equation modeling* (pp. 164–180). New York: Guilford Press.

Little, T. D., Bovaird, J. A., & Card, N. A. (Eds.). (2007). *Modeling contextual effects in longitudinal studies*. Mahwah, NJ: Erlbaum.

Longford, N. T. (1987). A fast scoring algorithm for maximum likelihood estimation in unbalanced mixed models with nested effects. *Biometrika, 74*, 817–827.

McArdle, J. J. (1994). Structural factor analysis experiments with incomplete data. *Multivariate Behavioral Research, 29*, 409–454.

Nelson, T. D., Aylward, B. S., & Steele, R. G. (2008). Structural equation modeling in pediatric psychology: Overview and review of applications. *Journal of Pediatric Psychology, 33*, 679–687. doi:10.1093/jpepsy/jsm107

Nesselroade, J. R., & Baltes, P. B. (1979). *Longitudinal research in the study of behavior and development*. San Diego, CA: Academic Press.

Nugent, G. C., Kunz, G. M., Pedersen, J., Houston, J., & Lee, S. C. (this volume). Technology-based coaching for rural teachers' science instruction. In G. C. Nugent, G. M. Kunz, S. M. Sheridan, T. A. Glover, & L. L. Knoche (Eds.) *Rural education research: State of the Science and emerging directions*. New York: Springer.

Oliver, J. S. (2007). Rural science education research and the frameworks that give it form. *The Rural Educator, 28*, 1–3.

Power, T., DuPaul, G., Shapiro, E., & Kazak, A. (2003). *Promoting children's health: Integrating school, family, and community*. New York: Guilford.

Raghunathan, T. E., & Grizzle, J. E. (1995). A split questionnaire survey design. *Journal of the American Statistical Association, 90*, 54–63. doi:10.1080/01621459.1995.10476488

Raudenbush, S. W., & Bryk, A. S. (2002). *Hierarchical linear models* (2nd ed.). Thousand Oaks, CA: Sage.

Ringle, C. M., Wende, S., & Will A. (2005). SmartPLS 2.0 (beta). Computer software. Downloaded from www.smartpls.de

Schaie, K. W. (1965). A general model for the study of developmental problems. *Psychological Bulletin, 64*, 92–107.

Shadish, W. R., Cook, T. D., & Campbell, D. T. (2002). *Experimental and quasi-experimental designs for generalized causal inference*. Boston: Houghton-Mifflin.

Sheridan, S. M., Bovaird, J. A., Glover, T. G., Garbacz, S. A., Witte, A., & Kwon, K. (2012). A randomized trial examining the effects of conjoint behavioral consultation and the mediating role of the parent–teacher relationship. *School Psychology Review, 41*, 23–46.

Sheridan, S. M., Kunz, G. M., Witte, A., Holmes, S., & Coutts, M. (2014). Rural parents and teachers as partners: Preliminary results of a randomized trial (R^2Ed Working Paper No. 2014-4). Retrieved from the National Center for Research on Rural Education: http:\\r2ed.unl.edu

Shoemaker, D. M. (1973). *Principles and procedures of multiple matrix sampling*. Cambridge, MA: Ballinger Publishing Company.

Snijders, T., & Bosker, R. (2012). *Multilevel analysis: An introduction to basic and advanced multilevel modeling* (2nd ed.). Thousand Oakes, CA: Sage.

Steele, R. G., & Aylward, B. S. (2010). An overview of systems in pediatric psychology research and practice. In M. C. Roberts & R. G. Steele (Eds.), *Handbook of pediatric psychology* (4th ed.). New York: Guilford.

Stroup, W. W. (2013). *Generalized linear mixed models: Modern concepts, methods and applications.* Boca Raton, FL: CRC Press.

Tonry, M., Ohlin, L. E., & Farrington, D. P. (1991). *Human development and criminal behavior: New ways of advancing knowledge.* New York: Springer.

U.S. Department of Education, Institute of Education Sciences, What Works Clearinghouse. (2013, March). *What works clearinghouse: Procedures and standards handbook (version 3.0).* Retrieved from http://whatworks.ed.gov

Wald, A. (1945). Sequential tests of statistical hypotheses. *The Annals of Mathematical Statistics, 16,* 117–186.

Watson, P. J., & Workman, E. A. (1981). The non-concurrent multiple baseline across-individuals design: An extension of the traditional multiple baseline design. *Journal of Behavior Therapy and Experimental Psychiatry, 12,* 257–259.

Wendorf, C. A. (2002). Comparisons of structural equation modeling and hierarchical linear modeling approaches to couples' data. *Structural Equation Modeling, 9,* 126–140.

Woertman, W., de Hoop, E., Moerbeek, M., Zuidema, S. U., Gerritsen, D. L., & Teerenstra, S. (2013). Stepped wedge designs could reduce the required sample size in cluster randomized trials. *Journal of Clinical Epidemiology, 66,* 752–758.

Wold, H. (1975). Path models with latent variables: The NIPALS approach. In H. M. Blalock, A. Aganbegian, F. M. Borodkin, R. Boudon, & V. Capecchi (Eds.), *Quantitative sociology: International perspectives on mathematical and statistical modeling* (pp. 307–357). New York: Academic.

Wold, H. (1982). Soft modeling: The basic design and some extensions. In H. Wold & K. Jöreskog (Eds.), *Systems under indirect observation: Causality, structure, prediction II* (pp. 589–591). Amsterdam: North-Holland.

Part II
Rural Education Research Findings Part 1: Teacher and School Influences

The Effectiveness of E-Coaching in Rural Science Classrooms

Gwen C. Nugent, Gina M. Kunz, James Houston, Irina Kalutskaya and Jon Pedersen

Abstract The Nebraska Center for Research on Children, Youth, Families and Schools, with funding from the U.S. Department of Education through the National Center for Research on Rural Education conducted a randomized controlled trial with 119 rural middle and high school science teachers across 109 schools in Nebraska and Iowa to investigate the effects of technology-delivered instructional coaching (e-coaching) focused on guided scientific inquiry. *CSI: Coaching Science Inquiry in Rural Schools* examined the impact of professional development, consisting of a summer face-to-face institute and e-coaching during the following school year (treatment) versus no *CSI*-delivered professional development (control) on teacher classroom practice and student inquiry skills. The coaching was grounded in teachers' day-to-day instruction and addressed their unique instructional needs. Use of low-cost technology also allowed rural teachers ongoing access to coaching in their home or school, without the need for teachers or coaches to travel. Project technology included video capture of classroom instruction using GoPro cameras, cloud computing to share large video files, and real-time video-conferencing to connect teachers with coaches located at the University of Nebraska—Lincoln. The chapter describes the technology utilized as well as research and evaluation findings.

Keywords Professional development · Coaching · Science inquiry · Video-based data collection · Video-based classroom observation

G.C. Nugent · G.M. Kunz · J. Houston · I. Kalutskaya
University of Nebraska—Lincoln, Lincoln, USA

G.C. Nugent (✉) · G.M. Kunz · J. Houston
Nebraska Center for Research on Children, Youth, Families and Schools,
University of Nebraska—Lincoln, 216 Mabel Lee Hall,
Lincoln, NE 68588-0235, USA
e-mail: gnugent@unl.edu

J. Pedersen
University of South Carolina, Columbia, SC, USA

© Springer International Publishing Switzerland 2017
G.C. Nugent et al. (eds.), *Rural Education Research in the United States*,
DOI 10.1007/978-3-319-42940-3_7

1 Introduction

Typical professional development (PD) in the United States has been described as "short, episodic and disconnected from practice" (Wei et al. 2010, p. 1) and with "a hodgepodge of providers, formats, philosophies, and content" (Hill 2007, p. 114). However, the growing body of teacher PD research is isolating features with positive impacts on teacher practice and student performance. A comprehensive review of the teacher PD literature sponsored by the National Staff Development Council (Darling-Hammond et al. 2009; Wei et al. 2010) identified several key characteristics that influence positive outcomes, including the need for follow-up support beyond the initial PD experience. One promising form of follow-up support is instructional coaching, with a growing research base showing positive effects (Campbell and Malkus 2011; Lockwood et al. 2010; Lotter et al. 2013). Although ongoing supports such as coaching are critical to ensuring that teachers can implement effective practices in their classrooms, rural teachers can have significant difficulty in attaining the level of on-site support needed to bolster their practice, with physical distance a major deterrent (Weitzenkamp et al. 2003). Recent advances in technology allow teachers to connect to expertise and specialized resources and can provide a means to develop quality experiences, provide personalized and ongoing support, and enhance integrity in the implementation of instructional programs. Technology-mediated coaching is emerging as an effective solution to deliver ongoing support to teachers (Powell et al. 2010; Allen et al. 2011). Its capability to provide access to specialized professional development resources makes it especially appropriate for rural teachers who are widely dispersed and find that typical materials and professional development training do not fit their needs (Best and Cohen 2014; Hardre 2012). Because coaching is intended to address the day-to-day realities of teaching, it is an ideal format to meet the unique needs of teachers in the rural context.

This chapter describes a federally funded project, *Coaching Science Inquiry in Rural Schools* (*CSI*), which utilized established and emerging technological solutions to support effective professional development and coaching. The research focused on determining the impact of professional development in guided science inquiry, consisting of a summer face-to-face institute and school-year e-coaching, on middle and high school teachers and their students in rural schools. For participant teachers, project technology included video capture of classroom instruction using GoPro cameras, cloud computing to share large video files, and real-time videoconferencing to connect rural middle and high school science teachers with project-based coaches located at the University of Nebraska-Lincoln.

This chapter also reports on the project's use of video-based data collection and coding as part of the research process. Video research in the learning sciences has become increasingly prominent because "video technologies provide powerful ways of collecting, sharing, studying, presenting, and archiving detailed cases of practice to support teaching, learning and intensive study of those practices" (Derry et al. 2010, p. 4). Video technologies provide a "microscope" for careful analysis of instructional events at varying levels of detail. A major portion of the *CSI* project involved video-based data collection focusing on the quality and quantity of guided-inquiry instruction and coaching as coded by independent, trained data coders.

1.1 Rural Science Education and Teacher Professional Development

The second edition of the *Handbook of Research in Science Education* contains a chapter on rural science education (Oliver 2007), which underscores the problem of identifying studies with samples that would qualify as rural based on demographic characteristics or governmental definitions. The author also reports that much of the existing research is anecdotal, characterized as "documentation and comment" rather than rigorous quantitative analysis. Other authors have confirmed that the current research base for science education in rural contexts is extremely limited (Harmon et al. 2003).

Evaluation data are available, however, for a major NSF-funded initiative begun in 1994 which aimed to improve rural science and mathematics education. Evaluations of projects funded through the Rural Systematic Initiative showed that teacher professional development activities were rated as having the highest impact (Boyer 2006), and those activities that were most valuable were ones that aimed at changing the ways that teachers perform (Oliver 2007). Barriers cited to science reform—money, equipment and materials, teacher turnover, community support—echoed challenges cited by other authors (Lynch 2000; Marlow and Cooper 2008). Other researchers have commented on the professional isolation, when a single teacher teaches all the science courses and represents the entire science department of a school (Annetta and Shymansky 2006). A national study of rural science teacher professional development showed that rural teachers reported fewer PD presentations by a colleague or a mentor/coach/lead teacher (Glover and Nugent 2011) than their non-rural counterparts. Rural teachers also have more difficulty connecting with universities and other sources of professional development (Jean-Marie and Moore 2004; Weitzenkamp et al. 2003; Williams 2010).

Other research has shown that rural science teachers have taken fewer science and science methods courses at the undergraduate and graduate levels (Arnold et al. 2004) and that many rural science teachers are teaching in a secondary teaching area or out of field (Reeves 2003), and in-service opportunities are often inadequate or unavailable (Harmon et al. 2003). Research has documented the challenges of providing professional development to teachers in rural areas and underscored the need to consider the rural context (Howley and Howley 2004; Sandholtz and Ringstaff 2013). However, rural teacher professional development literature is relatively sparse: A review of rural educational research showed that the percentage of studies dealing with teacher preparation is around 20 % (Cicchinelli 2011).

1.2 Coaching

Development of coaching models can be traced to the work of Joyce and Showers (1982), which became highly salient with the enactment of *No Child Left Behind* (NCLB) legislation. One key piece of NCLB was creating the *Reading First Initiative* in which coaching was suggested "as a viable way to provide sustained and effective PD support to teachers" (Denton and Hasbrouck 2009, p. 153). Further NCLB provisions created thousands of reading coaching positions by mandating that each *Reading First* school be served by a reading coach. This influx of coaches into the schools was the start of a next generation of teacher PD, and coaching was rapidly extended into mathematics. Unfortunately, this onset of coaching was not accompanied by empirical research on coaching effectiveness and its impact on students. The research base on coaching remains limited and often focuses on descriptive and case study approaches and reported best practices (Borman and Feger 2006; Cornett and Knight 2009). Recently, however, a few empirical studies in literacy and mathematics coaching have been conducted documenting impacts beyond teacher improvement to student achievement (Allen et al. 2011; Campbell and Malkus 2011; Lockwood et al. 2010; Powell et al. 2010). Science coaching studies are also showing the potential of coaching in helping teachers understand inquiry-based teaching practices (Lotter et al. 2013), in producing higher student science achievement compared to a control group (Vogt and Rogalla 2009), and in improving student achievement through a focus on teacher–student interactions (Allen et al. 2011).

Most of the research with instructional coaching has involved a site-based, face-to-face format. However, the limited research using technology-delivered coaching (Denton et al. 2007; Pianta et al. 2008; Rock et al. 2009) has shown promising results. Such coaching can replicate functions in a face-to-face format, while providing flexibility in scheduling and eliminating the costly need for coaches to travel from school to school. Similarly, the use of technology can allow rural teachers ongoing and flexible access to coaching in their home or school, without the need to travel.

1.3 Science Inquiry

The *CSI* PD program used the instructional approach of guided inquiry pedagogy. Guided scientific inquiry has been shown as effective in promoting student achievement (Lynch et al. 2005; Vandosdall et al. 2007; Wilson et al. 2010). The guided inquiry approach infuses instruction of scientific inquiry knowledge and skills with science content (e.g., physical, life, and earth science) and is aligned with the science and engineering practices presented in the *Next Generation Science Standards* (NGSS 2013). Typical science instructional practice generally involves teachers presenting science concepts and content through lecture, followed by reinforcing that content by having students confirm the information (e.g., confirmatory labs) (Hudson et al. 2002; Weiss et al. 2003). In contrast, the *CSI* PD used a guided scientific inquiry approach that is student centered, driven by student data collection and analysis, and leads to formulation of an underlying science concept or principle. It is also teacher facilitated, requiring extensive use of teacher questioning and scaffolding to guide students to greater understanding of science concepts, content, and process skills (i.e., inquiry).

2 Method

The project involved a randomized control trial aimed at addressing the following research question: *What is the impact of professional development on guided scientific inquiry with follow-up coaching (treatment) versus no professional development (control) on teacher classroom practice and student inquiry skills?* The evaluation component involved feedback from treatment teachers after they had received coaching and delivered their science inquiry unit.

2.1 Participants

There were 119 rural science teachers from 109 schools in Nebraska and Iowa participating in the *CSI* project (82 treatment and 37 control teachers). The gender split was 70 % female and 30 % male. The average teacher's age was 42 years (SD = 11.02); average teaching experience was 14 years (SD = 9.49); and 50 % of the teachers had a master's degree. Twenty-eight percent of the teachers taught in schools that served elementary, middle and high school students, and 92 % of the teacher participants taught multiple grades and science courses, with 75 % teaching biology and 71 % teaching physical science. Students of these teachers comprised the student study sample. There were 1640 students involved in this study, split approximately equally between middle (48 %) and high school (52 %); approximately 49 % were male and 51 % were female. In terms of ethnicity, 83 % were White (non-Latino), followed by Hispanic/Latino (8 %), and Multi-Racial (3 %). The rest were divided among Asian/Pacific Islander, Native American and Black/African-American.

2.2 CSI *Professional Development Intervention*

The *CSI* PD intervention consisted of an intensive 8-day summer institute for teachers (over two consecutive weeks) followed by 8–12 e-coaching sessions in the school year immediately following participation in the summer institute. These e-coaching sessions were delivered outside the classroom instruction time across a 6- to 8-week period during the school year while the teachers implemented a science unit using the *CSI* guided science instructional approach. Extensive coaching protocols for the coaches and the teachers were developed by the project researchers and utilized during the coaching sessions.

The *summer institute*, led by project researchers and coaches, aimed to promote knowledge and skills through use of content instruction through evidence-based practices including modeling and video examples by content experts and coaches, teacher practice of new skills, and feedback provided to teachers by content experts, including coaches. During the summer institute, project coaches and science educators introduced teachers to guided scientific inquiry by modeling inquiry lessons in which fellow teacher participants served as "students." Group discussion followed modeling to clarify concerns or questions. Teachers were also given sample middle and high school inquiry unit lessons spanning 6–8 weeks in life science, physical science, earth science, and chemistry as instructional models to be implemented in their classrooms during the following school year.

At the end of week one of the summer institute, teachers identified a sample lesson and prepared to present in week two of the summer institute. This presentation in week two gave teachers an opportunity to practice implementing a science lesson using the *CSI* guided science inquiry instructional approach and receive feedback from coaches and peers, and to see other teachers' lesson implementation, experiencing additional lessons. Time was allotted for teachers to practice using the technology (e.g., using GoPro cameras to record their lessons, sharing videos and documents with their coaches via Dropbox, and practice coaching sessions in WebEx). We interspersed discussions and exercises about teaching science concepts using a guided inquiry approach, instructional strategies for posing various types and levels of questions to students, and scaffolding student knowledge and skill acquisition. Live modeling and video examples of classroom teaching using the guided scientific inquiry instructional method were used throughout.

The *instructional coaching* involved bi-directional discussion and feedback based on video-recorded classroom lesson implementation. The e-coaching aimed to support teacher transfer of knowledge and skills gained in the summer institute to classroom practice. The coaching sessions were scheduled around the teacher's schedule and were delivered synchronously, one-on-one, for about 45 min to an hour approximately two times per week. Coaches followed a clear protocol that included the following: (a) positive feedback from the coach on the teacher strategies that led to desirable student outcomes; (b) detailed discussion of the lesson including sharing time-stamped video clips to show what worked well and/or needed improvement; (c) exchange of ideas about strategies to address areas for improvement; and (d) planning for the next video-recorded instructional classroom period. The teacher then implemented the plans developed during the coaching session. The cycle was repeated until the formal coaching sessions were mutually terminated by the teacher and coach (typically after 8–10 sessions). While the teacher–coach interaction was focused during the 6–8 week period, the coach typically had periodic additional phone and e-mail contact with the teacher prior to

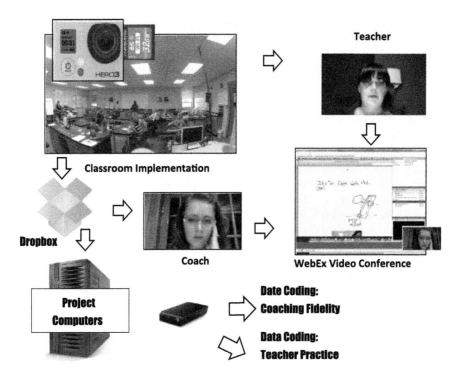

Fig. 1 Technology-supported coaching and research process

and following the coaching process. Coach skills building also was enhanced by weekly *CSI* team meetings including the coaches and research team members.

Figure 1 shows the technology-supported coaching system used in the *CSI* project. Teachers and coaches prepared for the e-coaching sessions by independently reviewing the video-recorded classroom period prior to each scheduled coaching session and completing preparation sections of the teacher or coach form of the coaching session protocols. The project technology was used for multiple purposes:

(1) To video-record classroom lesson implementation for review by coaches, teachers and data coders (to assess the quality and quantity of classroom guided inquiry instruction);
(2) To deliver video files from teachers to coaches and data coders;
(3) To connect teachers and coaches for the synchronous coaching sessions; and
(4) To video-record the e-coaching sessions for review by coaches (for self-reflection of coaching skills) and data coders (to assess the fidelity of the coaching sessions in the form of adherence to the coaching protocols)

Each of the steps in the process is discussed below, detailing the technology used to support the process.

Teacher recording of class instruction. Teachers were responsible for making digital recordings of their classroom instruction using GoPro cameras. These cameras worked remarkably well in our classroom settings. Their small size ($2\frac{1}{2}''$ wide $\times$ $1\frac{1}{2}''$ high $\times$ $1''$ deep) made them inconspicuous in the classroom; they were clearly not as intrusive as the physical presence of an external observer in the classroom. Developed originally for adventure or sports use, the GoPro cameras were rugged and virtually indestructible. A 178-degree wide-angle lens allowed video capture of an entire classroom. The cameras were simple to use, described by one teacher as "very good little devices, very dependable and easy to use." Most teachers found it easy to offload videos by either removing the storage card (holding 32 GB or about 10 h of video) or connecting to a USB port on their computer. The cameras were relatively inexpensive (around $250 apiece) and did not require the extra expense of a tripod.

Although the GoPro has a built-in microphone, we opted to microphone the teachers using Azden wireless lavalier microphones (approximately $150 apiece) because hearing teacher comments and instructional delivery was critical to our study outcomes. We found that the GoPro microphone seemed to capture almost every sound in the classroom, making isolation of the teacher difficult. The Azden microphones allowed us to capture the teacher audio, but only pick up voices of students who were in immediate range of the teacher. They were easy to use and portable. Some of the science teacher participants used them outside (i.e., when the class activity took place outside the classroom) with good success. We experienced minimal hardware failures with the wireless microphones.

Teacher review of video and transfer of video files to coaches. Once the recordings were made, teachers were responsible for uploading the files to their computer for their own review and for transfer to Dropbox. Dropbox allowed sharing of large files providing access to video from multiple computers from any geographic location. In order to meet the Dropbox storage limitations, the video files were copied to *CSI* servers and removed from the teachers' shared Dropbox folders by project developed software scripts. The time to transfer video files (about 3 GB) was as little as 10 min and as long as 2 days, and the discrepancy seemed related to the time of day, distance between the teacher's geographic location and the university, and bandwidth allocations set by local and regional network administrators.

Coaching sessions. The coaching sessions were conducted using WebEx, a web-based videoconferencing application. WebEx was chosen because of its support for two-way video and audio interaction, its ability to record coaching sessions and the capability to play back video examples of the classroom instruction during the coaching sessions for joint discussion by the coach and teacher. It also had the ability for the presenter and attendee to share documents and their desktop which greatly facilitated troubleshooting problems experienced by the teacher during the coaching session. WebEx was easily integrated into electronic calendars and provided easy access for teachers to the coaching sessions by simply clicking on a hot link that was embedded in an e-mail sent when the e-coaching session was scheduled and again when the session was initiated by the coach. The disadvantages of WebEx included the need to install software to view recorded sessions recorded in a proprietary WebEx format (.arf). At the time, the sharing of video was not supported for mobile devices (i.e., iPad, iPhone, Android) but compatibility issues have been addressed in subsequent software versions.

Video-based data collection. The use of video offered several advantages over in-person observational coding. A classroom environment is complex, with teacher instructional strategies changing throughout the instructional process while eliciting differing reactions from individual students. Coders were able to stop and review sections to verify the presence or absence of certain behaviors, helping to insure the accuracy of their data. Use of videos also eliminated the need for coders to travel to individual sites, resulting in tremendous travel savings of time, money and other resources (e.g., university or other rental cars). Our system also had the advantage that coders did not have to be on campus to view the files and complete online coding. Through the use of external hard drives containing the video files, coders were able to complete the coding anywhere they had access to a computer and the internet for entering coding online.

We also recorded the coaching sessions for coding coach fidelity to the established coaching protocols. Fidelity of coaching implementation was critical to assure that the coaching was being delivered as the developers intended and that there were not wide variations in the coaching process among individual coaches.

2.3 Teacher Instrumentation

Because the project focused on translation of guided inquiry skills into classroom instruction, we used three classroom observation instruments to assess teacher instructional practice (teacher dependent variable). Each instrument had its own purpose and set of behavioral indicators and was completed by independent coders blind to condition. To adhere to appropriate research practices, 25 % of our videos were coded by two raters to ensure appropriate inter-rater reliability. To ensure agreement between coders and to contribute to ongoing adherence to coding criteria, raters discussed and resolved any coding disagreements. Resulting Kappas for the three instruments ranged from 0.85 to 0.97.

Teacher Inquiry Rubric (TIR; Nugent et al. 2012, 2013) is a rubric assessing teacher proficiency in guiding students to develop skills in science questioning, investigating, explaining, collecting data, and communicating as specified in the standards. The culminating score is an overall, holistic rating reflecting the coder's assessment of the teachers' inquiry skills and practice. The instrument was designed with a 4-point scale, with a rating of 1 or 2 deemed "not proficient" and 3 and 4 as "proficient." "Not proficient" ratings indicated that teachers showed no evidence of promoting student acquisition of the skills or they instructed with a teacher-centered approach which precluded student practice and demonstration of the skills. "Proficient" ratings reflected teachers' use of guiding questions, experiences, and feedback to help students differentiate between examples and non-examples of the skill and ultimately to successfully perform inquiry.

EQUIP (Marshall et al. 2009) is a rubric assessing quality of inquiry instruction around four constructs: instruction, curriculum, assessment, and discourse. Although the rubric contains four levels for each of the constructs, as well as an overall score, we recoded the levels into "not proficient" (levels 1 and 2) and "proficient" (levels 3 and 4) to correspond to the TIR ratings.

The Partial Interval Classroom Inquiry Observation System-Teacher Version (PICI-T; Kunz et al. 2010; Nugent et al. 2013) uses a partial interval recording procedure (Cooper 1987) to code teacher instructional practices in the classroom that provide opportunities for students to engage in inquiry as aligned with the *CSI* conception of guided inquiry instruction (labeled as "inquiry") or that do not promote opportunities for student inquiry engagement (labeled as "non-inquiry"). Teaching sessions were divided into 15-s intervals. Coders coded each interval for whether the teacher was teaching with the "*CSI* guided inquiry approach" or a "non-inquiry approach." Percentages were calculated for each coded teaching session to identify the amount of class time in which the teachers engaged in "inquiry-based" or "non-inquiry-based" instructional practices.

Each of the teacher observation instruments focused on a different set of inquiry outcomes at a different resolution. For example, the TIR was content-based, focusing specifically on teacher abilities to promote specific student inquiry skills (such as questioning or investigating). EQUIP was based on key instructional constructs (such as assessment and classroom discourse), and the PICI-T provided an assessment of whether the teacher was presenting inquiry-based instruction.

Teacher evaluation results were obtained from a brief questionnaire that probed their assessment of key components of the coaching process (i.e., feedback, schedule, promotion of teacher self-reflection and improvement of instructional practices), as well as the technology. Questions utilized a 5-point Likert scale from 1 (Strongly Disagree) to 5 (Strongly Agree). Two open-ended questions asked for feedback about what teachers found particularly helpful about the coaching process and any recommendations they had for improvement.

2.4 Student Instrumentation

Just as we were focused on teacher classroom *practice*, we were also focused on student *performance* of inquiry skills, as well as their inquiry engagement (student dependent variables), which were assessed using two instruments:

Student Inquiry Rubric (Anthony and Person-Pandil 2001) was similar to the TIR in that it involved an overall rating of each student's inquiry abilities, and included indicators in the areas of questioning, investigating, collecting data, explaining, and communicating results. The instrument was adapted from a rubric created by Nebraska's Educational Service Unit #3 serving the Omaha area and was completed by the *teacher* for each student. As with the TIR, the 4-point scale was recoded into two categories, "proficient" or "not proficient." Non-proficient ratings indicated that the student was not able to perform the skill or performed the skill with some omissions or flaws. Proficient ratings indicated that the student could perform the skill successfully.

The *Partial Interval Classroom Inquiry Observation System-Student Version* (PICI-S; Kunz et al. 2010; Nugent et al. 2013), a direct classroom observation instrument, is a companion to the PICI-T (see description above). The PICI-S also uses a partial interval recording procedure (Cooper 1987) and generates an estimate of student inquiry engagement for the whole class based on rotational observation of individual students. One student is selected at random to observe and code behavior for four consecutive 15-s intervals (1 min). The observer randomly selects another student until all students are included. The instrument was used to code student behavior as "inquiry engaged" or "not inquiry engaged" based on whether they were on task (e.g., Austin and Soeda 2008; Haley et al. 2010; Kern and Dunlap 1994; Morrison et al. 2002; Northup et al. 1999; Ridgway et al. 2003) during an interval in which the teacher was coded as delivering an inquiry instructional practice.

2.5 Research/Evaluation Design and Data Analysis

The research utilized a randomized controlled design involving a treatment and control group. Because of the binary coding of the outcome variables, we used logistic regression to predict the probability of the treatment and control group being classified as proficient (TIR, EQUIP, SIR), presenting inquiry (PICI-T), or inquiry engaged (PICI-S-IE). The evaluation design focused on teacher evaluation of the coaching, using descriptive analysis.

3 Results

3.1 Teacher Research Results

Logistic regression analysis was employed to predict the probability that a participant would be rated as proficient in inquiry instruction as measured by the TIR and EQUIP study instruments. The predictor variable was the participant's condition assignment (0 = treatment, 1 = control).

Results of the logistic regression showed that condition assignment (treatment or control) was a valid predictor of inquiry proficiency performance for both teachers and students. Results from all three of the teacher observation measures showed that a high percentage of treatment participants were in the proficiency group.

Table 1 Frequencies of observed and predicted values for TIR and EQUIP models

Observed	Predicted		
	Not proficient	Proficient	Percentage correct
TIR			
Not proficient	46	19	70.8
Proficient	7	39	84.8
Overall percentage			76.6
EQUIP			
Not proficient	45	10	81.8
Proficient	8	48	85.7
Overall percentage			83.8

Note The cut value is 0.5

TIR. The model for TIR was able to correctly classify 71 % of those teachers who were rated "not proficient" in inquiry instruction and 85 % of those who were rated "proficient," for an overall success rate of 77 % (see Table 1). The odds of being rated as proficient in inquiry instruction for the treatment group were 2.05, and the odds for the control group were 0.15 (see Table 2). Overall, the model predicts that the odds of being rated as "proficient" in inquiry instruction are 14 times (2.05/.15) higher for participants in the treatment group than the control group. Consequently, our model predicts that the probability of being rated as "proficient" in inquiry instruction is 67 % for the treatment group and only 13 % for the control group.

EQUIP. The model for EQUIP was able to correctly classify 86 % of those who were rated "proficient" in inquiry instruction and 82 % of those who were rated "not proficient," for an overall success rate of 84 % (see Table 1). The odds of being rated as proficient in inquiry instruction for the treatment group were 4.80, and the odds for the control group were 0.18 (see Table 2). Overall, the model predicts that the odds of being rated as "proficient" in inquiry instruction are

Table 2 Logistic regression results predicting proficiency in inquiry instruction from group for TIR and EQUIP (N = 111 teachers)

	B	SE	Wald	Sig	Exp (B)	Probability	R^2	χ^2	df
TIR							0.28	35.87**	1
Treatment	0.72	0.28	6.61	0.010	2.05	0.67			
Control	−1.88				0.15	0.13			
Group difference	−2.60	0.49	27.87	0.000	0.07				
EQUIP							0.39	55.57**	1
Treatment	1.57	0.35	20.36	0.000	4.80	0.83			
Control	−1.73				0.018	0.15			
Group difference	−3.30	0.52	40.52	0.000	0.04				

Note **$p < 0.001$

Table 3 Summary of simple regression analysis for PICI-T (N = 111 teachers)

Variable	B	SE (B)	Beta	t	95 % C.I.	
					Lower	Upper
Constant	0.69	0.03		21.44**	0.62	0.75
Group	−0.46	0.05	−0.69	−9.97**	−0.55	−0.37

Note $R^2 = 0.69$; **$p < 0.001$

27 times (4.80/.18) higher for teacher participants in the treatment group than the control group. Consequently, our model predicts that the probability of being rated "proficient" in inquiry instruction is 83 % for the treatment group and only 15 % for the control group (see Table 2).

PICI-T: Teacher inquiry instruction. A simple regression analysis was conducted to evaluate how well the group assignment (e.g., treatment or control) predicted percent of the teacher inquiry instruction. Teacher inquiry instruction in classrooms ranged from 0 to 100 % (M = 47 %; SD = 34 %). Teacher inquiry instruction averaged 69 % (SD = 22 %) in the treatment classrooms and only 23 % (SD = 27 %) in the control classrooms. There was a significant difference between groups such that treatment teachers had on average 46 % more inquiry instruction in a classroom (t = −9.97, p < 0.001) compared to the control group (see Table 3).

The consistent results across the three teacher measures provide triangulated evidence of the effectiveness of the *CSI* professional development, including the summer institute and the follow-up coaching, which is further substantiated by the student impact results.

3.2   Student Research Results

SIR. Logistic regression analysis with the hierarchical linear modeling was conducted to evaluate how well the group assignment (e.g., treatment or control) predicted probability that a student would be rated as proficient in inquiry skills as reported by a teacher. The odds of being rated as proficient in inquiry skills for students in the treatment group were 3.11, and the odds for the control group were 2.05 (see Table 4). Overall, the model predicts that the odds of being rated as "proficient" in inquiry skills are 1.5 times higher (3.11/2.05) for student participants in the treatment group than the control group. Consequently, our model predicts that the probability of being rated "proficient" in inquiry skills is 76 % for students in the treatment group and only 67 % for students in the control group (see Table 4).

PICI-S: Student inquiry engagement. A simple regression analysis was conducted to evaluate how well the group assignment (e.g., treatment or control) predicted percent of student inquiry engagement in a classroom. Student inquiry engagement in classrooms ranged from 0 to 99 % (M = 45 %; SD = 32 %).

Table 4 Logistic regression results predicting proficiency in inquiry skills from group and school assignment for SIR (N = 1490 students)

	B	SE (B)	Exp (B)	Probability	df	F value	Sig.
Fixed effects							
Treatment	1.13	0.25	3.11	0.76			
Control	0.72		2.05	0.67			
Group difference	−0.42	0.37			1490	7.55	0.01
MiddleHigh	0.59	0.36			1490	1.36	0.24
Group × MiddleHigh	−0.58	0.51			1490	1.29	0.26
Random effects							
Intercept	1.21	0.26					

Note MiddleHigh = School Assignment (Middle or High School)

Table 5 Summary of simple regression analysis for students' inquiry engagement (N = 111 classrooms)

Variable	B	SE (B)	Beta	t	95 % C.I. for B	
					Lower	Upper
Constant	1.08	0.07		15.26**	0.94	1.23
Group	−0.43	0.05	−0.67	−9.50**	−0.52	−0.34

Note R^2 = 0.45; **$p < 0.001$

Student inquiry engagement averaged 65 % (SD = 22 %) in the treatment classrooms and only 22 % (SD = 26 %) in the control classrooms. There was a significant difference between groups such that students in the treatment group had on average 43 % more inquiry engagement in a classroom (t = −9.50, $p < 0.001$) compared to the control group (see Table 5).

3.3 Evaluation Results

Evaluation results from both quantitative and qualitative responses showed that teachers responded positively to the coaching. The overall rating of coaching was 4.87 on the 5-point scale. Teachers also reported that the coaching improved their teaching (M = 4.56, SD = 0.53). One teacher summed up the coaching process by reporting, "I believe that coaching was the essential link that had been missing from all of my previous training/workshops. Instead for a 1 day/week workshop, it continued the process through the year and more importantly in my classroom. It allowed me to see what I was doing well and what needed to be improved in a very concrete way." Another commented, "I wish I had a coach every day!" Teachers also reported that the technology was easy to use (M = 4.30 on a 5-point scale;

SD = 0.77), and that reviewing the videos of their teaching was valuable (M = 4.35, SD = 0.71) and that it encouraged them to self-reflect on their teaching (M = 4.66, SD = 0.60). Open-ended comments from the teachers also emphasized the impact of coaching. One teacher compared coaching to more traditional forms of professional development such as workshops, "We stuck with it [coaching] long enough for me to feel like I really made a change in my teaching. It wasn't just a one-time and done." Another commented on student impacts, "I found that once I got on the right track that the students' response and learning to the material far outweighed traditional methods of learning for most students." Another added, "My coach really helped me take my inquiry teaching up a level so the students were designing experiments without me dictating what to do. I would have never gotten to the level I am at without the coaching."

4 Discussion

CSI as a science inquiry PD intervention was grounded in research-based practices and utilized a technology-based solution to provide needed job-embedded professional development to rural teachers. It (a) embodied many critical evidence-based PD elements identified in the literature as high quality (e.g., modeling and practice with guided feedback); (b) focused on a teaching approach that is not prevalent in science classrooms (inquiry) and one that teachers are historically not successful in implementing; (c) included inquiry content knowledge, skills, and pedagogy grounded in solid research; (d) used instruction in both the summer institute and the coaching sessions that modeled the guided scientific inquiry approach; and (e) included needed follow-up support in the form of coaching to help teachers transfer knowledge to classroom practice. Results from both the research and evaluation substantiate teacher acceptance of the professional development including e-coaching and its positive impacts on their instructional practice. While there is considerable evidence that instruction delivered through various forms of technology (e.g., two-way video/audio, web-based) is effective (Russell 2001), most of the research has occurred within the framework of student-based instruction, not within the context of teacher professional development. This project provides evidence that technology-delivered coaching provides an efficient means of providing ongoing professional development to teachers, resulting in positive changes in teacher instructional practice and resulting positive impacts on students. The results revealed that treatment teachers were more likely than control teachers to be rated as "proficient" in inquiry on two different inquiry observation instruments. Analyses comparing the percent of inquiry instruction delivered by treatment versus control teachers showed a significantly higher percentage for the treatment teachers. Students of teachers who participated in the *CSI* professional development were also more likely to reach the proficient level in performing inquiry compared to the students of teachers in the control condition. Similarly, treatment group students were engaged in the instruction a higher percentage of the time than control students. Limitations to these results must be noted, however. Because the study relied on descriptive and correlational/probability analyses, causal inferences cannot be drawn.

Technology was a key feature in delivering the coaching to rural teachers. Simply stated, the teachers who received coaching in this project could not have received the same level of coach support without the technology delivery. The travel expenses would have been prohibitive, and the travel logistics impossible for our four coaches to travel to each individual site twice a week. This technology-supported coaching process exhibited the same "anywhere, anytime" advantages as any distance education or online professional development course could provide. Our rural teachers were able to receive ongoing professional development regardless of their location. Similarly, our four coaches could conduct their coaching sessions from anywhere—the office, their home, or place of travel. The system also provided tremendous flexibility. Teachers could review the video of their classroom session at their convenience to prepare for the coaching session. Teachers and coaches were able to schedule coaching sessions at available times for both the teacher and coach, including weekends, early mornings, and late evenings. While this required flexibility in working hours for the coach, it was critical to meet time constraints of rural teachers, most of whom were also involved in supporting numerous student extracurricular activities and had limited time during the school day.

We also found the "distant" aspect of our project and technology was viewed as an advantage because coaches were not physically located in the building and were not viewed as being directly connected with the local school administration. The physical separation between coach and teacher created a level of trust between the coach and teacher, who did not view the coach as an "evaluator" but instead as someone dedicated to improving their classroom instruction. As one teacher commented, it was great "just having an observer that wasn't 'evaluating' the teaching, I felt like she [coach] acted as a mentor, not like when administrators observe."

The use of videos for teacher review of their own instruction emerged as an important aspect of the project and supports other research underscoring its importance in impacting teacher change (Collett 2012; McConnell et al. 2008). As one teacher described the process, "I expected the coaching to be more evaluative, and it was much more reflection." After teachers got over the initial reality of watching themselves on a video recording, they began focusing on the teaching process, noting their teaching behaviors that positively impacted student performance outcomes. Critical to this process was the sharing of video clips during the coaching sessions, illustrating positives as well as targeted areas for change. Teachers commented that "the best part of the coaching process for me was being able to watch and reflect on my own process. It was very encouraging after a lesson that I thought was a disaster to see the good that came from it and have my coach point out positives throughout the lesson as well as helping me to improve for the next time." Teachers also used videos to observe students they did not typically notice or were not on their radar. The videos could be viewed multiple times with the ability to easily stop and repeat a section in order to fully observe behaviors of individual students and see how their instructional strategy was positively or negatively impacting particular students. A teacher reported that watching selected clips of her teaching during the coaching session was the most valuable part: "There were many times I said something at the moment but didn't realize what its impact was for the students." Another advantage of the videos was that they provided a video portfolio or archive of teaching, providing permanent documentation to share with administrators or possibly for national board certification. Further evidence that teachers were valuing the opportunity to record and review their lessons came from the fact that we received numerous requests from both teachers and administrators to purchase the cameras and microphones for local use after study participation had ended.

4.1   Challenges of Technology for Coaching and Research

Despite the advantages of e-coaching, we encountered some bumps in the road. Although the technology was generally reliable, we experienced periodic, unpredictable failures of the GoPro cameras, as well as unexpected outages of Dropbox and WebEx. We also found that our teachers had more experience using learning management systems and polycom videoconferencing than web-based videoconferencing. To help teachers get up to speed on project-specific applications and processes, teachers were encouraged to bring their own laptop computers to the summer institute where they had the opportunity to practice on their own computer systems. Teachers installed and utilized the necessary applications (Dropbox, WebEx, and GoPro cameras) during the PD in the same way they would need to when they returned to their classrooms. From the first year of the study we learned that having teachers *watch* the process of setting up the GoPro camera and microphone, connecting the camera to their computer, downloading videos to their computer, copying them to the shared Dropbox folder, and connecting to a WebEx meeting was ineffective for promoting teacher success on their own. Likewise, step-by-step tutorials were also problematic as the actual steps and screens changed with updates to the applications. Teachers needed to experience these steps first-hand, on their own devices, to more fully understand "how to do it" in their own classrooms.

Despite these efforts there still remained a steep learning curve at the outset of implementation for some teachers. Some did not realize that they had to have a webcam and microphone for their desktop computer to participate in WebEx sessions. Other problems involved moving the video to Dropbox and connecting the camera to the computer. We also ran into unexpected problems such as teachers closing their laptop during the uploading of videos to Dropbox, resulting in the computer going to sleep and disrupting the file transfer. The teachers were also unable to see what was being recorded without an additional purchase of an LCD screen, and it was very easy to accidentally select the "still" instead of "video" mode. In such cases, a series of still pictures was recorded instead of video of the lesson. Working with teachers required ongoing technology troubleshooting by our coaches, our project manager, regional service units, and local school personnel. The troubleshooting sometimes included backup plans such as using the chat feature in WebEx to type in instructions or communicate during a coaching session or connecting by phone. School issues included school firewalls and administrators' blocking installation of the Dropbox and/or WebEx software or blocking access to the Dropbox or WebEx sites. These issues occurred both at the regional and local levels. Unfortunately, we also found that rural schools often do not have adequate technology support for local troubleshooting.

We estimate we are storing approximately 1000 videos at roughly 3 GB per video (7 TB total) from the *CSI* project. The sheer number of videos and amount of data collected for this project presented unique problems. Coding nearly 1000 videos using three observational instruments was a laborious, time-consuming process. Our coders required approximately 2–3 h per video (approximately 40–50 min of classroom instruction equivalent to one class period) to code using all instruments. In addition, to adhere to appropriate research practices, 25 % of our videos were coded by two raters to insure appropriate inter-rater reliability. This practice obviously increased the number of times individual videos were reviewed and scored.

While these challenges discussed above focused on hardware and technology use issues, we also faced Institutional Review Board (IRB) challenges. Although Dropbox was approved by our Institutional Review Board as providing the necessary data security, IRB confidentiality requirements presented unique challenges in video recording classroom instruction. Specifically, we were required to provide parental notification letters for the schools to provide to each family that we would be video-recording classroom instruction as part of this research study and to outline a process for parents to request that their student's data not be included in the aggregated student classroom data. One school district had their attorney create an additional parental notification that further explained the parents' options to have their student's data removed from any data analysis as well as providing a district level contact to opt-out of study participation.

4.2 Future Directions

Results from direct observation of classroom practice showed that teachers who participated in the *CSI* intervention were more proficient in inquiry teaching practice compared to a "business as usual" control condition. While these results are encouraging, they do not address critical questions regarding the unique and combined effects of the two PD components—summer institute and follow-up coaching—nor do they provide insight into the underlying elements for coaching effectiveness. Because coaching is typically included with other forms of PD support (e.g., teacher in-service), understanding its unique effects is lacking. Systematic, rigorous research is necessary to discern the unique impact of instructional coaching and to identify the underlying mechanisms of coaching that promote positive outcomes for both teachers and students. Research is needed to determine whether there is a value-added effect of coaching when the coupled with a summer institute. Research is also needed to dig deeper into *why* or *how* coaching leads to outcomes. Only with an understanding of the underlying workings of coaching will we be able to design, implement and scale up appropriate interventions to meet diverse needs of rural science teachers and their students.

As always, availability and capabilities of technological resources changed over the course of the project. As a result, some of the tools we utilized will likely change in future project iterations. The advancement of cloud-based applications such as Google Drive has made it a viable option for replacing Dropbox and WebEx. The large size of the Google Drive (30 GB) as well as the integrative nature of the Google Apps [or Google Apps for Education (GAFE)] allow for the same anywhere, anytime access in a single location at no additional cost. For example, Google Docs would allow for joint modification of key coaching documentation such as lesson planning and observational notes. These documents easily track changes by contributor and can be linked to Google Forms which integrate information into a database/spreadsheet format for storage or easy export for further analysis. Google Hangouts, another feature of Google Apps, allows for recorded web conferencing similar to WebEx for no cost and across multiple mobile and desktop platforms. Google Drive would also allow for nearly immediate file sharing between teacher and coach to reduce the lag time between classroom video recording and subsequent coaching feedback. Perhaps the greatest advantage to utilizing Google Apps would include the accessibility for the teachers and the familiarity with its operations. We estimate that approximately one fourth to one third of our teachers are currently using some portion of Google Apps. This teacher familiarity could reduce the learning curve for the technology while increasing efficiency with an all-in-one suite. Many schools have not only opened up network access to Google Apps, but actually encouraged its usage by teachers thus minimizing the need for special access for study related processes. Given that teachers are already using this technology, expanding teacher networking through Google would appear to be a promising next step.

Acknowledgments This research was supported by the U.S. Department of Education's Institute of Education Sciences (R305C090022).

References

Allen, J., Pianta, R., Gregory, A., Mikami, A. Y., & Lun, J. (2011). An interaction-based approach to enhancing secondary school instruction and student achievement. *Science, 333*, 1034–1037. doi:10.1126/science.1207998

Annetta, L. A., & Shymansky, J. A. (2006). Investigating science learning for rural elementary school teachers in a professional-development project through three distance-education strategies. *Journal of Research in Science Teaching, 43*, 1019–1039.

Anthony, J., & Person-Pandil, S. (2001). *Inquiry student scoring rubric [Measurement instrument]*. Retrieved from www.education.ne.gov/science/Documents/Inquiry_Rubric.pdf

Arnold, M. L., Gaddy, B. B., & Dean, C. B. (2004). *A look at the condition of rural education research: Setting a direction for future research*. Aurora, CO: Mid-continent Research for Education and Learning.

Austin, J. L., & Soeda, J. M. (2008). Fixed-time teacher attention to decrease off-task behaviors of typically developing third graders. *Journal of Applied Behavior Analysis, 41*, 279–283.

Best, J., & Cohen, C. (2014). *Rural education: Examining capacity challenges that influence educator effectiveness (Policy brief)*. Denver, CO: McREL International.

Borman, J., & Feger, S. (2006). *Instructional coaching: Key themes from the literature*. Providence, RI: The Education Alliance at Brown University.

Boyer, P. (2006). *Building community: Reforming math and science education in rural schools*. Fairbanks, AK: University of Alaska.

Campbell, P., & Malkus, N. (2011). The impact of elementary mathematics coaches on student achievement. *The Elementary School Journal, 1*(111), 430–454. doi:10.1086/657654

Cicchinelli, L. (2011). *Rural schooling: Necessity is the mother of innovation*. Presentation to the National Center for Research in Rural Education Creating Connections Speaker Series, Lincoln, NE. Retrieved from http://r2ed.unl.edu/presentations/2011/012411_Cicchinelli/

Collett, V. (2012). Gradual increase of responsibility model: Coaching for teacher change. *Literacy Research and Instruction, 51*, 27–47.

Cooper, J. O. (1987). Measuring and recording behavior. In J. O. Cooper, T. E. Heron, & W. L. Heward (Eds.), *Applied behavior analysis* (pp. 59–80). Columbus, OH: Merrill.

Cornett, J., & Knight, J. (2009). Research on coaching. In J. Knight (Ed.), *Coaching: Approaches and perspectives* (pp. 192–216). Thousand Oaks, CA: Corwin.

Darling-Hammond, L., Wei, R. C., Andree, A., Richardson, N., & Orphanos, S. (2009). *Professional learning in the learning profession: A status report on teacher development in the United States and abroad*. Dallas, TX: National Staff Development Council. Retrieved from http://www.learningforward.org/docs/pdf/nsdcstudy2009.pdf

Denton, C. A., & Hasbrouck, J. A. N. (2009). A description of instructional coaching and its relationship to consultation. *Journal of Educational and Psychological Consultation, 19*, 150–175. doi:10.1080/10474410802463296

Denton, C. A., Swanson, E. A., & Mathes, P. G. (2007). Assessment-based instructional coaching provided to reading intervention teachers. *Reading and Writing, 20*, 569–590.

Derry, S. J., Pea, R. D., Barron, B., Engle, R. A., Erickson, F., Goldman, R., et al. (2010). Conducting video research in the learning sciences: Guidance on selection, analysis, technology, and ethics. *Journal of the Learning Sciences, 19*, 3–53.

Glover, T., & Nugent, G. (2011). *A national study of rural teachers' professional development, instructional knowledge, and classroom practice*. Paper presented at the 103rd National Rural Education Association Convention and Research Symposium, Hilton Head, SC.

Haley, J. L., Heick, P. F., & Luiselli, J. K. (2010). Use of an antecedent intervention to decrease vocal stereotypy of a student with autism in the general education classroom. *Child and Family Behavior Therapy, 32*, 311–321.

Hardre, P. (2012). Standing in the gap: Research that informs strategies for motivating and retaining rural high school students. *Rural Educator, 34*, 12–18.

Harmon, H. L., Henderson, S. A., & Royster, W. C. (2003). A research agenda for improving science and mathematics education in rural schools. *Journal of Research in Rural Education, 18*, 52–58.

Hill, H. C. (2007). Learning in the teaching workforce. *The Future of Children, 17*(1), 111–127. doi:10.1353/foc.2007.0004

Howley, A., & Howley, C. B. (2004). *High-quality teaching: Providing for rural teachers' professional development (AEL policy brief)*. Charleston, WV: AEL.

Hudson, S. B., McMahon, K. C., & Overstreet, C. M. (2002). *The 2000 national survey of science and mathematics education: Compendium of tables*. Chapel Hill, NC: Horizon Research Inc.

Jean-Marie, G., & Moore, G. (2004). The highly qualified teacher: Implications and recommendations for rural school districts. *Teacher Education and Practice, 17*(2), 146–161.

Joyce, B., & Showers, B. (1982). The coaching of teaching. *Educational Leadership, 40*, 4–10.

Kern, L., & Dunlap, G. (1994). Use of a classwide self-management program to improve the behavior of students with emotional and behavioral disorders. *Education and Treatment of Children, 17*, 445–458.

Kunz, G. M., Fluke, S., DeChenne, S. E., & Pedersen, J. (2010). *Partial Interval Classroom Inquiry (PICI) Observation System for Teachers (PICI-T) and Students (PICI-S)*. Unpublished measure, Lincoln, NE, University of Nebraska-Lincoln.

Lockwood, J. R., McCombs, J. S., & Marsh, J. (2010). Linking reading coaches and student achievement: Evidence from Florida middle schools. *Educational Evaluation and Policy Analysis, 32*, 372–388. doi:10.3102/0162373710373388

Lotter, C., Yow, J. A., & Peters, T. T. (2013). Building a community of practice around inquiry instruction through a professional development program. *International Journal of Science and Mathematics Education, 12*, 1–23. doi:10.1007/s10763-012-9391-7

Lynch, S. (2000). *Equity and science education reform: Listening to our better angels*. Mahwah, NF: Erlbaum.

Lynch, S., Kuipers, J., Pyke, C., & Szesze, M. (2005). Examining the effects of a highly rated science curriculum unit on diverse students: Results from a planning grant. *Journal of Research in Science Teaching, 42*, 912–946. doi:10.1002/tea.20080

Marlow, D., & Cooper, M. (2008). *The MetLife survey of the American teacher: Past, present, and future* (Report No. ED504457). New York, NY: MetLife.

Marshall, J. C., Smart, J., & Horton, R. M. (2009). The design and validation of EQUIP: An instrument to assess inquiry-based instruction. *International Journal of Science and Mathematics Education, 8*, 299–321.

McConnell, T. J., Zhang, M., Koehler, M. J., Lundeberg, M. A., Urban-Lurain, M., Parker, J. M., et al. (2008). A lesson in teaching starring you. *Journal of Staff Development, 29*(4), 39–42.

Morrison, R. S., Sainato, D. M., Benchaaban, D., & Endo, S. (2002). Increasing play skills of children with autism using activity schedules and correspondence training. *Journal of Early Intervention, 25*, 58–72. doi:10.1177/105381510202500106

NGSS Lead States. (2013). *Next Generation Science Standards: For states, by states*. Washington, DC: The National Academies Press.

Northup, J., Fusilier, I., Swanson, V., Huete, J., Bruce, T., Freeland, J., et al. (1999). Further analysis of the separate and interactive effects of methylphenidate and common classroom contingencies. *Journal of Applied Behavior Analysis, 32*, 35–50.

Nugent, G., Kunz, G., Pedersen, J., Luo, L., Berry, B., & Houston, J. (2012). *Teacher inquiry rubric*. Unpublished measure, Lincoln, NE, University of Nebraska-Lincoln.

Nugent, G., Marshall, J., Minner, D., Kunz, G., & Pedersen, J. (2013). *Understanding inquiry classroom practice through measurement of teacher inquiry skills*. Presentation to the National Association for Research in Science Teacher Conference, Rio Mar, Puerto Rico.

Oliver, S. (2007). Rural science education. In S. K. Abell & N. G. Lederman (Eds.), *Handbook of research on science education* (pp. 345–372). Mahway, NJ: Lawrence Erlbaum.

Pianta, R., Mashburn, A., Downer, J., Hamre, B., & Justice, L. (2008). Effects of web-mediated professional development resources on teacher–child interactions in pre-kindergarten classrooms. *Early Childhood Research Quarterly, 23*, 467–478.

Powell, D., Diamond, K., Burchinal, M., & Koehler, M. (2010). Effects on an early literacy professional development intervention of Head Start teachers and children. *Journal of Educational Psychology, 102*, 299–312. doi:10.1037/a0017763

Reeves, C. (2003). *Implementing the no child left behind act: Implications for rural schools and districts*. Naperville, Ill: NCREL.

Ridgway, A., Northup, J., Pellegrin, A., LaRue, R., & Hightshoe, A. (2003). Effects of recess on the classroom behavior of children with and without attention-deficit hyperactivity disorder. *School Psychology Quarterly, 18*, 253–268.

Rock, M. L., Gregg, M., Gable, R. A., & Zigmond, N. P. (2009). Virtual coaching for novice teachers. *Phi Delta Kappan, 91*(2), 36–41.

Russell, T. L. (2001). *The no significant difference phenomenon: A comparative research annotated bibliography on technology for distance education.* Montgomery, AL: IDECC.

Sandholtz, J., & Ringstaff, C. (2013). Assessing the impact of teacher professional development on science instruction in the early elementary grades in rural US schools. *Professional Development in Education, 39*, 678–697.

Vandosdall, R., Klentschy, M., Hedges, L. H., & Weisbaum, K. S. (2007). *A randomized study of the effects of scaffolded guided-inquiry instruction on student achievement in science.* Paper presented at the American Educational Research Association, Chicago, IL.

Vogt, F., & Rogalla, M. (2009). Developing adaptive teaching competency through coaching. *Teaching and Teacher Education, 25*, 1051–1060.

Wei, R., Darling-Hammond, L., & Adamson, F. (2010). *Professional development in the United States: Trends and challenges.* Dallas, TX: National Staff Development Council.

Weiss, I. R., Pasley, J. D., Smith, P. S., Banilower, E. R., & Heck, D. J. (2003). *A study of K–12 mathematics and science education in the United States.* Chapel Hill, NC: Horizon Research Inc.

Weitzenkamp, D. J., Howe, M. E., Steckelberg, A. L., & Radcliffe, R. (2003). The GOALS Model: Rural teacher preparation institutions meeting the ideals of a PDS through educational technology. *Contemporary Issues in Technology and Teacher Education, 2*(4). Retrieved from http://www.citejournal.org/vol2/iss4/currentpractice/article1.cfm

Williams, D. T. (2010). *The rural solution: How community schools can reinvigorate rural education.* Washington, DC: Center for American Progress.

Wilson, C., Taylor, J., Kowalski, S. M., & Carlson, J. (2010). The relative effects of equity of inquiry-based and commonplace science teaching on students' knowledge, reasoning, and argumentation. *Journal of Research in Science Teaching, 47*, 276–301. doi:10.1002/tea.20329

Accelerating the Mathematical Development of Young Navajo Children

Mark Sorensen and Derek Price

Abstract We describe a fulfilling 7-year relationship between educational practice and program evaluation at the STAR School, an Arizona public charter dedicated to providing excellent education for Navajo children in a rural, impoverished area. Previous literature had empirically identified Pre/K math and language skills as predictors of future school success. Therefore, a Montessori-based curriculum with trained teachers was implemented. It provided high quality preschool math education that was congruent with Navajo cultural values. Program evaluation and educators' insights comprised a long-term collaboration that guided annual improvement of the program. Children's data on growth in math, language, and social development are summarized for the most recent 3 years of the program, as are parental assessments of the school. Results indicate that this program has been highly successful with Pre and K students. They entered more than a year behind, on average, in math concepts and language. By the end of their Pre/K experience virtually all of the children were at or above grade level in math. We believe that our work underscores the value of creating long-term collaborative relationships between rural educators who are implementing promising educational practices and dedicated researchers who can offer beneficial empirical and theoretical perspectives.

Keywords Preschool/kindergarten · Math · Education · Rural · Montessori · Navajo culture · Bilingual · Qualitative and quantitative assessment · Sustained success

We dedicate this chapter to James Peshlakai, the Navajo educator who suggested our collaboration.

M. Sorensen (✉)
The STAR (Service to All Relations) School, 145 Leupp Road, Flagstaff,
AZ 86004, USA
e-mail: mark.sorensen@starschool.org

D. Price (✉)
Professor Emeritus, Psychology, Wheaton College, Norton, MA 02766, USA
e-mail: dprice@wheatonma.edu

© Springer International Publishing Switzerland 2017
G.C. Nugent et al. (eds.), *Rural Education Research in the United States*,
DOI 10.1007/978-3-319-42940-3_8

145

1   Introduction

Children's mathematical knowledge is important for their academic and life success. Children from disadvantaged minority backgrounds are particularly at risk for math failure. Research has shown that math skills in early elementary school strongly predict high school math abilities (Siegler et al. 2014). In addition, mathematics skills at the end of kindergarten even predict socio-economic status in mid-life (Ritchie and Bates 2013). This is equally true for girls and boys and across social classes (Duncan et al. 2007). The relationship between early and late math knowledge is roughly twice as great as between early and later reading abilities. Early success in math is critical: "Children from low-income backgrounds enter school with much less mathematical knowledge than their more affluent peers. These early deficits have long-term consequences; children who fall behind early in math generally stay behind" (Siegler 2009).

The chances of falling behind are especially great for impoverished rural children for whom isolation and cumulative risks loom large by age 3. Recent large-scale studies of representative samples of children in American rural families identify risks in multiple developmental and academic domains. The domains emerge by age 3 (Vernon-Feagans and Cox 2013) and include: executive functioning (e.g., systematic exploration), behavioral competence (e.g., resisting impulses), and language acquisition (e.g., receptive vocabulary). The profoundly rural domestic settings for Navajo children put them at risk for fewer educational materials, lower academic expectations, and lower enrollment in preschool. The rural risks are amplified by the poverty that is associated disproportionately with rural families. With respect to specific academic domains, young rural children score lower on standardized math and pre-reading measures than do suburban children (Miller and Votruba-Drzal 2013). The math score difference grows larger by eighth grade, and the math discrepancies were further amplified for rural and Native American children, especially in the western U.S. (Graham and Provost 2012).

Concerns about math education, specifically for Native American students, have been expressed for more than 30 years (Bradley 1984). Recent research by the National Assessment of Educational Progress (NAEP) indicates that while average math scores for White, Black, Hispanic and Asian students were higher in 2007 than in all previous assessments, American Indian scores had not risen (NAEP 2007). Thus, programming is needed that will support math development for Native American students. Programming within one charter school has been designed to address these concerns. The Service To All Relations (STAR) School is a public charter school located on the southwestern edge of the Navajo Nation in northern Arizona and dedicated to providing excellent education to the Native American children in the area. Ninety-nine percent of the students attending the STAR School are Native American.

The specifics of the educational and economic situation facing Native American children indicate that this is a rural population that is indeed at profound risk for school problems. Navajo Nation Census data (2000) indicated that 47 % of the

American Indian adults in the STAR School service area had never completed high school; 31 % dropped out before completing the ninth grade. U.S. Census data (U. S. Census Bureau 2000) indicated that 54.2 % of all American Indian families with children in the STAR School service area were far below the poverty level. In 2014, 80 % of students enrolled at STAR qualified for free or reduced lunch.

However, for Native American communities such as ours, the educational challenges created by high rates of poverty and low rates of successful schooling are compounded by the lack of available resources in this remote rural setting. The population density of the Navajo Nation chapters served by STAR School is six people per square mile. Navajo communities throughout the Navajo Nation, which is the largest land base of any Native American tribe (roughly equivalent to the size of the state of South Carolina), average around 1500 people and are often more than 20 miles from each other. It takes 30 min for an ambulance to reach STAR School, and much longer to reach the widely dispersed households. The nearest and largest Navajo community, from which most of the students come, has a population of 1400 and has no public library, police station, fulltime health care clinic or even a supermarket where fresh produce is available, and in the land surrounding the center of the community, nearly 30 % of homes do not have running water or electrical utilities provided (Navajo Nation Census 2000).

The students' poverty and social isolation is multifaceted and profound. For some STAR students there is no transportation beyond the school bus and no public transportation is available. Ten percent of students live with elders, some of whom speak no English. Children chop firewood and haul water. These contributing factors of high levels of poverty, remote rural conditions, and low levels of school education among their parents predict the students at STAR School to be at risk for future success in school.

In this chapter we will present emerging evidence of successful ways for meeting the educational needs for this group of students. We will provide (a) background on the foundational concepts for early math learning, (b) description of the evolution of the STAR School approach to supporting math development, and (c) qualitative and quantitative results that emerged through a collaborative partnership between empirical program evaluation and educational practice.

2 Teaching Math to Younger Children

Siegler (2009) and others have pointed out that a child's math skill upon entering school is a most powerful predictor of later reading and math success. Further, children from low-income backgrounds enter school with much less mathematical skill than children from higher income levels and these deficits are often difficult to change (Ramani and Siegler 2011), even more difficult than in other academic areas. Mathematics is a hierarchical domain; early foundational concepts are necessary for later learning.

Until recently, some early childhood education experts believed that direct instruction of math in preschool was wrong-headed, recommending instead that teachers create rich environments and take advantage of teaching opportunities as they naturally arise in play. Recent research indicates, however, that preschoolers' spontaneous interest in (and mastery of) math concepts can be nourished by teachers' initiatives, yielding richer math development across more children. The sequence of learning math concepts is remarkably regular and teachable in early childhood (Butterworth 2005; Spelke 2005). The National Association for the Education of Young Children and other national organizations now recommend organized math curricula for young children (Brenneman et al. 2011).

Children vary widely in their spontaneous focus on numbers (Hannula et al. 2005). Some children frequently notice numerical dimensions of their world while others rarely do so, and most are somewhere in between. This is true for all groups of children. To make the normative math transitions between 3 and 6 years of age, children must notice and explore the mathematical dimensions in their environments. Their exploration will lead to insights about the next level of math comprehension. Young children at first are learning math in what seem to be very small increments, but these actually are big hurdles for them. For example, moving from being a "2-knower" (who can, for example, accurately hand you two grapes when asked) to a "3-knower" to a "4-knower" are major accomplishments from about 2.5–4 years of age (Huang et al. 2010).

For all young children—but especially those with lower levels of spontaneous focus—adults' prompts to notice and discuss numbers, shape, and other math dimensions greatly enhance the children's math concepts. Children in households in which the adults are overwhelmed with the necessities of getting through the day are not as likely to get adult support in focusing on numbers or in learning the names for math concepts. This puts many poor and rural children at higher risk of falling behind. Specific intervention is needed to support skill development.

To be successful, programming must be developed in accordance with the known capacities and interests of young children. Fortunately, it is both possible and appropriate to teach math to preschool/kindergarten children (Ginsburg et al. 2008). As early as the preschool period, young children are interested and engaged in mathematical concepts. Developmentally appropriate curricula are needed to support and promote children's math knowledge.

3   STAR School

3.1   Background of STAR

STAR School was created in 2001 as a charter school designed to bridge the cultural gap in educating Navajo children (Sorensen, n.d.-a). STAR affirms and employs Navajo cultural values and practices in bicultural academic, ethical, and social practices. Navajo culture and language are still very much alive in northern Arizona, especially in the older generations. The complex interface of Navajo and European American cultures that STAR students navigate daily includes the risks of school failure, described above, but also implicitly provides rich educational opportunities. STAR School's intentionally hybrid academic culture integrates Navajo and European American practices by building upon four core values. These values are articulated as STAR's "Four R's": relationships, respect, responsibility, and reasoning which are the core values identified in traditional Navajo Peacemaking (Sorensen, n.d.-b).

These values are nominally similar across the two cultures, but deeper analysis reveals important cultural variations in the meaning of each term. For example, relationships are central in each culture but traditional Navajo relationships revolve around a complex matriarchal clan system that is hierarchical and obligatory, even across what seem to European Americans to be distant familial relationships. At STAR every child is related to many other children and often to staff members. In Navajo society respect, or acknowledging the value in another, is shown to everything in the natural world (Chisholm 1996) but especially to elders and is expressed, at times, via quiet listening, gaze aversion, and conversational reticence. Responsibility in Navajo society includes caring for clan elders, especially those who live in remote rural areas and need help with firewood and water. Reason refers in part to using observation and inference to identify problems and solve them, especially problems that trouble relatives.

These core values resonate with some of the strongest aspects of Navajo culture, particularly K'e, the concept of clanship and interrelatedness. Thus, when our school staff emphasizes these values while interacting with community members and when our students go home and practice these values, school is seen by parents and grandparents as less of a cultural intrusion and more as a way of strengthening children's cultural identities while also strengthening their education.

STAR's K-8 general approach did not, however, reliably lead to children's educational success during the first years of STAR's existence. Instead, there were problems with parental engagement and with children's socialization into school culture. Most of the children entering STAR's kindergarten or first grade already were far behind in mathematics and pre-literacy, and almost none of them spoke Navajo, the most widely spoken indigenous language in North America (McCarty 2008). Moreover, the establishment of a pervasive and effective Four R's school culture was proving difficult because there was no systematic orientation or early sustained teaching of the values and practices themselves. Five-year-old Navajo children were long since immersed in U.S. popular culture via the mass media that permeate (by satellite dish, cell phones, etc.) even remote rural Navajo households. Entering students lacked the self-regulation skills necessary in the classroom. The cultural catch-up gap for Navajo children entering the school at 5 or 6 years of age thus was proving too broad to surmount while also teaching a kindergarten curriculum. Kindergarteners themselves were not learning math or expanding their vocabularies. Therefore, in 2005 STAR leaders created a preschool program designed to address these problems.

3.2   Preschool Program Development

STAR leadership created a preschool program especially tailored to STAR's rural, Navajo population. STAR kindergartners were at high risk for immediate educational problems. Before the preschool was created, 90 % of the American Indian students entering kindergarten at STAR had no knowledge of letter names and no knowledge of print concepts. Eighty-five percent of our entering kindergarten students showed no ability to rhyme. These skills are considered to be standard readiness requirements for children entering kindergarten. Classroom testing of entering kindergarteners indicated that 85 % of the American Indian students entering kindergarten at the STAR School were At Risk (UO DIBELS 2015) for Initial Sound Fluency, with the remaining 15 % at Some Risk for Initial Sound Fluency. Testing also revealed that 85 % were also At Risk for Letter Naming Fluency. Our own recent data on the Woodcock-Johnson mathematics subscales (Woodcock et al. 2007) reveal that entering STAR preschoolers lacked rudimentary math abilities.

From its beginning the preschool program has employed Montessori pedagogy. Maria Montessori originally developed it for low SES Italian children who could benefit from an enriched environment in which to explore and discover—with guidance—the qualities and dimensions of the physical world, including mathematics (Boehnlein 1990). Montessori classrooms can facilitate the kinds of emotional support, classroom organization, and instructional interactions that are associated with successful early development (Hamre 2014). Fidelity to Montessori practices produces better outcomes in social problem solving, vocabulary, and mathematics (Lillard 2012). Ultimately, Montessori programming allowed the STAR preschool to find ways to transform the educational opportunities encountered by students through their complex interface of Navajo and European American cultures into a self-sustaining, supportive school culture whose practices enhance preschoolers' self-regulation (Raver et al. 2011; Grazzani and Ornaghi 2011) and academic learning in the key domains of mathematics (Siegler and Lortie-Forgues 2014) and pre-literacy (Bierman et al. 2014; Snow et al. 2007; Weiland and Yoshikawa 2013).

Recent reviews of the dimensions of excellent preschool math and science education (Brenneman et al. 2009) recommend approaches that closely match the STAR preschool in standards, curriculum, assessment, teacher development, and home–school connection. Stevenson-Boyd et al. (2008) developed the PRISM (Preschool Rating Instrument for Science and Mathematics) to guide preschool teachers in identifying the best materials and classroom practices for preschool children to begin to learn math and science concepts. PRISM recommendations closely match STAR's preschool Montessori materials and practices.

Virtually all of the STAR preschool students are Native American and come from a high poverty, rural area on or near the Navajo Nation. Most STAR preschool students now are involved in a fulltime, full year, 6.5 h per day, 5 days per week, 46 weeks per year, high fidelity Montessori preschool program for two consecutive years prior to their entry in kindergarten. Then they continue in the same classroom for a kindergarten year of Montessori education, but now as the "senior experts" in the eyes of the two younger preschool cohorts. Thus, a 3-year-old child may be in the STAR preschool for 2 years and then in kindergarten for yet another year in the same large classroom of approximately thirty children. The preschool and kindergarten are housed and taught together (known as *Alchini Bighan*—Navajo for "The Children's House") to foster beneficial modeling of peer relationships and skills. The preschool also features cultural adaptations that focus on inclusive, affirming relationships among staff, students and parents. For example, school rituals of belonging include a weekly gathering in which all preschool children are warmly greeted by all staff and by the rest of the students in the school.

3.3 Math Curricula at STAR Preschool

There is considerable variation in the math development of Navajo preschoolers upon STAR School entry. For example, in a recent year STAR School welcomed a typical group of 22 preschoolers who were 3 or 4 years old. That group included four children who scored at a math age-equivalent below 2 years of age, 15 who scored higher but still below their age level, and three other children entered at an age-equivalent of 5½ years of age or higher. Thus math programming is needed to address children's developmental levels. For the past 5 years the preschool has offered a Montessori program enhanced with guided focus on specific aspects of math. Specifically, the STAR preschool program enhances math development in three general ways.

The first is to create an exploratory environment that includes a wide array of objects that stimulate children's focus on specific dimensions of math and offers inviting objects to manipulate (Petersen and McNeil 2013). STAR School chose the Montessori approach because its highly structured and sequenced materials invite just such focus (Lillard 2012). Montessori pedagogy features guidance that scaffolds students' inquiry in many dimensions of math, such as geometry (Fisher et al. 2013). This can be a powerful stimulant to a growth spurt in mathematical development. For example, Siegler (2009) demonstrated that a relatively brief guided exposure to a number line dramatically improved African American preschoolers' math concepts immediately and several months later. In fact, simply playing the board game "Chutes and Ladders" stimulated measurable and lasting development of math concepts in young children. Hannula et al. (2005) found that directing Finnish children in daycare to focus on numbers of things in the environment led to both immediate improvements in their math concepts and continuous improvements months later. Well-constructed early math interventions can generate long-lasting effects.

The second mathematics enhancement is to create a rich language environment in the classroom. English language vocabulary strongly predicts school success and may contribute to math development as well (Negen and Sarnecka 2012; Zhang et al. 2014). Basic number name vocabulary affords a first step toward formal mathematical knowledge (Purpura et al. 2013). Preschool vocabulary strongly predicts grade four vocabulary and reading (Dickinson and Porche 2011). In fact, preschool may be a pivotal time for supporting language development, with effects detectable even a decade later (Bornstein et al. 2014). For our students the language environment also includes Navajo language, the most widely spoken indigenous language in North America. It also is rapidly disappearing, as evidenced in the generational changes in our students' families (Benally and Viri 2005). Math competence requires math vocabulary for numbers, shapes, and for all dimensions of the physical world.

The third way of enhancing math development among our population is to provide a school culture in which children feel supported, loved, respected, and cared for, and their parents also feel supported, respected, and effectively included in the educational process (Jones and Bouffard 2012; Kenyon and Hanson 2012). Among low SES minority students, two of the strongest predictors of resilient math outcomes in elementary school are a supportive community school model (which includes elements that actively shield children from adversity) and an early sense of competence in math (Borman and Overman 2004). The STAR preschool teachers aspire to relate to students in modes that are developmentally and pedagogically supportive (Hamre 2014). The goal of this pedagogy is an exploratory, play-based peer culture (Ramani 2012) in which even young children acquire and enforce peer social norms (Schmidt and Tomasello 2012). At STAR those norms are preschool versions of a supportive school-wide culture that can frame and direct students' development in mathematics.

4 Results from Program Evaluation

4.1 Iterative Measurement Process

STAR employs its own qualitative and quantitative data to guide its implementation and refinement of educational practices to address the three critical domains of (a) school culture, (b) English vocabulary, and (c) math. An iterative measurement process has been utilized wherein we work with Navajo staff and families to assess the subjective cultural validity (Solano-Flores and Nelson-Barber 2011) of European American quantitative, standardized instruments. A few Navajo adults were asked to examine a sampling of items from each of our assessments, identifying any that might be misunderstood for cultural or linguistic reasons. For example, on a standardized measure of English receptive language skills, the panel of Navajo employees at the school independently identified an item ("fence") that was indeed disproportionately missed by Navajo children, probably because the "correct" answer was to choose a picture of a white picket fence, something not seen in the high desert. Navajo children instead selected a picture of discarded construction material, something that adult Navajos also thought might be used for fencing. There were only four items that seemed culturally ambiguous and therefore were excluded from educational decisions regarding any one child.

Navajo staff and families also reviewed parent- and teacher-report measures. For example, our research team developed a checklist of Navajo cultural knowledge that was based on a published Navajo Nation government document (Office of Diné Culture, Language, and Community Service 2000) that identifies and specifies seven kinds of traditional cultural knowledge a young Navajo child should acquire at various ages. To recognize and honor Navajo educational values STAR created an assessment of young children's development through traditional Navajo eyes. We reorganized it into a checklist (The STAR School Inventory of Diné Culture and Language Development; Diné is what Navajos call themselves) and modified it to appropriately match cultural expectations. Navajo school employees first were asked to review the checklist for any inappropriate or incorrect items. Multiple people identified all questions regarding Navajo ceremonies and spirituality as inappropriate; consequently those were deleted, leaving a total of 53 items.

Following these review processes, we had the blessing of the Navajo staff and families to move forward with the collection and analyses of quantitative data. Fortunately, only a few items on any given assessment raised cultural questions. The Navajo families and the Navajo school employees and teachers all endorsed the use of the assessments despite such items, provided that the data were employed to assess students' progress in STAR School rather than to compare them inappropriately to other populations.

This approach to program evaluation yielded several benefits for program development. Students' parents and clan relatives were respected by the inclusion of their voices in program evaluation decisions. Trust was encouraged between families and the school. Data interpretations were culturally contextualized. Family participation in school activities of all kinds was enhanced. Furthermore, we did not require completion of evaluation measures but still enjoyed high participation rates that may be a function of our approach to measurement.

The academic intervention and the program evaluation research we have conducted annually at the STAR School have focused on low-SES, young Navajo children, specifically age 3 (preschool) to grade three. In three recent academic years (2010–2011 through 2012–2013) the preschool has generated sustained qualitative and quantitative success in each critical domain, preparing the children and families for elementary school. Sample sizes in those years were 16, 17, and 23 children, respectively. Nearly every child was included in every measure. In the following summary we include qualitative and quantitative empirical evidence for Navajo children's preschool progress in all three domains, including the social domain of supportive school culture, the related cognitive domain of language(s) development, and the focal domain of mathematics. We also provide evidence of the preschool's beneficial effects in the school, first in kindergarten and then in early elementary grades.

4.2 Supportive School Culture

Qualitative Evidence. STAR qualitatively assessed the school and classroom culture through systematic observations and interviews by a program evaluator from outside the school. His classroom and campus observations and interviews always occurred a few weeks into the school year and again a week before the end of that year. Observations and interviews were conducted from the 2006–2007 school year through 2012–2013. Occasionally additional interviews were organized around a specific topic (materials, satisfying state standards, teaching Navajo language, etc.). All were open conversations about subjects related to program development and fidelity. The teachers were enthusiastic and critical participants in all aspects of the evaluation, including setting agenda items and collecting and providing some of the program evaluation quantitative data.

The qualitative assessment process generated many important program improvements, with most initiated by teachers. They advocated the merger of preschool and kindergarten classrooms, now as one and known as Alchini Bighan The teachers continue to implement their program for a tri-lingual education, including American Sign, in Alchini Bighan. They also disseminate Montessori pedagogy at the request of collaborating STAR colleagues in the early elementary grades. In all cases, the teachers' initiatives were welcomed by administrators and seen as valuable challenges to be met through resourceful collaboration.

Montessori pedagogy proved highly flexible in accommodating a bicultural and multilingual emphasis. The STAR preschool classroom also provides objects and books drawn from Navajo culture. The Four R's values and practices were integrated into the pedagogy via frequent citations by the staff when addressing the children's social issues. The staffing always has included at least one teacher fluent in Navajo, and recently features one teacher who speaks only Navajo to the children, including during activities like counting and shape sorting. This provides the critical fluent input that can undergird language acquisition (McCabe et al. 2013). In addition, American Sign Language recently has been taught and employed to great practical effect during naptime and across physical distances, as on the playground.

Based on qualitative observations by the teachers and the program evaluator, peer transmission of school culture now occurs rapidly for preschoolers who eagerly follow the lead of experienced, confident kindergarteners. Currently, the preschool flourishes as two levels, 3- to 4-year-olds and 4- to 5-year-olds. Rich in diversity of materials and languages, the classroom is a quietly humming scene of child-initiated exploratory activity and related conversation, subtly managed by four well-trained and experienced teachers, at least one of which is Navajo at any given moment. Most kindergarteners have at least 1 year of STAR preschool experience and, by example, show the new preschoolers how to behave in the classroom. Such early peer influence is powerful and enduring (Schmidt and Tomasello 2012). Parents frequently visit and observe, following the teachers' entry and exit protocol that respects the children's classroom culture. This dynamic approximates STAR School's leaders' original vision of a pervasive school culture that is values-based, autonomous, and supportive to all.

Furthermore, the input of family and community has been instrumental. STAR has responded respectfully and programmatically to the ideas of Navajo teachers, parents, elders, and leaders, including members of STAR's Board of Directors. The education support deficits that seemed endemic to this population evolved into collaborative educational initiatives. For example, the STAR preschool at first implemented an obligatory home visit program for all families of children enrolled, as stipulated by the funding agency. Many families responded negatively to the idea that someone, also Navajo, was going to evaluate their home life and offer correctives to it. In keeping with Navajo values of maintaining harmony even in disagreements, the families' negative responses were expressed indirectly. For example, some families withdrew from the preschool program, some did not reply to scheduling requests, and some simply were not home at the appointed time. STAR therefore shifted to rallying the parents around educational school trips that required collaborative on-campus planning during the school year and the trip itself at the end of the year. This produced some beneficial effects but proved labor intensive for the teachers and only tangentially included parents in the school itself. Over three years, STAR therefore shifted to a goal of creating an on-campus culture that welcomes Navajo families to (a) meet individually with the teachers, (b) respond to a preschool newsletter, (c) attend open houses, (d) critique the preschool program, (e) visit the school on their own schedule, (f) participate in off-campus school activities, and (g) attend numerous school events that honor them. STAR systematically seeks each family's anonymous evaluation of the preschool program.

Now nearly every family interacts frequently and collaboratively with the preschool staff. The staff members report excellent working relationships with the families. The 2012–2013 school year concluded with a preschool graduation that attracted, for the first time, a standing-room-only gathering of Navajo elders, many of whom speak little English. This normally highly reserved audience loudly applauded, and some shed tears of joy when their grandchildren sang traditional songs in the Navajo language the children learned at STAR School.

Quantitative Evidence. In addition to the qualitative evidence, we quantitatively measured the strength of the preschool's supportive school culture in three ways, with all three measures collected pre- and post-program. Parents completed two paper and pencil measures at home or during a school visit. One measure of supportive school culture was parents' assessment of the child's development by Navajo cultural standards, using our checklist described above. In all, parents respond to 53 Likert-scale questions about behavioral frequencies in seven traditional Navajo domains, such as Nitsahakees, or "Thinking and Conceptualizing." One question in this domain is, for example, "Does this child use correct kinship terms?" An annual fall-to-spring increase in total reported traditional behaviors (Fig. 1) suggests that STAR may be helping students develop a traditional grounding in Navajo language and thought.

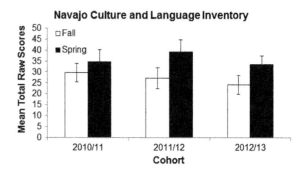

Fig. 1 Fall and spring mean raw score totals on the Navajo Culture and Language Inventory for three recent STAR preschool cohorts. *Note* Maximum possible score is 106. $N = 16, 17$, and 23 preschool children, respectively

The second quantitative assessment of Alchini Bighan's culture is a standardized evaluation of the parents' experience of the preschool program. The *Parent-Teacher Involvement Questionnaire: Parent Form* (Corrigan 2002) invites the family's responses to 26 Likert-scaled questions about four dimensions of the preschool (Table 1). The dimensions include (a) Frequency of Contact with Teacher (four items), (b) Quality of Relationship with Teacher (seven items), (c) Parent Involvement in School (11 items), and (d) Parent Endorsement of School (four items). The families' affirmation of the preschool was very high in all four dimensions for the recent 4 years. The dimension "Frequency of Contact with Teacher" illustrates a pattern that holds true for the other dimensions: Early STAR cohorts' scores were similar to those of the standardization sample but the recent four STAR cohorts scored statistically significantly higher, with ceiling effects on "Quality of Relationship with Teacher" and "Parent Endorsement of School." The recent small dips in scores for "Frequency of Contact" and "Parent Involvement"

Table 1 Parents' evaluation of STAR preschool: annual mean item scores on the Parent-Teacher Involvement Questionnaire: Parent Form

National 2002			STAR school year			
Subscale	Item mean (SD)	Previous[a]	09/10	10/11	11/12	12/13
N	387	21	10	16	19	16
Frequency of contact w/teacher	0.81 (0.62)	0.90	1.42[b]*	1.63[b]*	1.87[b]*	1.78[b]*
Quality of relationship w/teacher	3.17 (0.77)	3.28	3.60[b]*	3.62[b]*	3.65[b]*	3.67[b]*
Parent involvement in school	1.23 (0.59)	1.52	1.58	1.92[b]*	1.92[b]*	1.79[b]*
Parent endorsement of school	3.33 (0.65)	3.38	3.80[b]*	3.78[b]*	3.79[b]*	3.85[b]*

Note Maximum score = 4.00. Zero = lowest frequency rating of behavior, or lowest level of agreement with values statement
* $p < 0.05$, two-tailed
[a]Previous = scores for STAR preschool years of 06/07, 07/08, and 08/09 combined
[b]Mean is significantly greater than both the National 2002 mean and the STAR "previous" means

may reflect the increasing use of texting among STAR teachers and parents, a dimension not included in the standardized assessment. At the suggestion of the preschool lead teacher, STAR added two texting items to the end of the assessment in the final year of our data collection. We found those item averages to be the highest of all items across both "Quality of Relationship…" and "Parent Endorsement…" indicating that this instrument now has outlived its content validity. The technological revolution in interpersonal communications has measurably altered the modes of relationships between STAR and its families in this most rural of areas.

Our third quantitative measure of supportive school culture is the Social Skills Improvement System (SSIS; Gresham and Elliott 2008) a teacher-completed standardized assessment of each child's development of classroom social skills and problem behaviors. We focused on skills because those are more predictive of later school success (Claessens and Dowsett 2014). One Navajo teacher scored half the preschoolers while a European American teacher scored the other half. The teachers' average scores for students varied slightly in magnitude but were otherwise similar. Implemented in the 2011–2012 school year (replacing a parent-completed assessment), the SSIS, in contrast to other social development measures, has the virtues of being (a) completed by the teachers, (b) focused on school behavior, and (c) less correlated with measures of other domains. The SSIS also offers a diagnostic analysis that focuses on specific social skills and problem behaviors, information that may help staff members identify an individual student's needs in school adjustment.

The preschoolers' SSIS fall and spring social skills results for the recent 2 years provide an encouraging picture of classroom social development (Fig. 2). At the beginning of each year STAR preschoolers' average scores were at approximately the 30th percentile, well below the middle for their national age peers. These scores appear discouraging but must be carefully interpreted, given the rural and cultural differences between STAR preschoolers and the standardization sample. Indeed, by the end of the school year the average SSIS score for STAR preschoolers was approximately the 60th percentile. Nearly every student's score improved markedly, and 75 % of students in both cohorts passed the U.S. government's GPRA

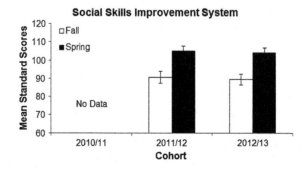

Fig. 2 Social Skills Improvement System mean fall and spring standard scores for two STAR preschool cohorts. *Note* Normative score = 100. Earlier cohorts were assessed on a different social development measure. *N* = 17 and 23 preschool children, respectively

(Government Progress Reporting Act) standards (Heinemeier and Troppe 2010). Successive cohorts of STAR preschoolers have significantly improved their social skills in the school setting.

On the basis of the convergence of qualitative observations and quantitative assessments of families' and children's relationships to school and to peers in school, STAR School is providing a supportive school culture in which the children also should be improving on assessments of their nascent language and mathematical skills.

4.3 Gains in English Language

Qualitative Evidence. The observations revealed that STAR teachers implemented multiple evidence-based changes in language pedagogy over 5 years, steadily encouraging each preschool cohort to extend their linguistic communications. These changes in pedagogy included (a) speaking to students using adult vocabulary, (b) leading analytic talk about books (Dickinson and Porche 2011), and (c) communicating in more than one language (Hirata-Edds 2011).

Furthermore, qualitative observations revealed that the multilingual classroom sometimes led to helpful language and math insights. For example, Navajo students realized that English is irregular in its counting sequence of "...10, 11, 12, 13...", which oddly offers "eleven, twelve" instead of "oneteen, twoteen." In contrast, Navajo systematically adds a new standard syllable for numbers 10 through 19. With respect to a different math domain, a Hopi teacher in a higher grade realized that Hopi identifies geometric shapes by the number of pointed junctions instead of sides.

Quantitative Evidence. We directly assessed the receptive language development of children by employing the Peabody Picture Vocabulary Test, 4th Edition (PPVT4; Dunn and Dunn 2007). The PPVT4 assesses English language development by measuring a child's receptive vocabulary, proven to be a strong indicator of current and future language development. In this assessment the child simply looks at sets of four pictures and selects the one that illustrates a word spoken by the adult conducting the test. The child need not speak.

For 5 years STAR preschoolers' average PPVT4 scores lingered below the age norm (Fig. 3, for the recent 3 years). Successive preschool cohorts began the school year with mean standard scores between 93 and 96 but hardly changed by the end of the year, never reaching the standardization mean of 100 and seeming to verify the adage about falling behind. In the final year, however, the students' average standard score in the spring was 103, a significant increase.

This accomplishment is more incremental if considered by GPRA standards in the most recent 4 years of data. Then the proportion of students passing PPVT4 GPRA standards moves from roughly one in three in 2009–2010 to about half for the next 2 years. In the fourth year (2012–2013) the proportion rises to about 8 of 10, concluding a remarkable improvement.

Fig. 3 Mean fall and spring standard scores on the Peabody Picture Vocabulary Test 4th Ed. for three recent STAR preschool cohorts. *Note* Normative score = 100. N = 16, 17, and 23 preschool children, respectively

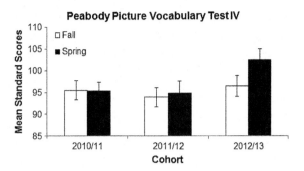

In summary, we found that our enrichment of spoken English, principled commitment to offering Navajo language, and our practical employment of American Sign Language contributed to a hard-won gain in English language skills for our students. The STAR preschool seems to demonstrate that a multilingual language-rich environment can support significant improvement in English language development.

4.4 Gains in Preschool Math

4.4.1 Qualitative Evidence

In the first years of the preschool program we were concerned with the issue of students' spontaneous focus on Montessori mathematics activities. Given free choice, some children opted out even when encouraged by a teacher. Therefore, we implemented weekly activity cards for each child. The card featured pictures of activities that must be completed by that child that week. This strategy worked only to a degree but it gave us anecdotal insight into a better strategy. For example, the kindergarten buddies of a preschool boy were eager to go outside and became impatient with his progress on a neglected math activity. They therefore demonstrated it for him and talked him through it, yielding his quick understanding and success. On the basis of repeated observations of spontaneous, successful peer tutoring, and on Montessori principles of age-integrated classrooms, the teachers successfully lobbied for the integration of preschool and kindergarten into a single room (The Children's House).

4.4.2 Quantitative Evidence

Our new preschoolers have begun each year with math assessment scores that average well below the national mean on the standardized Woodcock-Johnson III Math Subscales of Concepts (18a) and Sequences (18b) (Woodcock et al. 2007). By the end of the first year, these students have improved in math much faster than the normative rate with their year-end averages equal to or above the national standard. Kindergarteners improve similarly even when they already gained significantly in their preschool years. Each of the recent three preschool cohorts began the year behind the age norms for the Woodcock-Johnson math scales (Fig. 4). By the end of the year the children in these cohorts typically gained 17 months on their average "test age equivalence" scores in just 10 months of school (the Woodcock-Johnson does not provide standard scores for these subscales). The most recent cohort ended the year with an average test-age score 6 months ahead of their average chronological age. All but one of those children scored at the entry level for kindergarten or higher. It is noteworthy that, although last year's cohort was the first to enter the STAR preschool with an average test age close to their chronological age, the magnitude of their gains over the year nevertheless matched those of previous cohorts. (There are no GPRA standards for these math subscales.)

STAR's math intervention now meets its goals at the preschool level but is it also related to successful math learning in subsequent grades? Trends in Woodcock-Johnson scores for children in preschool through third grade suggest that the math intervention effects are positively related to math success in grades after preschool (Table 2). Note that in Table 2, preschool now is broken into two cohorts: (a) 3-year-olds who just entered the program and will stay for 2 years, and (b) 4-year-olds who either newly entered the program or who returned after completing a first year of STAR Preschool. Both preschool-age cohorts gained substantially in math, achieving average scores that match or exceed the entry score for kindergarten. Gains were similar in magnitude across the two preschool cohorts, though students started with fewer skills at age three than at age four. Looking beyond preschool, the average spring Woodcock-Johnson scores for the 14 kindergarten students in 2012–2013 also far exceed the standardized norms for

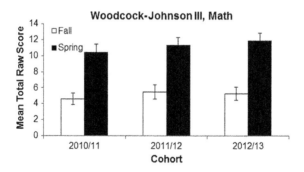

Fig. 4 Mean total items correct on the Woodcock-Johnson III Mathematics Subscales 18a (Math Concepts) and 18b (Math Sequences) for three recent STAR preschool cohorts. *Note* Total items = 57. Normative total raw score for children entering kindergarten is nine correct items. N = 16, 17 and 23 preschool children, respectively

Table 2 Woodcock-Johnson III Mathematics (18a and 18b) item scores for the six recent STAR preschool cohorts

Grade enrolled in 2012/2013	N	Mean items correct		Woodcock-Johnson III	Percentage achieving (%)
		Fall	Spring	Entry norm for	Entry norm
Preschool I[a] (3-year-olds)	6	3.17	9.17	K = 9 correct	83
Preschool II[a] (4-year-olds)	10	6.50	13.50	K = 9 correct	100
Kindergarten[a]	14	13.29	17.71	1st = 16 correct	93
First grade[a]	15	19.40	23.73	2nd = 23 correct	67
Second grade[a]	8	23.88	27.50	3rd = 28 correct	63
Third grade[b]	7	24.14	27.43	4th = 31 correct	29

Note Table includes only students for whom complete data are available
[a]Experienced fully developed STAR preschool math program
[b]Did not experience fully developed STAR preschool math program

children entering first grade. Taken together, of the 30 children in preschool and kindergarten cohorts in the spring of 2013, 28 scored at or above the entry norm for their next year of school. Beneficial preschool program effects may also be inferred from the Woodcock-Johnson scores of the 30 students in First, Second, and Third Grades. Seventeen of these students met or exceeded the entry score for his or her grade. The Third Grade comprises students who did not experience the fully developed STAR preschool math program of the last 3 years. Their weaker Woodcock-Johnson performance may reflect that gap. Data in the coming years will clarify the relationship between the preschool program and later math performance.

To summarize the evidence regarding preschool math development, our goals were fully realized. Qualitatively, the children and their families are fully engaged in the students' discovery and exploration of the mathematical dimensions of their surroundings. Quantitatively, during both years of preschool nearly every student is eagerly mastering normative math concepts and by the end of kindergarten the students are already mastering math concepts associated with First Grade. Two thirds of current First and Second Graders score at or above the normative math score.

5 Conclusions/Discussion

The STAR School's Montessori-based math instruction at the preschool level has produced consistent and significant gains in students' math abilities for a very rural, high poverty population of Navajo children. These children began preschool with poor math scores, but over the course of 1 year caught up to or surpassed national age norms. This was achieved within a matrix of evidence-based sociocultural and linguistic enrichment that was guided by skilled and dedicated teachers in the classroom. The children's significant gains in language development and social development were welcome byproducts of a multidimensional math program that was fully embraced by the children's families. Our work contributes to the growing body of knowledge regarding positive development for minority children (Cabrera 2013).

The small size of our program is both a virtue and a liability. One virtue is our ability to adapt quickly on many levels. For example, over 6 years the preschool program was delivered in three different classrooms. Each structural change was strongly recommended by the teachers and then funded by grants awarded to the school. This process ultimately aggregated the preschoolers and kindergarteners in one open classroom, a key element, in our estimation, in the preschoolers' math, social, and language gains. Our size is a liability, however, in convincing other professionals of the broader significance of our work. Despite our significant empirical results, the fight to achieve funding for those classrooms was difficult.

It is our belief that even though our sample sizes are indeed very small the robustness of the results indicates not only the need for other remote rural schools to consider such a high quality preschool program in their own communities but also the need for more collaborative research between individual researchers and school faculty, to be conducted at small rural schools wishing to implement promising practices. The collaborative, multi-year relationships among the program evaluator, the school administration, and the faculty, as demonstrated in this chapter, allowed the STAR program to improve steadily in response to qualitative and quantitative research results. As we adjusted to strengthen the program, we saw the breadth and magnitude of the gains become even greater. Our work underscores the value of creating long-term collaborative relationships between small rural schools that are implementing promising educational practices and dedicated researchers who can offer beneficial empirical and critical perspectives.

Our examples demonstrate how program adjustments are often made in response to community feedback as well as to quantitative and qualitative research results. Rural schools and rural communities are often isolated and distant from one another; therefore it is incumbent upon us to find ways to coalesce the unique strengths of our very rural schools. Promising practices can be documented effectively, publicized, and improved over time. Effective education dealing with a particular challenge can be replicated and perhaps made ready to be shared and implemented at other rural schools. If rural education in America is to progress, we would argue, we need approaches to educational research that allow us to include multi-year small research projects on promising programs in small rural schools.

References

Benally, A. C., & Viri, D. (2005). Diné bizaad (Navajo language) at a crossroads: Extinction or renewal? *Bilingual Research Journal, 29,* 85–108.

Bierman, K. L., Nix, R. L., Heinrichs, B. S., Dimitrovich, C. E., Gest, S. D., Welsh, J. A., et al. (2014). Effects of Head Start REDI on children's outcomes 1 year later in different kindergarten contexts. *Child Development, 85*(1), 140–159.

Boehnlein, M. M. (1990). Research and evaluation summary of Montessori programs. In D. Kahn (Ed.), *Implementing Montessori education in the public sector* (pp. 476–483). Cleveland, OH: North American Montessori Teachers' Association.

Borman, G. D., & Overman, L. T. (2004). Academic resilience in mathematics among poor and minority students. *Elementary School Journal, 104,* 177–195. doi:10.1086/499748

Bornstein, M. H., Hahn, C., Putnick, D. L., & Suwalsky, J. T. D. (2014). Stability of core language skill from early childhood to adolescence: A latent variable approach. *Child Development, 85,* 1346–1356.

Bradley, C. (1984). Issues in mathematics education for Native Americans and directions for research. *Journal for Research in Mathematics Education, 15,* 96–106.

Brenneman, K., Stevenson-Boyd, J., & Frede, E. C. (2009). *Math and science in preschool: Policies and practice* (Policy brief). Retrieved from www.nieer.org/resources/policybriefs/20.pdf

Brenneman, K., Stevenson-Garcia, J., Jung, K., & Frede, E. (2011). *The Preschool Rating Instrument for Science and Mathematics (PRISM)* (ERIC Report No. ED528753). Retrieved from eric.ed.gov/?id=ED528753.

Butterworth, B. (2005). The development of arithmetical abilities. *Journal of Child Psychology and Psychiatry, 46,* 3–18.

Cabrera, N. J. (2013). Positive development of minority children. *Society for Research in Child Development Social Policy Report, 27,* 1–22.

Chisholm, J. S. (1996). Learning respect for everything. In C. P. Hwang, M. E. Lamb, & I. E. Sigel (Eds.), *Images of childhood* (pp. 167–183). Mahwah, NJ: Lawrence Erlbaum.

Claessens, A., & Dowsett, C. (2014). Growth and change in attention problems, disruptive behavior, and achievement from kindergarten to fifth grade. *Psychological Science, 25,* 2241–2251. doi:10.1177/0956797614554265

Corrigan, A. (2002). *Parent–Teacher Involvement Questionnaire: Parent version.* Retrieved from http://www.fasttrackproject.org/techrept/p/ptp/ptp1tech.pdf

UO DIBELS data system. (2015). Eugene, OR: University of Oregon Center on Teaching and Learning. Retrieved from https://dibels.uoregon.edu

Dickinson, D. K., & Porche, M. V. (2011). Relation between language experiences in preschool classrooms and children's kindergarten and fourth-grade language and reading abilities. *Child Development, 82,* 870–886.

Duncan, G. J., Dowsett, C. J., Claessens, A., Magnuson, K., Huston, A. C., Klebanov, P., ... Duckworth, K. (2007). School readiness and later achievement. *Developmental Psychology, 43,* 1428–1446.

Dunn, L. M., & Dunn, D. M. (2007). *The Peabody Picture Vocabulary Test, Fourth Edition (PPVT™-4).* Bloomington, MN: Pearson.

Fisher, K. R., Hirsch-Pasek, K., Golinkoff, R. M., & Newcombe, N. (2013). Taking shape: Supporting preschoolers' acquisition of geometric knowledge through guided play. *Child Development, 84,* 1872–1878.

Ginsburg, H. P., Lee, J. S., & Boyd, J. S. (2008). Mathematics education for young children: What it is and how to promote it. *Social Policy Report, 22*(1), 3–12.

Graham, S., & Provost, L. (2012). *Mathematics achievement gaps between suburban students and their rural and urban peers increase over time* (Issue Brief No. 52). Durham, NH: Carsey Institute, University of New Hampshire.

Grazzani, I., & Ornaghi, V. (2011). Emotional state talk and emotion understanding: A training study with preschool children. *Journal of Child Language, 38,* 1124–1139.

Gresham, F., & Elliott, S. N. (2008). *Social skills improvement system (SSIS) rating scales manual.* Bloomington, MN: Pearson.

Hamre, B. K. (2014). Teachers' daily interactions with children: An essential ingredient in effective early childhood programs. *Child Development Perspectives, 8,* 223–230. doi:10.1111/cdep.12090

Hannula, M. M., Mattinen, A., & Lehtinen, E. (2005). Does social interaction influence 3-year-old children's tendency to focus on numerosity? A quasi-experimental study in day-care. In L. Verschaffel, E. de Corte, G. Kanselaar, & M. Valcke (Eds.), *Powerful learning environments for promoting deep conceptual and strategic learning* (pp. 63–80). Leuven, Belgium: Leuven Press.

Heinemeier, S., & Troppe, P. (2010). *Guidance to Indian education demonstration grants program grantees on Government Performance Results Act (GPRA) data collection and reporting.* Washington, DC: U.S. Department of Education, Office of Indian Education.

Hirata-Edds, T. (2011). Influence of second language Cherokee immersion on children's development of past tense in their first language, English. *Language Learning, 61,* 700–733. doi:1111/j.1467-9922.2011.00655.x

Huang, Y., Spelke, E., & Snedeker, J. (2010). When is four far more than three? Children's generalization of newly acquired number words. *Psychological Science, 21,* 600–606. doi:10.1177/0956797610363552

Jones, S. M., & Bouffard, S. M. (2012). Social and emotional learning in schools from programs to strategies. *Social Policy Report, 26*(4), 1–22.

Kenyon, D. B., & Hanson, J. D. (2012). Incorporating culture into positive youth development programs with American Indian/Alaska Native youth. *Child Development Perspectives, 6,* 272–279.

Lillard, A. S. (2012). Preschool children's development in classic Montessori, supplemented Montessori, and conventional programs. *Journal of School Psychology, 50,* 379–401.

McCabe, A., Tamis-LeMonda, C. S., Bornstein, M. H., Cates, C. B., Golinkoff, R., Guerra, A. W., et al. (2013). Multilingual children: Beyond myths and towards best practices. *Social Policy Report, 27*(4), 3–9.

McCarty, T. (2008). Native American languages as heritage mother tongues. *Language, Culture, and Curriculum, 21,* 201–225.

Miller, P., & Votruba-Drzal, E. (2013). Early academic skills and childhood experiences across urban and rural schools. *Early Childhood Research Quarterly, 28,* 234–248.

Navajo Nation Census. (2000). Window Rock, AZ: Navajo Nation Vital Records, Census Office. Retrieved from http://www.navajonationcensus.com

National Assessment of Educational Progress. (2007). National Center for Education Statistics. Retrieved from http://www.nces.ed.gov/nationsreportcard/

Negen, J., & Sarnecka, B. (2012). Number-concept acquisition and general vocabulary development. *Child Development, 83,* 2019–2027.

Office of Diné Culture, Language, & Community Service. (2000). *Diné cultural content standards for students. READINESS: Pre-school through 4th grade,* R1-R10. Retrieved from http://www.odclc.navajo-nsn.gov/books

Petersen, L. A., & McNeil, N. M. (2013). Effects of perceptually rich manipulatives on preschoolers' counting performance: Established knowledge counts. *Child Development, 84,* 1020–1033.

Purpura, D. J., Baroody, A. J., & Lonigan, C. J. (2013). The transition from informal to formal mathematical knowledge: Mediation by numeral knowledge. *Journal of Educational Psychology, 105,* 453–464. doi:10.1037/a0031753

Ramani, G. B. (2012). Influence of a playful, child-directed context of preschool children's peer cooperation. *Merrill-Palmer Quarterly, 58,* 159–190. doi:10.1353/mpq.2012.0011

Ramani, G. B., & Siegler, R. S. (2011). Reducing the gap in numerical knowledge between low-and middle-income preschoolers. *Journal of Applied Developmental Psychology, 32,* 145–159. doi:10.1016/j.jappdev.2011.02.005

Raver, C. C., Jones, S. M., Li-Grining, C., Zhai, F., Bub, K., & Pressler, E. (2011). CSRP's impact on low-income preschoolers' pre-academic skills: Self-regulation as a mediating mechanism. *Child Development, 82*, 362–378.

Ritchie, S. J., & Bates, T. C. (2013). Enduring links from childhood mathematics and reading achievement to adult socioeconomic status. *Psychological Science, 25*, 1–8. doi:10.1177/0956797612466268

Schmidt, M. F. H., & Tomasello, M. (2012). Young children enforce social norms. *Current Directions in Psychological Science, 21*, 232–236. doi:10.1177/096372144865

Siegler, R. S. (2009). Improving the numerical understanding of children from low-income families. *Child Development Perspectives, 3*(2), 118–124.

Siegler, R. S., Duncan, G. J., Davis-Kean, P. E., Duckworth, K., Claessens, A., Engel, M., et al. (2014). Early predictors of high school mathematics achievement. *Psychological Science.* doi:10.1177/0956797612440101

Siegler, R. S., & Lortie-Forgues, H. (2014). An integrative theory of numerical development. *Child Development Perspectives, 8*, 144–150.

Snow, C. E., Porche, M. V., Tabors, P. O., & Harris, S. R. (2007). *Is literacy enough?*. Baltimore, MD: Brookes Publishing.

Solano-Flores, G., & Nelson-Barber, S. (2011). On the cultural validity of science assessments. *Journal of Research in Science Teaching, 38*, 553–573.

Sorensen, M. (n.d.-a). *Welcome to the Navajo Peacemaking Project website.* Retrieved May 6, 2015, from http://www.navajopeacemaking.org

Sorensen, M. (n.d.-b). *Welcome to the STAR School's website.* Retrieved May 6, 2015, from http://www.starschool.org

Spelke, E. (2005). Sex differences in intrinsic aptitude for mathematics and science? *American Psychologist, 60*, 950–958.

Stevenson-Boyd, J., Brenneman, K., Frede, E., & Weber, M. (2008). *Preschool Rating Instrument for Science and Math.* New Brunswick, NJ: National Institute for Early Education Research.

U.S. Census Bureau. (2000). *United States Census 2000: American Indian and Alaska Native areas.* Retrieved from https://www.census.gov/census2000/states/us.html

Vernon-Feagans, L., & Cox, M. (2013). The Family Life Project: An epidemiological and developmental study of young children living in poor rural communities. *Monographs of the Society for Research in Child Development, 78*(5), 1–150. doi:10.1111/MONO.12046

Weiland, C., & Yoshikawa, H. (2013). Impacts of a prekindergarten program on children's mathematics, language, literacy, executive function, and emotional skills. *Child Development, 84*, 2112–2130.

Woodcock, R., McGrew, K., & Mather, N. (2007). *Woodcock-Johnson III.* Rolling Meadows, IL: Riverside Publishing.

Zhang, X., Koponen, T., Rasanen, P., Aunola, K., Lerkkanen, M., & Nurmi, J. (2014). Linguistic and spatial skills predict early arithmetic development via counting sequence knowledge. *Child Development, 85*, 1091–1107. doi:10.1111/cdev.12173

Investigating Teacher Professional Development with Distance Coaching to Promote Students' Response to Reading Interventions in Rural Schools

Todd A. Glover

Abstract This chapter examines emerging research on professional development with coaching for rural teachers to promote students' response to early reading instruction (early reading RTI). The purpose of this chapter is to (a) provide a brief discussion of the importance of research on teacher professional development to promote early reading RTI; (b) present a rationale for conducting rigorous investigations that take into account contexts of rural schools and study teacher professional development considerations within a well-defined theory of change; (c) provide examples of key studies on teacher professional development designed for rural schools to promote students' response to early reading instruction; (d) present a research example illustrating the investigation of potential mediating variables within a proposed theory of change; and (e) propose several next steps for advancing practically-relevant research on professional development for rural school teachers.

Keywords Instructional coaching · Response to intervention · Distance coaching · Intervention · Prevention · Professional development

A growing body of research on rural education has focused on unique attributes of rural schools and instructional practices (e.g., Schafft and Jackson 2010), as well as the efficacy of approaches designed to advance student achievement and support individual learning needs (e.g., Glover et al. 2015; Vernon-Feagans et al. 2013). With increased attention over the past decade to early prevention and intervention as a means of advancing students' acquisition of foundational skills, recent studies in rural schools have begun to focus on instructional practices and/or behavioral support systems that optimize student learning in early elementary grades (e.g., Glover et al. 2015; Kratochwill et al. 2007). Given the importance of reading as a prerequisite for all school learning, emerging research has focused on efforts to improve reading skills instruction in schools that is responsive to individual school

T.A. Glover (✉)
Rutgers University, 41 Gordon Rd., Suite C, Piscataway, NJ 08854, USA
e-mail: todd.glover@rutgers.edu

© Springer International Publishing Switzerland 2017
G.C. Nugent et al. (eds.), *Rural Education Research in the United States*,
DOI 10.1007/978-3-319-42940-3_9

and student needs (e.g., Glover and Vaughn 2010; Wanzek and Vaughn 2010). The purpose of this chapter is to (a) provide a brief discussion of the importance of research on teacher professional development designed to promote students' response to early reading instruction; (b) present a rationale for conducting rigorous investigations that takes into account contexts of rural schools and investigates teacher professional development considerations within a well-defined theory of change; (c) provide examples of key studies on teacher professional development designed for rural schools to promote students' response to early reading instruction; (d) present a research example illustrating the investigation of potential mediating variables within a proposed theory of change; and (e) propose several next steps for advancing practically-relevant research on professional development for rural school teachers.

1 Professional Development to Promote Rural Students' Response to Early Reading Intervention

In response to increased attention to school accountability, educators have advocated for the use of data to formatively guide instructional decisions and interventions to support *all* students. Federal efforts to advance early literacy instruction and the consideration of students' response to scientifically-based instruction and interventions have also prompted schools to seek out professional development to train teachers in new practices (e.g., Elementary and Secondary Education Act 2002; Individuals with Disabilities Education Improvement Act 2004). Although access to such professional development has increased for rural schools, the quality and sustainability of training has varied widely. (e.g., American Institutes of Research 2004; Deussen et al. 2007; Marsh et al. 2008; Neufeld and Roper 2003).

Ongoing professional development with opportunities for modeling, practice, and feedback in the context of the classroom is required for rural teachers to adequately promote students' response to early reading instruction. Although many rural teachers are knowledgeable about core literacy curricula and instructional approaches, they are typically less familiar with the application of skill-specific interventions and the use of assessments for identifying and monitoring students' instructional needs. To sufficiently meet learning objectives, teachers often need assistance with identifying specific skills where students' require additional support, providing appropriately matched interventions, monitoring students' progress in response to intervention, and making instructional changes when necessary to reach desired goals (Glover et al. 2015; Glover and Vaughn 2010).

Although findings from existing studies suggest that teachers can be trained to implement early reading interventions to meet students' needs (e.g., Fletcher and Vaughn 2009; Wanzek and Vaughn 2010), it is also important to explore approaches for sustaining teachers' application of a student assessment and intervention process over time within an authentic classroom environment. This work has started to emerge via investigations of teacher professional development with coaching. However, ongoing research is needed to best understand optimal practices and conditions for supporting teachers within a rural context (e.g., Glover et al. 2015; Vernon-Feagans et al. 2013).

2 Considerations for Conducting Rigorous Rural Professional Development Research

In investigating rural teacher professional development in practices that promote students' response to early reading instruction, it is important to take into account the unique rural context while also considering training and instructional processes and outcomes within a testable theory of change. For example, it may be useful to consider rural school personnel resources and prerequisite teacher knowledge and skills pertaining to early reading and/or data-based decision making, as well as leadership structures that can advance professional development activities. Many rural schools do not have personnel specifically assigned to the provision of student reading intervention or regular monitoring or analysis of student reading performance data. Further, opportunities for ongoing, in-classroom support may be limited and extensive travel may be required to access high quality professional development in practices for promoting students' response to early reading instruction. Innovative leadership may be required to integrate effective training opportunities into school activities.

Further, to adequately investigate rural teachers' professional development, research must not only evaluate the impact on teacher and student outcomes via rigorous experimental methods, but also take into account mediating and moderating influences within rural contexts via a well-defined theory of change. As Mercer et al. (2014) note, incorporating mediating variables into a testable theory of change is useful for examining mechanisms responsible for the relationship between a provided intervention (e.g., professional development) and teacher or student outcomes. For example, mediating influences such as increases in teacher knowledge, perceptions, or practices may be responsible for observed relationships between teacher professional development and student achievement. Mercher and colleagues add that examinations of moderating variables can also be useful for exploring contextual influences on observed effects (Mercer et al. 2014). Contextual variables (i.e., moderators) such as teachers' prerequisite knowledge and/or perceptions about reading instruction or unique staffing or classroom configurations may have a mediating influence.

Although not within the context of experimental efficacy studies, there is a precedent for studying mediating and moderating influences in rural contexts. For example, Howley and Howley (2004), exploring the influence of socioeconomic status (SES) in mediating the relationship between school size and academic achievement (an important consideration in evaluating achievement in small rural schools), found that appropriate class size varied based on SES (with greater benefits found for those from a lower SES). Likewise, another class size study by the Texas Education Agency (1999) found that the lower the grade level, the better the benefits for students. While there is a promising trend of attending to mediating and moderating influences in rural education research, this is primarily limited to correlational studies (e.g., Arnold et al. 2005). In addressing questions about the impact of professional development practices in rural schools (examinations of efficacy), mediation and moderation analyses can have an added benefit in unpacking the context of observed findings.

Consideration of specific attributes of rural schools and their unique contributions on student learning is, by itself, insufficient for advancing practice. By developing and empirically-testing theories of change that incorporate professional development interventions, factors presumed to influence the learning process for teachers and students, and desired outcomes, researchers can address specific questions about which professional development approaches are effective in which context and why. Emerging research in the area of teacher professional development to support students' response to early reading intervention has begun this approach.

3 Key Studies on Rural Teacher Professional Development to Promote Students' Response to Early Reading Instruction

Although there is an emerging database of studies investigating professional development for teachers in the use of practices to promote students' response to early reading instruction (e.g., Fletcher and Vaughn 2009; Wanzek and Vaughn 2010), very few studies have explored teacher support within a rural context. Further, most studies fail to take into account unique attributes of rural schools in designing and evaluating specific professional development approaches.

Two studies that do consider unique aspects of rural context include (a) an evaluation of the Targeted Reading Intervention, a program designed to support kindergarten and first-grade teachers in assisting struggling readers by facilitating re-reading for fluency, word work, and guided oral reading (Vernon-Feagans et al. 2013); and (b) an investigation of the impact of K-3 teacher and school-based interventionist support for data-based decision making and the implementation of early interventions targeting the "Big Five" in reading (phonemic awareness, phonics, fluency, vocabulary, and comprehension; National Institute of Child Health and Human Development 2000; Glover et al. 2015). Both studies consider personnel constraints and travel distances for training in rural communities in their investigations of approaches that utilize technology-mediated distance coaching. Further, the flexible formats of the professional development approaches under investigation accommodate variations in scheduling and instructional programming. In this chapter, two studies are presented as examples of research that is responsive to the rural context, and recommendations are provided for further extending this work.

Vernon-Feagans et al. (2013). Vernon-Feagans and colleagues evaluated the impact of the Targeted Reading Intervention, a web-based teacher coaching program, on students' early reading performance. They randomly assigned 15 rural schools to an experimental coaching condition or control group. Five students with reading difficulties and 5 students without reading difficulties were randomly selected from each kindergarten and first-grade classroom to participate in the study. Teachers in the experimental condition attended a 3-day summer training institute. In addition, they participated in biweekly one-on-one, webcam-facilitated coaching sessions along with each of the students who had reading difficulties, working individually with each student until he or she made reading progress. These teachers received real-time input from their coach in the form of modeling and feedback during the delivery of reading interventions designed to promote re-reading for fluency, word work, and guided oral reading with each student. Results indicated that the students with reading difficulties who were in classrooms where their teacher received coaching outperformed their control counterparts in the areas of word attack, letter word identification, passage comprehension, and spelling of sounds. Although students with reading difficulties improved their performance at the same rate as those without reading difficulties, they did not reach the same level of performance.

The professional development approach utilized by Vernon-Feagans and colleagues was responsive to the rural context. In the rural schools, teachers providing reading instruction had varying levels of expertise in individualizing interventions based on specific student needs. Further, the resources to train and support these teachers would not have been available onsite, and would have required extensive travel to receive professional development support. By individualizing the professional development experience for each teacher and by offering coaching from a highly-trained coach from a distance, this approach helped to accommodate unique resource needs for rural teachers (Vernon-Feagans et al. 2013).

Glover et al. (2015). Glover and Ihlo and their colleagues evaluated the impact of professional development with distance, webcam-facilitated coaching designed to promote students' response to early reading interventions. They randomly assigned 61 schools to one of two conditions for teacher support—*business as usual* or *professional development with coaching*. Within each school assigned to professional development with coaching, 1–4 kindergarten through third-grade home-room teachers and 1–4 reading interventionists (i.e., school-based personnel who could provide reading intervention outside of regular classroom instruction) attended summer institute training (5 days for home-room teachers and 4 days for school-based interventionists) and received regular support from a highly-trained instructional coach throughout the school year. Coaching support for homeroom teachers took place via videoconferencing at a time outside of instruction. It focused on a process of data-based decision making, whereby all students were screened for early reading skill difficulties, students with like skill needs were placed into intervention groups, and regular data collection took place to monitor students' response to intervention and to adjust intervention planning. Coaching support for school-based interventionists focused on the provision of individualized reading instruction via a toolkit of published, research-based interventions collectively targeting phonemic awareness, phonics, fluency, vocabulary, and comprehension. It took place via a webcam during intervention implementation with small-groups of students. This allowed for immediate opportunities for modeling, feedback, and teacher practice during instructional delivery. A strict protocol was followed during coaching sessions to promote teachers' understanding and application of data-based decision making and reading intervention practices.

Results from an efficacy investigation (Glover et al. 2015) indicated that, relative to their control counterparts, teachers and interventionists assigned to professional development with coaching exhibited greater increases in knowledge, perceptions about self-efficacy, and practices in data-based decision making (teachers) or intervention delivery (interventionists). Further, students in coached teachers' classrooms exhibited greater benefits than control students on measures of kindergarten and first-grade alphabetic principal and phonics, and second- and third-grade oral reading fluency, as assessed by the Dynamic Indictors of Early Literacy Skills—Next assessment (Good et al. 2011). In addition, these students exhibited higher end-of-year performance on letter/word identification and word attack, as measured by the Woodcock Johnson Tests of Achievement—III (Woodcock et al. 2004). All of these results were statistically significant.

As with Vernon-Feagans et al. (2013), the professional development approach utilized by Glover et al. (2015) was responsive to the rural context. Outside of the study, the rural teachers providing reading instruction had very little access to professional development in data-based decision making for their students. Given personnel constraints common in rural schools (e.g., limitations with the availability of instructional specialists and intervention teachers; Johnson et al. 2014), additional support was needed to train teachers in the use of specific reading interventions to meet students' needs. As with the teachers participating in the Vernon-Feagans and colleagues study, the training and support resources would not have been available onsite, and would have required extensive travel or cost-prohibitive regular in-classroom visits from an external consultant to receive professional development support. By providing systematic professional development responsive to the needs of each teacher and interventionist and by offering coaching from a highly-trained coach from a distance, this approach helped to accommodate unique resource needs in rural schools.

Although Glover et al. (2015) provide an important contribution in advancing research on coaching and identifying the efficacy of a sustainable form of professional development for promoting students' response to early reading intervention, this initial contribution did not explore the mechanisms responsible for the observed impact of coaching on students' performance. Importantly, Glover, Ihlo, and their colleagues followed up their initial efficacy investigation with a study of potential mediators contributing to the observed effects (Glover et al., in preparation). Specifically, they examined the mediating influences of teachers' (a) knowledge of data-based decision making (e.g., interpreting early reading data and selecting interventions based on the data) and reading instructional practices (i.e., instruction pertaining to phonemic awareness, phonics, fluency, vocabulary, and comprehension); (b) perceived utility of specific data-based decision making and instructional practices; (c) self-efficacy pertaining to the implementation of data-based decision making practices and reading instruction; and (d) practices pertaining to the use of data (e.g., screening, using data to inform skill-based interventions, progress monitoring) and interventional delivery (e.g., providing opportunities to respond, academic feedback, positive praise, etc.). Their hypothesized theory of change is shown in Fig. 1.

Based on existing research exploring relationships between teacher support (e.g., professional development with coaching) and teachers' knowledge, perceptions, and practices (e.g., Gamse et al. 2008; Garet et al. 2001; Glover et al. 2016; Matsumura et al. 2013; Rim-Kauffman and Sawyer 2004), they hypothesized that teachers' knowledge, perceived utility of classroom practices, and self-efficacy would partially mediate the relationship between the condition for professional development (*professional development with coaching* or *business as usual*) and teachers' practice, which would then influence student early reading skill performance. Although investigations of the mediating influence of teacher and instructional variables are rare within experimental education research, especially in the areas of coaching for early reading RTI, Glover and colleagues' (in preparation) proposed theory of change was based on limited extant research separately investigating the mediating influence of teacher knowledge, perceptions, and practice on student outcomes. For example, Matsumura et al. (2013), through a randomized

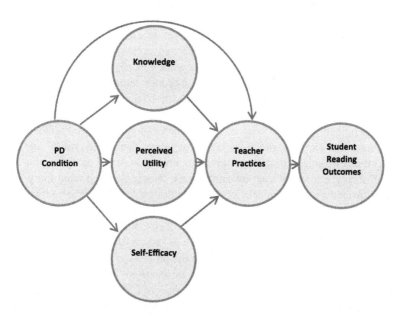

Fig. 1 Theory of change for professional development with coaching

trial investigation of the mediating impact of teacher literacy instruction (i.e., classroom practice) on the relationship between content-focused coaching and student outcomes, found that the positive effect of their coaching program on student reading achievement was mediated through the quality of classroom instruction. Likewise, Gamse et al. (2008), in evaluating the impact of the Reading First initiative, found that changes in instructional variables mediated the impact of Reading First training on students' early print and letter knowledge achievement.

Garet et al. (2001), in a large-scale survey study of mathematics and science teachers' professional development, found that enhanced knowledge and skills had a large positive influence on change in reported teacher practice. This work supported the key contribution of pedagogical content knowledge on classroom instruction.

There is also limited support for the relationship between (a) perceived self-efficacy and/or the utility of instruction and (b) classroom practices. For example, Rim-Kauffman and Sawyer (2004), in an investigation of the Responsive Classroom (RC) teaching approach, found that teachers who reported implementing more RC practices reported greater self-efficacy and perceived utility pertaining to RC-aligned practices. In a study of rural and non-rural teachers' reading, science, mathematics, and data-based decision making professional development, Glover et al. (in preparation) also found that teachers' perceived utility of practices was significantly related to their reported implementation of those practices.

By integrating mediating variables from previous educational research into their proposed theory of change, Glover et al. (in preparation) explored potential mechanisms for change influencing the relationship between professional development with coaching and student reading outcomes. Given past relationships between knowledge and/or perceptions (i.e., self-efficacy, perceived utility) and practice, as well as the mediating influence of teacher practice on professional development and student outcomes, Glover and colleagues proposed the model shown in Fig. 1. Although exploratory, this work was needed to examine potential causal relationships that could further be tested in future experimental research. Glover, Ihlo, and their colleagues used structural equation modeling to conduct mediation analyses with the teachers, interventionists, and students from the 61 schools participating in their original randomized experimental study (Glover et al., in preparation). These exploratory analyses were conducted within the larger context of a randomized trial. Appropriate examination of the mediating influences required disaggregation of data by grade-level, which placed limited the power to detect statistically significant relationships. Although several of the pathways were not found to be statistically significant, Glover and colleagues found relationships of interest. For third-grade homeroom teachers, they found that data-based decision-making practices (measured by logs administered to all participating teachers) mediated the relationship between the professional development condition (*professional development with coaching* or *business as usual*) and students' reading fluency. This finding was similarly observed for third-grade interventionists, with instructional practices (measured by coded observations of instruction) mediating the relationship between the professional development and students' reading. These observed mediating influences were statistically significant. Glover et al. (in preparation) also found, for kindergarten interventionists, that the relationship between the professional development condition and knowledge (measured by a pedagogical content knowledge assessment) as well as between knowledge and reading instructional practices were significant (though when statistically tested, the mediation effect was not significant, potentially due to insufficient sample size).

The additional follow-up mediation analyses for the impact study by Glover et al. (2015) is an important initial step in exploring potential variables that influence professional development outcomes in rural contexts. A recommended next step would include measuring and exploring the influence of specific variables unique to rural contexts (e.g., teacher characteristics, unique classroom configurations) in these and other similar efficacy investigations. This would better enable researchers, policymakers, and practitioners to understand how context contributes to the efficacy of practices for training teachers and advancing student learning environments. Given its importance in informing educational decisions, this should be at the forefront of the research agenda on teacher professional development in rural schools.

Previous debates among researchers have contrasted the merits of various methods for determining the influence of unique contexts in rural communities (e.g., qualitative, correlational, case study, or experimental methods) (e.g., Arnold et al. 2005). By considering potential mediating and moderating influences within proposed theories change, experimental research can help to address existing concerns about an overly narrow, one-size-fits-all approach to examining the efficacy of professional development for teachers in rural schools. This chapter presents an initial example for how this can take place with respect to professional development with coaching to promote students response to early reading instruction.

4 Conclusion

Collectively, the investigations by Vernon-Feagans et al. (2013) and Glover et al. (2015, in preparation) offer important contributions to the literature on teacher professional development designed to promote students' response to early reading instruction in rural schools. Vernon-Feagans explored the impact of coaching with homeroom teachers in the provision of a reading intervention focusing on early reading skills. Glover et al. (2015) further evaluated the benefits of professional development with coaching in an approach that capitalized on coordination between the homeroom teacher and an interventionist in providing reading intervention that was responsive to students' needs and growth while at the same time taking into account limited resources, scheduling concerns, and time constraints in teachers' classroom environment in rural schools. Importantly, Glover et al. (in preparation), through mediation analyses, tested a clearly-specific theory of change, examining questions about how and why the professional development with coaching resulted in improved reading outcomes for students. This was an important initial step in reducing one-size-fits-all conclusions about intervention efficacy in rural contexts. Additional work is currently underway by these investigators to further explore coaching components and the integration of data-based decision making and reading intervention delivery into rural school systems of change.

5 Next Steps for Advancing Research with Implications for Practice

Although the investigations described herein have been useful for determining the efficacy of professional development with coaching for rural teachers in promoting students' response to early reading intervention, ongoing research is needed to better understand (a) additional factors that mediate or moderate the relationship between professional development and observed outcomes, (b) school stakeholders' perceptions about the professional development and implementation process, and (c) the differential impact of various professional development (coaching) elements. Glover et al. (in preparation) illustrate the utility of exploring mediating variables such as teacher knowledge, perceptions, and practice for developing an understanding of the relationship between rural teacher professional development and student reading outcomes. Future extensions of this work will be useful for clarifying the influence of factors the enable student learning to take place, as well as the role that contextual variables, such as leadership infrastructure or characteristics of teachers in rural schools, play in moderating the impact of professional development.

Additional research is also needed better understand how to best integrate new practices that result from rural teachers participation in professional development into schools' existing infrastructure. This research could directly explore (a) whether specific elements of the professional development process meet educational stakeholders' needs and (b) stakeholders' perceptions and recommendations for future changes to both the support that is offered and the resulting practices.

Given the complexity of data-based instructional decisions for reading, it would be helpful to explore the use of various methods of support for teachers in rural schools in guiding data use and the application of instruction and interventions. For example, Powell and Diamond and colleagues (e.g., Powell et al. 2010) have used case-based video exemplars of early literacy instructional via hypertext embedded in feedback provided by coaches. Pianta and colleagues (e.g., Downer et al. 2012) have also provided teachers with access to online video exemplars of intervention activities. Future research is warranted to examine the application of such approaches with teachers in rural schools and within a data-based instructional decision-making framework.

In future investigations, it would be useful to experimentally manipulate aspects of the professional development/coaching process that are relevant to rural teacher support to determine their impact on teacher and student outcomes. For example, the coaching under investigation by Glover et al. (2015) and Vernon-Feagans et al. (2013) involved real-time modeling conducted by a coach from a distance. It would also be helpful to explore the differential impact of this aspect of coaching relative to other alternatives such as the use of hyper-linked case examples demonstrating instruction. This research could be guided by hypothesized theories of change that could be tested to help determine the influence of variables of interest on the relationship between the provided intervention and observed outcomes within the rural context. This work would help to advance research beyond one-size-fits-all efficacy investigations. As a result, these additional evaluations of variations in professional development approaches would be useful for determining optimal methods of support for rural teachers in specific contexts.

Acknowledgments This research was supported by a grant awarded to the University of Nebraska by the U.S. Department of Education's Institute for Education Sciences (R305C090022). The lead investigators for this project were Todd A. Glover (Rutgers University), Tanya Ihlo (University of Nebraska-Lincoln), and Edward S. Shapiro (Lehigh University).

References

American Institutes for Research. (2004). *Conceptual overview: Coaching in the professional development impact study*. Washington, DC: American Institutes for Research.

Arnold, M. L., Newman, J. H., Gaddy, B. B., & Dean, C. B. (2005, April 27). A look at the condition of rural education research: Setting a difference for future research. *Journal of Research in Rural Education, 20*(6). Retrieved January 15, 2015, from http://jrre.psu.edu/articles/20-6.pdf

Deussen, T., Coskie, T., Robinson, L., & Autio, E. (2007). *"Coach" can mean many things: Five categories of coaches in Reading First (Issues & Answers Report, REL 2007-No. 005)*. Washington, DC: U.S. Department of Education, Institute of Education Sciences, National Center for Education Evaluation and Regional Assistance, Regional Educational Laboratory Northwest.

Downer, J. T., Pianta, R. C., Fan, X., Hamre, B. K., Mashburn, A., & Justice, L. (2012). Effects of web-mediated teacher professional development on the language and literacy skills of children enrolled in prekindergarten programs. *NHSA Dialog, 14*(4), 189–212.

Elementary and Secondary Education Act, Public Law 107–110, 107th Cong. (2002).

Fletcher, J. M., & Vaughn, S. (2009). Response to intervention: Preventing and remediating academic difficulties. *Child Development Perspectives, 3*(1), 30–37.

Gamse, B. C., Bloom, H. S., Kemple, J. J., & Jacob, R. T. (2008). *Reading First Impact Study: Interim Report*. Washington, DC: National Center for Education Evaluation and Regional Assistance, Institute of Education Sciences, U.S. Department of Education.

Garet, M. S., Porter, A. C., Desimone, L., Birman, B., & Suk Yoon, K. (2001). What makes professional development effective? Results from a national sample of teachers. *American Educational Research Journal, 38*(4), 915–945.

Glover, T. A., Ihlo, T., Howell Smith, M. C., Martin, S. D., Wu, C., & Bovaird, J. A. (in preparation). A randomized experimental study of an RTI reading coaching approach: Examining the mediating influences of teacher knowledge, perceptions, and practices.

Glover, T. A., Ihlo, T., Martin, S. D., Howell Smith, M. C., Wu, C., McCormick, C. & Bovaird, J. A. (2015, February). *Professional development with coaching in RTI reading: A randomized study.* Paper presented at the Annual Meeting of the National Association of School Psychologists, Orlando, FL.

Glover, T. A., Nugent, G. C., Chumney, F. L., Ihlo, T., Shapiro, E., Guard, K, Koziol, N., & Bovaird, J. A. (2016). Investigating rural teachers' professional development, instructional knowledge, and classroom practice. *Journal of Research on Rural Education, 31*(3), 2–16.

Glover, T. A., & Vaughn, S. (Eds.). (2010). *The promise of response to intervention: Evaluating current science and practice.* New York, NY: Guilford Press.

Good, R. H., Kaminski, R. A., Cummings, K. D., Dufour-Martel, C., Petersen, K., Powell-Smith, K., et al. (2011). *DIBELS next.* Eugene, OR: Dynamic Measurement. Group available http://dibels.org/

Howley, C. B., & Howley, A. A. (2004, September 24). School size and the influence of socioeconomic status on student achievement: Confronting the threat of size bias in national data sets. *Education Policy Analysis Archives, 12*(52). Retrieved February 2, 2015, from http://epaa.asu.edu/epaa/v12n52/

Individuals with Disabilities Education Improvement Act, Public Law 108–446, 108th Cong. (2004).

Johnson, J., Showalter, D., Klein, R., & Lester, C. (2014). *Why rural matters: The condition of rural education in the 50 states.* Washington, D.C.: Rural School and Community Trust.

Kratochwill, T. R., Volpiansky, P., Clements, M., & Ball, C. (2007). Professional development in implementing and sustaining multitier prevention models: implications for response to intervention. *School Psychology Review, 36*(4), 618–631.

Matsumura, L. C., Garnier, H. E., & Spybrook, J. (2013). Literacy coaching to improve student reading achievement: A multi-level mediation model. *Learning and Instruction, 25*, 35–48.

Marsh, J. A., McCombs, J. S., Lockwood, J. R., Martorell, F., Gershwin, D., Naftel, S., et al. (2008). *Supporting literacy across the sunshine state: A study of Florida middle school reading coaches.* Santa Monica, CA: RAND.

Mercer, S. H., Idler, A. M., & Bartfai, J. M. (2014). Theory-driven evaluation in school psychology intervention research: 2007–2012. *School Psychology Review, 43*, 119–131.

National Institute of Child Health and Human Development (NICHD). (2000). Report of the National Reading Panel. *Teaching children to read: An evidence-based assessment of the scientific research literature on reading and its implications for reading instruction: Reports of the subgroups* (NIH Publication No. 00-4754). Washington, DC: U.S. Government Printing Office.

Neufeld, B., & Roper, D. (2003). *Coaching: A strategy for developing instructional capacity: Promises and practicalities.* Providence, RI: Annenberg Institute for School Reform.

Powell, D. R., Diamond, K. E., Burchinal, M. R., & Koehler, M. J. (2010). Effects of an early literacy professional development intervention on head start teachers and children. *Journal of Educational Psychology, 102*(2), 299–312.

Rim-Kauffman, S. E., & Sawyer, B. E. (2004). Primary-grade teachers' self-efficacy beliefs, attitudes toward teaching, and discipline and teaching practice priorities in relation to the "responsive classroom" approach. *The Elementary School Journal, 104*(4), 321–341.

Schafft, K. A., & Jackson, A. Y. (Eds.). (2010). *Rural education for the twenty-first century: Identity, place, and community in a globalizing world.* University Park, PA: The Pennsylvania State University Press.

Texas Education Agency. (1999). School size and class size in Texas public schools. Report Number 12. Document Number GE9 600 03. Austin, TX: Texas Education Agency Office of Policy Planning and Research.

Vernon-Feagans, L., Kainz, K., Hedrick, A., Ginsberg, M., & Amendum, S. (2013). Live webcam coaching to help early elementary classroom teachers provide effective literacy instruction for struggling readers: The targeted reading intervention. *Journal of Educational Psychology, 105*(4), 1175–1187.

Wanzek, J., & Vaughn, S. (2010). Research-based implications from extensive early reading interventions. Reprinted with permission. In T. A. Glover & S. Vaughn (Eds.), *The promise of response to intervention: Evaluating current science and practice* (pp. 113–142). New York: Guilford.

Woodcock, R. W., Mather, N., & Schrank, F. (2004). *WJ III diagnostic reading battery*. Rolling Meadows, IL: Riverside.

Rural Language and Literacy Connections: An Integrated Approach to Supporting Low-Income Preschool Children's Language and Literacy Development

Lisa L. Knoche and Dawn L. Davis

Abstract High-quality preschool programs that promote early literacy through oral language, phonological awareness, print and word awareness, and alphabet knowledge prepare children to be more successful in kindergarten and more effective readers. Additionally, interventions that connect home and school literacy environments and create literacy-rich home environments are associated with children's positive academic outcomes. Integrated programming to support early literacy skills at home and school is important because children's skill levels and readiness at the time they enter school are strongly related to later school success. Few early childhood programs effectively integrate supports across home and preschool settings. This chapter will describe Rural Language and Literacy Connections, an ecologically-based early language and literacy intervention for rural, low-income preschool children and their families that integrates preschool classroom instruction with family and environmental supports. The intervention includes the implementation of scientifically-based literacy curricula and as well as enriched literacy environments in rural preschools, child care settings, and children's homes through the provision of supplemental literacy-based opportunities. Details of the intervention, including professional development supports for early childhood teachers, as well as language and literacy outcomes for children will be discussed.

Keywords Early childhood · Language · Literacy · Preschool · Family engagement · Intervention · Professional development · Rural

L.L. Knoche (✉) · D.L. Davis
Nebraska Center for Research on Children, Youth, Families and Schools,
University of Nebraska–Lincoln, 238 Teachers College Hall, Lincoln,
NE 68588-0345, USA
e-mail: lknoche2@unl.edu

© Springer International Publishing Switzerland 2017
G.C. Nugent et al. (eds.), *Rural Education Research in the United States*,
DOI 10.1007/978-3-319-42940-3_10

1 Introduction

Children's early academic performance has significant and lasting implications for their future success; children who prosper early are more likely to maintain positive outcomes well beyond high school graduation. Numerous longitudinal studies have shown pre-literacy and language skills are among the strongest predictors of later academic success (e.g., La Paro and Pianta 2000; Kurdek and Sinclair 2000; Reynolds 1998). Literacy and language skills provide the foundation for learning and social interaction and participation (Farran et al. 2006). Literacy skills at kindergarten entry predict grade retention, referral to special education services, and achievement test scores (Pianta and McCoy 1997). Thus, intervention programming implemented during the early childhood period (birth to age 8 years) is significant for promoting children's healthy development. This chapter outlines the important contribution of children's early language and literacy development, and describes an ecologically-based intervention program (Rural Language and Literacy Connections; *Rural LLC*) designed to support language and literacy skills for nearly 500 children who attended preschool in a rural Midwestern community. Immediate and sustained results on children's skill development, as well as teacher and classroom-level outcomes will be discussed.

1.1 Significance of Early Language and Literacy Development

Competence in reading is an essential developmental achievement that predicts success in almost all facets of contemporary society. In many ways, reading serves as the gateway to children's learning. Students who do not learn to read early in their academic careers experience extreme difficulties when expected to read to learn later on. Juel (1988) reported a .88 probability that children who were poor readers at the end of 1st grade would also be poor readers at the end of their 4th grade year. Decades of early literacy research have shown that young children's early literacy skills predict later academic success (Barnett and Belfield 2006; Barnett et al. 2005; Dickinson and Neuman 2006). An alarming 85–90 % of students with serious reading problems in the primary grades fail to graduate from high school (NICHD 2000). Furthermore, children who read well also read more and thus attain more knowledge across a variety of domains (Cunningham and Stanovich 1998; Echols et al. 1996) than their peers who do not read well. Stanovich (1986) termed this the "Matthew effect," in which poor readers fall further behind their more literate peers in all academic areas. Additionally, literacy skills are closely tied to positive societal outcomes such as employment and participation in society (Heckman and Masterov 2007; Kirsch et al. 1993). Given the predictive nature of early literacy skills, it is imperative that we develop integrated systems of prevention and intervention to assure competence in early literacy for all young children.

Learning to read depends on the foundational skills of *oral language, phonological awareness, print awareness, and alphabet knowledge* (Dickinson et al. 2003; NICHD 2000; Storch and Whitehurst 2001; Whitehurst and Lonigan 1998). A meta-analysis of early childhood literacy research in the National Early Literacy Panel (NELP) report (2008) identified key literacy skills shown to predict later academic success. The skills found to have medium to large predictive relationships with later literacy achievement in decoding, reading comprehension or spelling include (a) alphabet knowledge, (b) phonological awareness, (c) rapid automatic naming of letters or digits, (d) rapid automatic naming of colors or objects, (e) name writing, and (f) phonological memory. These associations hold true for children across community settings, including children who reside in rural communities. Thus, these early literacy skills must be targeted in effective interventions.

1.2 Instructional Settings in Classrooms and Homes

The environments that children experience are important in promoting these key literacy skills. These environments may include early childhood settings, such as child care or preschool, as well as home and family environments. Instruction for young children around the key literacy skills is most effective when it is language-rich, provides frequent opportunities for children to hear diverse and complex vocabulary (Hart and Risley 1999), includes shared book reading (Whitehurst et al. 1994a), and incorporates conversations into daily life experiences (Snow et al. 2001). Children benefit from intensive classroom-based instruction (Dickinson 2001). While many prekindergarten programs, including Head Start, implement a general curricula, a number have also adopted more a more specialized literacy curriculum (Hulsey et al. 2011). These literacy curricula have specified scope and sequence to support the age-appropriate developmental progression of language and literacy skills.

Furthermore, several studies have documented the effectiveness of various types of shared book reading in improving young children's early language and literacy outcomes. All involve an adult reading a book to a single child or small group of children; the most effective strategies use a variety of techniques to engage the children in the text (Justice and Ezell 2002; Sénéchal et al. 1996). One specific approach to shared book reading is dialogic reading, in which adults elicit children's active involvement in reading and discussing books through interactive reading strategies (e.g. open-ended questions, expansions, following a child's lead; Arnold et al. 1994). Improvements are evident for children across socioeconomic strata with gains for low-income children maintained for at least 6 months (Lonigan et al. 1999; Wasik and Bond 2001; Whitehurst et al. 1994b). Moderate effect sizes have been found in parent—(Jordan et al. 2000) and teacher-delivered interventions (Lonigan and Whitehurst 1998).

Significantly, research has shown evidence that the combination of high-quality language and literacy experiences (Barone 2011; Hart and Risley 1999) along with family involvement is advantageous to young children. Parent support for children's literacy during the preschool years, such as book reading, pretend play, and mealtime conversations, all promote oral language and predict children's later language and literacy competence (Beals 2001; DeTemple 2001). Moderate effect sizes are found when parents read to children, listen to their child read, or use specific instructional techniques (Neuman and Gallagher 1994; Nye et al. 2006; Taverne and Sheridan 1995). These findings point to the importance of parent involvement in early learning.

Children develop and learn within multiple contexts, and these setting variations must be taken into account when designing effective interventions. Children's development is optimal and the greatest gains are evident when learning and literacy experiences are integrated across contexts and continuities among these major systems are created (Rimm-Kaufman and Pianta 2000; Taylor and Pearson 2004). Explicit and integrated literacy-based interactions between teachers and children, between parents and children, and between the home and school enhance children's learning opportunities across all settings children encounter daily (Pinto et al. 2013; Tabors et al. 2001) and support academic outcomes (Espinosa 2002). Efforts to enhance the "curriculum of the home," and to create integrated opportunities for learning within and across home and school contexts offer promising foci for promoting early reading (Hill 2001). For example, dialogic reading interventions implemented across school and home have been found to be significantly more effective at increasing children's expressive vocabulary than school-only and control conditions (Whitehurst et al. 1994a), with home-school intervention effect sizes at least twice as large as classroom-only effect sizes (Lonigan and Whitehurst 1998). The nature of family involvement has been found to mediate expected effects, with the most effective interventions being those that (a) promote active dialogue and home-school communication systems, (b) monitor children's behavior and performance, (c) teach parents methods for assisting their child in learning new academic skills, and (d) engage in family-school consultation to address individual child needs (Christenson and Carlson 2005). These must be considered in intervention design for rural children and families.

The importance of literacy skills and their contribution to academic achievement is unquestioned and an abundant number of programs, interventions and supports have been developed to target this area in young children. The preschool years seem to be a principally sensitive time to make these lifelong impacts. Preschool children's interactions with, and participation in their environment (e.g., home, school, and community), contribute to learning; therefore, ecologically focused interventions are needed to maximize children's literacy development (Gonzalez and Uhing 2008).

Ecological preschool interventions designed to support language and literacy are particularly relevant for children and families living in rural communities. Available evidence suggests that students in large urban and rural communities come to kindergarten less academically prepared in the areas of reading and math than their small urban and suburban counterparts (Miller and Votruba-Drzal 2013). Rural children are 60 % more likely to be placed in special education in kindergarten than their non-rural counterparts (Grace et al. 2006). Significantly, rates of child poverty are higher and parents' levels of education are lower than in urban communities (Garrett-Peters and Mills-Koonce 2013; USDA 2014). Furthermore, the parenting skills, expectations for children's development as well as knowledge of child development are all lower for rural parents than their urban counterparts (Miller and Votruba-Drzal 2013). Additionally, disparities exist in specialized developmental services and resources in rural communities thereby limiting access for children and families to potentially valuable developmental supports, including access to high quality center-based child care programs (Smith 2010; Vernon-Feagans et al. 2008). These unique needs and characteristics of families who live in rural communities must be considered in the development, design and execution of optimal early childhood services (Smith et al. 2008). One such ecological intervention is the Rural Language and Literacy Connections (*Rural LLC*), an intensive, literacy-based early learning program for rural, low-income preschool children.

1.3   Intervention Description

Rural Language and Literacy Connections (*Rural LLC*) was originally funded as an Early Reading First Project. Early Reading First was part of the "Good Start, Grow Smart" initiative authorized under Title I, Part B, of the *No Child Left Behind* Act in 2002. Early Reading First projects were funded for three-year periods from 2002 through 2009 with an average of 30 awards funded per year for amounts ranging between $250,000 and $3 million. The goal of these projects was to promote the development of early literacy skills within high quality programs for at-risk children (U.S. Department of Education).

Overview of Approach. *Rural LLC* was grounded in strong preschool/Head Start classroom curriculum instruction and rich environmental supports in literacy and language, as well as literacy supports for supplemental child care (family home or center-based) settings and children's homes to enhance children's oral language, phonological awareness, print awareness, and alphabet knowledge (Fig. 1). The primary emphasis of the intervention was on center-based preschool settings but a secondary emphasis on supplemental child care settings and homes was necessary given the particular milieu of children's everyday lives in this community. The intentional focus on these two levels maximizes language opportunities and provides a highly intensive experience designed to put children at risk for educational failure on successful reading trajectories.

Rural LLC included three primary objectives. First, the intervention involved implementation of *scientifically-based reading curricula* in center-based preschool classrooms, supplemental child care settings and children's homes. Second, the project worked to *enrich literacy environments* in preschool classrooms, supplemental child care settings attended by *Rural LLC* children, and children's homes.

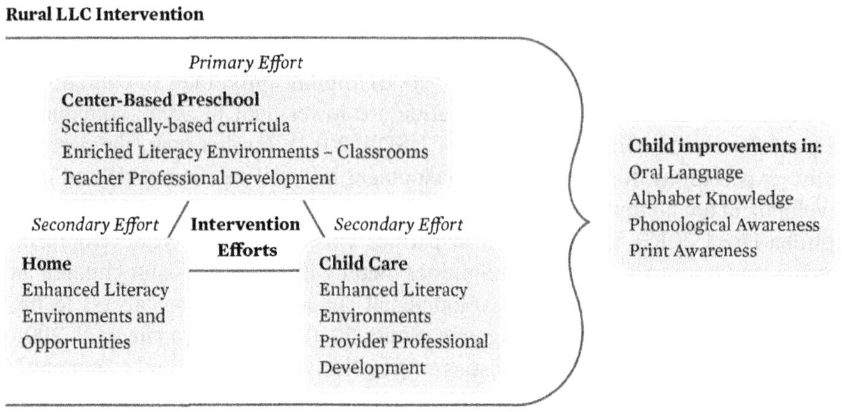

Rural LLC Intervention

Fig. 1 Intervention design and theory of change for Rural LLC

Finally, the project was concerned with *providing intensive and systematic professional development* around literacy/language curricula and scientifically-based practices, as well as *supplemental literacy-based opportunities* to families.

Description of Partners. Rural LLC was developed in collaboration with a University-Community team. The Nebraska Center for Research on Children, Youth, Families and Schools at the University of Nebraska-Lincoln worked in partnership with Head Start Child and Family Development Program (HSCFDP), and Grand Island Public Schools-Early Childhood (GIPS-EC) in central, rural Nebraska to develop and implement the literacy intervention. The intervention was developed with the particular needs of the community in mind. In the agricultural community involved in *Rural LLC*, many parents were employed in meat packing plants that operated in three round-the-clock shifts. Parents often worked more than one job. Additionally, 10 % of families were migrant and left the community during the summer for agricultural jobs. As a result, families often required supplemental childcare, as well as language and literacy services beyond the typical preschool day to provide equitable services for all children. Thus, integration across the multiple settings children encountered on a daily basis (i.e. home, school, child care) was a particularly salient design for this rural community.

Classroom Based Instruction. The primary focus of the intervention was on center-based preschool classroom settings. The project selected a scientifically based preschool literacy curriculum, Opening the World of Learning (OWL; Schickedanz et al. 2005) to systematically build the foundational skills of oral language, phonological awareness, print awareness, and alphabet knowledge in the preschool classrooms (Table 1). The curriculum had also shown to have positive child impacts in previous studies (Schickedanz et al. 2005). One to 2.5 h (part-day classrooms) and 3–4.5 h (full-day classrooms) of dedicated, curriculum-supported time were spent developing children's language, cognition and early reading skills daily, in addition to informal time for extended conversation and language practice

Table 1 Mapping child literacy skills to curricula components

Skill	OWL curricula components
Oral language	• Story time • Teacher- and child-led discussions, extended discourse and exchange of information • Key vocabulary words in each book, used during activity time • Vocabulary relevant to real life
Phonological awareness	• Songs, predictable books, sing-along CD's, teacher-led alliteration, rhyming activities
Print awareness/alphabet knowledge	• Teacher-led games and child-initiated activities focused on letter recognition • Use of letters in rich literacy environment • Support of early writing

that occurred more frequently each day. The OWL daily schedule included a morning meeting, center time, group read alouds with multiple readings of books over several days, small group activities, songs and word play and activities designed to build upon children's background knowledge or address social and emotional topics. OWL has a clearly specified scope and sequence and provides detailed instructions for teachers. OWL uses children's books, poems, music and small group activities to develop literacy skills in preschool children. The curriculum also includes teacher resources and a teacher's guide with detailed information about each lesson.

OWL is scientifically-based to incorporate a full range of age-appropriate experiences with words, sounds, letters, print, books, and conversations. OWL provides an instructional program that is comprehensive, begins with teacher-directed and moves toward child-directed activities, and systematically teaches children essential literacy concepts, while building children's background knowledge (units e.g. *Wind and Water* and *Family*).

Modifications to the arrangement of the day were made to individualize the curriculum for specific teacher/classroom/child needs. For children who were Dual Language Learners (DLL), books and materials were made available in English and Spanish. Appropriate modifications, including individualized support for children with identified speech and/or language delays, were made for children by collaborating with other service providers to ensure specific goals and modifications were included in their Individual Education Plans (IEPs).

Supplemental Instructional Opportunities. As a secondary effort, *Rural LLC* aimed to increase the language and print richness of child care and home environments. This secondary focus was implemented to increase the intensity of language exposure for children, and create coherent opportunities for learning within and across home and school contexts. A second evidence-based curriculum was used for this purpose, Read Together, Talk Together (Pearson Early Learning 2006; RTTT). RTTT was integrated with OWL to reinforce the oral language skills of children, enrich and extend children's vocabularies and help teachers, parents and child care partners talk with children about books. RTTT was a good choice for the secondary effort because limited training was needed (a training video was available) and materials were readily available and accessible for Spanish and English-speaking families and providers. Child care partners and parents were encouraged to use RTTT at least two times each day in structured book-reading activities, and more frequently during informal dialogue with children.

Additional efforts were also implemented to encourage enrichment of child care and home settings. *Family literacy events* (FLE) took place in preschool classrooms two times per month. FLEs were intentionally developed to promote the active engagement between parent and child around interesting language and literacy activities. FLE activities were designed to meet eight key objectives (see Table 2). The FLEs provided opportunities for parents to learn about the skills their children were working on in the classroom and how these skills might extend to and be supported at home. Additionally, parents were provided materials and suggestions for additional literacy activities that would correspond to the activities of the classroom, as well as a monetary incentive for participating in each event. The events were implemented from a family-centered perspective; the strengths, needs and priorities of families were central to each FLE. In addition, OWL Family Connection Plans outlining specific literacy games and activities for parents, older siblings, and relative providers to do with children were provided.

As appropriate, children's child care providers were encouraged to attend the family literacy events. Child care partners also selected materials to enhance their child care settings, and received guidance and support from *Rural LLC* coaches for environment set-up. Additionally, Family Service Workers, who conducted monthly home visits, supported families in the use of RTTT, OWL Family Connection Plans, and parents' conversational skills to expand children's background knowledge. Incentives for child care partners and Family Service Workers were offered for enrolling in the program, attending events and completing activities.

Professional Development Supports. Professional development that is high quality, sustained and intensive was important for effective implementation of the

Table 2 Objectives for family literacy event (FLE) activities	*The FLE activity*
	• Is focused on child-parent interaction
	• Requires minimal direction and is handed off to be parent or child-directed
	• Relates to the current curriculum unit theme and early literacy skill
	• Is open-ended and focused on process between parent and child
	• Is based in active learning
	• Can be extended to the home environment
	• Is appropriate for children with varying developmental skills and abilities
	• Is fun and interesting for parents and children

curriculum components (OWL/RTTT). The primary goal for the *Rural LLC* professional development series was to ensure that teachers understood the underlying principles of child language and literacy development as well as OWL and RTTT curricula, including effective instructional strategies, appropriate use of materials, and effective techniques to engage participation of parents and other family members who routinely engage with the child at home.

For preschool teachers, the professional development series included a 2-day curriculum training, refresher half-day workshops and ongoing group and individual coaching throughout the academic year. A coaching model of consultation was utilized. *Rural LLC* literacy coaches worked with 1–3 teachers each week. Literacy coaches completed at least 2 h of classroom observations each week. During the observations, literacy coaches made notes about teaching strategies and practices, modeled teaching practices, worked with individual children, collected data (implementation fidelity data and child assessments) and provided general support to teaching staff. Literacy coaches met with teaching staff for 30–60 min a week. During these coaching sessions, staff worked together to set goals, document progress towards goals, plan for lessons, discuss individualizing instruction, review data from observations and child assessments, and discuss topics determined by the group. Preschool teachers were eligible to receive 6 credits per academic year for participation in the professional development series. Courses were applicable for undergraduate or graduate credit and post baccalaureate certification renewal, with tuition and fees paid by project resources. Monthly stipends were provided.

Professional development was also provided to the child care partners (CCPs), including initial training in use of the RTTT curriculum, other language/literacy in-service opportunities (for Community College Credit) and bi-monthly support from *Rural LLC* coaches who visited centers or child care homes and offered recommendations to improve literacy environments and implement RTTT. In addition to the continuing education opportunities, literacy materials and a stipend were made available to CCPs as an incentive for participating in *Rural LLC*.

1.4 **Rural LLC** *Results and Outcomes*

The preschool classrooms, teachers and child care partners experienced positive outcomes from the intervention in areas of classroom quality, education and professional development and enhanced home-school connections. Additionally, children's language and literacy skill development was enriched. Details regarding the primary and supplemental instructional settings are provided, along with the results experienced in each setting. The language and literacy outcomes demonstrated by children over the course of the intervention period are then highlighted.

1.5 Settings

Primary Center-Based Preschool Environments. Eleven preschool classrooms were involved in the project; two classrooms operated full-day, full-year schedules and nine classrooms operated half-day, two sessions per day, part-year programs. All classrooms received Head Start funding and, as such, adhered to Head Start standards and procedures related to activities, daily schedules, materials and classroom practices. All center-based preschool classrooms were accredited by the National Association for the Education of Young Children (NAEYC). Classrooms were large and were well equipped with a variety of materials, and had dedicated areas for book reading, manipulatives, small group time and other activities. Materials were rotated and new materials and displays were brought in throughout the year to support the current unit theme. Classroom placement of children was conducted to ensure there were no more than 18 children per classroom and a fairly equal distribution of gender, home language, and age (3–5 years).

Twenty lead preschool teachers participated in the project over 4 years. The average teacher age was 33.85 years (SD = 9.88) and all were Caucasian and female. Eighty percent of teachers had a 4-year degree or higher and 20 % had a 2-year degree. Teachers had an average of just over 6 years of early childhood experience but this varied (SD = 6.87 years).

Supplemental Child Care Environments. Fifteen different child care programs, both center-based and home-based, participated in *Rural LLC*. Child care partners (CCPs) were provided with all materials to implement the RTTT curriculum including books and question cards. In addition, CCPs received funds to make improvements to their environments based on the results of assessments of the literacy environment and consultation with their literacy coaches.

Twenty-one CCPs participated in the project over the 4 years. The average age was 30.29 years (SD = 9.06 years) and all were female. Most CCPs were Caucasian (76.2 %), 9.5 % were African American, 4.8 % were Hispanic, 4.8 % were American Indian/Alaska Native and 4.8 % were Native Hawaiian/Other Pacific Islander. CCPs were less educated than the preschool teachers, with only 19 % holding a 4-year degree or beyond, 28.6 % had a 2-year degree, 33.4 % had some college/training and 19 % had a high school diploma. CCPs had an average of almost five and a half years of early childhood education experience (SD = 4.28).

Children and Families. The 4-year project involved a total of 488 children. For this group of children, 48 % were female; 42 % were Caucasian; 3.2 % were African American; 51.7 % were Latino/Hispanic; 1.1 % American Indian and 2 % identified ethnicity as "other." English was the primary language at home for 73.8 % of the children. About one-third of parents (37.4 %) reported earning less than a high school diploma, with another third (34.5 %) reporting a high school diploma as their highest educational level.

1.6 Primary Environment: Center-Based Preschool Classroom and Teacher Results

Classroom Results. The ECERS-R (Harms et al. 1998) was used as a measure of global classroom quality. This tool consists of seven subscales and an overall total quality score; scores range from 1–7. A score of 5 or above reflects a high quality environment. Total quality scores on the ECERS-R prior to the implementation of *Rural LLC* were above the cut off for high quality environments (overall average scores of 6.1); this provided an indication that the settings were providing a high quality experience for children upon initiation of the intervention. Following implementation of *Rural LLC*, quality measures were collected each fall and spring of the project. Throughout the project period, preschool classrooms were able to maintain these high levels of quality (ECERS-R overall means were above 5.7 at each fall and spring assessment). Following the completion of the classroom observations, literacy coaches met with teachers to discuss results and make action plans for improving areas that scored below 5 on the measure. These results suggest that though the addition of the intervention required additional focus and resources, high quality environments for young children were supported and maintained over the course of *Rural LLC*.

Teacher Results. Furthermore, we set out to enhance professional development opportunities for preschool teachers. Teacher professional development was a cornerstone of the project. The professional development offered through *Rural LLC* supported teachers in developing knowledge about best practices in language and literacy through trainings on curriculum, literacy/language development, assessment, and using data-based decision making. Furthermore, teachers experienced individualized coaching and college courses. Three indicators provide evidence of enhanced supports including (a) participation in professional development offerings, including college coursework; (b) knowledge and application of best practices, including fidelity to the curriculum; and (c) quality of teacher-child interactions. Together, these indicators provide evidence that the intervention helped teachers to improve their instructional practices in support of children's language and literacy skills.

Overall, teachers received over 108 h of training over the 4 years of the project and approximately 36 h of coaching each year. In addition to these training experiences, 14 of the 20 teachers (70 %) took part in college credit offered through the project. The courses included an independent study course in which teachers reflected on the implementation of the intervention and their classroom practices, as well as courses on child development and early language and literacy. An area of need for rural teachers is access to college-level course credit and we were able to provide opportunities for teachers to advance their education through the project.

Teachers' classroom practices were observed by coaches weekly and an OWL curriculum fidelity checklist-Revised (Modified from Jonathan Fribley, Education Consulting St Cloud MN and Candi Foltz-Hall, Shannon County School District) was completed by coaches annually in the fall and spring. The fidelity checklist assessed teacher's adherence to the curriculum design and the quality of teacher-child interactions occurring. Scores on the fidelity checklist consistently increased from fall to spring each year with overall averages of fidelity in the spring above 80 %. One aspect of particular interest assessed by the fidelity checklist was teacher interaction with children. The 5-point scale (1 = basic and 5 = exemplary) assessed teachers interactions with children during center time (i.e., teacher engages in conversations with children, models vocabulary word use, promotes child choice). The data indicate that teachers had positive interactions with children (e.g. average interaction ratings above 4.0 at each assessment).

In addition, during the third year of the project, teachers completed the Preschool Teacher Language and Literacy Beliefs Questionnaire (Hindman and Wasik 2008; TLLB). The 30-item TLLB addresses teachers' beliefs about preschool children's development in the areas of decoding (e.g. "I believe that children need plenty of drill and practice to learn the sounds of letters"), oral language (e.g. "I believe that children should not talk during meals"), book reading (e.g. "I believe that children should look at books to help the learn to read") and writing (e.g. "I believe that children should write without worrying about spelling."). Teachers respond to items using a 5-point Likert scale (1 = strongly disagree to 5 = strong agree). Mean scores are calculated with higher means indicating more developmentally appropriate beliefs. The overall mean score was 4.4, indicating teachers held developmentally appropriate and evidence-based practice beliefs by the third year of implementation.

Results from these measures, paired with comments from teachers collected during annual focus groups, indicate that teachers' classroom practices and beliefs about literacy were supported and enriched by the *Rural LLC* project. Teachers described feeling supported by coaches and learning from trainings provided. Teachers stated that the support received from the project (specifically the material preparation, coaching and professional development) helped them implement the intervention curriculum. Teachers reported that seeing changes in child behavior and skills demonstrated in the classroom and increased child assessment scores was evidence for teachers that the intervention was effective. In addition, some teachers shared that positive parent comments and feedback about the intervention and child skills further encouraged teachers to implement the intervention with fidelity.

1.7 Supplemental Environments: Child Care and Home Results

Child Care Results. Environment quality measures were completed each fall and spring in the supplemental child care settings using measures that were similar to those collected in the preschool classrooms. Comparable quality measures were collected in family home child care environments. Results from the quality measures in the center- and family home- child care settings indicated that the child care environments were typically of low quality and fall to spring improvements occurred for only a few CCPs. This outcome was not unexpected, as the primary intervention efforts in *Rural LLC* were occurring in the center-based preschool classrooms and the ability of the project to impact global quality in the child care settings was limited.

The CCPs were provided similar education and professional development opportunities as the preschool staff, although at a lower level of intensity. Five of the 21 CCPs (24 %), as compared to 70 % of the center-based preschool providers, participated in the college-credit courses offered through the project. These courses were offered through collaboration with a local community college. Additionally, CCPs were invited to attend the trainings provided to the preschool staff and several CCP did throughout the project. CCPs received an average of 5 h of coaching per academic year. During focus groups, CCPs reported increasing the number of literacy activities they did with children and being more intentional in their interactions as a result of the project. These changes were likely beneficial to children, but were not identified on the global measures of quality.

Home Results. *Rural LLC* targeted enhanced home-school connections, and enriched environments at home. One approach for encouraging engagement of families was the offering of Family Literacy Events (FLE). Parents and staff viewed these events as opportunities to engage in one-on-one activities with their children and gather ideas for supporting literacy development at home. Over the course of the project, 53 FLE were conducted. Overall, 39 % of families attended more than 1 event, 14 % of families attended one event and 47 % of families did not attend any events while their child was in the program. The events were well received and results from parent satisfaction surveys collected at each event indicated that parents enjoyed the activities with overall satisfaction ratings above 4.5 on a 5-point scale. Additionally, home-school connections were strengthen by the creation of newsletters by teachers, use of OWL Family Connections documents, and participation in RTTT. Parents' voiced satisfaction with this experience in focus groups that were conducted each year. During these focus groups, parents reflected on the intervention components and impacts, reporting changes in their children's literacy and language skills, increased engagement in literacy activities at home, and benefits of participating.

1.8 Children's Language and Literacy Outcomes

While all children were part of *Rural LLC*, not all children experienced the full ecological intervention (i.e. home and/or child care enrichments in addition to classroom). Some only experienced the preschool classroom-based curriculum and enhancements. We were interested in exploring how the language and early literacy skills varied for children who participated in Center-based programming versus Center-based Plus (preschool in addition to child care and/or family literacy events) programming at Kindergarten transition (Knoche et al. 2011b). Forty-seven percent of children ($n = 229$) participated in classroom-based activities alone; 53 % ($n = 259$) participated in the ecological programming across settings. These groups were not pre-determined but identified post hoc based on actual experience. Demographic characteristics across groups were not statistically significantly different, and baseline scores were equivalent. After controlling for baseline scores, significant differences at the end of preschool were observed in children's alphabet knowledge as measured by the number of upper case letters identified, as well as print awareness.

Children who experienced the full ecological intervention had significantly higher alphabet knowledge skills than children who experienced classroom-based programming alone ($b = 1.94$, $t(443) = 2.63$, $p = .009$). Furthermore, children who experienced the full ecological intervention had significantly higher print awareness skills than children who experienced classroom-based programming alone ($b = .49$, $t(309) = 2.68$, $p = .008$). Early literacy skills appear to be most affected by ecological programming.

Furthermore, a small follow up study was conducted to compare the kindergarten progress of children who had participated in *Rural LLC* (Osborn et al. 2010). Data were gathered from 212 *Rural LLC* students in kindergarten, and 720 peers who were identified as receiving free and reduced lunch. There were no significant differences identified between children who had participated in the *Rural LLC* intervention in preschool and those who had not. This finding could indicate that in fact the early literacy intervention supported children in developing skills to make them more equivalent to their peers upon school entry. A significant difference was identified in attendance rate $t(460) = 3.24$, $p < .01$, demonstrating that children who participated in the *Rural LLC* intervention attended school at a significantly higher rate than children who had not participated in the *Rural LLC* intervention.

Specific analyses investigated outcomes for dual language learners who were involved in project (n = 185); (Knoche et al. 2011a). Sixty-one percent of dual language learners participated in classroom-based activities alone; 39 % participated in the ecological programming across settings. After controlling for baseline scores, children who experienced the full ecological intervention had significantly higher alphabet knowledge skills at the end of preschool than children who experienced classroom-based programming alone. No differences between groups were identified on oral language phonological awareness or print awareness measures. Additionally, children who experienced the ecological intervention had significantly higher rates of attendance during preschool than children who experienced classroom-based alone ($b = 0.02$, $t(134) = 2.06$, $p = .04$). Furthermore, some gains persisted through kindergarten. At the end of kindergarten, dual language learners who had participated in ecological preschool programming were less likely to be identified as at risk on a measure of letter naming fluency, relative to their peers of the same age (χ^2 (1, N = 81) = 6.09, $p < .05$).

2 Future Research Needs

The ecological, cross-setting focus of *Rural LLC* was well-suited for preschool children in this rural, agricultural community. While the intervention was not highly individualized, the breadth of services accommodated the needs of the diverse children and families who were involved in programming. The continuity of educational supports across preschool, home and supplemental child care settings encouraged children's literacy skill development during preschool. Furthermore, the preschool teachers and child care partners also benefited from the intervention. There are, however, additional areas of research that would aid in the ongoing implementation of *Rural LLC*.

First, issues surrounding infrastructure are worthy of future investigation. In the federally-funded *Rural LLC* project, monetary resources were made available to programs; materials were purchased, literacy coaches were provided and participants (teachers, families, CCP) received incentives for participation. Once the funding cycle was complete, modifications were necessary to sustain some features of the program. For example, literacy coaches were hired as part of programmatic practice to support ongoing implementation of language and literacy supports. The use of evidence-based early learning curricula was incorporated into all center-based preschool classrooms. But other features, like incentives for families to participate in family literacy events could not be sustained. Research that explores how programs can sustain demonstration projects is needed, particularly in rural communities with restricted resources. Use of technology for intervention implementation should be explored (e.g. provision of early childhood literacy coaching via web conference).

Future research should also examine closely the environmental enrichments that are taking place in the homes of rural preschool children. The opportunities and experiences afforded to children in rural settings is likely to be unique. Some of these unique experiences are reported in this volume (Clarke et al., this volume). Understanding exchanges in the homes of rural children would allow for more effective intervention programs to be developed that build on the strengths and needs of rural families. Additionally, a systematic follow up of children into and through third grade who participated in *Rural LLC* would yield important longitudinal information about the sustained effects of an ecological intervention designed to support young children's language and literacy skills.

Acknowledgments This research was supported by a grant awarded to Drs. Lisa Knoche and Helen Raikes by US Department of Education. The opinions expressed herein are those of the investigators and do not reflect the funding agencies (GRANT ED S359B070074).

References

Arnold, D. H., Lonigan, C. J., Whitehurst, G. J., & Epstein, J. N. (1994). Accelerating language development through picture book reading: Replication and extension to a videotape training format. *Journal of Educational Psychology, 86*, 235–243.

Barnett, W. S., & Belfield, C. R. (2006). Early childhood development and social mobility. *Future of Children, 16*(2), 73–98.

Barnett, W. S., Lamy, C., & Jung, K. (2005). *The effects of state prekindergarten programs on young children's school readiness in five states*. Brunswick: National Institute for Early Education Research, Rutgers University.

Barone, D. (2011). Welcoming families: A parent literacy project in a linguistically rich, high-poverty school. *Early Childhood Education Journal, 38*, 377–384.

Beals, D. E. (2001). Eating and reading: Links between family conversations with preschoolers and later language and literacy. In D. K. Dickinson & P. O. Tabors (Eds.), *Beginning literacy with language: Young children learning at home and school* (pp. 75–92). Baltimore: Paul H. Brookes.

Christenson, S. L., & Carlson, C. (2005). Evidence-based parent and family intervention in school psychology: State of scientifically-based practice. *School Psychology Quarterly, 20*, 525–527.

Cunningham, A. E., & Stanovich, K. E. (1998). Early reading acquisition and its relation to reading experience and ability 10 years later. *Developmental Psychology, 33*(6), 934–945.

DeTemple, J. (2001). Parents and children reading books together. In D. K. Dickinson & P. O. Tabors (Eds.), *Beginning literacy with language: Young children learning at home and in school* (pp. 31–51). Baltimore: Brookes Publishing Company.

Dickinson, D. K. (2001). Putting the pieces together: The impact of preschool on children's language and literacy development in kindergarten. In D. K. Dickinson & P. O. Tabors (Eds.), *Beginning literacy with language: Young children learning at home and school*. Baltimore: Brookes Publishing Company.

Dickinson, D. K., McCabe, A., Anastasopoulos, L., Peisner-Feinberg, E., & Poe, M. D. (2003). The comprehensive language approach to early literacy: The interrelationships among vocabulary, phonological sensitivity, and print knowledge among pre-school-aged children. *Journal of Educational Psychology, 95*, 465–481.

Dickinson, D. K., & Neuman, S. B. (2006). Introduction. In D. K. Dickinson & S. B. Neuman (Eds.), *Handbook of early literacy research* (2nd ed., pp. 1–8). New York: The Guilford Press.

Echols, L. D., West, R. F., Stanovich, K. E., & Zehr, K. S. (1996). Using children's literacy activities to predict growth in verbal cognitive skills: A longitudinal investigation. *Journal of Educational Psychology, 88*(2), 296.

Espinosa, L. (2002). High-quality preschool: Why we need it and what it looks like. *Preschool policy matters, 1*. New Brunswick, NJ: NIEER. Available at http://nieer.org/resources/policybriefs/1.pdf

Farran, D. C., Aydogan, C., Kang, S. J., & Lipsey, M. W. (2006). Preschool classroom environments and the quantity and quality of children's literacy and language behaviors. *Handbook of early literacy research, 2*, 257–268.

Garrett-Peters, P., & Mills-Koonce, R. (2013). The description of the families and children. In L. Vernon-Feagans, M. Cox, & The FLP Key Investigators (Eds.), *The family life project: An epidemiological and developmental study of young children living in poor rural communities. Monographs of the Society for Research in Child Development, 78,* 36–52.

Gonzalez, J. E., & Uhing, B. M. (2008). Home literacy environments and young Hispanic children's English and Spanish oral language: A communality analysis. *Journal of Early Intervention, 30*, 116–139.

Grace, C., Shores, E. F., Zaslow, M., Brown, B., Aufseeser, D., & Bell, L. (2006). *Rural disparities in baseline data of the early childhood longitudinal study: A chartbook* (Rural Early Childhood Report No. 3). Mississippi State, MS: National Center for Rural Early Childhood Learning Initiatives, MS State University Early Childhood Institute.

Harms, T., Clifford, R., & Cryer, D. (1998). *Early childhood environment rating scale* (Revised edition). New York: Teachers College Press.

Hart, B., & Risley, T. R. (1999). *The social world of children: Learning to talk.* Baltimore: Paul H. Brookes.

Heckman, J. J., & Masterov, D. V. (2007). The productivity argument for investing in your children. *Review of Agricultural Economics, 29,* 446–493.

Hill, N. E. (2001). Parenting and academic socialization as they relate to school readiness: The role of ethnicity and family income. *Journal of Educational Psychology, 93,* 686–697.

Hindman, A. H., & Wasik, B. A. (2008). Preschool teacher language and literacy beliefs questionnaire. *Early Childhood Research Quarterly, 23,* 479–492.

Hulsey, L. K., Aikens, N., Kopack, A., West, J., Moiduddin, E., & Tarullo, L. (2011). *Head start children, families, and programs: Present and past data from FACES. OPRE Report 2011-33a.* Washington, DC: Office of Planning, Research and Evaluation, Administration for Children and Families, U.S. Department of Health and Human Services.

Jordan, G. E., Snow, C. E., & Porche, M. V. (2000). Project EASE: The effect of a family literacy project on kindergarten students' early literacy skills. *Reading Research Quarterly, 35,* 524–556.

Juel, C. (1988). Learning to read and write: A longitudinal study of 54 children from first through fourth grades. *Journal of Educational Psychology, 80,* 437–447.

Justice, L. M., & Ezell, H. K. (2002). Use of storybook reading to increase print awareness in at-risk children. *American Journal of Speech-Language Pathology, 11,* 17–29.

Kirsch, I. S., Jungeblut, A., Jenkins, L, & Kolstad, A. (1993). *Adult literacy in America: A first look at the results of the National Adult Literacy Survey.* Washington, DC: Office of Educational Research and Improvement, U.S. Department of Education, NCES 93275, September 1993. Retrieved from http://nces.ed.gov/pubsearch/pubsinfo.asp?pubid=93275

Knoche, L. L., Kupzyk, K. A., & Plata-Potter, S. I. (2011a). *Sustained effects of an ecologically-based preschool intervention on the early language and literacy development of dual-language learners in a rural community.* Paper presented at the Society for Prevention Research Conference, Washington, DC.

Knoche, L. L., Plata-Potter, S. I., Raikes, H. H., & Kupzyk, K. A. (2011b). *Findings from Rural Language and Literacy Connections: An integrated approach to supporting low-income preschool children's language and literacy development.* Paper presented at the biennial meeting of the Society for Research in Child Development, Montreal, Canada.

Kurdek, L. A., & Sinclair, R. J. (2000). Psychological, family, and peer predictors of academic outcomes in first-through fifth-grade children. *Journal of Educational Psychology, 92*(3), 449.

La Paro, K. M., & Pianta, R. C. (2000). Predicting children's competence in the early school years: A meta-analytic review. *Review of Educational Research, 70*(4), 443–484.

Lonigan, C. J., & Whitehurst, G. J. (1998). Relative efficacy of parent and teacher involvement in a shared-reading intervention for preschool children from low-income backgrounds. *Early Childhood Research Quarterly, 13,* 263–290.

Lonigan, C. J., Anthony, J. L., Bloomfield, B. G., Dryer, S. M., & Samwel, C. S. (1999). Effects of two shared-reading interventions on emergent literacy skills of at-risk preschoolers. *Journal of Early Intervention, 22,* 306–322.

Miller, P., & Votruba-Drzal, E. (2013). Early academic skills and childhood experiences across the urban-rural continuum. *Early Childhood Research Quarterly, 28,* 234–248.

National Institute of Child Health and Human Development. (2000). *Report of the National Reading Panel. Teaching children to read: An evidence-based assessment of the scientific research literature on reading and its implications for reading instruction* (NIH Publication No. 00-4769). Washington, DC: U.S. Government Printing Office.

National Early Literacy Panel. (2008). *Developing early literacy: Report of the National Early Literacy Panel.* Washington, D.C: National Institute for Literacy. Retrieved from http://www.nifl.gov/earlychildhood/NELP/NELPreport.html

Neuman, S. B., & Gallagher, P. (1994). Joining together in literacy learning: Teenage mothers and children. *Reading Research Quarterly, 29,* 383–401.

Nye, C., Turner, H. M., & Schwartz, J. B. (2006). *Approaches to parental involvement for improving the academic performance of elementary school children in grades K–6*. London: The Campbell Collaboration. Available at http://campbellcollaboration.org/docpdf/Nye_PI_Review.pdf

Osborn, A. Q., Raikes, H., & Knoche, L. L. (2010, June). *Benefits of an early literacy preschool intervention: Follow-up findings in kindergarten*. Poster presented at the Head Start Tenth National Research Conference, Washington, DC.

Pearson Early Learning. (2006). *Read together, talk together*. Retrieved from http://www.pearsonearlylearning.com

Pianta, R. C., & McCoy, S. J. (1997). The first day of school: The predictive validity of early school screening. *Journal of Applied Developmental Psychology, 18*(1), 1–22.

Pinto, A., Pessanha, M., & Aguiar, C. (2013). Effects of home environment and center-based child care quality on children's language, communication, and literacy outcomes. *Early Childhood Research Quarterly, 28*, 94–101.

Reynolds, A. J. (1998). *The Chicago Child-Parent Center and Expansion Program: A study of extended early childhood intervention social programs that work* (pp. 110–147). New York, NY: Russell Sage Foundation.

Rimm-Kaufman, S. E., & Pianta, R. C. (2000). An ecological perspective on the transition to kindergarten: A theoretical framework to guide empirical research. *Journal of Applied Developmental Psychology, 21*, 491–511.

Schickedanz, J. A., Dickinson, D. K., & Charlotte-Mecklenburg Schools. (2005). *Opening the world of learning: A comprehensive early literacy program*. Parsippany, NJ: Pearson Early Learning.

Sénéchal, M., LeFevre, J., Hudson, E., & Lawson, P. (1996). Knowledge of storybooks as a predictor of young children's vocabulary. *Journal of Educational Psychology, 88*, 520–536.

Smith, L. (2010). *Child care in rural areas: Top challenges*. Arlington, VA: National Association of Child Care Resource and Referral Agencies. Retrieved from http://www.naccrra.org/sites/default/files/default_site_pages/2012/rural_top_concerns_070910.pdf

Smith, M., Patterson, K., & Doggett, L. (2008). *Meeting the challenge of rural Pre-K*. Retrieved from www.preknow.org

Snow, C. E., Tabors, P. O., & Dickinson, D. K. (2001). Language development in the preschool years. In D. K. Dickinson & P. O. Tabors (Eds.), *Beginning literacy with language* (pp. 1–25). Baltimore: Paul H. Brookes.

Stanovich, K. E. (1986). Matthew effects in reading: Some consequences of individual differences in the acquisition of literacy. *Reading Research Quarterly*, 360–407.

Storch, S. A., & Whitehurst, G. J. (2001). The role of family and home in the literacy development of children from low-income backgrounds. *New Directions for Child and Adolescent Development, 2001*(92), 53–72.

Tabors, P. O., Snow, C. E., & Dickinson, D. K. (2001). Homes and schools together: Supporting language and literacy development. In D. K. Dickinson & P. O. Tabors (Eds.), *Beginning literacy with language: Young children learning at home and school*. Baltimore, MD: Brookes Publishing.

Taverne, A., & Sheridan, S. M. (1995). Parent training in interactive book reading: An investigation of its effects with families at-risk. *School Psychology Quarterly, 10*, 41–64.

Taylor, B. M., & Pearson, P. D. (2004). Research on learning to read-at school, at home, and in the community. *Elementary School Journal., 105*(2), 168–181.

U.S. Department of Agriculture Economic Research Service. (2014). *Rural poverty and well-being. Poverty overview*. Retrieved from http://www.ers.usda.gov/topics/rural-economy-population/rural-poverty-well-being/poverty-overview.aspx#.U4YGEvldV8E

Vernon-Feagans, L., Gallagher, K., & Kainz, K. (2008). The transition to school in rural America: A focus on literacy. In J. Meece & J. Eccles (Eds.), *Handbook of research on schools, schooling, and human development*. New York, NY: Routledge, Taylor, & Associates.

Wasik, B. A., & Bond, M. A. (2001). Beyond the pages of a book: Interactive book reading and language development in preschool classrooms. *Journal of Educational Psychology, 93*, 243–250.

Whitehurst, G. J., Arnold, D. H., Epstein, J. N., Angell, A. L., Smith, M., & Fischel, J. E. (1994a). A picture book reading intervention in day care and home for children from low-income families. *Developmental Psychology, 30*, 679–689.

Whitehurst, G. J., Epstein, J. N., Angell, A. L., Payne, A. C., Crone, D. A., & Fischel, J. E. (1994b). Outcomes of an emergent literacy intervention in Head Start. *Journal of Educational Psychology, 86*(4), 542–555.

Whitehurst, G. J., & Lonigan, C. J. (1998). Child development and emergent literacy. *Child Development, 69*, 848–872.

Part III
Rural Education Research Findings Part 2: Family and Community Influences

Rural Parenting: Cumulative Risk and Parenting Process

Irina L. Mokrova, Lynne Vernon-Feagans and Patricia Garrett-Peters

Abstract In this chapter, we describe the Family Life Project, a large-scale longitudinal study that chronicles the lives of African American and non-African American children and their families living in two poor rural areas of the US: Appalachia and the Black South. The breadth of the Family Life Project data allows us to expand the previous literature on rural poverty and to highlight the notion that the effects of poverty are not limited to low levels of income, but are rather fused with several "correlated constraints" that co-occur with poverty: low maternal education, low job prestige, non-standard work hours, single parenthood, residential instability, and neighborhood safety. We use a cumulative risk perspective as a comprehensive way to describe the life in rural poverty and the disproportionate burden it puts on rural families as they navigate day-to-day life. We also look at two examples of parenting—the quality of mothers and fathers language input and the quality of mothers and fathers emotion talk—as we examine (1) parenting as a mediating link in the relation between cumulative risk and children's literacy skills, and (2) the role of fathers in the process of child development.

Keywords Parenting · Poverty · Rural families · Child development · Cumulative risk · Low income

1   Introduction

Seminal works by McLoyd (1990, 1998), Duncan and Books-Gunn (1997), and others have highlighted the importance of social and economic capital in affecting the quality of parenting and child development. Among the components that

I.L. Mokrova (✉)
Frank Porter Graham Child Development Institute, The University of North Carolina, CB#8040, Chapel Hill, NC 27599-8040, USA
e-mail: irina.mokrova@unc.edu

I.L. Mokrova · L. Vernon-Feagans · P. Garrett-Peters
The University of North Carolina, Chapel Hill, USA

© Springer International Publishing Switzerland 2017
G.C. Nugent et al. (eds.), *Rural Education Research in the United States*,
DOI 10.1007/978-3-319-42940-3_11

comprise social and economic capital, poverty has been implicated as perhaps the largest contributor to the lower quality of parenting and negative child outcomes. Most of the previous research in this area has focused on urban poverty while much less is known about the challenges of families who live in geographically isolated poor communities. These rural families may have unique challenges and supports compared to urban areas that create a somewhat different context for processes of parenting and children's development (Vernon-Feagans et al. 2012).

In this chapter, we describe the Family Life Project (FLP), an epidemiological longitudinal study that chronicles the lives of children and their families growing up in low wealth rural America. We use the FLP data to expand the previous literature on how families navigate the challenges of poverty and examine closely the exacerbating effects of being poor in African American and non-African American families who live in rural communities. While all the FLP families live in rural settings, the FLP sample allows us to contrast poor African American and non-African American families with their not poor counterparts. In this chapter we highlight the notion that effects of poverty are not limited to low levels of income, but are rather fused with several "correlated constraints" that co-occur with poverty. We provide a brief review of the previous research on poverty and rurality and discuss the use of a cumulative risk index, a theoretically-based and empirically-validated composite that incorporates most-often co-occurring concomitants of poverty, as a comprehensive way to describe the life in rural poverty.

We also highlight the disproportionate burden of poverty that poor rural families, and particularly African American poor families, experience as they navigate day-to-day life.

In the second part of the chapter we elaborate on two examples of parenting quality that the FLP project has examined: the quality of mothers and fathers language input and the quality of mothers and fathers emotion talk. We highlight the role of both mothers and fathers as important for their child's successful development. In the case of parental language input we also trace its role as a mediating link in the relation between cumulative risk index and children's literacy skills in early childhood. Based on the results from the FLP data we show that greater parental language input and greater levels of emotion talk among poor parents can buffer children from poor families, and particularly from poor African-American families, from the adverse effects of poverty.

1.1 The Family Life Project

The Family Life Project is a multidisciplinary longitudinal study that used an epidemiological sampling frame to recruit a sample of 1292 infants and their families residing in six poor rural counties in North Carolina and Pennsylvania. Poor families in North Carolina and Pennsylvania and African-American families in North Carolina were oversampled. The sampling frame in the Family Life Project was unique compared to previous research on rural populations and many previous studies of poverty. Of the four rural areas in the US identified with high rates of rural poverty (Dill 1999), two areas are located east of Mississippi: Appalachia and the "African American South". The FLP recruited a representative sample of families residing in six counties (3 contiguous counties in Pennsylvania and 3 contiguous counties in North Carolina) that contained mid-size and small towns and that are distant from urban centers (see Chap. 2 in Vernon-Feagans et al. 2013). As such, the FLP sample is generalizable to other populations residing in rural Appalachian Mountains and African American South. To increase the representativeness and generalizability of our sample, the FLP contacted over 90 % of mothers who gave birth to a baby in six target counties between September 2003 and September 2004, the targeted recruitment period. Eighty percent of eligible mothers agreed to participate in our study. This is an extremely high rate of contact and acceptance and these rates did not differ by race or socioeconomic status. Moreover the FLP was able to maintain a high level of participant retention, with over 75 % of families actively participating in the study 90 months after its inception.

As a multidisciplinary longitudinal study, the FLP placed a focus not only on the development of children who were born to parents living in low wealth rural comminutes, but also examined the overall functioning of families, with an emphasis on parenting. Primary caregivers, who were overwhelmingly biological mothers, were the most constant adults in the study children's lives but data were also collected on the secondary caregiver, usually fathers. As such, the FLP collected an unprecedented wealth of data about the mothers and fathers of young children living in poor rural communities. Data were collected on family life during multiple home visits and phone interviews over a seven year period, collecting a wide variety of developmental, contextual, and demographic information that helps to understand the development and functioning of children and adults in these families.

2 Families Living in Rural America: Correlated Constrains

Rural living has long had an image of picturesque landscapes, charming small towns, and close-knit communities. When urban/suburban dwellers think about rural settings, they envision a measured life style, with time for friends and family and with close proximity to nature. But the reality for many families who live in rural settings is often quite different from this idealistic view. Most rural areas of the US did not gain during the economically prosperous years of 1990s and early 2000s, which produced high level of economic growth on the heels of the technological revolution. The increased productivity and subsequent economic advances that resulted from incorporation of technology into all spheres of business were centered mainly in urban/suburban areas (Regional Educational Laboratory Network 2004). Moreover, the growing availability of imported foods, emergence of multi-national farming corporations, and mechanization of agriculture led to the demise of many small family-owned farms. Currently, only a very small percentage of all jobs in rural areas are farm-related (O'Hare and Johnson 2004). In addition, there has been a dramatic decrease in mining and manufacturing jobs as those largely relocated overseas in pursuit of cheaper labor force (Duncan 1999; O'Hare and Johnson 2004). These larger economic trends of globalization especially impacted many rural communities where mining, steel, textile, and furniture-related businesses had employed many rural adults in the past but now these industries have gone overseas. The higher-paying industrial jobs that were able to afford middle-class life styles to its workers 30–40 years ago were replaced by service sector jobs, particularly for adults without college education. The service sector jobs often entail low pay, low occupational prestige, few benefits, irregular work hours, and limited job security (Weber et al. 2002). Due largely to these economic changes as well as lack of educational and occupational opportunities, by the end of the 20th century there was a gradual out-migration of talented young adults from rural to urban areas, leaving behind an elderly population and a smaller, less-educated, young adult population (O'Hare and Johnson 2004; Weber et al. 2005).

2.1 Poverty in Rural America

One of the unwelcome consequences of this economic shift was an increase in poverty in rural America and a growing gap in poverty rates between urban/suburban and rural areas (Mattingly et al. 2011). Nationally, more than half (51 %) of rural families with children have incomes below 200 % of the federal poverty line (which is often an eligibility criterion for public services and is generally considered the minimal subsistence income level), compared to only 37 % of urban families with children in the same income bracket. This high rural poverty rate occurs despite the fact that 80 % of all rural families have a family member working full-time (Rivers 2005). Moreover, one-quarter of rural poor families who had two or more employed household members were still living in poverty. These data suggest that low-wage jobs, combined with geographic isolation, and limited access to higher education or vocational training are likely to impede poor rural families' chances of climbing out of poverty (Lichter et al. 2003). The out-migration of talented young adults from rural areas also contributes to the growing economic disparity between rural and urban/suburban areas: talented young adults are leaving their rural communities because of limited opportunities for life advancement; and once they leave, the overall social capital of their rural communities diminishes. That in turn leaves fewer resources, particularly in terms of social capital, for people who stay behind, including children.

The FLP project adopted a detailed and inclusive way to measure poverty and income levels of the participating families. We used the approach taken by Hanson et al. (1997) of basing household income on anyone who resides in the household, not simply those people related by blood, marriage, or adoption. At each home visit,

Fig. 1 Average
income-to-needs ratios, by
race and poverty status

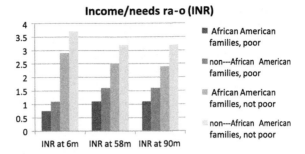

the primary caregiver reported on the annual income of members of the household and all other sources of income available to family members, such as unemployment insurance, social security retirement, child support, regular help from relatives or friends, or other incomes. An annual household total income then was calculated and divided by the federal poverty threshold for a household of that particular size and composition to create the income/needs ratio. For instance, a household of 2 adults and 2 children making $19,157 in 2004 would have an income/needs ratio of 1 or 100 % of the poverty line while this same family constellation making double that amount or $38,314 would have an income/needs ratio of 2 or 200 % of the poverty threshold. Because many anti-poverty programs have developed eligibility requirements up to 200 % of poverty, the FLP considered a family poor if they were below 200 % of the poverty line for that family size.

Our in-depth approach to measuring poverty revealed that about 68 % of the FLP families had income below 200 % poverty during their child's early years of life. Of all African American families participating in the FLP, over 80 % of families had income below 200 % poverty during their child's early years. This large difference in poverty rates indicates that rural African American families were disproportionately more poor compared to rural non-African American families. As Fig. 1 indicates, for most families in the FLP sample income levels did not change significantly during the first 7 years of their child's life. Moreover, the proportion of families, both African American and non-African American, who lived below 200 % poverty appeared fairly stable from 6 months to 7 years of age.

2.2 Educational Attainment in Rural America

Another demographic indicator that often co-occurs with poverty is low levels of education. With the broader economic changes of the last several decades, educational attainment is becoming a more significant predictor of financial stability than ever, where people who obtain college degrees are able to achieve middle class life styles, or "board the escalator upwards" to the higher income levels, whereas high school graduates are losing financial ground (Carnevale et al. 2010; Vernon-Feagans et al. 2015). Educational attainment of the FLP mothers

Fig. 2 Average levels of educational achievement, by race and poverty status

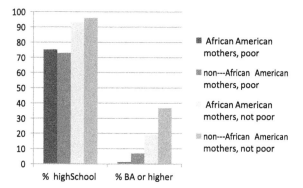

corresponds to the national data on levels of education in rural settings. Nation-wide, 30 % of urban/suburban adults have a college degree while only 17 % of rural adults have a college degree (USDA Economic Research Service 2012). Figure 2 shows percentages of high school and 4-year college degrees among African American and non-African American poor and not poor mothers. Overall, about 15 % of all FLP mothers did not complete high school and about 70 % of the mothers had a high school degree or its equivalent. In contrast, college graduation rate was only 15 %. Among poor mothers, only 1 % of African American women had a college degree and about 7 % of non-African American women had a college degree. Among not poor mothers, 19 % of African American women had a college degree and 37 % of non-African American women had a college degree. Thus, we observed striking, but unfortunately not surprising differences in the levels of educational attainment between poor and not poor mothers. Moreover, we do not see, on average, lower levels of education among African American mothers in our rural sample in comparison to their non-African American counterparts. Thus the educational differences between our poor and non poor are fairly dramatic with really no race differences. As we showed elsewhere (see Vernon-Feagans et al. 2015), it is precisely the difference between having and not having a 4-year college degree that sets people on divergent tracks in life with college educated women doing increasingly better than women who have a high school degree or less.

2.3 Parental Work and Work Hours in Rural America

Rural parents are likely to work longer hours but earn less than their urban counterparts. A common trend among rural families in recent decades was the increase in non-standard work hours and the increase in multiple jobs (Mather and Scopilliti 2004). The changes in work schedules from day-time standard work hours (approximately 9 a.m. to 5 p.m.) to non-standard work hours (i.e., evening, overnight, rotating, seasonal, or unpredictable hours) have disproportionately affected adults with lower levels of education. Currently, about 40 % of American labor force is working non-standard work hours, with lower educated adults are likely to have non-standard shift jobs both in rural and urban/suburban settings (Presser 2004). It had been argued, however, that with the disappearance of key industries that previously employed rural residents, there are now less opportunities in rural areas to find stable, standard work hour jobs (Vernon-Feagans et al. 2010). As such, many rural adults have no other choice but to accept service-sector or other non-standard types of work available to them.

Further, rural families commute longer distances to work and services, with only 40 % of rural areas having access to public transportation (Friedman 2003), which makes daily routines even harder to follow. In sum, non-standard work hours, multiple jobs, and long commutes translate into fewer hours that parents are able to devote to interacting with their children and being involved in their lives.

As a consequence in this shift in work patterns, combined with low levels of education and income, many aspects of family life are being negatively affected (Enchautegui 2013; Smith and Tickamyer 2011). For example, mothers who work non-standard hours during the early years of their child's life tend to have children with poorer language and cognitive skills at 36 months of age compared to mothers who work standard hours (Han 2005). In examining the African American families in FLP, findings were consistent with Han's findings that nonstandardwork schedules were associated with detrimental effects on children's early expressive language and uniquely identified maternal positive engagement and negative work–family spillover as partial mediators through which the association between mother's work schedules and children's expressive language ability might be explained (Odom et al. 2013).

In the Family Live Project, we observed several factors that contribute to hardship for rural parents and are likely to exert negative influence on parental ability to provide optimal parenting for their children. For example, many parents in our sample were working non-standard work hours (defined as any second shift, nigh shift. Over 15 % of families in the FLP sample did not have access to a working vehicle, which created additional barriers in accessing services and navigating day-to-day life. Overall, 64 % of mothers in our sample participated in labor force, either full time or part time, during the early childhood years of the study children. Of the working mothers, 38 % of poor mothers and about 25 % of not poor mothers had non-standard shifts (see Fig. 3 for the full race by poverty status percentages). Many not poor mothers, who were working non-standard hours, were employed at occupationally prestigious jobs, such as nurses or managers, and their employers provided health insurance, paid vacation leave, and other benefits. In contrast, many poor mothers with non-standard work hours were employed at less occupationally prestigious jobs, such as retail and food service industries, and often did not have employer-sponsored health insurances or other benefits.

Moreover, the quality of working conditions, aside from the standard/non-standard work shift differences, also varied greatly for mothers from poor and not poor groups. Working mothers' occupational self-direction was much higher for not poor mothers than for poor mothers.

Fig. 3 Percent of non-standard work hours, by race and poverty status

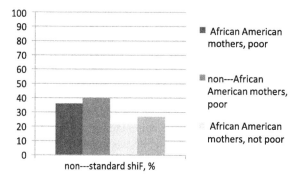

Occupational self-direction was defined as the degree of self-supervision, control of others, and decision-making power of the job; and was measured through mothers self-report on a number of questions such as making decisions about when to come and leave work, how to perform one's work, who to hire, etc. (Crouter et al. 2001; Lennon 1994). Prior evidence suggests that occupational self-direction of parents is associated with the quality of their parenting, such as ability to organize optimal environments for their children, provide less restrictive parenting, and offer more appropriate emotional and educational supports for their children (e.g., Kohn and Schooler 1978; Schooler and Schoenbach 1994). Parents who live in rural areas and have lower levels of occupational self-direction are the least likely to interact with their children in developmentally appropriate and nurturing ways than any other group of parents (Goodman et al. 2008). Ultimately, higher levels of occupational self-direction have been related to child cognitive and behavioral outcomes; and parenting processes have been indicated as mediating links in these relations (Crouter and McHale 2005; Menaghan and Parcel 1991).

Of other aspects of working conditions, poor working mothers in the FLP sample reported lower levels of supervisor support, lower levels of job flexibility (i.e., ability to deal with family matters during work hours or to arrange for flexible work hours to accommodate family needs), less employer-sponsored benefits, such as health insurance, retirement plan, and paid time-off, and higher levels of negative work-to-family spillover effects. The cumulative toll of these less than desirable factors depletes working mothers' ability to cope with life's challenges, increases their levels of stress, and diminishes psychological, social, and temporal resources available for their children.

2.4 Single Parenthood

Before the broader economic shift of the last four decades that has affected rural Americans' income standing, about 77 % of rural children lived in two-parent families compared to 72 % of urban children who lived in two-parent families. Since then, family structure in rural settings has been changing alongside the economic and educational opportunities. By 2007, only 66 % of rural children compared to 70 % of urban children lived in two-parent families (O'Hare 2009).

The decline in two-parent families with children in rural areas has direct implications for increasing rates of child poverty, as two parent families are less likely to live in poverty than other types of family structure. Despite the gradual decline in poverty rates among female-headed households after the welfare reform of 1996, families of single mothers in rural areas have continued to experience higher rates of poverty than families of single mothers in urban areas. This difference in poverty rates exists despite the fact that rural single mothers tend to work longer hours than their urban counterparts do, once again pointing to the fact that rural mothers have less access to or less skills required for higher paying jobs (Lichter and Jensen 2001).

The aggregated data on single mothers masks the large racial differences in terms of single parenthood in rural areas. African American women who live in rural areas are twice as likely to be single mothers and to be poor in comparison to other women (Graefe and Lichter 2002). One-parent family structure generally provides children with a smaller economic base and less access to parental time. It also puts greater pressure on the parent who is the sole provider and caregiver to his or her children. Moreover, single mothers of young children in rural areas, as compared to single mothers in urban areas, are likely to have more barriers to sustaining work due to the difficulties of finding reliable transportation to child care and to work. This may be an even greater challenge for African American single mothers because they tend to be much poorer than non-African American single mothers (Bratsch 2008).

The data from the Family Life Project confirms these major trends. As Fig. 4 indicates, poor African American mothers in the FLP sample were twice as likely to be single mothers as other mothers were. Overall, only 8 % of not poor mothers were single mothers at the time of their child's birth, whereas almost half of poor mothers (47 %) reported to be single mothers; and these differences did not change dramatically over the children's early childhood years. Being a single parent undoubtedly adds psychological and economic pressure on any mother. Single mothers living in rural contexts tend to be poorer than urban/suburban single mothers, but there are also protective factors that may be unique to families living in

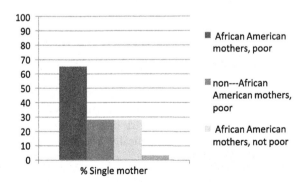

Fig. 4 Single parenthood, percent, by race and poverty status

rural contexts. For example, rural single mothers report greater levels of religiosity, support from relatives and friends, and greater levels of neighborhood safety compared to urban single mothers (Brody and Flor 1998; Murry and Brody 1999). In the FLP sample, single mothers also reported high levels of social support from family, friends, and religious organizations, and there were no large differences in these forms of support between poor and not poor mothers. These findings reiterate the notion of the importance of social support for families residing in rural settings (Seiling et al. 2011), as more formal types of support, such as social service programs, may not be readily available for parents and children in rural communities. That makes informal, community-based social supports ever more valuable for rural populations.

2.5 Poverty and Associated Risks: A Cumulative Risk Index

Low levels of income are seldom the only attributes of poverty. A number of factors that tend to co-occur with poverty contribute to parental hardship and less than optimal development among rural children, including diminished academic achievement, lower levels of physical and mental health, and higher levels of behavior problems. Low levels of education, long commutes and non-standard work hours, higher levels of residential instability, and greater likelihood of single-parent status are likely not independent of each other but likely co-occur and have been called "correlated constraints" on development because they are bundled with other risk factors (Burchinal et al. 2000, 2006, 2008; Cairns et al. 1998; Vernon-Feagans et al. 2013). Moreover, the effects of poverty on child development and achievement cannot be easily separated from the effects of these highly related risk factors. The work of Sameroff, Rutter, and Garmezy (Garmezy and Rutter 1988; Haggerty et al. 1996; Rutter 1990; Sameroff and Chandler 1975; Sameroff and Seifer 1995) has focused on the development of a cumulative risk framework as an overarching and omnipresent context in which families affected by poverty live. Based on this framework, prior research with the FLP data showed that a quantifiable index of cumulative risk can be calculated using a combination of many of the individual risk factors. The FLP successfully used this index as a measure of the magnitude of hardship experienced by poor families in rural America on daily basis. Cumulative risk index can also serve as a comprehensive predictor of parenting behaviors (see Burchinal et al. 2008; Vernon-Feagans et al. 2013). Moreover, previous work that documented the high level of co-variation between poverty and its associated factors also showed that this concomitance of risks predicts poor child outcomes better than any risk factor did alone (e.g., Burchinal et al. 2000, 2006; Vernon-Feagans et al. 2013).

   To create the cumulative risk index, the FLP team carefully selected individual risk factors that were theoretically and empirically linked to negative child outcomes in early childhood.

These individual factors included the following: level of maternal education, single parenthood status, employment hours, family income/needs ratio, occupational prestige, household density, and neighborhood safety. A series of factor analysis models confirmed that these individual risk factors indeed form one factor of cumulative risk and that this factor was reliable ($\alpha = 0.76–0.79$) and stable over time ($0.82 < r < 0.91$). The higher cumulative risk index was represented as a factor-score of these individual risks, The higher the index, the higher level of risk a particular family faced, and by extension, the higher level of negative developmental outcomes could be expected for children in that family. Given that African American families had lower levels of income, lower levels of occupational prestige, higher rates of single parenthood, and higher levels of household density than non-African American families, it was anticipated that African American families had higher level of cumulative risk. Indeed, when the "correlated constraints" of poverty are aggregated together, they show that overall African American families in the FP sample face more risk that non-African American families do; and that the racial gap in the level of risk is still present when only poor African American and poor non-African American families are compared (see Fig. 5).

Such vast disparities faced by rural African American families in general and by poor African American families in particular indicate a high level of vulnerability to negative outcomes among parents and children in these families. In that, the FLP findings supported prior studies reporting higher levels of poverty and risk among African American rural families (O'Hare 2009). The FLP also found that relying on informal, community-based support systems, such as churches, religious groups, and extended families was often times the most readily available source of support for families living in rural settings, especially poor families.

As documented in detail elsewhere (see Vernon-Feagans et al. 2013), the FLP data indicated that higher levels of cumulative risk are associated with negative child outcomes partially through suboptimal parenting practices. In the second part of the chapter, we use parental language input as a specific example of mediating role of parenting practices in the relation between cumulative risk and children's literacy skills. Moreover, we focus on the role of fathers as unique contributors to child development, as well as on the role of mothers and fathers' emotion talk in children's social-emotional development. In situations when we as society cannot

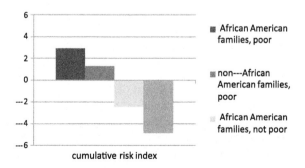

Fig. 5 Cumulative risk index, by race and poverty status

alleviate the burdens of poverty to a degree where the poverty does not pose a risk for the development of children, perhaps we should focus on helping poor parents to acquire adequate parenting skills that could, ideally, protect children from the worst brunt of growing up in poverty. Additionally, we should focus on strengthening social support systems available to mothers of young children, particularly those who reside in the context of rural poverty. As the FLP data illuminates on the fathers' role in child development, the presence of a second adult in a family can improve children's developmental outcomes in early childhood years. We would like to highlight that it is likely the presence of a second caring and capable adult that makes this difference rather than the presence of a father per se. As such, in the discussion below we receive fathers as a specific and the most common example of a secondary caregiver to young children.

3   The Quality of Parental Language Input in Low Wealth Rural America

It is likely that no matter where a family lives, poverty exerts its greatest impact on early child development through the way parents engage with their children and through parental ability to provide the resources that promote the optimal child development, such as books in the home and children's participation in enrichment activities. Recent evidence suggested that the gap between more educated middle income families and less educated lower income families with respect to these important resources is growing wider, with college educated parents spending increasingly more time and resources on their children compared to non-college educated parents (Duncan and Murnane 2011; Reardon 2011; Vernon-Feagans et al. 2015). There is now some evidence that poverty indirectly influences child development through parental educational levels that may be a proxy for "good parenting". For example, a recent study by Kalil et al. (2012) examined the relationship between maternal education and the amount of time mothers spent in various activities with their children at different ages. College-educated mothers shifted their time with children in response to child developmental needs. These mothers spent more time talking with and teaching their children in early childhood, but at school age they spent more time helping manage children's activities.

This shift in time allocation was not apparent in the non-college-educated mothers' time. The gap in parenting quality and provision of resources between mothers with and without college degree may be even greater in the rural United States because only a small percentage of adults living in rural America have a college degree.

One of the critical elements of good parenting for children's school readiness is high quality parental language interactions with children starting early in life. Research has generally focused on maternal language input, measuring the diversity of the vocabulary as well as the complexity of talk that mothers use while interacting with their young children (Bornstein et al. 1998; Hart and Risley 1995;

Hoff 2003; Huttenlocher et al. 1991; Pan et al. 2005; Vernon-Feagans et al. 2013; Weizman and Snow 2001). These studies have measured mother language input in a variety of contexts, including toy play, mealtime, and book activities. Although these previous studies have clearly demonstrated the importance of parental language for children's early language and literacy development, very few of these studies have examined language input by fathers as well as mothers and even fewer have examined mother and father language input in rural and/or minority families.

There is growing evidence on the importance of both mothers and fathers for the development of their children. A recent theoretical article on the role of fathers in addition to that of mothers (Cabrera et al. 2014) suggests both the complementary and unique contributions of fathers to various domains of child development. The literature within the field of language development supports these propositions. For example, fathers from African-American families across a spectrum of SES were found to vocalize more and to be more affectionate with their 3–4-month-old infants, while mothers were more available to their infants and fed them more (Roopnarine et al. 2005). Fathers of 2-year-old children from rural Caucasian families used more language that presented conversational challenges to their children (Rowe et al. 2004) and used more different words in their interactions with their children, resulting in better children's expressive language skills one year later (Pancsofar and Vernon-Feagans 2006). Language input is one of the ways fathers may play a unique role in helping children develop the skills they will need for success in school. This may be especially important in rural families, where there are fewer resources outside of the home and fewer opportunities to interact with others outside of the family. The presence of a second caregiver may also be important for African American families where the rates of single parenthood are higher than in other racial groups.

3.1 Mother and Father Language in the FLP

The FLP data was used in a series of studies that have examined mother and father language input across early childhood in the subsample of families with a continuously present father figure in the home. On average this included approximately 500 of the nearly 1300 children in the sample. The data on language interactions came from videotaped sessions in which mothers and fathers shared a wordless picturebook with their child in separate sessions. This kind of book sharing by parents and children has been linked to children's later literacy skills through the enhancement of children's vocabularies and other mechanisms (Neuman 1997; Payne et al. 1994; Ninio 1983; Sénéchal et al. 1996). Because of the ethnic diversity of the families in the FLP sample, all books that were used in the picturebook task were photo-shopped to create racially ambiguous book characters. These sessions were later transcribed using system that calculated the mean length of utterance, length of dialogues, proportion of complex conjunctions, and number of different words.

Results from the Family Life Project analysis in early and later preschool years indicated that fathers' language contributions made a difference for children's literacy skills. In early childhood, the FLP found that the language input during the picturebook session in the home yielded important differential prediction to child language by mothers and fathers, even though there were no mean differences between mothers and fathers in the total number of words or the number of different words during the picturebook sessions. The analysis indicated that maternal education, but not maternal vocabulary, was related to children's later language skills; while both father education and father vocabulary were related to more advanced child language skills (Pancsofar et al. 2010). Another FLP study (Baker and Vernon-Feagans 2015), examined father language input during the picturebook session just prior to kindergarten entry in relation to end of kindergarten literacy and math skills (measured through Woodcock-Johnson III-R achievement tests). There were no differences between mother and fathers in terms of language complexity during the picturebook session at this age, but both mother and father language complexity appeared to be important predictor of child academic skills. After controlling for demographic characteristics, fathers' complexity of language predicted children's math literacy skills above and beyond mothers' language input. Interestingly, father education was no longer a significant predictor of child outcomes while mothers' education remained significant. Thus by 60 months, both mother and father language complexity, and maternal level of education seem to be uniquely and independently contributing to children's literacy skills at the end of kindergarten year.

3.2   Cumulative Risk, Maternal Language and Child Outcomes in FLP

Although poverty and education have consistently been linked to poorer outcomes for children, FLP has argued that it is important to consider the combined risks of poverty for children who live in low resourced environments. As presented in detail in a recent monograph of the SRCD (Vernon-Feagans et al. 2013), the FLP examined the relation between cumulative risk index over the first 3 years of life and children's skills by the age of three. Parenting was proposed as an important mediator in this relation. Here we discuss the findings regarding the quality of maternal language input as one example of such mediation. The FLP created stable longitudinal composites of maternal language that represented maternal language input and complexity during the picturebook sessions at four home visits over the children's first 3 years of life. We found that the complexity of maternal language was an important predictor of child language and a mediator between family's cumulative risk score and child language skills. Our findings confirm other reports in literature that found similar associations between quality of parental language input and child skills (Hoff 2003; Huttenlocher et al. 2002; Pan et al. 2005).

It is hard to compare our findings to previous studies that have not used a cumulative risk framework or have not used a rural sample. Yet, the FLP cumulative risk models accounted for 22 % of the variance in 36-month expressive language and 25 % of the variance in receptive language. In studies that relied on maternal education or an SES composite in predicting children's early language, much less variance in child language outcomes was explained (Feagans and Farran 1994; Hart and Risley 1995; Hoff 2006). For instance, Hoff and Tian (2005) reported that maternal SES accounted only for 5 % of the variance in children's early vocabulary. It is likely that the combination of various types of risks creates an overarching context for child development that may be conducive, if risks are small, or detrimental, if risks are large, to optimal child development and that is the reason behind the cumulative risk index explaining large variance of children's language skills. It also may be the case that cumulative risk index accounts for more of the variance in language outcomes in a rural environment because children have been more geographically isolated in rural areas with less access to other stimulating resources that are found in urban areas, such as libraries. In a rural context these outside the family influences may not be accessible to many children, thus contributing to the greater influence of the family as well as the cumulative risk index on child development.

4 Parent Internal State Language: Emotion and Mental State Language

In the final section of this chapter we draw attention to one unique aspect of parental language—emotion and mental state language—that can serve as another example of protective process in low wealth rural areas, and that was found to be particularly prominent among African American families in the FLP sample. Human language is unique in that it permits talk about the abstract and objects that are outside our immediate perceptual experience. This discourse can take many forms, such as talk about memories of the past, a hypothetical future, or imaginary objects such as "a flying pink elephant". Human language also affords us ability to talk about internal psychological experiences. Talk about internal states can take many forms including discourse about emotions, such as "happiness", "anger, or "sadness", and mental states, such as verbs like "think", "know", and "want" (Harris 2007).

Of empirical interest has been to understand how families socialize their children through their talk about the psychological world, as well as to describe the positive developmental consequences of children's exposure to parents' internal state language. In the Family Life Project, we have also sought to identify the characteristics of parents who tend to use internal state language, and hence, potentially support children's adaptive functioning by drawing attention to and thinking about internal psychological experiences. First, we describe some of the previous literature outlining the positive developmental consequences of two types of parent internal state language (i.e., emotion language and mental state language), followed by summaries of research using the FLP aimed at identifying characteristics of parents who are predisposed to use these types of internal state language with their children. Identifying the characteristics of parents who are likely to provide this enriched language environment to their children is particularly important in the context of rural poverty where risks to parenting and child development are often greater than in higher resourced and more urban areas.

4.1 Parent Emotion Language: Developmental Consequences

By engaging in emotion-related discourse, parents can heighten children's awareness of emotional states and experiences and promote children's emotion-related conceptual systems (Malatesta and Haviland 1982). Indeed, mothers' willingness to engage in emotion-related discussions has been found to contribute positively to children's own use of emotion language and their awareness and understanding of others' emotional states (Denham et al. 1994; Dunn et al. 1991; LaBounty et al. 2008; Martin and Green 2005). In seminal works, Dunn et al. (1987, 1991) found that observed references to feeling states by mothers and older siblings when toddlers were 18 months old predicted toddlers' references to feeling states 6 months later. Additionally, mothers' emotion talk to 36 month olds was positively associated with children's use of emotion terms and emotion understanding at 40 months and 6 years of age. This early exposure to maternal discussion of emotions likely contributes to emotion understanding by facilitating children's ability to identify and discuss emotions.

Children who possess these emotion understanding skills are able to engage in more prosocial behaviors, have more successful peer relationships (Ensor and Hughes 2005; Fabes et al. 2001), exhibit fewer aggressive behaviors with peers, and demonstrate greater social competence and fewer behavior problems in both preschool and elementary school (Castro et al. 2015; Denham et al. 2002; Garrett-Peters et al. 2015; Hughes et al. 1998). Mothers who engage in early emotion discussions likely promote these social-emotional competencies by providing a context in which children are primed for the processing of emotional aspects of the environment thereby facilitating the early socialization of emotion awareness, understanding, and regulation.

4.2 Parent Emotion Language: Predictors in the Family Life Project

Given the wealth of research supporting the developmental advantages of children's frequent exposure to parent emotion language, we used data from the FLP to identify characteristics of parents who provided this enriched language environment in the context of rural poverty. Identifying parents who set the stage for children's early emotion awareness and understanding is particularly important among low-income families such as those in the FLP, because low-income children tend to be less advanced in social cognitive development in the preschool years (Pears and Moses 2003), and they benefit from emotion understanding by having fewer behavior problems later in life (Schultz et al. 2001).

In our studies of parents in the FLP, we adopted a multivariate ecological framework (Bronfenbrenner and Evans 2000) to examine factors at multiple levels, including family demographics, family context, child, and parent qualities to identify characteristics of mothers' and fathers' who were predisposed to reference positive and negative emotions when viewing a wordless picture book of baby faces showing different emotions with their 7 month old infants. We examined parent talk to infants, as opposed to older children, because preverbal infants cannot directly elicit emotional discourse from their parents (e.g., through questioning). Thus, our assessment of parent emotion talk with infants provides a more precise and untainted measure of parents' emotion language than studies of parent language with older children.

We found that mothers who were African American, had higher income, or who demonstrated more positive engagement with their infant during a separate parent-child play task referenced positive emotions more often during the picture book interaction (Garrett-Peters et al. 2008).

Positive emotions were referenced more often for fathers also if they were African American, or if their partners (i.e., the child's mother) also frequently referenced positive emotions, or if their infants were more attentive during the picture book task (Garrett-Peters et al. 2011) However, only those African American fathers who showed more negative intrusiveness during a separate play task had high rates of positive emotion talk. This finding points to the possibility that group differences in cultural processes and beliefs about childrearing may lead African American fathers to view their negative intrusive behaviors as indicative of care, involvement, and concern for the proper socialization of their children (Garrett-Peters et al. 2011; Gibson-Davis and Grassman-Pines 2010).

Identifying the characteristics of parents who were more likely to reference negative emotions during the picture book interaction was less straight forward given that social context variables (i.e., ethnicity and income) moderated several significant effects. Only a few of those findings will be reviewed here. (For a full discussion of results see Garrett-Peters et al. 2008, 2011). Once again, African American parents referenced negative emotions more frequently than did non-African American parents. However, this was true for African American mothers more often when their children were attentive during the picture book task. For African American fathers, this was true for those with higher household income levels.

Perceived discrimination has been cited as a possible factor that heightens the salience of emotional stimuli among African Americans and may consequently lead to more freqent emotion references in the parent-child discourse of African American parents, as they prepare their children to be vigilant and aware of the emotional expressions of others (Garrett-Peters et al. 2008, 2011; Odom et al. 2014). We found support for this proposition in a study of FLP families that focused exclusively on African American mothers (Odom et al. 2014). Mothers who reported higher perceived discrimination and had fewer psychological supports referenced emotions more often during a picture book interaction with their 24 month old toddlers than did mothers who reported lower perceived discrimination.

4.3 Parent Mental State Language: Developmental Consequences

There is a growing consensus that parent mental state talk plays a critical role in children's early social cognitive understanding (Taumoepeau and Ruffman 2008). Variations in mothers' mental state talk occurring as early as 6 and 15 months have been linked to children's later use of mental state talk, emotion understanding, and false belief understanding (Meins et al. 2002, 2003; Taumoepeau and Ruffman 2006, 2008). Specifically, mothers who use more early mental state language have children who later use more mental state talk and perform better on tasks of emotion understanding and false belief understanding by preschool. These studies suggest that variation in maternal mental state language predicts individual differences in children's early social cognitive development.

Children are exposed to different levels of mental state talk in their families (Jenkins et al. 2003), and contributions of other family members, particularly fathers, have received increasing attention. Research indicates that fathers' appropriate references to their 6 month old infants' internal states (e.g., knowing, thinking, feelings) are associated with attachment security at 12 months of age (e.g., Arnott and Meins 2007). LaBounty et al. (2008) reported that fathers' use of explanation around desire terms (e.g., want, like) when children were 3½ years old was related to children's theory of mind performance both concurrently and at age 5. These findings suggest that fathers who talk about mental states with their young children provide an important context for the development of their children's socio-cognitive understanding. Although rarely studied, it is particularly important to examine parents' use of mental state language among poor and/or minority families whose children may be at risk for social cognitive deficits (Ensor and Hughes 2007).

4.4 Parent Mental State Language: Parent Predictors in the Family Life Project

In a study of the FLP families, many of whom are at risk due to poverty and/or minority status, we examined the extent to which social contextual factors, family factors, and parent characteristics contributed to individual variation in parents' use of mental state language with their infants during the same parent-infant picture book interaction described above (Garrett-Peters et al. 2009, 2011). We found that mothers referenced mental states more often than fathers during the picture book interaction. In addition, those mothers and fathers who showed more warmth/sensitivity toward their infant during a separate parent-child play task referred to mental states more often. African American parents were more likely to use mental state language if their partner did also, suggesting that there may be more partner coherence in mental state talk among African American families and a greater likelihood of mutual influence among parents (King 1994; Coley and Chase-Lansdale 1999).

In sum, our studies of internal state language use among parents in the FLP suggest that, even in at-risk families, parents are providing enriched language environments as early as the infancy years in the form frequent talk about internal psychological states (i.e., emotion language and mental state language). Not surprisingly, FLP parents who were more positively engaged, sensitive, and responsive with their infants were, in general, more likely to provide these enriched language environments. Perhaps most striking was our finding that, in general, these enriched language environments were more often observed in our African American families who are poorer than our non-African American families and who face increased risk due to concomitants of poverty and to minority status. However, questions remain unanswered regarding the extent to which the use of internal state language by parents in the FLP might facilitate and support children's social, cognitive, and emotional development in this high poverty rural sample.

5 Summary

The purpose of this chapter was to describe the context of lives of parents and children who participate in the Family Life Project, a multidisciplinary longitudinal study of nearly 1300 families living in rural areas of Appalachia and the South. We described the contexts of lives of poor and not poor African American and non-African American families in our sample, indicating that African American families tend to be poorer than non-African American families, even though there are few differences in levels of education between African American and non-African American parents. We also introduced the framework of cumulative risk indices, a combination of social risk factors, such as income levels, maternal education, single parenthood, parental work conditions and occupational status, residential instability, and neighborhood risks, as a more comprehensive and overarching descriptor of the context of lives of families living in poverty. We discussed the fact that cumulative risk index often serves as a stronger predictor for various child outcomes than any of the individual risk factors that are associated with poverty, primarily for two reasons. First, poverty has many correlated constraints, all of which contribute to the level of stress in navigating day-to-day life, and by extension diminishing parental resources that are available to their children. Second, risk factors that constitute cumulative risk index, describe multiple aspects of social context in which children and their family live. These risk factors can be viewed as comprehensive, omnipresent characteristics of family life and its social fabric, and as such can indeed have great effects on child developmental trajectories.

Given that cumulative risk framework has been shown to be useful in describing parenting processes and their relations to child outcomes, in the second part of the chapter we reviewed research conducted with the FLP data that traced the relations between cumulative risk index and children's literacy skills, with the quality of parental language input servings as a mediating factor. That clearly was only one of many parenting processes that can be viewed as process mechanisms through which cumulative risk is associated with diminished child outcome. More comprehensive analyses on this topic are presented in the Monographs of the SRCD (Vernon-Feagans et al. 2013). We also examined the developmental outcomes and parenting practices, especially with an emphasis on fathers, that were observed in the FLP in relation to mother talk and child language. In a series of studies, fathers appeared to play an important and maybe an even more important role in children's early language and academic skills than mothers. FLP also examined the role of parental emotion and mental state language. We found that African American parents, on average, provide more emotion and mental state language talk to their children, which can serve as a protective factor particularly for children from poor families.

6   Future Directions

The Family Life Project has been the only large epidemiological and developmental study of rural families living in low wealth communities. The strength of the study is in its epidemiological frame so the study was able to recruit a representative sample of children while oversampling for African American and poverty status. The extremely low attrition from 2 to 10 % over early childhood and early school years is a testament to the expertise and commitment of our staff of the Family Life Project who live in these communities, with most of the staff still with our project after almost 12 years. In addition, the multidisciplinary team of investigators (including developmental psychologists, sociologists, educators, and physicians) allowed a multifaceted picture of the children and their families. Thus, this study has been able to depict the lives of families and their children in a deeper and more interdisciplinary way than other studies through many home, childcare, and school visits (Vernon-Feagans et al. 2013). The portrait of these families who live in low wealth rural America in the Eastern part of the United States gives a window into the struggles they have faced as they raise their children with fewer resources than other families. The carefully planned visits to families many times in the early part of the children's lives yielded impressive data that can now be accessed as a public use data set at the University of Michigan. The findings presented in this chapter are but a small part of the information gathered and published on the children in this study. Our findings suggest the powerful role of poverty and parenting in understanding children's early development, with a special emphasis in this chapter on the language input of both African American and non-African American parents. Our findings demonstrate the powerful interconnections among poverty and its related risks as well as how parenting may be compromised by the many challenges families face with fewer resources and less predictability in their work and home lives.

Yet, there are many unanswered questions that remain about the lives of rural children and their families. The Family Life Project did not focus on all rural families and thus many Midwestern and Western areas of the United States were not included in this study. These other parts of the country have areas of greater wealth (Midwest farm belt) and also pockets of greater poverty (Native American reservation areas). It would be important to have other studies to examine whether there would be similar findings in other rural areas of the country. A major limitation of this study was the lack of Hispanic families. The growing Hispanic population in rural areas has not been studied intensively, even though we have evidence that Hispanic family life may be more cohesive and important than in other families (Cabrera and Bradley 2012; Coll et al. 1998).

Future studies might include a more diverse group of children and families in other rural areas of the United States to examine the role of family, fathers, and other factors that might influence children's early development. It would also be helpful to have comparison groups of children growing up in urban and suburban areas who are somewhat matched to the children in rural America. These studies might focus more on not only the nuclear family but the importance of extended family and friends, jobs, and services outside the family. It may also be important to examine institutions that might support families, such as religious organizations and other formal support groups. As children grow older parenting may still play a major role but other influences become more salient, such as children's schools, peers, and outside activities that have been found to play an important role in studies of rural adolescence (Brody et al. 2010; Conger 2013; Conger et al. 1994; Murry et al. 2005). Thus, the context and risk factors may change as children get older and those factors need to be included to understand how development occurs in the context of changing risk and protective factors in rural America in comparison to more urban America.

It does appear that the context for development may be somewhat different in rural America and thus implications for intervention and prevention programs may need to be tailored to fit the rural context (Murry et al. 2005, 2008; Simons et al. 2006). For instance, the role of fathers may be more important in rural America and could be a target for intervention strategies within the family, given our findings about the importance of father language for children's language and academic skills. Using the more advanced emotion talk skills of African American mothers and fathers may provide information about the strength of African American families relative to other families and provide a way to tailor interventions to build on that strength. In general this chapter would suggest that although poverty is pervasive in the families studied in the FLP, parenting may be a particularly important place to begin thinking about interventions that can help support parenting that can lead to better outcomes for children.

References

Arnott, B., & Meins, E. (2007). Links among antenatal attachment representations, postnatal mind-mindedness, and infant attachment security: A preliminary study of mothers and fathers. *Bulletin of the Menninger Clinic, 71*(2), 132–149.

Baker, C. E., & Vernon-Feagans, L. (2015). Fathers' language input during shared book activities: Links to children's kindergarten achievement. *Journal of Applied Developmental Psychology*, 3653–3659. doi:10.1016/j.appdev.2014.11.009

Bornstein, M. H., Haynes, M. O., & Painter, K. M. (1998). Sources of child vocabulary competence: A multivariate model. *Journal of Child Language, 25*, 367–393.

Bratsch, M. (2008). *Rural African American families' child care placement: Examined through child age, economic, education, social support, and geographic isolation measures.* M.A. dissertation. Retrieved June 25, 2010, from Dissertations & Theses @ University of North Carolina at Chapel Hill (Publication No. AAT 1454477).

Brody, G. H., Chen, Y., & Kogan, S. M. (2010). A cascade model connecting life stress to risk behavior among rural African American emerging adults. *Development and Psychopathology, 22*(3), 667–678. doi:10.1017/S0954579410000350

Brody, G. H., & Flor, D. (1998). Maternal resources, parenting practices, and child competence in rural, single-parent African-American families. *Child Development, 69*, 803–816.

Bronfenbrenner, U., & Evans, G. W. (2000). Developmental science in the 21st century: Emerging questions, theoretical models, research designs and empirical findings. *Social Development, 9* (1), 115–125.

Burchinal, M. R., Roberts, J. E., Hooper, S., & Zeisel, S. A. (2000). Cumulative risk and early cognitive development: A comparison of statistical risk models. *Developmental Psychology, 36*, 793–807.

Burchinal, M. R., Roberts, J. E., Zeisel, S. A., Hennon, E. A., & Hooper, S. (2006). Risk and resiliency: Protective factors in early elementary school years. *Parenting: Science and Practice, 6*, 79–113. doi:10.1207/s15327922par0601_4

Burchinal, P, Vernon-Feagans, L. & Cox, M. & The Family Life Project Investigators (2008). Cumulative social risk, parenting, and infant development in rural low-income communities. *Parenting: Science and Practice, 8*(1), 41–69.

Cabrera, N. J., & Bradley, R. H. (2012). Latino fathers and their children. *Child Development Perspectives, 6*(3), 232–238. doi:10.1111/j.1750-8606.2012.00249.x

Cabrera, N. J., Hofferth, S. L., & Hancock, G. (2014). Family structure, maternal employment, and change in children's externalizing problem behaviour: Differences by age and self-regulation. *European Journal of Developmental Psychology, 11*(2), 136–158.

Cairns, R. B., Cairns, B. D., Rodkin, P., & Xie, H. (1998). New directions in developmental research: Models and methods. In R. Jessor & R. Jessor (Eds.), *New perspectives on adolescent risk behavior* (pp. 13–40). New York, NY: Cambridge University Press. doi:10.1017/CBO9780511571138.003

Carnevale, A. P., Smith, N., & Strohl, J. (2010). *Help wanted: Projections of job and education requirements through 2018*. Lumina Foundation.

Castro, V. L., Halberstadt, A. G., & Garrett-Peters, P. (2015). A three-factor structure of emotion understanding in middle childhood. *Social development* (Manuscript submitted for publication).

Coley, R. L., & Chase-Lansdale, P. L. (1999). Stability and change in paternal involvement among urban African American fathers. *Journal of Family Psychology, 13*(3), 416–435.

Coll, C. G., Lamberty, G., Jenkins, R., McAdoo, H. P., Crnic, K., Wasik, B. H., et al. (1998). An integrative model for the study of developmental competencies in minority children. In M. E. Hertzig, E. A. Farber, M. E. Hertzig, & E. A. Farber (Eds.), *Annual progress in child psychiatry and child development: 1997* (pp. 437–463). Philadelphia, PA: Brunner/Mazel.

Conger, R. D. (2013). Rural children at risk. *Monographs of the Society for Research in Child Development, 78*(5), 127–138. doi:10.1111/mono.12055

Conger, R. D., Elder, G. J., Lorenz, F. O., Simons, R. L., & Whitbeck, L. B. (1994). *Families in troubled times: Adapting to change in rural America*. Hawthorne, NY: Aldine de Gruyter.

Crouter, A. C., Bumpus, M., Head, M., & McHale, S. M. (2001). Implications of overwork and overload for the quality of men's family relationships. *Journal of Marriage and Family, 63*, 404–417.

Crouter, A. C., & McHale, S. M. (2005). Work, family, and children's time: Implications for youth. *Work, family, health, and well-being* (pp. 49–66).

Denham, S. A., Caverly, S., Schmidt, M., Blair, K., De Mulder, E., & Caal, S. (2002). Preschool understanding of emotions: Contributions to classroom anger and aggression. *Journal of Child Psychology and Psychiatry, 43*(7), 901–916.

Denham, S. A., Zoller, D., & Couchoud, E. A. (1994). Socialization of preschoolers' emotion understanding. *Developmental Psychology, 30*(6), 928–936.

Dill, B. T. (1999). *Poverty in the rural U.S.: Implications for children, families, and communities*. Literature review prepared for The Annie E. Casey Foundation.

Duncan, C. M. (1999). *Worlds apart: Why poverty persists in rural America*. New Haven: Yale University Press.

Duncan, G., & Brooks-Gunn, J. (Eds.). (1997). *Consequences of growing up poor*. New York: Russell Sage Foundation.

Duncan, G. J., & Murnane, R. J. (Eds.). (2011). *Whither opportunity? Rising inequality, schools, and children's life chances*. New York: Russell Sage Foundation.

Dunn, J., Bretherton, I., & Munn, P. (1987). Conversations about feeling states between mothers and their young children. *Developmental Psychology, 23*(1), 132–139.

Dunn, J., Brown, J., & Beardsall, L. (1991). Family talk about feeling states and children's later understanding of others' emotions. *Developmental Psychology, 27*(3), 448–455.

Enchautegui, M. E. (2013). *Nonstandard work schedules and well-being of low income families (Paper# 26)*. Washington, DC: Urban Institute.

Ensor, R., & Hughes, C. (2005). More than talk: Relations between emotion understanding and positive behaviour in toddlers. *British Journal of Developmental Psychology, 23*(3), 343–363.

Ensor, R., & Hughes, C. (2007). Executive function and theory of mind: Predictive relations from ages 2 to 4. *Developmental Psychology, 43*(6), 1447–1459.

Fabes, R., Eisenberg, N., Hanish, L., & Spinrad, T. (2001). Preschoolers' spontaneous emotion vocabulary: Links to likability. *Early Education and Development, 12*(1), 11–27.

Feagans, L. V., & Farran, D. C. (1994). The effects of daycare intervention in the preschool years on the narrative skills of poverty children in kindergarten. *International Journal of Behavioral Development, 17*, 503–523.

Friedman, P. (2003). *Meeting the challenge of social service delivery in rural areas*. The Finance Project, 7(2), Welfare Information Network. Retrieved from http://76.12.61.196/publications/meetingthechallengeIN.htm

Garmezy, N., & Rutter, M. (1988). *Stress, coping, and development in children (Johns Hopkins paperbacks ed.)*. Baltimore: Johns Hopkins University Press.

Garrett-Peters, P., Castro, V., & Halberstadt, A. (2015). *Parents' emotion related beliefs, children's emotion knowledge, and social competence in school*. Poster presented at the meeting for the Society for Research in Child Development, Philadelphia, PA.

Garrett-Peters, P., Mills-Koonce, R., Adkins, D., Vernon-Feagans, L., Cox, M., & The Family Life Project Key Investigators (2008). Early environmental correlates of maternal emotion talk. *Parenting: Science and Practice, 8*(2), 117–152.

Garrett-Peters, P., Mills-Koonce, R., Zerwas, S., Cox, M., & Vernon-Feagans, L. (2011). Fathers' early emotion talk: Associations with income, ethnicity, and family factors. *Journal of Marriage and Family, 73*(2), 335–353.

Garrett-Peters, P.T., Zerwas, S., Bratsch, M., Vernon-Feagans, L., & The Family Life Project Key Investigators (2009). Early mental state language of rural mothers and fathers living in poverty: Child, parent, and family factors. In L. M. Armstrong & C. H. Hughes (Eds.), *Steps in a scaffold: From child communicative skills and parent-child talk to children's socio-emotional understanding.* Symposium conducted at the meeting for the Society for Research in Child Development, Denver, CO.

Gibson-Davis, C. M., & Grassman-Pines, A. (2010). Early childhood family structure and mother-child interactions: Variation by race & ethnicity. *Developmental Psychology, 46*(1), 151–164.

Goodman, J. C., Dale, P. S., & Li, P. (2008). Does frequency count? Parental input and the acquisition of vocabulary. *Journal of child language, 35*(3), 515.

Graefe, D. R., & Lichter, D. T. (2002). Marriage among unwed mothers: Whites, Blacks and Hispanics compared. *Perspectives on Sexual and Reproductive Health, 34*, 286–293.

Haggerty, R., Sherrod, L., Garmezy, N., & Rutter, M. (1996). *Stress, risk, and resilience in children and adolescents: Processes, mechanisms, and interventions.* Cambridge: Cambridge University Press.

Han, W. (2005). Nonstandard work schedules and child care decisions: Evidence from the NICHD Study of Early Child Care. *Early Childhood Research Quarterly, 19*(2), 231–256.

Hanson, T. L., McLanahan, S., & Thomson, E. (1997). Economic resources, parental practices, and children's well-being. In G. Duncan & J. Brooks-Gunn (Eds.), *Consequences of growing up poor* (pp. 190–221). New York: Russell Sage Foundation.

Harris, P. L. (2007). Social cognition. *Handbook of child psychology,* (Vol. 2, pp. 811–858). Hoboken, NJ: John Wiley & Sons, Incorporated.

Hart, B., & Risley, T. (1995). *Meaningful differences in the everyday experience of young American children.* Baltimore: Brookes.

Hoff, E. (2003). The specificity of environmental influence: Socioeconomic status affects early vocabulary development via maternal speech. *Child Development, 74*(5), 1368–1378.

Hoff, E. (2006). How social contexts support and shape language development. *Developmental Review, 26*(1), 55–88.

Hoff, E., & Tian, C. (2005). Socioeconomic status and cultural influences on language. *Journal of Communication Disorders, 38*, 271–278.

Hughes, C., Dunn, J., & White, A. (1998). Trick or Treat?: Uneven understanding of mind and emotion and executive dysfunction in "hard-to-manage" Preschoolers. *Journal of Child Psychology and Psychiatry, 39*(7), 981–994.

Huttenlocher, J., Haight, W., Bryk, A., Seltzer, M., & Lyons, T. (1991). Early vocabulary growth: Relation to language input and gender. *Developmental Psychology, 27*(2), 236–248.

Huttenlocher, J., Vasilyeva, M., Cymerman, E., & Levine, S. (2002). Language input and syntax. *Cognitive Psychology, 45*, 337–374.

Jenkins, J. M., Turrell, S. L., Kogushi, Y., Lollis, S., & Ross, H. S. (2003). A longitudinal investigation of the dynamics of mental state talk in families. *Child Development, 74*(3), 905–920.

Kalil, A., Ryan, R., & Corey, M. (2012). Diverging destinies: Maternal education and the developmental gradient in time with children. *Demography, 49*(4), 1361–1383.

King, V. (1994). Nonresident father involvement and child well-being. *Journal of Family Issues, 15*, 78–96.

Kohn, M. L., & Schooler, C. (1978). The reciprocal effects of the substantive complexity of work and intellectual flexibility: A longitudinal assessment. *American Journal of Sociology*, 24–52.

LaBounty, J., Wellman, H. M., Olson, S., Lagattuta, K., & Liu, D. (2008). Mothers' and fathers' use of internal state talk with their young children. *Social Development, 17*(4), 757–775.

Lennon, M. (1994). Women, work, and well-being. *Journal of Health and Social Behavior, 35*, 235–247.

Lichter, D., & Jensen, L. (2001). Poverty and welfare among rural female-headed families: Before and after PRWORA. *Rural America, 16*(3), 28–35.

Lichter, D. T., Roscigno, V., & Condron, D. (2003). Rural children and youth at risk. In D. Brown & L. E. Swanson (Eds.), *Challenges for rural America in the twenty-first century* (pp. 97–108). University Park, PA: The Pennsylvania State University Press.

Malatesta, C. Z., & Haviland, J. M. (1982). Learning display rules: The socialization of emotion expression in infancy. *Child Development, 53*(4), 991–1003.

Martin, R. M., & Green, J. A. (2005). The use of emotion explanations by mothers: Relation to preschoolers' gender and understanding of emotions. *Social Development, 14*, 229–249.

Mather, M., & Scopilliti, M. (2004). *Multiple jobholding rates higher in rural America.* Population Reference Bureau, September. Available online at http://www.prb.org/rfdcenter/MultipleJobholdingRates.htm

Mattingly, M. J., Johnson, K. M., & Schaefer, A. (2011). More poor kids in more poor places: Children increasingly live where poverty persists. *Carsey Institute Issue Brief, 38*, 1–8. Durham, NH: University of New Hampshire.

McLoyd, V. C. (1990). The impact of economic hardship on black families and children: Psychological distress, parenting, and socioemotional development. *Child Development, 61*, 311–346.

McLoyd, V. C. (1998). Socioeconomic disadvantage and child development. *American Psychologist, 53*, 185–204. doi:10.1177/02711214040240040401

Meins, E., Fernyhough, C., Wainwright, R., Clark-Carter, D., Gupta, M. D., Fradley, E., et al. (2003). Pathways to understanding mind: Construct validity and predictive validity of maternal mind-mindedness. *Child Development, 74*(4), 1194–1211.

Meins, E., Fernyhough, C., Wainwright, R., Gupta, M. D., Fradley, E., & Tuckey, M. (2002). Maternal mind-mindedness and attachment security as predictors of theory of mind understanding. *Child Development, 73*(6), 1715–1726.

Menaghan, E. G., & Parcel, T. L. (1991). Determining children's home environments: The impact of maternal characteristics and current occupational and family conditions. *Journal of Marriage and the Family*, 417–431.

Murry, V. M., & Brody, G. H. (1999). Self-regulation and self-worth of black children reared in economically stressed, rural, single mother-headed families the contribution of risk and protective factors. *Journal of Family Issues, 20*(4), 458–484.

Murry, V. M., Brody, G. H., McNair, L. D., Luo, Z., Gibbons, F. X., Gerrard, M., et al. (2005). Parental involvement promotes rural African American youths' self-pride and sexual self-concepts. *Journal of Marriage and Family, 67*(3), 627–642. doi:10.1111/j.1741-3737.2005.00158.x

Murry, V. M., Harrell, A. W., Brody, G. H., Chen, Y., Simons, R. L., Black, A. R., et al. (2008). Long-term effects of stressors on relationship well-being and parenting among rural African American women. *Family Relations: An Interdisciplinary Journal of Applied Family Studies, 57*(2), 117–127. doi:10.1111/j.1741-3729.2008.00488.x

Neuman, S. B. (1997). Guiding young children's participation in early literacy development: A family literacy program for adolescent mothers. *Early Child Development and Care, 127*(128), 119–129.

Ninio, A. (1983). Joint book reading as a multiple vocabulary acquisition device. *Developmental Psychology, 19*(3), 445–451.

O'Hare, W. P., & Johnson, K. M. (2004). Child poverty in rural America. Population Reference Bureau. *Reports on America, 4*(1), 1–19.

Odom, E. C., Garrett-Peters, P., Vernon-Feagans, L., & The Family Life Project Investigators. (2014). Racial discrimination as a correlate of African American mothers' emotion talk to young children. *Journal of Family Issues*, 1–27. doi:10.1177/0192513X14521196

Odom, E. C., Vernon-Feagans, L., Crouter, A. C., & Family Life Key Investigators. (2013). Nonstandard maternal work schedules: Implications for African American children's early language outcomes. *Early Childhood Research Quarterly, 28*(2), 379–387. doi:10.1016/j.ecresq.2012.10.001

O'Hare, W. P. (2009). *The forgotten fifth: Child poverty in rural*. Carsey Institute, 1–24. Report. Retrieved from http://carseyinstitute.unh.edu/publications/Report-OHare-ForgottenFifth.pdf

Pan, B. A., Rowe, M. L., Singer, J. D., & Snow, C. E. (2005). Maternal correlates of growth in toddler vocabulary production in low-income families. *Child Development, 76*, 763–782.

Pancsofar, N., & Vernon-Feagans, L. (2006). Mother and father language input to young children: Contributions to later language development. *Journal of Applied Developmental Psychology, 27*(6), 571–587.

Pancsofar, N., Vernon-Feagans, L., & The Family Life Project Investigators. (2010). Fathers' early contributions to children's language development in families from low-income rural communities. *Early Childhood Research Quarterly, 25*(4), 450.

Payne, A. C., Whitehurst, G. J., & Angell, A. L. (1994). The role of home literacy environment in the development of language ability in preschool children from low-income families. *Early Childhood Research Quarterly, 9*, 427–440.

Pears, K., & Moses, L. (2003). Demographics, parenting, and theory of mind in preschool children. *Social Development, 12*, 1–20.

Presser, H. B. (2004). The economy that never sleeps. *Contexts, 3*, 42–49.

Reardon, S. (2011). The widening academic achievement gap between the rich and the poor: New evidence and possible explanations. *Whither Opportunity? Rising inequality, schools, and children's life chances*. New York, NY: Russell Sage Foundation.

Regional Educational Laboratory Network. (2004). *The name assigned to the document by the author. This field may also contain sub-titles, series names, and report numbers*. Responding to Regional Needs & National Priorities. Annual Report.

Rivers, K. (2005). *Rural southern children falling behind in well-being indicators* (population reference bureau brief). Accessed online March 25, 2010 at http://www.prb.org/Articles/2005/RuralSouthernChildrenFallingBehindinWellBeingIndicators.aspx?p=1

Roopnarine, J. L., Fouts, H. N., Lamb, M. E., & Lewis-Elligan, T. Y. (2005). Mothers' and fathers' behaviors toward their 3-to 4-month-old infants in lower, middle, and upper socioeconomic African American families. *Developmental Psychology, 41*(5), 723–732.

Rowe, M. L., Coker, D., & Pan, B. A. (2004). A comparison of fathers' and mothers' talk to toddlers in low-income families. *Social Development, 13*(2), 278–291.

Rutter, M. (1990). Psychosocial resilience and protective mechanisms. In J. E Rolf, A. Matsen, & D. Cicchetti (Eds.), *Risk and protective factors in the development of psychopathology*. Hoboken, NJ: Wiley.

Sameroff, A., & Chandler, M. (1975). Reproductive risk and the continuum of caretaking casualty. In F. D. Horowitz, E. M. Hetherington, S. Scarr-Salapatek, & G. Siegel (Eds.), *Review of child development research* (Vol. 4, pp. 187–244). Chicago: University of Chicago Press.

Sameroff, A., & Seifer, R. (1995). Accumulation of environmental risk and child mental health. In H. Fitzgerald, B. Lester, & B. Zuckerman (Eds.), *Children of poverty* (pp. 233–254). New York: Garland Publishing Inc.

Schooler, C., & Schoenbach, C. (1994). Social class, occupational status, occupational self-direction, and job income: A cross-national examination. *Sociological Forum, 9*, 431–458.

Schultz, D., Izard, C. E., Ackerman, B. P., & Youngstrom, E. A. (2001). Emotion knowledge in economically disadvantaged children: Self-regulatory antecedents and relations to social difficulties and withdrawal. *Development and Psychopathology, 13*, 53–67.

Seiling, S. B., Manoogian, M. M., & Son, S. (2011). "I don't know how we would make it"—Social support in rural low-income families. In *Rural families and work* (pp. 157–183). New York: Springer.

Sénéchal, M., LeFevre, J., Hudson, E., & Lawson, E. (1996). Knowledge of storybooks as a predictor of children's vocabulary. *Journal of Educational Psychology, 88*, 520–536.

Simons, L. G., Chen, Y., Simons, R. L., Brody, G., & Cutrona, C. (2006). Parenting practices and child adjustment in different types of households: A study of African American families. *Journal of Family Issues, 27*(6), 803–825. doi:10.1177/0192513X05285447

Smith, K. E., & Tickamyer, A. R. (Eds.). (2011). *Economic restructuring and family well-being in rural America*. University Park: Penn State Press.

Taumoepeau, M., & Ruffman, T. (2006). Mother and infant talk about mental states related to desire language and emotion understanding. *Child Development, 77*(2), 465–481.

Taumoepeau, M., & Ruffman, T. (2008). Stepping stones to others' minds: Maternal talk relates to child mental state language and emotion understanding at 15, 24, and 33 months. *Child Development, 79*(2), 284–302.

USDA Economic Research Service (2012). *Rural education*. Washington, DC: ERS. Retrieved from http://www.ers.usda.gov/topics/rural-economy-population/employment-education/rural-education.aspx

Vernon-Feagans, L., Burchinal, M., & Mokrova, I. (2015). Diverging destinies in rural America. *Families in an era of increasing inequality* (pp. 35–49). New York: Springer International Publishing.

Vernon-Feagans, L., Cox, M., & The Family Life Project Key Investigators (2013). The Family Life Project: An epidemiological and developmental study of young children living in poor rural communities. *Monographs of the Society for Research in Child Development, 78*, 1–150.

Vernon-Feagans, L., Gallagher, K., & Kainz, K. (2010). The transition to school in rural America: A focus on literacy. In J. Eccles & J. Meece (Eds.), *Handbook of research on schools, schooling, and development* (pp. 163–184). Mahweh, NJ: Erlbaum.

Vernon-Feagans, L., Garrett-Peters, P., DeMarco, A., & Bratsch, M. (2012). Children living in rural poverty: The role of chaos in early development. In V. Maholmes & R. King (Eds.), *The Oxford handbook of poverty and child development* (pp. 448–466). Oxford: Oxford University Press.

Weber, B. A., Duncan, G. J., & Whitener, L. A. (2002). *Rural dimensions of welfare reform*. Kalamazoo, MI: W.E. Upjohn Institute for Employment Research.

Weber, B., Jensen, L., Miller, K., Mosley, J., & Fisher, M. (2005). A critical review of rural poverty literature: Is there truly a rural effect. *International Regional Science Review, 28*, 381–414.

Weizman, Z. O., & Snow, C. E. (2001). Lexical output as related to children's vocabulary acquisition: Effects of sophisticated exposure and support for meaning. *Developmental Psychology, 37*(2), 265–279.

The Effects of Rurality on Parents' Engagement in Children's Early Literacy

Brandy L. Clarke, Natalie A. Koziol and Susan M. Sheridan

Abstract Investigations of urban-rural context on children's educational experiences have produced somewhat inconsistent findings, but one thing is clear, parent engagement in children's early learning positively impacts academic outcomes. Research identifying conditions that uniquely influence parents' early engagement in learning and literacy in rural settings are needed. An illustrative example of a study investigating the effects of rurality on parent engagement and children's literacy using a nationally representative dataset (Early Childhood Longitudinal Study, Birth Cohort, ECLS-B; n = 6550) is discussed. Contextual differences in parents' use of technology and community resources and children's reading scores were revealed. The important role of technology and structural characteristics of rural communities in young children's early literacy development was demonstrated; however, further research is needed to better understand the impact of these and other contextual influences. A proposed agenda for future research in this area is discussed.

Keywords Parent engagement · Early language and literacy · Rural contexts · Preschool · Literacy resources · Home environments

B.L. Clarke (✉)
Munroe-Meyer Institute, University of Nebraska Medical Center, Omaha, USA
e-mail: brandy.clarke@unmc.edu

N.A. Koziol · S.M. Sheridan
Nebraska Center for Research on Children, Youth, Families and Schools,
National Center for Research on Rural Education, University of Nebraska–Lincoln,
Lincoln, USA
e-mail: nkoziol@unl.edu

S.M. Sheridan
e-mail: ssheridan2@unl.edu

1 Parent Engagement, Reading Readiness and Rural Settings

Reading skills are critical to children's academic success (Duncan et al. 2007), and the effects of poor early reading are compounded over time (Arnold and Doctoroff 2003). Language skills that influence reading abilities are formed in the beginning stages of life; children's early language experiences not only set the stage for their learning potential, but they also greatly influence their academic trajectory (Heckman 2006; Whitehurst and Lonigan 2001). Thus, the effects of undermined language and literacy development can be seen early on and have lasting consequences. Specifically, poor language and literacy skills at the time of school entry have been linked to increased remedial education and school dropout (Dickinson and Tabors 2001).

High quality early experiences in childcare and preschool settings significantly impact children's skill development, and as children's first teachers, parents play a critical role in establishing a stimulating learning environment that will optimize their overall development (National Institute of Child Health and Human Development Early Child Care Research Network 2006). Early parent engagement in language and literacy activities is important for young children's overall learning and school readiness (Sheridan et al. 2011; Weigel et al. 2006) and has been linked to children's increased vocabulary and language skills (Hart and Risley 1995; Hindman and Morrison 2012), alphabet knowledge (Hindman et al. 2008; Sénéchal 2006), and learning behaviors, such as self-regulation, cooperation and compliance (Hindman and Morrison 2012). Furthermore, early reading experiences in the home have been shown to predict later language and literacy readiness in kindergarten and reading skills in early elementary school, demonstrating longitudinal effects of early parent engagement (Forget-Dubois et al. 2009).

Parent engagement, as defined here, refers to practices and provisions that support early language and literacy skills for preschoolers. Establishing a home learning environment that provides accessible language and literacy resources for children, both material and relational, is an important method by which parents support early learning (Bradley 2002). Interactive shared book-reading experiences between parents and children are among the most influential methods for expanding vocabulary (Fielding-Barnsley and Purdie 2003; Jordan et al. 2000). A language rich environment includes other forms of language-based interaction, such as telling stories, singing songs, and reciting nursery rhymes, which support oral narrative skills linked to later reading comprehension (Hester 2010), reading fluency (Reese et al. 2010), vocabulary development (Hart and Risley 1995), and phonological awareness (Tabors et al. 2001). Providing access to print materials in the home, especially children's books, creates a literacy environment conducive to vocabulary development (Burgess et al. 2002; Dever and Burts 2002). Access to computers has also been shown to positively influence children's early literacy skills (Macaruso and Rodman 2011; Shamir et al. 2012). Additionally, accessing community resources, such as libraries or museums, expand cultural experiences and provide opportunities for engagement in language- and literacy-based activities, promoting early reading skills (Neuman and Celano 2001, 2004).

Several factors influence parent engagement in language and literacy interactions, such as socioeconomic status and education. One level of influence on early parental literacy engagement that deserves more attention is geographical location. Structural characteristics within one's neighborhood or community have been shown to influence parenting behavior and children's literacy outcomes (Froiland 2011). For example, exposure to community-based resources, including libraries, zoos, museums, parks and/or playgrounds fosters children's positive early learning outcomes (Froiland et al. 2014). However, more research is needed to understand the unique determinants of setting conditions on early parent-child literacy interactions. Specifically, little is currently known about the similarities or differences between rural and urban settings in the manner by which parents engage in language and literacy activities with their young children and the effect of their engagement on children's reading readiness.

Conditions in rural settings may differentially impact the ways in which parents are engaged in early learning activities and the degree to which parents' behaviors impact later academic skill development. Some have argued that the diminished resources and income potential in rural communities may negatively influence parents' educational aspirations for their children and in turn depress their efforts to promote learning in the home (Durham and Smith 2006; Roscigno and Crowley 2001). Although some research indicates that parents in rural communities place less emphasis on academic achievement (Lampard et al. 2000) and invest and engage less in educational experiences (Roscigno et al. 2006) than their urban counterparts, others have demonstrated that parent involvement in children's education in rural settings produces similar benefits for student achievement for children in rural schools as it does for children in urban and suburban settings (Keith et al. 1996). Specifically, rural parent involvement in school-based literacy activities has been shown to positively affect kindergarten children's reading skills (Porter DeCusati and Johnson 2004). Yet, more research is needed to better understand the effects of geographic locale on parent engagement in early literacy and children's academic development.

2 An Investigation of Geographical Context on Parent Engagement in Early Literacy

Rigorous methodological investigations of setting conditions impacting family engagement in children's education are lacking (Arnold et al. 2005; Coladarci 2007). Most studies that claim to study a rural phenomenon do not include comparison conditions that explain differences of rural relevance (Coladarci 2007; Semke and Sheridan 2012). Previous examinations of parents' engagement in early language and literacy activities have included rural samples (Barnyak 2011; Dever and Burts 2002); however, they have not included urban comparison groups, thereby making it difficult to draw conclusions about the unique impact of the different settings. Thus, our current understanding of the effects of rural setting on parents' language and literacy behaviors is based on speculation and conjecture about presumed universal practices or influences and their relationship to children's outcomes, based largely on research conducted in urban or nonspecified settings. An additional challenge with conducting research in rural communities is obtaining large enough samples to allow for robust analyses of contextual variability. Conducting a generalizable evaluation of the effects of geographic setting on parental behavior and child literacy outcomes requires a large, representative sample from each locale. Studies of this magnitude would demand significant resources; fortunately, large-scale secondary datasets allow for such evaluations.

Few studies have explored the extent to which parents' engagement and children's early literacy vary across geographic contexts. To partially fill this void, we conducted a study that examined variation in engagement and literacy between rural settings and city, suburban, and town settings. Specifically, we examined the relationships among rurality, parents' early language and literacy engagement behaviors, and children's kindergarten literacy. Our primary research question concerned the total effect of geographical context on parents' literacy engagement in preschool and children's literacy in kindergarten. Second, we investigated whether parent engagement mediated the pathway between context and child outcomes. The specific research questions examined in this study were:

1. What is the effect of geographic setting—living in a rural setting versus city, suburban, or town setting—on (a) children's kindergarten literacy, and (b) parents' preschool literacy engagement?
2. Does parent literacy engagement during preschool mediate the relationship between geographic setting and children's kindergarten literacy?

As demonstrated in previous research (Froiland 2011), we hypothesized that setting would have a unique effect on parents' preschool literacy engagement and children's kindergarten literacy. Given the differences in community resources (i.e., libraries) in urban and rural communities, it was expected that rural families would access these resources less frequently during preschool than their urban counterparts, which may negatively impact their kindergarten literacy scores. However, we hypothesized that parent literacy behavior during preschool (i.e., reading, singing, story-telling, providing access to literacy materials [books and computers] in the home) would look similar across settings, which may address some of the gaps in resources and support later reading skill development.

This study was conducted via a secondary data analysis of the Early Childhood Longitudinal Study, Birth Cohort (ECLS-B) study sponsored by the National Center for Education Statistics (NCES), U.S. Department of Education. The ECLS-B was designed to examine the systemic interactions of the child, family, childcare, health care, educational system, and community on children's overall health, social-emotional development, and intellectual capacity that influence children's school readiness (Andreassen and West 2007). The longitudinal information provided by the ECLS-B database made it possible to examine temporal relations between parent engagement and child literacy; no other studies of this magnitude have allowed for such longitudinal investigations. Studies that have collected longitudinal data tend to be based on relatively small samples, whereas the ECLS-B provided a large, nationally representative sample across various geographical contexts and time points that allowed us to conduct a statistically powerful and generalizable evaluation of the effects of setting on parent engagement and child literacy using sophisticated analytic methods.

3 Methods

Participants and selection procedure. A stratified, multistage sampling design involving unequal selection probabilities was used by ECLS-B researchers to obtain the sample of eligible children (Snow et al. 2009). See Bethel et al. (2005) for information regarding the ECLS-B sampling design. Information was obtained from approximately 10,700[1] children and their parents, early child care providers, and kindergarten teachers, across five waves of data collection. The present study utilized data collected during the preschool (Wave 3; 2005–2006) and kindergarten waves (Waves 4 and 5; 2006–2007 and 2007–2008, respectively) (Snow et al. 2009). The second wave of kindergarten data collection was necessary to gather information about children who were not yet in kindergarten in 2006 (Wave 4) or who repeated kindergarten. For the present study, Waves 4 and 5 were combined into a single kindergarten wave so that inferences could be made about children in their kindergarten year. Data were obtained from Wave 4 for children first entering kindergarten in 2006 (including children who first entered kindergarten in 2006 but repeated kindergarten in 2007) and from Wave 5 for children first entering kindergarten in 2007.

Home-schooled children, children in ungraded programs, children with no kindergarten experience, and children for whom grade was unknown, were excluded from the analyses. Furthermore, children reported as Native Hawaiian or other Pacific Islander/non-Hispanic, were excluded from the analyses due to the very small sample size which resulted in non-convergence of the models when child race/ethnicity was included as a covariate. Upon excluding all ineligible cases, the effective sample size for this study was $n = 6550$, although missing item-level data resulted in some variation in sample size across analyses. Weighted descriptive statistics for this sample are provided in Table 1.

Study Variables and Measures. Parent interview data were collected by ECLS-B field staff via a structured computer-assisted personal interviewing (CAPI)

---

[1]To protect confidentiality of the data, all sample sizes have been rounded to the nearest 50 per Institute of Education Sciences reporting requirements.

Table 1 Weighted descriptive statistics[a] for the reduced sample (n = 6550)

Study variable	Statistic
Child	
Male	51.340 %
Race/ethnicity	
White	53.448 %
Black	14.000 %
Hispanic	25.523 %
Asian	2.536 %
American Indian or Alaska Native	0.498 %
More than 1 race	3.995 %
Kindergarten assessment age in months	68.163 (4.420)
Parent[b]	
Primary respondent is biological mother[c]	95.593 %
Family[b]	
Highest parent education level	
Less than a high school degree	10.985 %
High school degree or equivalent	23.177 %
Vocational or technical program degree	5.833 %
Some college	27.550 %
Bachelor's degree	16.614 %
Advanced schooling beyond Bachelor's	15.840 %
At or above 100 % poverty threshold	75.638 %
2 or more adults[d] in the home	86.644 %
Primary language in home is English	81.411 %

[a]Percentages for categorical variables and means (SD) for continuous variables
[b]Statistics are based on Wave 3 data
[c]Remaining respondents included biological fathers, other mother and father types, non-parent relatives, and non-relatives
[d]Individuals 18 years of age or older. Percentages may not sum to 100 due to rounding error

program (Snow et al. 2009). See Snow et al. (2009) for a detailed description of interview procedures.

Geographic Setting. Household ZIP codes from the Wave 3 parent interview were combined with data from the American Community Survey to create a composite location variable based on the Urban-Centric Locale Codes defined by the National Center for Education Statistics (Snow et al. 2009). The 12 locations included large city, mid-size city, small city, large suburban area, mid-size suburban area, small suburban area, fringe town, distant town, remote town, rural fringe, distant rural, and remote rural. For this study, locations were collapsed into four groups, city (*n* = 1950), suburban (*n* = 2550), town (*n* = 850), and rural (*n* = 1100). The Urban-Centric Locale Codes take into account locations' population size and proximity to urban areas (i.e., principal cities, urbanized areas, and urban clusters). Urban areas are classified based on population size and density, and economic and social integration and prominence. We chose this classification system because it provides a finer discrimination than a simple urban versus rural designation. Furthermore, it utilizes information about proximity to urban areas, which is likely to be more related to parent engagement and child literacy than population size alone.

The Urban-Centric Locale Codes were applied at the level of household ZIP codes. Thus, all rural inferences generated by this study exist, by definition, at the level of ZIP codes. It is important to bear in mind that rural, as defined by this study, cannot explain differences in parent engagement and child literacy within ZIP codes, because all households within a ZIP code were assigned the same location code.

Parental Preschool Literacy Engagement. Parent-reported literacy engagement variables were obtained from the Home Environment section of the Wave 3 parent interview. Four parental engagement characteristics were selected: home literacy materials, access to computer technology, children's exposure to the library, and parental language and literacy behaviors.

Home Literacy Materials. Home literacy materials were assessed via access to children's books in the home. A one-item measure, "About how many children's books does [child] have in your home now, including library books?" was used to determine number of books in the home. Unweighted statistics computed for our sample indicated that households had an average of 68.021 (SD = 86.317) children's books, with a minimum of 0 and a maximum of 900 books. Due to the highly skewed nature of this variable, a log-transformed version was used for all analyses.[2]

Access to Computer Technology. Children's use of computers was measured via the question, "In a typical week, how often does [child] use the computer?" with possible response options 1 = *Never*, 2 = *Once or twice a week*, 3 = *Three to six times a week*, and 4 = *Every day*. The unweighted average response was 1.843 (SD = 0.947).

Exposure to the Library. Four dichotomous (*No* = 0, *Yes* = 1) questions on library use were summed to create a composite score of children's library exposure. These questions were (a) "In the past month, has anyone in your family visited a public library with [child]?" and (b) "In the past month, did you use the public library to...Borrow books to read aloud to [child] or for [him/her] to read? (c) Borrow materials other than books, such as cassettes, CDs, videos, or toys, to share with [child]? (d) Take [child] to a story hour or program?" Parents who responded "No" to the first question did not complete the remaining three questions; in these cases, the remaining three questions were scored as '0'. The unweighted Kuder–Richardson 20 (KR20) coefficient for the four items was 0.861. Sample composite scores ranged from 0 to 4 with higher scores representing greater exposure. The unweighted average composite score was 1.122 (SD = 1.470).

---

[2]A value of one was added to all observations prior to the transformation in order to avoid taking the log of zero, which equals infinity.

Parent Behaviors. Three questions measured parent language and literacy behaviors: "In a typical week, how often do you or any other family member… (a) Read books to your child? (b) Tell stories to your child? (c) Sing songs with your child?" The four possible response options were *Not at all*, *Once or twice*, *3 to 6 times*, and *Everyday* with higher scores representing more frequent behaviors. Unweighted Cronbach's alpha for the three items was 0.576. Parent language and literacy behavior trait scores were computed using confirmatory factor analysis (CFA) as described in the Sects. 4 and 5. The unweighted average trait score was 0.003 (SD = 0.535) with a minimum score of −1.451 and a maximum score of 0.848.

Children's Kindergarten Literacy. Children's early literacy was evaluated by the early reading assessment of the direct child assessment. Most of the 85 items that comprised the assessment came from the *PreLAS 2000* (Duncan and De Avila 1998), PPVT-III (Dunn and Dunn 1997), or Preschool Comprehensive Test of Phonological and Print Processing (Pre-CTOPPP; Lonigan et al. 2002), but some items were created specifically for the ECLS-B (Najarian et al. 2010).

Child scores and item parameters were estimated according to the three-parameter logistic (3PL) model commonly used in item response theory (Najarian et al. 2010). The unweighted average kindergarten theta score for the reduced sample was 0.647 (SD = 0.803) with a minimum theta score of −2.115 and a maximum theta score of 3.086. Reliability of the kindergarten theta scores as reported in the ECLS-B kindergarten 2006 and 2007 Data File User's Manual was 0.920 for Wave 4 (2006) and 0.930 for Wave 5 (2007) (Snow et al. 2009). See page 56 of Snow et al. (2009) for more information on the reliability calculations.

Child and Family Covariates. Three child covariates were included in the analyses: race/ethnicity (also used as a proxy for family race/ethnicity), age at kindergarten assessment, and sex. Child race/ethnicity and sex were obtained through parent report. The present study used a single, mutually-exclusive composite variable that classified children into one of eight categories: White, non-Hispanic; Black or African American, non-Hispanic; Hispanic, race specified; Hispanic, no race specified; Asian, non-Hispanic; Native Hawaiian or other Pacific Islander, non-Hispanic; American Indian or Alaska Native, non-Hispanic; or More than one race, non-Hispanic (Snow et al. 2009). The categories of "Hispanic, race specified" and "Hispanic, no race specified" were collapsed into a single category. Child age at kindergarten assessment was computed as the difference, in months, between the date of the kindergarten direct child assessment and the child's birthdate as recorded on the child's birth certificate.

One family covariate, socioeconomic status, was also included in the analyses. The SES standardized composite variable available in the ECLS-B restricted datafile is comprised of five parent/household variables, including father/male guardian's education and occupation prestige, mother/female guardian's education and occupation prestige, and household income (Snow et al. 2009). The Wave 3

SES composite scores were used in the present analyses. The unweighted average SES for the present sample was −0.003 (SD = 0.847) with a minimum SES of −2.250 and a maximum SES of 2.090.

4 Data Analysis

All data were analyzed in M*plus* Version 6.1 (Muthén and Muthén 1998–2010) using full-information maximum likelihood estimation to account for item-level missing data. A design-based approach was used to account for the ECLS-B complex sampling design. Specifically, parameter estimates were weighted by the WKR0 weight appropriate for longitudinal analyses involving child assessment data and/or parent interview data obtained from the wave in which the child first entered kindergarten (Snow et al. 2009), and variance estimation was performed using a paired jackknife replication method (Wolter 1985).

Confirmatory factor analysis (CFA) was performed to evaluate the hypothesized structure of the parent behavior construct. Three parent-reported indicators of parent language and literacy behavior—reads books to child, tells stories to child, and sings songs with child—were specified to measure a single latent factor. The indicators were deemed to be good measures of the latent construct (i.e., unstandardized factor loadings were significant at the $\alpha = 0.050$ level and all standardized factor loadings were greater than 0.400). Expected a priori estimation was used to obtain latent trait scores based on the CFA model. These scores were then used in the primary analyses.

Structural equation modeling (SEM) was used to evaluate the primary research questions. Model fit was evaluated according to the root mean square error of approximation (RMSEA) and standardized root mean square residual (SRMR), with the joint criteria of RMSEA < 0.060 and SRMR < 0.090 indicating good model fit (Hu and Bentler 1999). Standardized path coefficients were provided as measures of effect size with absolute values of $\beta < 0.10$ suggesting a "small" effect, near 0.30 suggesting a "medium" effect, and at or above 0.50 suggesting a "large" effect. Coefficients of determination (R^2 values) were provided with R^2 values less than 0.01, near 0.06, and at or above 0.14 suggesting small, medium, and large effects, respectively (Cohen 1988).

The total effect of geographic setting on children's early literacy was first examined by evaluating an SEM without the hypothesized mediating parental literacy engagement variables. The indirect effect of geographic setting on children's early literacy was then examined by evaluating an SEM with the hypothesized mediating parental literacy engagement variables. Sobel's (1982) test was used to evaluate the significance of the indirect effect. Geographic setting was represented by three dummy variables (city, suburban, and town) with the rural setting as the reference group. Thus, negative coefficients indicated that rural individuals were higher on the endogenous (dependent) variable. Child race/ethnicity, kindergarten assessment age, gender, and family SES variables were included in both models as covariates.

5 Results

Preliminary analysis. Item parameter estimates from the CFA of the parent behaviors construct are presented in Table 2. With only three indicators, the model was fully saturated so absolute model fit could not be established. However, all unstandardized factor loadings were significant at the $\alpha = 0.001$ level, and all standardized factor loadings were greater than 0.400 ($\hat{\lambda} = 0.565$, 0.724, and 0.448 for read books to child, tell stories to child, and sing songs with child, respectively) suggesting that each of the indicators adequately reflects the latent construct.

Primary analyses. Table 3 provides the weighted descriptive statistics, by geographic setting, for all study variables used in the primary analyses.

Table 2 Item parameter estimates from a confirmatory factor analysis of the parent language and literacy behaviors construct

Item	Unstandardized factor loading	Standardized factor loading	R^2
Read books to child	0.489***	0.565	0.320
Tell stories to child	0.668***	0.724	0.524
Sing songs with child	0.399***	0.448	0.200

Note $n = 6550$. Estimates were weighted using the WKR0 longitudinal weight. Standard errors were computed using a paired jackknife replication method
***$p < 0.001$

Table 3 Weighted descriptive statistics[a] by geographic setting

Study variable	City	Suburban	Town	Rural
Child sex				
Male (%)	51.8	51.1	52.4	50.5
Female (%)	48.2	48.9	47.6	49.5
Child race/ethnicity				
White (%)	38.5	51.7	61.4	78.2
Black (%)	20.5	13.0	9.1	8.2
Hispanic (%)	33.5	28.8	21.6	6.5
Asian (%)	3.2	3.5	0.8	0.4
American Indian or Alaska Native (%)	0.3	0.2	1.3	1.2
More than 1 race (%)	4.0	2.9	5.7	5.5
Child age in months[b]	68.136 (4.365)	68.123 (4.387)	68.086 (4.419)	68.354 (4.646)
Family SES[c]	−0.220 (0.838)	0.075 (0.783)	−0.221 (0.771)	−0.149 (0.706)
Number of children's books[c]	58.611 (76.292)	71.724 (81.462)	70.344 (88.832)	81.021 (91.977)
Child computer use[c]	1.764 (0.932)	1.938 (0.940)	1.767 (0.907)	1.766 (0.902)
Child library exposure[c]	1.060 (1.434)	1.147 (1.466)	0.951 (1.406)	0.836 (1.308)
Parent lang/lit behaviors[c]	−0.021 (0.541)	0.009 (0.527)	−0.015 (0.522)	0.034 (0.557)
Child reading score[b]	0.544 (0.809)	0.743 (0.760)	0.561 (0.744)	0.588 (0.738)

Percentages may not sum to 100 due to rounding error. Estimates were weighted using the WKR0 longitudinal weight. Standard errors were computed using a paired jackknife replication method
[a]Percentages for categorical variables and means (SD) for continuous variables
[b]Statistics are based on kindergarten Wave data
[c]Statistics are based on Wave 3 data

Research Question 1a: What Is the Effect of Setting on Children's Kindergarten Literacy? Parameter estimates for the model containing the total effect of setting on children's early literacy controlling for the effects of child race/ethnicity, kindergarten assessment age, and gender, and family SES are displayed in Table 4. The model is fully saturated, so absolute model fit could not be assessed. Together, the predictors accounted for approximately 26 % of the variance in children's early literacy. Holding the other variables in the model constant, child reading scores significantly differed across suburban and rural settings such that suburban children had higher reading scores in kindergarten than rural children ($\hat{\beta} = 0.072$, $p = 0.013$). There were no differences in reading scores between rural settings and city and town settings.

Research Question 1b: What Is the Effect of Setting on Parents' Preschool Literacy Engagement? The full model including the parental literacy engagement variables demonstrated acceptable model fit, RMSEA = 0.030 (90 % CI = 0.023–0.038), SRMR = 0.008. Parameter estimates are given in Table 5. Together, the predictors accounted for 39.6 % of the variance in the number of children's books in the home, 6.2 % of the variance in child library exposure, 7.7 % in parent language/literacy behaviors, 7.4 % in children's computer use, and 28.1 % of the variance in child reading scores. Holding the other variables in the model constant, city and suburban children were exposed to the library significantly more than rural children ($\hat{\beta} = 0.105$, $p < 0.001$ and $\hat{\beta} = 0.102$, $p < 0.001$, respectively). There was no significant difference between town and rural children's library exposure. In addition, suburban children had significantly greater computer access in the home

Table 4 Parameter estimates from a structural equation model examining the total effect of rurality on children's early literacy

Parameter	Unstandardized estimate	Standardized estimate	R^2
Child reading score *regressed on*			0.261
City	0.023	0.014	
Suburban	0.113*	0.072	
Town	0.037	0.015	
Black	−0.012	−0.006	
Hispanic	−0.125**	−0.070	
Asian	0.238***	0.049	
American Indian or Alaska Native	−0.258**	−0.023	
Multiple races	−0.016	−0.004	
SES	0.341***	0.351	
Child age	0.052***	0.300	
Child gender	0.119***	0.077	

Note $n = 6350$. Rural was the reference group for the geographic setting variable. White/non-Hispanic was the reference group for the child race/ethnicity variable. Estimates were weighted using the WKR0 longitudinal weight. Standard errors were computed using a paired jackknife replication method

***$p < 0.001$; **$p < 0.010$; *$p < 0.050$

Table 5 Parameter estimates from a structural equation model examining the indirect effect of rurality on children's early literacy through parental language and literacy engagement

Parameter	Unstandardized estimate	Standardized estimate	R^2
Number of books[a,b,c] (log transformed) *regressed on*			0.396
City	−0.061	−0.025	
Suburban	−0.046	−0.020	
Town	−0.022	−0.006	
Black	−0.852***	−0.261	
Hispanic	−0.872***	−0.336	
Asian	−1.019***	−0.142	
American Indian or Alaska Native	−0.713***	−0.044	
Multiple races	−0.215***	−0.037	
SES	0.536***	0.379	
Child computer use[a,d,e] *regressed on*			0.074
City	0.057	0.028	
Suburban	0.139**	0.074	
Town	0.039	0.014	
Black	−0.107*	−0.040	
Hispanic	−0.131**	−0.062	
Asian	0.148**	0.025	
American Indian or Alaska Native	−0.273**	−0.021	
Multiple races	−0.047	−0.010	
SES	0.259***	0.222	
Child library exposure[b,d,f] *regressed on*			0.062
City	0.329***	0.105	
Suburban	0.295***	0.102	
Town	0.181	0.041	
Black	−0.102	−0.025	
Hispanic	−0.278**	−0.085	
Asian	0.248*	0.027	
American Indian or Alaska Native	−0.069	−0.003	
Multiple races	0.062	0.009	
SES	0.339***	0.190	
Parent language/literacy[c,e,f] behaviors *regressed on*			0.077
City	0.021	0.018	
Suburban	−0.006	−0.006	
Town	−0.013	−0.008	
Black	−0.171***	−0.110	
Hispanic	−0.169***	−0.137	
Asian	−0.124**	−0.036	
American Indian or Alaska Native	−0.179***	−0.023	

(continued)

Table 5 (continued)

Parameter	Unstandardized estimate	Standardized estimate	R^2
Multiple races	−0.035	−0.013	
SES	0.122***	0.182	
Child early literacy *regressed on*			0.281
City	0.014	0.008	
Suburban	0.101*	0.064	
Town	0.032	0.013	
Number of books (log transformed)	0.057***	0.083	
Children's computer use	0.057***	0.068	
Child library exposure	0.019^	0.035	
Parent language/literacy involvement	0.094***	0.065	
Black	0.062	0.028	
Hispanic	−0.047	−0.026	
Asian	0.294***	0.060	
American Indian or Alaska Native	−0.184*	−0.017	
Multiple races	0.001	0.000	
SES	0.278***	0.287	
Child age	0.053***	0.302	
Child gender	0.105***	0.068	

Note n = 6450. Residual correlations = [a]0.070; [b]0.112; [c]0.258; [d]0.073; [e]0.119; [f]0.170
Rural was the reference group for the geographic setting variable. White/non-Hispanic was the reference group for the child race/ethnicity variable. Estimates were weighted using the WKR0 longitudinal weight. Standard errors were computed using a paired jackknife replication method
***$p < 0.001$; **$p < 0.010$; *$p < 0.050$; ^$p = 0.053$

than rural children ($\hat{\beta} = 0.074$, $p = 0.001$). Living in a rural community did not significantly influence number of children's books in the home nor parent behaviors.

Research Question 2: Does Parental Literacy Engagement in Preschool Mediate the Relationship Between Setting and Children's Kindergarten Literacy? Indirect effects of setting on children's kindergarten literacy through parental literacy engagement in preschool were examined for combinations of variables in which both sets of pathways—parental preschool literacy engagement regressed on setting and children's kindergarten literacy regressed on parental preschool literacy engagement—were significant. Children's computer access, parent behaviors, and number of children's books in the home significantly predicted child reading scores in kindergarten ($\hat{\beta} = 0.068$, $p < 0.001$; $\hat{\beta} = 0.065$, $p < 0.001$; and $\hat{\beta} = 0.083$, $p < 0.001$, respectively), and children's library exposure marginally significantly predicted children's reading scores ($\hat{\beta} = 0.035, p = 0.053$). However, only library exposure and computer access were predicted by setting. Thus, only two sets of indirect effects were evaluated: (1) the effect of setting on children's kindergarten literacy through children's preschool exposure to the library, and (2) the effect of setting on children's kindergarten literacy through children's preschool computer access. There was a small but marginally significant indirect effect of setting, city versus rural ($\hat{\beta}$ = 0.004, p = 0.091) and suburban versus rural ($\hat{\beta}$ = 0.004, p = 0.070), on children's kindergarten reading scores through children's preschool exposure to the library. There was also a small but significant indirect effect of setting, suburban versus rural ($\hat{\beta}$ = 0.005, p = 0.016), on children's kindergarten reading scores through children's preschool computer access. These results indicate that setting indirectly impacts children's kindergarten reading scores by limiting access to libraries and computers, which in turn negatively impacts reading scores (see Fig. 1).

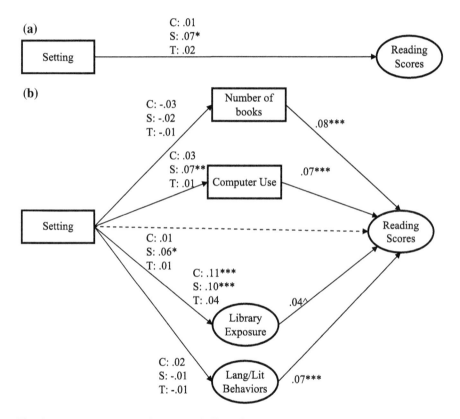

Fig. 1 Path diagrams illustrating the total effect of geographic setting on children's kindergarten literacy (**a**) and indirect effect of geographic setting on children's kindergarten literacy through parents' preschool literacy engagement (**b**). Rural was the reference group for the geographic setting variable. *C* city versus rural, *S* suburban versus rural, *T* town versus rural. Residual correlations and covariate effects are not shown for sake of simplicity. *Rectangles* indicate manifest variables and *ovals* indicate latent variables. *Values* represent standardized coefficients. ***p < 0.001; **p < 0.010; *p < 0.050; ^p = 0.053

6 Discussion

The primary aim of this study was to examine the effect of setting (as defined by population, density, and proximity to urban areas) on parent engagement in language and literacy during preschool, and children's early literacy as measured by their kindergarten reading scores. This study was conducted via a secondary analysis of the ECLS-B dataset which represents an extensive nationally-representative sample. Findings from this study revealed that living in a rural community influences some parenting variables that are important in predicting language and literacy in kindergarten entry, but not others. Specifically, residing in a rural community did not appear to influence the number of children's books in the home nor parent-child language and literacy interactions during preschool. Stated in another way, being in close proximity to urban areas or resources did not make a difference regarding parents' provision of children's literacy materials or their verbal interactions (i.e., reading, singing, telling stories) with their young children. Thus, beliefs that rural conditions may depress parents' engagement in learning activities are not supported by these findings, as parents in rural settings appear to be equally engaged in stimulating parent-child interactions as parents in urban communities.

Not surprisingly, however, given the structural context of small, distal communities, the variables affected by setting appear to be those related to access to resources (i.e., library and home computer access). Preschoolers in rural settings used computers in the home less frequently than those in suburban areas and had lower kindergarten reading scores. Results also showed that living in rural settings limits parents' access to resources in the community (i.e., libraries) during the preschool years, which negatively impacted children's kindergarten literacy. Specifically, preschool children in rural areas were exposed to the library less than preschool children in city and suburban areas, which negatively influenced rural children's kindergarten reading scores.

As was demonstrated in previous research, this study supports the notion that structural characteristics of the community in which one lives may play an important role in young children's early literacy development. Cognitively stimulating resources, such as libraries and museums, may be limited in rural communities due to financial resources, population scarcity, and lack of proximity to metropolitan areas. Institutions, such as libraries, operate on property taxes and other public funds that may be restricted in some rural communities relative to other (e.g., city, suburban) communities. Furthermore, geographic isolation may prohibit families from accessing public resources in rural communities. Community resources that stimulate language and literacy have been shown to impact children's early skill development and preparedness for school (Froiland 2011; Lareau 2000).

However, as technology advances, learning tools such as e-readers and iPads may play a larger role in supporting the learning of young children (Macaruso and Rodma 2011; Shamir et al. 2012). Increasing access to and use of these learning tools in home settings may compensate for the lack of other resources found in rural communities. As of yet, few studies have specifically explored the use of these types of technology in rural homes and its impact on early learning. Such research will have important implications for the fields of early intervention and education in understanding the systemic variables that influence child learning and methods to support rural children to achieve optimal learning outcomes.

Our findings also suggest that other mediating factors need to be considered. Interestingly, when attempting to understand the role of setting on parent engagement and children's reading, there was no difference in rural and city children's reading scores, despite the differences in their library and computer exposure. Hence, it appears likely that there are additional mediator variables for which rural children are advantaged over city children, compensating for their limited exposure to the library and home computers. For example, children in rural communities may have greater access to safe, green spaces (e.g., yards, parks, and fields) that afford young children safe opportunities for outdoor play and discovery, providing a unique context for cognitively stimulating experiences. This may help to offset their limited access to community libraries or technological resources.

Similarly, it appears that there are additional mediating variables not included in our model that would explain why suburban children have higher kindergarten entry reading scores than rural children, even after controlling for computer use, library exposure and other demographic variables (i.e., race/ethnicity, age, sex, and SES). Families in suburban areas often have access to both technology and community resources, as well as green space (e.g., yards and parks). Collectively, suburban areas may have the best of both urban and rural communities, which may play a role in the overall differences in kindergarten reading scores.

Structural factors unique to geographic settings, such as social organization, also warrant further exploration. Community identity and social relatedness may uniquely differ across setting conditions and play a role in children's early learning outcomes. Families in urban neighborhoods with lower levels of social organization interact less with others in their community as a means of protection from potential negative influences (APA 2005). Families in other areas (i.e., suburban, small town, or rural communities) may experience a closer sense of social community and more frequent, positive social interactions (van den Berg et al. 2007). Levels of social disorder and strong social networks have been shown to influence parent engagement in learning activities and children's early academic skill development (Froiland et al. 2014). Thus, further investigation is needed to determine what structural factors unique to setting conditions, such as social organization or natural environments, serve to support early parent engagement in stimulating language and literacy interaction and young children's overall reading development.

7 Limitations

It is important to consider these findings in light of how rural was defined. Population, density and proximity to urban areas do not fully define rural communities and any inferences drawn about rural settings are limited to our use of the

Urban-Centric Locale Codes to define rural locations. More sensitive, comprehensive locale definitions may have produced different findings, and may also explain the lack of differences seen between rural and town settings.

Furthermore, this study focused on only a select number of parent language and literacy engagement variables during preschool that impact children's reading scores. Although the variables included in this study have been used across various studies as indications of parent language and literacy behaviors (Burgess et al. 2002; Dever 2001; Dever and Burts 2002), other possible mediating factors need to be considered. Social organization may be an important consideration, especially for rural communities (Froiland 2011). The social structures within rural communities may serve to buffer the effects of limited resources associated with rural settings and should be further explored. A related limitation is the exclusive use of self-report data to measure parent engagement rather than observational ratings. Although the ECLS-B datafile includes observational ratings of parents' literacy engagement, these ratings are only available for approximately 11 % of cases (Najarian et al. 2010). Retaining the direct observations would have reduced the sample by approximately 89 %. Nevertheless, relying on parents' reports of their engagement activities and behaviors may have produced an upward bias in our measures of parent language and literacy engagement due to socially desirable responding. Finally, parent engagement data were collected in 2005–2006; therefore, interpretations must be made in terms of resources that were available and parenting practices that were reflective of that time period. Certain indicators of parental preschool literacy engagement may have changed since the time these data were collected in both rural and non-rural contexts. Again, this is an area in need of further study.

8   Conclusions and Future Research Directions

This study provides a unique look into the influence of geographic setting on early parent engagement and children's kindergarten language and literacy development. Findings suggest that parents across rural and urban settings are equally engaged in establishing interactive home literacy environments during the preschool period. However, preschool children's access to resources (i.e., libraries and computers) is limited in rural areas compared to children in urban areas, which in turn negatively impacts rural children's kindergarten reading scores.

Yet, as demonstrated by the lack of differences in kindergarten scores for children in rural and city settings and overall higher scores for children in suburban communities, it is likely that other variables may uniquely serve to enhance early literacy skill development in both rural and suburban settings that were not accounted for in this model and warrant further study. These findings have important implications for future research examining the effects of geographic settings on parent engagement in home learning activities. Conditions in rural settings need to be better understood to determine factors that promote strong literacy skills and ultimately, academic success for rural children. Future studies need to include rigorous evaluations of distinctive features of rural contexts to better explain setting differences and identify important mediating factors influencing academic outcomes for children in rural education systems.

Acknowledgments The research reported here was supported by the Institute of Education Sciences, U.S. Department of Education, through Grant R305C090022 to the University of Nebraska-Lincoln. The opinions expressed are those of the authors and do not represent views of the Institute of Education Sciences or the U.S. Department of Education.

References

Andreassen, C., & West, J. (2007). Measuring socioemotional functioning in a national birth cohort study. *Infant Mental Health Journal, 28*, 627–646. doi:10.1002/imhj.20157

Arnold, D. H., & Doctoroff, G. L. (2003). The early education of socioeconomically disadvantaged children. *Annual Review of Psychology, 54*, 517–545. doi:10.1146/annurev.psych.54.111301.145442

Arnold, M., Newman, J., Gaddy, B., & Dean, C. (2005). A look at the condition of rural education research: Setting a direction for future research. *Journal of Research in Rural Education, 20*, 1–25.

Barnyak, N. C. (2011). A qualitative study in a rural community: Investigating the attitudes, beliefs, and interactions of young children and their parents regarding storybook read alouds. *Early Childhood Education Journal, 39*, 149–159.

Bethel, J., Green, J. L., Nord, C., Kalton, G., & West, J. (2005). *Early childhood longitudinal study, birth cohort (ECLS–B): Methodology report for the 9-month data collection (2001–02): Volume 2: Sampling (NCES 2005-147)*. Retrieved from http://files.eric.ed.gov/fulltext/ED485636.pdf

Bradley, R. H. (2002). Environment and parenting. In M. H. Bornstein (Ed.), *Handbook of parenting: Biology and ecology of parenting* (2nd ed., Vol. 2, pp. 281–314). Mahweh, NJ: Lawrence Erlbaum.

Burgess, S., Hecht, S., & Lonigan, C. (2002). Relations of the home literacy environment (HLE) to the development of reading-related abilities: A one-year longitudinal study. *Reading Research Quarterly, 37*, 408–426.

Cohen, J. (1988). *Statistical power analysis for the behavioral sciences* (2nd ed.). Hillsdale, NJ: Lawrence Erlbaum Associates.

Coladarci, T. (2007). Improving the yield of rural education research: An editor's swan song. *Journal of Research in Rural Education, 23*, 1–9.

Dever, M. T. (2001). Family literacy bags: A parent vehicle for parent education and involvement. *Journal of Early Education and Family Review, 8*(4), 17–28.

Dever, M. T., & Burts, D. C. (2002). An evaluation of family literacy bags as a vehicle for parent involvement. *Early Child Development and Care, 172*, 359–370.

Dickinson, D. K., & Tabors, P. O. (Eds.). (2001). *Beginning literacy with language: Young children learning at home and school*. Baltimore, MD: Paul H. Brookes.

Duncan, G. J., Dowsett, C. J., Claessens, A., Magnuson, K., Huston, A. C., Klebanov, P., … Japel, C. (2007). School readiness and later achievement. *Developmental Psychology, 43*, 1428–1446. doi:10.1037/0012-1649.43.6.1497

Duncan, S. E., & De Avila, E. A. (1998). *PreLAS 2000*. Monterey, CA: CTB/McGraw-Hill.

Dunn, L. M., & Dunn, L. M. (1997). *Examiner's manual for the Peabody Picture Vocabulary Test* (3rd ed.). Upper Saddle River, NJ: Pearson.

Durham, R. E., & Smith, P. J. (2006). Nonmetropolitan status and kindergarteners' early literacy skills: Is there a rural disadvantage? *Rural Sociology, 71*, 625–661.

Fielding-Barnsley, R., & Purdie, N. (2003). Early intervention in the home for children at risk of reading failure. *Support for Learning, 18*, 77–82. doi:10.1111/1467-9604.00284

Forget-Dubois, N., Dionne, G., Lemelin, J.-P., Perusse, D., Tremblay, R. E., & Boivin, M. (2009). Early child language mediates the relation between home environment and school readiness. *Child Development, 80*, 736–749.

Froiland, J. M. (2011). Examining the effects of location, neighborhood social organization, and home literacy on early cognitive skills in the United States. *International Journal of Psychology, 9*, 29–42.

Froiland, J. M., Powell, D. R., & Diamond, K. E. (2014). Relations among neighborhood social networks, home literacy environments, and children's expressive vocabulary in suburban at-risk families. *School Psychology International, 35*, 429–444. doi:10.1177/0143034313500415

Hart, B., & Risley, T. R. (1995). *Meaningful differences in the everyday experience of young American children*. Baltimore, MD: Paul H. Brookes.

Heckman, J. J. (2006). Skill formation and the economics of investing in disadvantaged children. *Science, 312*, 1900–1902. doi:10.1126/science.1128898

Hester, E. J. (2010). Narrative correlates of reading comprehension in African American children. *Contemporary Issues in Communication Sciences and Disorders, 37*, 73–85.

Hindman, A. H., Connor, C. M., Jewkes, A. M., & Morrison, F. J. (2008). Untangling the effects of shared book reading: Multiple factors and their associations with preschool literacy outcomes. *Early Childhood Research Quarterly, 23*, 330–350.

Hindman, A. H., & Morrison, F. J. (2012). Differential contributions of three parenting dimensions to preschool literacy and social skills in a middle-income sample. *Merrill-Palmer Quarterly, 58*, 191–223.

Hu, L., & Bentler, P. M. (1999). Cutoff criteria for fit indexes in covariance structure analysis. Conventional criteria versus new alternatives. *Structural Equation Modeling, 6*, 1–55.

Jordan, G. E., Snow, C. E., & Porsche, M. V. (2000). Project EASE: The effect of a family literacy project on kindergarten students' early literacy skills. *Reading Research Quarterly, 35*, 524–546.

Keith, T. Z., Keith, P. B., Quirk, K. J., Coehen-Rosenthal, E., & Franzese, B. (1996). Effects of parental involvement on achievement for students who attend school in rural America. *Journal of Research in Rural Education, 12*, 55–67.

Lampard, J. E., Voigt, M., & Bornstein, M. H. (2000). Urban and rural parenting. In L. Balter (Ed.), *Parenthood in America: An encyclopedia* (pp. 442–444). Santa Barbara, CA: ABC-CLIO Press.

Lareau, A. (2000). *Home advantage: Social class and parental intervention in elementary education* (2nd ed.). Lanham, MD: Rowman and Littlefield.

Lonigan, C. J., Wagner, R. K., Torgesen, J. K., & Rashotte, C. A. (2002). *Preschool comprehensive test of phonological and print processing*. Unpublished assessment.

Macaruso, P., & Rodman, A. (2011). Efficacy of computer-assisted instruction for the development of early literacy skills in young children. *Reading Psychology, 32*, 172–196.

Muthén, L. K., & Muthén, B. O. (1998–2010). *Mplus user's guide* (6th ed.). Los Angeles, CA: Authors.

Najarian, M., Snow, K., Lennon, J., Kinsey, S., & Mulligan, G. (2010). *Early childhood longitudinal study, birth cohort (ECLS-B), preschool—kindergarten 2007 psychometric report* (NCES 2010-009). Retrieved from http://nces.ed.gov/pubs2010/2010009.pdf

National Center for Education Statistics. (n.d.). *School locale definitions*. Retrieved from http://nces.ed.gov/surveys/ruraled/definitions.asp

National Institute of Child Health and Human Development. (2006). *Report of the National Reading Panel. Teaching children to read: An evidence-based assessment of the scientific research literature on reading and its implications for reading instruction* (NIH Publication No. 00-4769). Washington, DC: U.S. Government Printing Office.

Neuman, S. B., & Celano, D. (2001). Access to print in low- and middle-income communities: An ecological study of four neighborhoods. *Reading Research Quarterly, 36*, 8–26.

Neuman, S. B., & Celano, D. (2004). Save the libraries. *Educational Leadership, 61*, 82–85.

Porter DeCusati, C. L., & Johnson, J. E. (2004). Parents as classroom volunteers and kindergarten students' emergent reading skills. *The Journal of Educational Research, 97*, 235–246.

Reese, E., Suggate, S., Long, J., & Schaughency, E. (2010). Children's oral narrative and reading skills in the first three years of reading instruction. *Reading and Writing, 23*, 627–644. doi:10.1007/s11145-009-9175-9

Roscigno, V. J., & Crowley, M. L. (2001). Rurality, institutional disadvantage, and achievement/attainment. *Rural Sociology, 66*, 268–293.

Roscigno, V. J., Tomaskovic-Devey, D., & Crowley, M. (2006). Education and the inequalities of places. *Social Forces, 84*, 2121–2145.

Semke, C. A., & Sheridan, S. M. (2012). Family-school connections in rural educational settings: A systematic review of the empirical literature. *School Community Journal, 22*(1), 21–48.

Sénéchal, M. (2006). Testing the home literacy model: Parent involvement in kindergarten is differentially related to grade 4 reading comprehension, fluency, spelling, and reading for pleasure. *Scientific Studies of Reading, 10*, 59–87. doi:10.1207/s1532799xssr1001_4

Shamir, A., Korat, O., & Fellah, R. (2012). Promoting vocabulary, phonological awareness and concept about print among children at risk for learning disability: Can e-books help? *Reading and Writing, 25*, 45–69. doi:10.1007/s11145-010-9247-x

Sheridan, S. M., Knoche, L. L., Kupzyk, K. A., Edwards, C. P., & Marvin, C. A. (2011). A randomized trial examining the effects of parent engagement on early language and literacy: The Getting Ready intervention. *Journal of School Psychology, 49*, 361–383. doi:10.1016/j.jsp.2011.03.001

Snow, K., Derecho, A., Wheeless, S., Lennon, J., Rosen, J., Rogers, J., ..., Einaudi, P. (2009). *Early childhood longitudinal study, birth cohort (ECLS-B), kindergarten 2006 and 2007 data file user's manual (2010–010)*. Washington, DC: U.S. Department of Education, Institute of Education Sciences, National Center for Education Statistics.

Sobel, M. E. (1982). Asymptotic confidence intervals for indirect effects in structural equation models. In S. Leinhardt (Ed.), *Sociological methodology 1982* (pp. 290–312). Washington, DC: American Sociological Association.

Tabors, P. O., Roach, K. A., & Snow, C. E. (2001). Home language and literacy environment: Final results. In D. K. Dickinson & P. O. Tabors (Eds.), *Beginning literacy with language: Young children learning at home and school* (pp. 111–138). Baltimore, MD: Paul H. Brookes.

van den Berg, A. E., Hartig, T., & Staats, H. (2007). Preference for nature in urbanized societies: Stress, restoration, and the pursuit of sustainability. *Journal of Social Issues, 63*, 79–96. doi:10.1111/j.1540-4560.2007.00497.x

Weigel, D. J., Martin, S. S., & Bennett, K. K. (2006). Contributions of the home literacy environment to preschool-aged children's emerging literacy and language skills. *Early Child Development and Care, 176*, 357–378. doi:10.1080/03004430500063747

Whitehurst, G. J., & Lonigan, C. J. (2001). Emergent literacy: Development from prereaders to readers. In S. B. Neuman & D. K. Dickensen (Eds.), *Handbook of early literacy research* (pp. 11–29). New York, NY: Guilford Press.

Wolter, K. M. (1985). *Introduction to variance estimation*. New York, NY: Springer.

Improving Education Outcomes for American Indian Children: Community and Family Influences on Rural Student Academic Success

Judy Pfannenstiel and Marsha Gebhardt

Abstract This chapter describes the Parents as Teachers (PAT) home visiting model as a strategy for improving education outcomes for American Indian (AI) children in rural communities and the challenges posed by geographic isolation and poverty in these communities. It describes the lingering impacts of a federal trust role that initially sought to eradicate the influences of AI/AN culture and language in these communities and relatively recently adopted principles of self-determination and self-governance. It includes a history of PAT's work in tribal communities since 1990 in implementing home visiting programs that have moved early childhood to the forefront in AI communities at the earliest stages of child development—prenatal to age three, including the Family and Child Education (FACE) program, the Investing in Innovations (i3) Baby FACE program, and the recent Tribal MIECHV programs. Home-based strategies that address challenges and strengths of rural AI families are described. Research findings specific to PAT models in AI rural community settings and concerns for the conduct of research in these settings are provided. The chapter concludes with suggestions for future directions to advance rural research for AI communities.

Keywords American Indian · Parents as Teachers · Rural education research · Home-based strategies

While many student groups have demonstrated gains on national tests, students of American Indian and Alaskan Native (AI/AN) descent are in an academic rut, according to a 2012 study of the National Assessment of Education Progress. Achievement gaps on the Nation's Report Card have remained stagnant for AI/AN students in reading since 2005 (Sparks 2012). Reaching AI/AN children at the

J. Pfannenstiel (✉)
Research & Training Associates, Inc., 11030 Oakmont Street, Suite 200,
Overland Park, KS 66210-1100, USA
e-mail: jpfannenstiel@rtainc.com

M. Gebhardt
Parents as Teachers National Center, St. Louis, MO, USA

© Springer International Publishing Switzerland 2017   251
G.C. Nugent et al. (eds.), *Rural Education Research in the United States*,
DOI 10.1007/978-3-319-42940-3_13

earliest opportunity in their development in order to change this trajectory of low achievement, as well as providing an evidence-base for programmatic success, is high on the agenda for advancing student achievement in AI/AN communities.

Some researchers have concluded that AI/AN children are not as prepared to begin school relative to children of other racial or ethnic groups (Flanagan and Park 2005; Strang et al. 2002) and indicators of school readiness for rural AI/AN children are less than half the level of non-rural AI/AN children (National Center for Rural Early Childhood Learning Initiatives 2005). Lacking support for early childhood development programs, and exacerbated by conditions of unemployment, underemployment, and poverty in AI/AN communities, these children and families often experience an irreparable gap already at school entry.

Whereas programs and funds have focused primarily on educational outcomes for the AI/AN K-12 student population, this chapter focuses on the earliest opportunities for improving educational outcomes—prenatal to school entry. This chapter describes the ecological influences that provide challenges for learning in rural AI/AN communities and the lingering impacts of a federal trust role that initially sought to eradicate the influences of AI/AN culture and language in these communities. It includes a history of PAT's work in tribal communities since 1990 in implementing home visiting programs that have moved early childhood ages prenatal to three to the forefront in AI communities, including the Family and Child Education (FACE) program, the Investing in Innovations (i3) Baby FACE program, and the recent Tribal Maternal, Infant, and Early Childhood Home Visiting (Tribal MIECHV) program. Home-based strategies that address challenges and strengths of rural AI families are described. Research findings specific to PAT models in rural AI rural community settings and concerns for the conduct of research in these settings are provided. The chapter concludes with suggestions for future directions to advance rural research for AI communities.

1 Ecological Influences on Learning in Rural AI/AN Communities

Typical factors that distinguish rural education settings are heightened or more intense in rural American Indian communities. Most Bureau of Indian Education (BIE) schools meet the criteria outlined in the Small Rural School Achievement (SRSA) or Rural and Low-Income School (RLIS) program: geographic remoteness, high levels of poverty, and daily attendance at almost all schools serving K-6 students having fewer than 600 students. Of the approximately 150 BIE schools serving K-6 students, one-fourth of schools have fewer than 100 students; two-thirds of schools have fewer than 200 students (Bureau of Indian Education 2012). Other salient variables for the rural AI reservation context are their dispersion across many state bureaucracies; limited employment opportunities; high percentages of mothers with less than a high school education; higher percentages of single-parent households; dual language households, and limited access to literacy resources in the community and in the homes.

Two variables warrant further description because of their theoretical and empirical relationship to the well-being of young children: poverty and mother's educational level. Rural AI/AN communities have the highest poverty levels of all racial/ethnic groups. During the years spanning 2007–2011, 14.3 % of the U.S. population had income below the poverty level; this compares with a poverty rate of 25.8 % for Black/African Americans; 23.2 % for Hispanics; and 27.0 % for the AI/AN population (Macartney et al. 2013). The *highest* poverty levels (36 %) are experienced for the smaller AI population living on reservations (DeVoe and Darling-Churchill 2008). And among AI reservations, in 2010, western South Dakota was home to the three counties with the nation's highest poverty rate and has four counties in the top 10 highest poverty counties nationwide, with poverty rates exceeding 50 % (Lengerich 2012).

The intergenerational transfer of low levels of literacy continues. Nearly half of AI/AN students nationally fail to graduate each year (Alliance for Excellent Education 2010). Approximately one-third of mothers of entering kindergartners in schools operating FACE programs in 2004 and 2008 had a high school diploma or GED as their highest level of education when their child was born. Only 4 % of these American Indian children, compared with 23 % of children nationally, are born to mothers with a college degree (Pfannenstiel et al. 2006). Comparatively, 10 % of entering kindergartners nationally live in a household where the highest level of educational attainment is less than high school (U.S. Department of Education 2012). Nationwide, gaps in learning and development are known to occur from the earliest ages and large gaps between economic classes can be detected as early as nine and 24 months of age (Halle et al. 2009). As much as half of school failure may be attributable to gaps in early learning and development that exists before school entry (Lee and Burkham 2002; Rouse et al. 2005).

2   Historical Context for Education in Rural AI Communities

Some understanding of the history of the relationship between the federal government and AI/AN reservation communities is required to understand current successes and challenges in implementing and researching early childhood education in these rural communities. The federal government's historic relationship with the tribes initially denied the AI/AN community and its families the right to meet the academic, social and spiritual needs of their children, most notably through the creation of Indian Boarding Schools. The rural and economic challenges of the geographic areas the reservations encompass contributed to a lengthy history of poor educational outcomes for AI/AN communities. Federal laws and policies enacted by the Bureau of Indian Affairs since its establishment in 1824 were initially designed to subjugate and assimilate AI/AN communities; the path to Indian self-determination was long and fraught with uncertain implications for the provision of Indian education services.

A major change in policy was embodied in the Indian Reorganization Act (IRA) of 1934. It ended the allotment policy of the Dawes Act, banned the further sale of Indian land, decreed that any unallotted land not yet sold should be returned to tribal control, and granted AI communities some governmental and judicial autonomy—the beginning of today's tribal governments. Importantly, the IRA introduced the teaching of Indian history and culture in BIA schools. Despite its best intentions, the IRA had limited resources for developing self-sustaining lives for more than 100,000 landless American Indians. The migration of American Indians from rural to urban centers rapidly increased (Reynher and Education Week Staff 2013).

In 1974, in response to a Congressional directive to provide an analysis of the need for a program in early childhood education together with recommendations for carrying out such programs in the future, the Office of Indian Education published a report citing the critical need for parent-focused early childhood education programs for AI/AN children birth to five and programs for children age 5–8 (U.S. Bureau of Indian Affairs 1976). Although the need for early education for AI children was made apparent in this report, it would take almost 15 years before a birth-to-age eight BIA program was funded.[1]

The Indian Nations at Risk Task Force was chartered in 1990 by the U.S. Department of Education (U.S. Department of Education 1991). The Task Force was charged with studying the status of Native education in the United States and with issuing a report and recommendations to set the stage for improving the quality of educational institutions that AI/AN children attend and for improving their academic performance. The Task Force joined Goals 2000 in identifying school readiness as the first national goal for education: "By the year 2000 all Native children will have access to early childhood education programs that provide the language, social, physical, spiritual, and cultural foundations they need to succeed in school and to reach their full potential as adults" (p. i).

3 Programs that Have Moved Early Childhood Education Forward in AI Communities

Despite the need for early childhood services identified decades earlier, not until 1990 was the Early Childhood/Parent Involvement Pilot Program designed and implemented by the Bureau of Indian Affairs Office of Indian Education Program (now the BIE) in six pilot sites to address the common characteristics of

---

[1]The tribally-operated Head Start program was established in 1965 under the Civil Rights legislation.

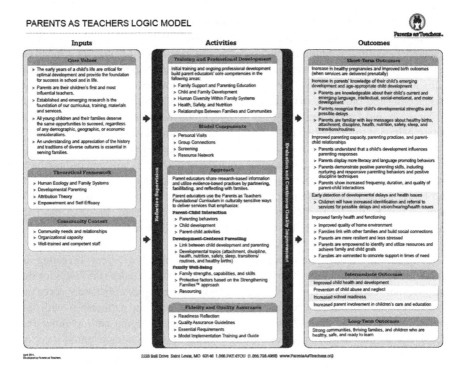

Fig. 1 The PAT logic model

low-achieving AI/AN children. The Early Childhood program was designed as a two-generational program comprised of a pre-birth to age three home-based component (provided by the Parents as Teachers model), a center-based program for preschoolers and their parents (provided by the National Center for Family Literacy), and a model for classrooms serving K-3 children and their families (provided by High/Scope).[2] The program was renamed the Family and Child Education (FACE) program in 1992.

The PAT home visiting model is based on theoretical beliefs and research which indicate that the early years of a child's life are critical for optimal development and provide the foundation for success in school and in life and that parents are their children's first and most influential teachers. The model annually provides 24 personal visits, periodic child health and developmental screenings to allow the early detection of developmental delays and health issues, resources and referrals, and monthly group connections for families. Trained and certified Parent Educators provide the services. The PAT Logic Model is depicted in Fig. 1.

---

[2]In the 2005–2006 program year, the K-3 component was eliminated from the Early Childhood FACE program in light of funding from other sources for the professional development that had formerly been funded by the FACE program.

PAT's current and expanded approach of parent education and family support includes three key areas of emphasis throughout the curriculum: development-centered parenting, parent-child interaction, and family well-being. The blend of personal visit plans and guided planning tools allow parent educators enough flexibility to individualize services for families while maintaining consistency required to produce desired outcomes. This approach and curriculum also helps organize discussions around family well-being, child development, protective factors, and parenting behavior to strengthen the parent educator and family relationships.

Although the program was expanded beyond the pilot sites throughout the following decade, some AI communities that desired a FACE program did not have the population size or school resources to implement the center-based component of the FACE model. For these communities, implementing the home-based component of FACE, the PAT home visiting model, was achievable. In 2002, the BIE awarded grants to 60 schools in AI communities to implement only the PAT home-based component as the Baby FACE program.[3]

In 2010, the U.S. Department of Education awarded a 5-year Investing in Innovations (i3) grant to the Parents As Teachers National Center (PATNC) for the purposes of expanding and developing innovative practices that can serve as models of best practices, encouraging grantees to work in partnership with the private sector and the philanthropic community, and identifying and documenting best practices that can be shared and taken to scale based on demonstrated success. The pre-birth to age three Baby FACE program was implemented in 22 rural and geographically distant American Indian reservations in six states based on growing research findings that demonstrate that achievement gaps are evident in infancy.

Additional home-based resources initiated through a federal policy initiative are now available in some AI/AN communities. The Tribal MIECHV program, established under the Patient Protection and Affordable Care Act, supports the development of happy, healthy and successful AI/AN at-risk pregnant women and children through a coordinated home visiting system that begins before birth. Several home visiting models, including Parents as Teachers, are used for this initiative, and PAT has been the most frequently-selected model. The accompanying federal initiative to encourage the use of evidence-based programs was launched in 2009 through the Home Visiting Evidence of Effectiveness (HomVEE) review process (Avelar et al. 2014). A review of the home visiting research literature for programs that serve families with pregnant women and children from birth to age 5 concluded that "more evidence is needed about the effectiveness of home visiting models for different types of families with a range of characteristics" (Avelar et al., p. 14). The i3 Baby FACE grant and its study seeks to provide further evidence of the effectiveness of home visiting for the population of children and families residing in AI communities.

---

[3]Though highly-desired by the schools, the funding for these PAT/Baby FACE programs ended after 3 years due to a ruling that rights of tribal sovereignty required decisions about the use of funds to be made at the local tribal, not BIE, level of governance. A few of the schools were able to continue funding their Baby FACE programs locally.

4   Home-Based Strategies that Address Challenges and Strengths of Rural AI Families

Geographic isolation and poverty—the most dire poverty nationwide in some of these rural tribal communities—greatly affect family well-being and children's school readiness, the foci of PAT home-based intervention strategies. Key strategies of the PAT model, and the i3 Baby FACE program specifically, are designed to help families ameliorate at least some of the impacts of isolation and poverty.

The effects of isolation in these extremely rural communities are many. Poorly maintained roads, great distances, lack of transportation, minimal communication technology and almost no internet access render it difficult or impossible to locate and access available services and resources. Home-based service delivery is an obvious solution. Information, resources, and materials are brought to the homes of families who would not be able to access them if they had to rely on their own transportation or technology resources. A prime example is the problem that these communities have no public libraries. The strategy of the Baby FACE program to infuse children's books into the homes of Baby FACE families greatly enhances the home literacy environment and renders it capable of supporting children's literacy and school readiness. Parent educators bring three age-appropriate children's books each month. These books are introduced during the personal visit; the parent educator models effective book sharing techniques and provides parents opportunities to practice and become more skillful in promoting literacy development and the joy of reading.

Other effects of poverty result in difficulty meeting the basic needs of families, such as a lack of continuous/reliable employment, non-existent or unreliable transportation, lack of money for gas, housing and food insecurity, and child/family health and safety issues. The key strategies used by PAT parent educators include goal-setting and the resource/referral component of the model. For example, a parent educator might help a parent work through the goal setting tool from the curriculum to identify specific steps and timelines for completing a GED or enrolling in college; applying for and obtaining employment; or accessing housing, food, counseling and other resources. This process may include direct assistance in connecting the parent with the appropriate resource, and evaluating monthly progress toward the goal.

In addition to isolation and poverty, a serious challenge for rural tribal education is the disproportionate placement of K-12 AI/AN students into special education programs and services beginning in early grades—14 % of AI/AN students compared to 12 % of Black/African American, 9 % of White, 8 % of Hispanic, and 5 % of Asian/Pacific Islander students between ages 6 and 21 receive special education services (U.S. Department of Education 2009). The PAT home visiting programs over time have increasingly focused on early detection and systematic screening for developmental delays, including physical, social-emotional, cognitive and receptive and expressive language development. The percentage of home-based FACE children who received screening services increased from less than 47 % in 1997 to

91 % in 2013 (Yarnell et al. 2014). Subsequent home visits include information and activities to support any identified concerns or deficits. If still more support is needed, referrals are made to community-based resources such as Indian Health Services (IHS) and early intervention.

The preservation and use of native language is highly valued by the 566 federally recognized tribes. Meeting the needs and supporting the strengths of dual language households is an important challenge for home-based programs—20 % of AI/AN children between 5 and 17 years of age live in a home where a language other than English is spoken (DeVoe and Darling-Churchill 2008). Both the FACE and Baby FACE programs were continually modified over time in ways that explicitly integrated the language and culture of the tribal communities through processes that have been found effective, including ongoing communication with parents and the community about teaching within a culturally relevant context; building a sense of belongingness and community through ritual and cultural events; and respecting children, families, and community (Gilliard and Moore 2007; Romero-Little 2010). For example, a parent educator will support the family in practicing the tribe's traditions around a child's development, such as the baby's first laugh ceremony. Parent educators also encourage parents to incorporate their Native language and images in the homemade books and toys from the curriculum's Activity Pages.

The PAT home-based programs have also promoted the integration of culture and language by an emphasis on hiring tribal community members as parent educators, and have provided the training and support needed when few tribal members initially had the credentials for the positions. Now almost all parent educators (96 %) are American Indian and are from the community they serve, which enables them to be effective and enthusiastic supporters of language and culture (Yarnell et al. 2014).

In the implementation of the PAT model in FACE and Baby FACE programs, predictable obstacles have existed in these very rural, very poor American Indian communities. Hiring and retention of qualified staff is a continual challenge (Lambson et al. 2005). Although PAT standards recommend that parent educators have a BA degree, approximately 50 % of the FACE and Baby FACE parent educators have a BA. In rural American Indian communities it is more difficult to find staff with both the interpersonal skills required of parent educators and a 4-year degree. The need is intensified by the relatively small amount of time that supervisors, usually principals, have available for training and supporting the program staff. To address this need, on-going professional development and technical assistance are especially important and have been provided on a continual basis. On-site technical assistance is provided twice a year for the first 3 years of a FACE or Baby FACE program and once a year thereafter. Systematic distance technical assistance is delivered through monthly calls with individual parent educators. Face-to-face professional development events occur annually, and group webinars and conference calls occur more frequently.

Other program strategies address the two problems that loom large among obstacles to program implementation: recruitment and the sustained participation of families. Hiring staff with prior experience working with families in the community, in-person recruitment and direct referrals are reported to be the most successful outreach strategies (Valorose et al. 2015). The small size of many tribal communities facilitates in-person recruitment at grocery stores, schools, hospitals and clinics, or door-to-door. Regular and sustained participation by families is a key factor in achieving expected outcomes. Participation rates are regularly analyzed; strategies to increase participation are developed and shared among programs through regularly scheduled site-specific reflective supervision, professional development, and technical assistance. Successful strategies that have evolved include making participation comfortable and convenient by establishing trusting relationships and providing services in the home; intensifying persistence and support for families experiencing multiple crises; and providing services and materials that are valued by families, such as parent-child activities, developmental information, children's books, and basic needs such as diapers and gas cards. A more recent strategy for reducing no-shows has been the use of social media such as Facebook for scheduling and reminding participants of home visits and group meetings (Valorose et al. 2015.) Social media also proved to be an effective communication tool for families who moved frequently, had no land-line phone access, or ran out of minutes on their mobile phones.

5   Early Childhood Research Base in AI/AN Communities

In his review of the research on early childhood for AI/AN populations, Demmert (2001) concluded that studies on "the effects of early environment and educational programs on the intellectual development of Native children are scarce. In contrast, the body of research on these topics for non-Native groups is growing in significance and volume" (p. 6). In their review of programs and strategies that meet the literacy needs of AI/AN families more than a decade later, Faircloth and Thompson (2012) similarly conclude that:

> ...with the exception of FACE and Head Start/Early Head Start, limited data have been collected documenting outcomes and impacts of these programs. What literature does exist is primarily based on program evaluations and associated reports. While this information is important, it fails to adequately meet the need for empirically validated data (p. 265).

A significant amount of past research has been conducted for the FACE program and a significant study of the Baby FACE program is underway. While the FACE program encompasses both home-and center-based components and the Baby FACE program is comprised of only the home-based component, the research presented is largely a summary of findings for PAT's home-based component.

This research was facilitated by the PATNC's continual focus on clearly articulating the PAT model's theoretical underpinnings through the development of a program logic model, comprised of inputs to the program; activities that support implementation; and short-, medium, and long-term outcomes. Expectations for fidelity of implementation (FOI) of the service delivery model and levels of participation were outlined. PAT's logic model formed the basis for research on the relationships among FOI, levels of participation, and program outcomes.

Three FACE Impact Studies collected school readiness data in the fall of 2004, 2008 and 2012 from approximately 1500 kindergartners in each study. Together with annual evaluations of the FACE program conducted since the program's inception in 1990, these studies form the primary sources for research on the FACE program. The FACE Impact evaluations were specifically designed to be mindful of the BIE's need to link early learning experiences to longer-term measures of school readiness. Nonetheless, impacts on shorter- and medium-term outcomes were included in these studies.

The initial FACE Impact Study was a quasi-experimental design study conducted at 25 tribal schools which had been participating in the FACE program for a sufficient length of time to have participants at the kindergarten entry age. Two comparison groups were formulated. One comparison group was comprised of 19 tribal schools which had not operated FACE programs and were matched to the 25 FACE tribal schools on tribal affiliation and geographic proximity.

A second comparison group, and the one used in the subsequent impact studies, was comprised of entering kindergartners at the FACE tribal schools who had not participated in the FACE program prior to school entry.

The FACE impact studies obtained measures of school readiness that were consistent with the BIE's vision of how to assess AI children. In the three impact studies, the Work Sampling System (WSS) was used. The WSS employs teacher observational rating checklists completed during 6 weeks of observation at the beginning of the kindergarten year on domains that include language and literacy, mathematics, and personal and social development. Additionally, kindergarten teachers rated each child on their preparation for kindergarten with a three-point scale that included above average preparation, average preparation, and below average preparation. The 2004 study additionally required the use of a nationally standardized test (Stanford Achievement Test, Edition 10), consistent with the direction for direct student assessment emphasized at that time. In 2012, consistent with a bureau-wide adoption of a computerized direct assessment of student performance, the Northwest Evaluation Association's (NWEA) kindergarten entry assessment was used for the impact study.

Parents of kindergartners were also surveyed for each study to provide information on their child(ren's) pre-kindergarten experiences (e.g., participation in Early Childhood Special Education and participation in preschool—including Early Head Start, Head Start, FACE preschool, other public preschool, or private preschool), frequency of home literacy activities, number of children's books in the home, and parent involvement in the school.

Structural equation modeling was used to test relationships among characteristics of study participants, program characteristics, quantitative and qualitative aspects of participation, and program outcomes; and to explore alternative structural models that investigated the mediating effects of type and length of preschool participation and the home literacy environment. Several strategies for establishing evidence of causality were used in these investigations. Data were collected that have an established temporal order; the program's logic model was used to identify the intervening mechanisms by which the FACE program promotes child outcomes such as school readiness; dose/response relationships were measured (e.g., intensity of program participation and preschool attendance); and control techniques for background characteristic (e.g., age, gender, mother's educational level) were made explicit (Johnson 2001).

The results of these studies indicate that a pre-birth to kindergarten culturally-relevant program provides a structure of supports at home and in center-based settings that predict school readiness for AI children in mostly rural reservation settings. The studies reaffirmed findings that sequentially receiving a home-visiting program followed by a preschool program is of considerable value in altering the trajectory for children experiencing low achievement (Administration for Children and Families 2006; Pfannenstiel et al. 2002); this combination of services was found to be especially effective for special needs AI preschoolers (Pfannenstiel and Lente-Jojola 2011). Structural equation findings reveal that frequent home visits from birth to age three predict school readiness through two intervening variables—the length of preschool attendance and the frequency of home literacy activity (Pfannenstiel et al. 2002; Pfannenstiel and Lente-Jojola 2011). The FACE program has impacts on increased parent involvement, increased frequency of use of the tribal language in the home, increased access to literacy resources in the home, and increased frequency of home literacy activity in the home.

National data indicate that children of the most highly educated mothers are more than twice as likely to attend early childhood care and education programs (71 %) than are children of mothers without a high school diploma (29 %) (Federal Interagency Forum on Child and Family Statistics 2012). A second source of national data in 2011 indicated that 64 % of mothers with at least a B.A. compared with 34 % of mothers with less than a high school/GED degree enrolled their children in preschool (U.S. Department of Health and Human Services 2014). Contrary to these findings, FACE Impact study findings in each year indicate that significantly more FACE mothers who lacked a high school diploma at their child's birth reported that their child attended preschool (98 % in 2004, 97 % in 2008 and 86 % in 2012). Of mothers who lacked a high school diploma and did not participate in FACE, only 58 % reported in 2012 that their child attended preschool. Thus, participation in FACE mitigates the deleterious effects of a mother's low educational level on preschool attendance.

The FACE program has also demonstrated some level of success in breaking the cycle of intergenerational low literacy. FACE children whose mothers lacked a high school diploma or GED at their child's birth entered school with average preparation for school as rated by kindergarten teachers. Children whose mothers did not have a high school diploma and whose mother did not participate in FACE entered school with a below average preparation rating. Thus, participation in the FACE program also mitigates the deleterious effects of a mother's low educational level on children's school readiness.

6 Concerns for Research in AI/AN Communities

The issues of tribal sovereignty, self-determination, and preservation of language and culture that guided the development of the FACE/Baby FACE programs have their corollary in emerging policies and procedures guiding the design of research, data collection, and use and ownership of data in AI/AN communities. The history of the conduct of research on AI/AN populations, not surprisingly, contains many parallels to the assimilationist policies of the past. While Demmert's research review cited the paucity of early childhood and educational research specific to AI/AN populations, Sahota's research concludes that the AI/AN population has been heavily studied for medical science research (Sahota 2007). Her search on one of the nation's largest search engines for medical science articles dating from the 1950s yielded more than 3000 articles reporting research in AI/AN communities. The high prevalence of health concerns (i.e. diabetes, heart disease, and alcohol use) and priorities in federal funding for research with ethnic minority groups are cited as reasons for this focus (Brugge and Missaghian 2003). Research missteps have included the failure to gain informed consent, the use of data for purposes other than those cited in the research design, the use of data for unauthorized purposes, and the publication of papers containing sensitive information on identified AI tribes without their review or approval (Sahota 2007).

As sovereign nations, tribal communities responded to these transgressions by formulating strategies for regulating research conducted on tribal members and their communities. Building on federal policy contained in The Code of Federal Regulation's Protections of Human Subjects (Department of Health and Human Services 2005) and the Institutional Review Board (IRB) process, these efforts seek to extend the federal policy that largely focuses on the rights of individual tribal members to also include the rights of the tribal community. "This means that AI/AN communities should not be identified in research results without their 'explicit consent' and that, like individual research participants, they can refuse to participate in a study or withdraw at any time" (Sahota, p. 4). The IHS has established IRBs for its Area Offices and requires proof that tribal governments have approved the research, often in the form of a tribal resolution or letter of support. An increasing number of tribes have established their own IRBs.

As Sahota points out, while these efforts promote tribal sovereignty and self-determination in the control and regulation of research, potential conflicts of interest and limitations to research exist. The federal government, for instance, supports research which is in the public interest, supports academic freedom, and has requirements for data sharing for federally-funded research. The data sharing federal requirement has implications for tribal regulation and control when tribes desire to apply for federal grants and the data use requirements of the federal grant conflict with tribal policy.

Other concerns for research in these rural communities stem from the many federal agencies with trust obligations to the tribes. While studies of the FACE program and AI/AN Head Start/Early Head Start program may provide the bulk of the research on early childhood and family programs in rural AI settings, the data for FACE research is restricted to participants in FACE programs and the data for AI/AN Head Start/Early Head Start programs is restricted to AI/AN Head Start/Early Head Start programs and participants—despite the fact that these programs operate in many of the same communities and share participants. Of the 44 FACE programs in program year 2013, for example, 86 % also had Head Start Programs in their community and three also operated Early Head Start programs (Yarnell et al. 2014). Most AI communities, similar to many rural areas, are unable to link data across early childhood programs in order to answer critical policy questions (Johnson et al. 2014).

Dual funding agencies with separate research agendas also render it difficult to identify unique program effects (Pfannenstiel and Lente-Jojola 2012). The FACE impact study findings, which primarily focus on school readiness as the major outcome variable, found that approximately 70 % of FACE children had attended Head Start preschool for at least part of their preschool experience Identifying the quantitative and qualitative aspects of preschool attendance and its impact on school readiness is a complex undertaking in these communities.

FACE impact study findings consistently find that no more than one in three children entering kindergarten in schools where the FACE program has been implemented for a sufficient number of years to have children of kindergarten age have participated in any FACE component prior to school entry. Only one in ten students in FACE schools had participated in both home-based and center-based components of the FACE model prior to kindergarten entry. Whereas the number of sites participating in the FACE program has increased over time, within-site participation has remained stable due to a combination of level-funding and difficulties in providing services to families with young children, including high mobility. This relatively low level of program "reach" and comparatively small numbers of research subjects raises questions about the extent to which the FACE program can currently be expected to impact school readiness for AI/AN children.

Well-known to the AI/AN community is the propensity for children and their families to be excluded from national studies, largely due to their wide geographic dispersion and small sample size. In cases where AIs are not excluded, they are often aggregated with "other" minorities (Pavel and Curtin 1997), rendering the data of limited value for informing the 566 federally-recognized tribes. Acknowledging the lack of AI/AN representation in its studies, the Department of Health and Human Services established the AI/AN Head Start Research Center (AIANHSRC); it focuses on community-based participatory research projects and requires tribal review and approval before results can be disseminated outside the tribal community.

Other concerns for limits on the generation of research that supports the information needs of rural tribal communities and tribal control of the research process are encountered when tribal needs meet federal funding and research requirements. The study design for the i3 Baby FACE program, by way of example, was guided by the National Evaluation of i3 (NEi3), which was based on the What Works Clearinghouse (WWC) Procedures and Standards Handbook to define the criteria for what constitutes high-quality research for this effort (U.S. Department of Education 2014). The difficulties in meeting adequate sample size for treatment and control or comparison groups in AI tribal communities are profound, particularly for interventions that extend beyond a school year and encompass a pre-birth to age 3 timeframe—or a pre-birth to kindergarten timeframe. In some AI communities, sustaining participation in multi-year interventions is highly problematic and is characterized by multiple program entry and exit.

A final research concern for rural AI communities is a long-standing concern—the instruments that are commercially available for assessing intellectual or achievement outcomes for populations with unique language and culture (and which would meet psychometric standards for high quality research) are non-existent or extremely limited. For the evaluation of the Baby FACE program, a paramount concern was the need to assess 3-year-old children using assessors from the AI community to the extent possible. In almost every site, this requirement meant that the instrument employed could be administered by persons who did not have to be certified to do so. Only three commercially available instruments with the required psychometric characteristics were available.

For early childhood programs which have a goal of increasing the use of the tribal language, assessments that focus only on English language acquisition do not measure the efforts devoted to tribal language acquisition and preservation or the learning of the children. Research on early language acquisition concludes that birth-to-three is a critical timeframe for children. "Infants quickly learn to identify different languages by their rhythms, their characteristic phonemes, and other cues. Though bilingual children have a smaller vocabulary in a particular language than monolingual children of the same age, bilingual children know more words in total if you count both languages" (Aamodt and Wang 2011, p. 53). Aamodt and Wang argue that a too-early focus on English-only language acquisition can be detrimental to dual-language acquisition.

7 Future Directions to Advance Rural Education Research for AI Communities

The lack of progress in closing the achievement gap for K-12 students has increased the urgency in AI/AN communities to close the achievement gap at school entry. While an increased focus on early childhood programs is promising for improving education outcomes for AI children, future directions for research require a longer-term approach. All early childhood programs operating in rural AI communities would benefit from a longitudinal research design that spans the intervention years of pre-birth to school entry and extends to the critical third grade benchmark for reading. Future research would also benefit from the measurement of interventions as they are experienced by families across federal funding sources rather than past and current attempts to isolate the independent effects of programs operated from a specific funding source.

One effort with this potential is the study of the prenatal to age three i3 Baby FACE program, which supports research for the very important early stages of development and assesses children's cognitive and socio-emotional development at age three. While this is important research specifically focused on a population with little research, the longer-term goal of the home-based programs is to close the achievement gap at school entry. Sources for funding the extension of the study to include kindergarten readiness are being sought. This longitudinal research, as well as future research, will be aided by the BIE's facilitation of access to computer-based assessments at kindergarten entry in BIE and tribally-operated schools. This systematic assessment will readily provide a measure of school readiness that has been largely unavailable in the past.

References

Aamodt, S., & Wang, S. (2011). *Welcome to your child's brain.* New York, NY: Bloomsbury.

Administration for Children and Families. (2006). *Preliminary findings from the Early Head Start pre-kindergarten follow-up.* Washington, DC: United States Department of Health and Human Services.

Alliance for Excellent Education. (2010). *Current challenges and opportunities in preparing rural high school students for success in college and careers: What federal policymakers need to know.* Washington, DC: Author.

Avelar, S., Paulsell, D., Sama-Miller, E., Del Grosso, P., Akers, L., & Kleinman, R. (2014). *Home visiting evidence of effectiveness reviews: Executive summary.* Washington, DC: Office of Planning, Research and Evaluation, Administration for Children and Families, U.S. Department of Health and Human Services.

Bureau of Indian Education. (2012). *Native American student identification system kindergarten students [data file].* Albuquerque, NM: Author.

Brugge, D., & Missaghian, M. (2003). *Protecting the Navajo people through tribal regulation of research.* Retrieved from http://www.researchethics.org/articles.asp?viewrec=27

Demmert, W. (2001). *Improving academic performance among Native American students: A review of the research literature.* Charleston, WV: ERIC Clearinghouse on Rural Education and Small Schools.

Department of Health and Human Services. (2005). *Code of federal regulations, title 45, public welfare,* part 46, protection of human subjects. Retrieved from http://www.hhs.gov/ohrp/humansubjects/guidance/45cfr46.htm

DeVoe, J., & Darling-Churchill, K. (2008). *Status and trends in the education of American Indians and Alaska Natives* (NCES 2008-084). Washington, DC: National Center for Education Statistics, Institute of Education Sciences, U.S. Department of Education.

Faircloth, S., & Thompson, N. (2012). Meeting the needs of American Indian and Alaska Native families. In B. Wasik (Ed.), *Handbook of family literacy* (2nd ed., pp. 270–288). New York, NY: Routledge.

Federal Interagency Forum on Child and Family Statistics. (2012). *America's children: Key national indicators of well-being, 2011.* Washington, DC: U.S. Government Printing Office.

Flanagan, K., & Park, J. (2005). *American Indian and Alaska Native children: Findings from the base year of the early childhood longitudinal study, birth cohort (ECLS-B) (NCES 2005-116).* Washington. DC: U.S. Department of Education, National Center for Education Statistics.

Gilliard, J. L., & Moore, R. A. (2007). An investigation of how culture shapes curriculum in early care and education programs on a Native American Indian reservation: "The drum is considered the heartbeat of the community". *Early Childhood Education Journal, 34*(4), 251–258.

Halle, T., Forry, N., Hair, E., Perpe, K., Wandner, L., & Whittaker, J. (2009). *Disparities in early learning and development: Lessons from the early childhood longitudinal study—Birth cohort.* Bethesda, MD: Child Trends.

Johnson, B. (2001). Toward a new classification of nonexperimental quantitative research. *Educational Researcher, 30*(2), 3–13.

Johnson, J., Showalter, D., Klein, R., & Lester, C. (2014). *Why rural matters 2013–14: The condition of rural education in the 50 states.* Washington, DC: The Rural School and Community Trust.

Lambson, T., Yarnell, V., & Pfannenstiel, J. (2005). *BIA Baby FACE program evaluation study.* Overland Park, KS: Research and Training Associates Inc.

Lee, V., & Burkham, D. (2002). *Inequality at the starting gate: Social background differences in achievement as children begin school.* Washington, DC: Economic Policy Institute.

Lengerich, R. (2012). Nation's top three poorest counties in western South Dakota. *Rapid City Journal.* Retrieved from http://rapidcityjournal.com/news/nation-s-top-three-poorest-counties-in-western-south-dakota/article_2d5bb0bc-44bf-11e1-bbc9-0019bb2963f4.html

Macartney, S., Bishaw, A., & Fontenot, K. (2013). *Poverty rates for selected detailed race and Hispanic groups by state and place: 2007–2011* (pp. 13–20). Washington, DC: US Census Bureau.

National Center for Rural Early Childhood Learning Initiatives. (2005). *American Indian and Alaska native young children: Findings from the ECLS-K and ECLS-B baseline data (rural early childhood brief no. 4).* Mississippi State, MS: Mississippi State University Early Childhood Institute.

Pavel, D., & Curtin, T. (1997). *Characteristics of American Indian and Alaska Native education: Results from the 1993–94 and 1990–91 schools and staffing survey.* Washington, DC: U.S. Department of Education.

Pfannenstiel, J., & Lente-Jojola, D. (2011). The Family and Child Education (FACE) program and school readiness: A structural model approach in an American Indian reservation context. *Journal of American Indian Education, 50*(2), 84–96.

Pfannenstiel, J., & Lente-Jojola, D. (2012). *The family and child education program: Unpacking the effects of preschool on school readiness.* Paper Presented at the Annual Conference of the National Center for Family Literacy, San Diego, CA.

Pfannenstiel, J., Seitz, V., & Zigler, E. (2002). Promoting school readiness: The role of the Parents as Teachers program. *NHSA Dialog, 6,* 71–86.

Pfannenstiel, J., Yarnell, V., Stromberg-Kettelhake, R., & Lambson, T. (2006). *Impact study of the family and child education program.* Washington, DC: Department of Interior, Bureau of Indian Affairs, Office of Indian Education Programs.

Reynher, J., & Education Week Staff. (2013). 1819–2013: A history of American Indian Education. *Education Week.* Retrieved from: http://www.edweek.org/ew/projects/2013/native-american-education/history-of-american-indian-education.html

Romero-Little, M. E. (2010). How should young indigenous children be prepared for learning? A vision of early childhood education for indigenous children. *Journal of American Indian Education, 49*(1 & 2), 7–27.

Rouse, C., Brooks-Gunn, J., & McLanahan, S. (2005). Introducing the issue. School readiness: Closing racial and ethnic gaps. *The Future of Children, 15*(1), 5–13.

Sahota, P. (2007). *Research regulation in American Indian/Alaska Native communities: Policy and practice considerations.* Washington, DC: National Congress of American Indian Policy Research Center. Retrieved from http://www.ncaiprc.org/research-regulation-papers

Sparks, S. (2012). NAEP scores still stalled for Native American students. *Education Week.* Retrieved from http://www.edweek.org/ew/articles/2012/07/03/36indian.h31.html

Strang, W., von Glatz, A., & Hammer, P. (2002). Setting the agenda: American Indian and Alaska Native education research priorities. *ERIC Digest* EDO-RC-02-14. Retrieved from http://files. eric.ed.gov/fulltext/ED471718.pdf

U.S. Bureau of Indian Affairs. (1976). *Young Native Americans and their families: Educational needs assessment and recommendations.* Washington, DC: ERIC Document Reproduction Service No. ED127021.

U.S. Department of Education. (2014). What Works Clearinghouse[TM]; procedures and standards handbook version 3.0. Washington, DC: Author. Retrieved from http://ies.ed.gov/ncee/wwc/ pdf/reference_resources/wwc_procedures_v3_0_standards_handbook.pdf

U.S. Department of Education, National Center for Education Statistics. (2012). *Early childhood longitudinal study, kindergarten class of 2010–11 (ECLS-K:2011),* preliminary restricted-use data file. See Digest of Education Statistics 2012, table 136.

U.S. Department of Health and Human Services. (2014). *Trends in the use of early care and education, 1995–2011.* Washington, DC: U.S. Government Printing Office.

U.S. Department of Education. (1991). *Indian nations at risk: An educational strategy for action: Final report of the Indian Nations at Risk Task Force.* Washington, DC: Author. Retrieved from http://www2.ed.gov/rschstat/research/pubs/oieresearch/research/natatrisk/report.pdf

U.S. Department of Education, Office of Special Education and Rehabilitative Services, Office of Special Programs. (2009). *28th Annual Report to Congress on the Implementation of the Individuals with Disabilities Education Act, 2006* (Vol. 1). Washington, DC: Author.

Valorose, J., Johnson, N., Steele, M., & Chase, R. (2015). *Baby FACE qualitative evaluation.* St. Louis: Parents as Teachers National Center.

Yarnell, V., Lambson, T., & Pfannenstiel, J. (2014). *Evaluation of the BIA family and child education program for program year 2012–13.* Overland Park, KS: Research and Training Associates Inc.

Family-School Partnerships in Rural Communities: Benefits, Exemplars, and Future Research

Susan M. Sheridan, Gina M. Kunz, Shannon Holmes
and Amanda Witte

Abstract Research has established that families significantly influence students' development, with parental engagement positively predicting academic and social-behavioral adjustment. When families and schools partner in students' education, positive benefits for the students as well as their families and teachers are realized. Although rural schools are uniquely positioned to foster and benefit from family-school partnerships, limited resources, logistical barriers and lack of familiarity challenge the development of effective partnerships in rural settings. This chapter will examine *Teachers and Parents as Partners* (TAPP), a structured, indirect intervention that focuses both on promoting students' social-behavior and academic success and strengthening family-school partnerships. Research on TAPP has documented its positive effects on students' behavioral, academic and social-emotional functioning across home and school settings; this chapter will outline its efficacy and utility in rural settings. Authors will review results from a four-year randomized controlled trial investigating the effects of TAPP in rural schools and provide suggestions for future research considerations of family-school partnerships in the rural context.

Keywords Rural home-school partnerships · Teachers and parents as partners · Rural parent-teacher partnerships · Rural education research on parent-teacher partnerships · Parents and teachers as partners · Rural education research partnerships · Rural education research

S.M. Sheridan (✉) · G.M. Kunz · S. Holmes · A. Witte
Nebraska Center for Research on Children, Youth, Families
and Schools, National Center for Research on Rural Education,
University of Nebraska–Lincoln, 216 Mabel Lee Hall, Lincoln,
NE 68588-0235, USA
e-mail: ssheridan2@unl.edu

© Springer International Publishing Switzerland 2017
G.C. Nugent et al. (eds.), *Rural Education Research in the United States*,
DOI 10.1007/978-3-319-42940-3_14

1 Introduction to Family-School Partnerships

Student learning is a dynamic, interactive process. It occurs through experiences within and across many interconnected systems and environments. Grounded in ecological theory (Bronfenbrenner 1979, 1992), attention to methods for augmenting proximal learning environments (microsystems, characterized as homes *or* schools) and relationships among them (mesosystems, characterized as homes *with* schools) is necessary for maximizing student academic and social-behavioral outcomes. Because students spend the majority of their time within and between the home and school systems, promoting cohesion across these two systems is a particularly relevant goal. The ways in which families and schools work together are important, and it is only when parents and teachers engage in partnership with one another that positive benefits for students are maximized (Christenson and Sheridan 2001; Semke and Sheridan 2012).

Family influences, practices, and relationships have a significant effect on students' development. It is now widely accepted that parents' attitudes, behaviors, and the provision of personal and educational resources to support a child's learning and development (i.e., parent engagement) is strongly related to students' academic and social-behavioral adjustment (Henderson and Mapp 2002; Hoover-Dempsey et al. 2005). Families can be engaged in their child's education in several ways. Definitions espousing a *family involvement* frame emphasize the unique roles and contributions of families, and activities they practice to support education (Fantuzzo et al. 2000). When family involvement is extended in specific ways to include shared responsibilities of parents and teachers in relationships that are viewed as mutual and collaborative, there is a shift from isolated contributions to *partnerships* between home and school settings (Christenson and Sheridan 2001; Henderson et al. 2007; Witte and Sheridan 2011).

Rural schools and families are uniquely positioned to foster and benefit from family-school partnerships. Limited availability of specialized student support resources, logistical barriers for accessing supports, and lack of familiarity with and routine use of services challenge the development and practice of effective family-school partnerships in rural settings. This chapter will examine Teachers and Parents as Partners (TAPP; also known as Conjoint Behavioral Consultation; Sheridan et al. 1996; Sheridan and Kratochwill 2008), a structured, indirect service delivery model that focuses both on promoting students' academic and social-behavioral success *and* strengthening connections between parents and teachers as a means for supporting family-school partnerships in rural communities. We provide an overview of family-school partnerships and the research supporting their efficacy, describe TAPP and its application in rural communities, and conclude with a discussion on future research directions for family-school partnerships in rural settings.

2   What are Family-School Partnerships?

Family-school partnerships are student-centered actions wherein parents and educators cooperate, coordinate, and collaborate to enhance opportunities and success for children and adolescents (Christenson and Sheridan 2001; Sheridan et al. 2014a). A hallmark of family-school partnerships is the centrality of students in every interaction between home and school. In true partnerships, families and schools come together for the common purpose of supporting a student's positive growth and development. The goals of family-school partnerships are to (a) improve learning experiences and outcomes for students; (b) strengthen relationships within and among systems in a student's life (parent-child, parent-teacher, teacher-student); (c) address concerns for students across home and school settings; and (d) increase cooperation and collaboration between home and school settings. Family-school partnerships are poised to increase shared commitments between parents and schools; enhance mutual understandings of problems, challenges or needs of students; and establish joint ownership for solutions, rather than assign blame (Christenson and Sheridan 2001).

Partnerships between families and schools are couched in relationships, developed and refined through intentional interactions over time. Effective partnerships place priority on the relationship between home and school, rather than the distinct roles that each serves. Elements of trust, mutual respect, bi-directional communication and joint planning are foundational components of effective family-school partnership approaches (Sheridan et al. 2014a). There is a close collaboration between parents and schools as they share information, perspectives and resources.

3   Importance of Partnerships Between Families and Schools

When families and schools engage in effective partnership practices, students' educational, behavioral and social-emotional outcomes are enhanced (for review see Fan and Chen 2001). Decades of research show that when families and schools work together, students demonstrate (a) increased achievement and performance (Galindo and Sheldon 2012), (b) long-term academic success and school completion (Barnard 2004), and (c) fewer problems related to school discipline (e.g., fewer occurrences of suspensions and detentions; Sheldon and Epstein 2002). In fact, benefits of quality family-school partnership intervention programs are evident for even the youngest students. Galindo and Sheldon (2012) reported significant increases in math and reading gains for students in kindergarten, and Miedel and Reynolds (1999) reported fewer occurrences of students in preschool and kindergarten being retained a grade. Beyond academic improvements, family-school partnership programs have been shown to reduce students' disruptive behaviors

(Pearce 2009; Sheridan et al. 2013) and ADHD symptoms (Owens et al. 2008), and increase adaptive behavior and social skills (Sheridan et al. 2012).

Parents and schools also benefit from quality family-school partnership programs. Greater knowledge of school functioning and increased levels of participation on school decision-making committees has been associated with high quality parent engagement programs (Sheldon and Van Voorhis 2004). Significant gains in parental competence in problem-solving, home-school communication, and family and classroom functioning have been noted in research on collaborative family-school intervention programs (Owens et al. 2008; Sheridan et al. 2014c).

4   The Value of Family-School Partnerships in the Rural Context

Several research studies examining the role of family involvement and family-school partnerships in rural communities found these programs to be critical for rural students' achievement. In fact, in a review of six types of rural family-school-community connections, parent involvement was recognized as a predictor of student success (e.g., Epstein 1995 and Tompkins and Deloney 1994, in Bauch 2001). Similarly, Barley and Beesley (2007) found that success for students in high-performing, high-needs rural schools was strongly linked to supportive relationships with families and communities.

Benefits associated with *involving* parents in rural students' education are evident across age and grade ranges, ethnicity, and various rural geographic locations. One study examined the relationship between parent involvement and student outcomes for middle-school (e.g., 9–12 years) African American students in rural schools (Brody et al. 1995). They found that involvement from mothers mediated the relationship between parental demographic characteristics (education, SES) and student functioning (academic skills and self-regulation). Another study examined the relationship between family involvement and student language outcomes for predominantly Hispanic, immigrant families in rural schools (St. Clair et al. 2012). Findings revealed that students of families who participated in the family involvement training program scored higher on language measures than the students of families who did not participate in the program. Even for older students, parental involvement remains important. Schools in rural Appalachia that employed successful efforts to secure parent involvement in their children's education found this resulted in the highest levels of students enrolling in college (King 2012). This study identified parental involvement as one of the factors that contributed the most to students' decisions to enroll in college.

Benefits of rural families and schools *partnering* on behalf of students have also been documented (for review see Semke and Sheridan 2012). Notably, Owens and colleagues (2008) examined the effects of a family-school partnership intervention with a sample of students with disruptive behaviors in a rural community in the Appalachian region. Of the students (grades K-6) that participated, those that received the treatment, which was comprised of a daily report card intervention, biweekly consultation meetings, and behavioral parenting sessions, showed significant improvements in behavioral functioning (i.e., hyperactivity, impulsivity, and conduct disorder symptoms). Moreover, parents and teachers that received the intervention reported better relationships with the participating students, as well as improvements in classroom and family functioning.

Indications point to the likelihood of success for rural schools that implement programs to engage parents in true family-school partnerships. The benefits to the students, as well as to the families and schools are clear. Additionally, when schools do not employ family-school partnership programs, they lose an opportunity to capitalize on parents as a valuable resource for students' education. Rural schools stand much to gain and little to lose in implementing effective family-school partnerships. Recommendations for establishing family-school partnerships in rural schools are presented in Table 1.

Table 1 Recommendations for establishing family-school partnerships in rural communities	*Provide the context for parents to feel empowered* • Always consider parents/families as a resource and help them to recognize themselves as resources • Communicate to parents that they have power, dignity, and authority in rearing their children and contributing to their child's education • Empower parents in an intentional and ongoing way by demonstrating respect, belief, and expectations so that parents can gain greater access to and control over resources
	Negotiate roles and responsibilities • Include parents in decision making for their child • Explain to parents the importance of families to their child's learning, right away and often • Expect parents to be engaged in helping their child learn at home and other out-of-school settings • Clarify how parents can help; provide options that are meaningful and acceptable to them • Encourage parents to be assertive • Develop a family-school agreement
	Reduce barriers • Have contact with parents early in the school year • Establish ongoing communication systems; include "good news" phone calls • Use two-way communication formats that are both school-to-home and home-to-school • Bridge the language gap; strive to have the best communication between school and home with all parents, including those who speak a language other than English
	Create a spirit of cooperation • Explore what goals parents have for their child • Devise opportunities for engagement that parents see as practical and meaningful

(continued)

Table 1 (continued)	• Reach out to parents with warmth, friendliness and sensitivity

	Take parents' perspectives
	 • Identify why parents might not be involved
	   – Diverse background experiences of parents with schools
	   – Economic and time constraints
	   – Diverse linguistic and cultural norms
	 • Recognize that resistance is a form of communication
	   – Failure to achieve a connection between home and school highlights the lack of understanding about what is important to each party rather than the presence of resistance
	   – Rather than defining parents as resistant, appreciate that they may simply hold different perspectives that need to be understood

	Make the school welcoming and family friendly • Create a physical appearance that is inviting and open to all • Consider whether the affective climate (unwritten and unspoken messages and attitudes about students and families) fosters warmth, sensitivity, and trust, or judgment and preconceived notions
	Consider a range of other strategies • Use technology-mediated forms of communication that preclude the need to be physically present (e.g., Skype, Facetime, text messaging) • Offer flexible scheduling • Provide information and data in advance of meetings, and explain planning/partnering processes • Create opportunities to connect with parents when they are already attending school events • Use multiple efforts; no one way will work for all families • Make events fun for families • Plan for logistical barriers (e.g., work schedules, transportation, child care) and build in flexibility • Invite parents to help determine the best way for them to be involved • Meet parents "on their turf" • Identify a parent in the school who can help spread positive messages • Make sure roles for parents are meaningful to them
	Adapted from Sheridan et al. (2014a)

5 Challenges of Family-School Partnerships in the Rural Context

Despite the overwhelming support for family-school partnerships, in general, and in the rural context, in particular, there are challenges associated with the practice of family-school partnerships in rural communities. Realities faced by rural schools as well as families pose unique context-specific practice challenges to family-school partnerships.

5.1 Increased Demands and Limited Access to Services

Schools in rural communities are expected to meet multiple needs of students, including those that are educational, behavioral and social-emotional in nature (National Education Association 2008; Roeser and Midgley 1997; Witte and Sheridan 2011). Unfortunately, the geographic isolation of rural schools often results in limited resources to support efforts to meet the educational demands placed on them, and they are further limited in their access to additional or specialized resources to meet a wider range of student needs (Arnold et al. 2005; Howley and Howley 2004; Monk 2007). In a real sense, they are expected to "do more with less" (Barley and Beesley 2007). While the demands on schools to increase student achievement levels continue to rise, further complications result from a myriad of realities in the rural school context: school closures and consolidations, high rates of teacher turnover, and a large number of teachers who are early in their careers and might lack the experience necessary to meet increased student demands beyond traditional educational needs (Barley and Beesley 2007; Jerald 2002; Monk 2007).

Given the limited resources for rural schools and families and high demands placed on rural educators to meet student needs, families have the potential to serve as a significant resource (Witte and Sheridan 2011). In some cases, the physical locations of school buildings, families' homes, and teachers' residences creates distance barriers for collaborative, relationship-building meetings between parents and teachers. School consolidations have increased the distance from homes to schools for many rural educators and families (Phillips et al. 2007), creating challenges associated with access to parents and effective, frequent family-school interactions. Distance also creates difficulties when specialized staff are necessary to structure or support the partnership; such specialized service providers (e.g., school psychologists) frequently work across multiple school districts, travel extensively for their jobs (McLeskey et al. 1984), and may therefore be unavailable for participation. Indeed, parents and teachers have reported that the physical locations of school buildings, families' homes, and teachers' residences creates distance barriers and further constraints on their time for collaborative, relationship-building meetings (Kushman and Barnhardt 2001; McBride et al. 2002). Finally, school personnel (e.g., teachers and administrators) often lack training in how to effectively engage families as a partner in students' education, including effective communication strategies and cultural sensitivity (Agbo 2007; Dornbusch and Glasgow 1996; Witte and Sheridan 2011).

5.2 Relational Characteristics of Rural Communities

Lack of availability and access to specialized services for rural families is not the only challenge. For some families, partnerships focus on addressing student concerns regarding academic, behavioral or social-emotional functioning. Due to the small size of rural communities and multiple relationships among their residents, there may be challenges associated with lack of privacy, stigma associated with seeking help for problems, lack of trust of outside professionals, and fear of judgment from community members (Beloin and Peterson 2000; Owens et al. 2007). Rural communities have closely connected professional and social networks, enabling information and attitudes to spread quickly among community members. Parents may fear that other family members, friends, and colleagues will discover their need for intervention or other private information (Larson and Corrigan 2010), and react with skepticism even when confidentiality is promised. Realities that might further hinder families' abilities or desires to access specialized services are linked to demographic factors of the changing face of rural communities, including high poverty rates, parents with lower levels of formalized education, immigrant families or single parents (Grey 1997; Schafft et al. 2008).

Despite the potential for families to partner with schools as a viable resource in supporting the educational success of their students, families in rural settings experience certain realities that pose challenges to effective practice of family-school partnerships. In a study of rural, Hispanic families, Smith and colleagues (2008) found that despite parents' desires to be involved in their children's education, they lacked the knowledge of how to become involved in a meaningful ways that contributed to their children's education, and they did not feel welcomed in their children's schools. Previous, negative histories of interactions between parents and their children's teachers can hinder families' desires to partner with school personnel. It is not uncommon in rural communities for teachers of current students to also have taught the parents of those students. Thus, parents and teachers in rural communities may have long-standing relationships and histories of previous interactions (some predating current school situations) that influence their initial abilities to work together as partners.

6   Teachers and Parents as Partners (TAPP)

One family-school partnership intervention that demonstrates promise in rural communities is Teachers and Parents as Partners (TAPP; also known as Conjoint Behavioral Consultation; Sheridan et al. 1996; Sheridan and Kratochwill 2008). TAPP is a consultative approach wherein parents and teachers work as joint consultees under the guidance of a trained consultant to address students' academic delays and social-behavioral challenges through structured, collaborative problem-solving interactions. Consistent with other family-school partnership interventions, the primary goals of TAPP are to improve students' academic, behavioral, socioemotional functioning at home and school and build the capacity of parents and teachers to effectively work together to support students' healthy development (see Table 2 for a detailed list of the goals of TAPP). In TAPP, positive outcomes for students are realized when constructive and quality relationships are established and supported between parents and teachers allowing them

Table 2 Goals and objectives of CBC

Goals
1. Promote healthy development of children through cross-system intervention development
2. Build the capacity of families and educators for data-based decision making and evidence-based intervention implementation
3. Establish and strengthen home-school partnerships
Outcome objectives
1. Obtain comprehensive, functional progress monitoring data over time and across settings
2. Establish intervention plans across home and school and program for generalization and maintenance of intervention effects
3. Improve skills, knowledge, and behavior of families and educators for immediate and ongoing problem-solving
Relational objectives
1. Establish and strengthen relationship within and across home and schools
2. Improve communication, knowledge, and understanding across home and school to maximize opportunities to meet the needs of the family, child, and school
3. Promote perspective taking, shared ownership of educational goals, and joint responsibility for problem solution
Adapted from Sheridan et al. (2014b)

to engage in collaboration, problem-solving, and evidence-based intervention implementation (Sheridan et al. 2012).

6.1 TAPP Objectives and Stages

Meaningful changes in students' behaviors during TAPP are accomplished through attaining specific relational and structural objectives that co-operate to support positive, working relationships between parents and teachers, allowing them to engage in constructive and meaningful problem-solving (Sheridan et al. 2014b). The relational objectives of the TAPP intervention are concerned with building and promoting partnerships to provide the foundation for parents and teachers to work together to support student success. The structural objectives, which are concerned with student-focused results that occur with successful problem-solving, provide the means and organization for effectively addressing students' difficulties across home and school.

Relational and structural objectives of TAPP are met through a four stage collaborative problem-solving sequence in which parents and teachers share responsibility for identifying the strengths and prioritizing a concern to address for each student and conjointly contribute to the development, implementation, and evaluation of evidence-based intervention plans across home and school (Sheridan and

Kratochwill 2008). Semi-structured interviews and ongoing, reciprocal contacts among parents, teachers, and a trained consultant are used to guide the consultation team through the problem-solving objectives of each stage of TAPP (see Fig. 1 for a depiction of TAPP meeting objectives).

During the *Building on Strengths* interview, the consultant and consultees (i.e., parents and teachers) work together to set goals for consultation and establish a collaborative, working relationship. The team jointly identifies the assets of the student, family, and school and agrees upon and operationally defines a behavioral concern that will be targeted during the process. Consultees collaboratively set meaningful and achievable behavioral goals for the student and identify the unique environmental conditions that may impact the presentation and maintenance of the target behavior. Hypotheses are generated about the function the student's behavior may serve at home and school (e.g., access to adult attention, escape from demands) and valid procedures for collecting pre-plan, baseline data are established. After baseline data have been collected, individualized home and school behavior plans

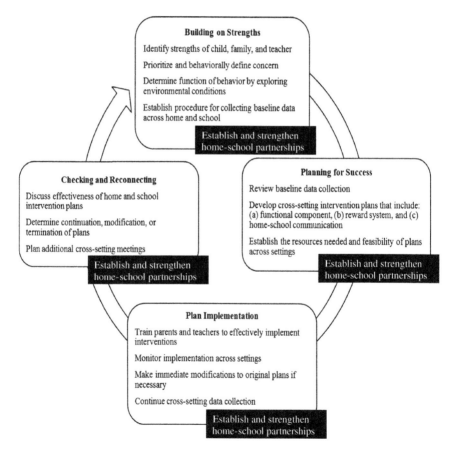

Fig. 1 TAPP stages and meeting objectives

are discussed during the *Planning for Success* interview. Cross-setting intervention plans are collaboratively developed that build upon the competencies of the student, parents, and teacher; address the hypothesized function of the target behavior; reward the student's progress toward behavior goals; and create methods for consistent and frequent communication between home and school. Consultants support parents' and teachers' implementation of the cross-setting behavior plans during the *Plan Implementation* stage. During this stage, consultants remain in close contact (e.g., phone calls, personal visits, e-mail communication) with parents and teachers to support accurate implementation of the developed interventions. Consultants provide parents and teachers with ongoing coaching and skills-based training, including performance feedback regarding their implementation of the plan (Noell et al. 2005) and modeling and rehearsing plan steps. Consultees continue to monitor their adherence to the plan (Swanger-Gagne et al. 2009) to ensure the intervention fits within each home and school context (Durlak and DuPre 2008) and can be implemented with fidelity. The efficacy of the intervention plans are evaluated during the *Checking and Reconnecting* interview. Data collected during baseline and the plan implementation stages are used to determine the attainment of consultation goals and discuss the need to continue the intervention, terminate the process, and/or plan for maintenance and follow-up. Plans for future partnering and problem-solving between the parent and teacher are developed through reviewing the relevance of the skills established and strategies used during the process, identifying methods for continued open communication, and preparing for future collaborative problem-solving meetings.

6.2 Research Support for TAPP

Decades of randomized controlled trial (Sheridan et al. 2012) and single case experimental research (Sheridan et al. 2001) conducted in non-rural settings support TAPP as an effective intervention to improve the functioning of students and their family homes and teachers' classrooms. Individual experimental studies have examined the use of TAPP to address a variety of student difficulties. These small-*n* and single case studies have shown TAPP effectively addresses student academic concerns (e.g., Galloway and Sheridan 1994; Weiner et al. 1998), social problems (e.g., Sheridan et al. 1990), and disruptive behaviors (e.g., Ray et al. 1999). These outcomes have been replicated with large-scale experimental studies of TAPP. Sheridan and colleagues (2012) conducted a randomized controlled trial with a sample of kindergarten through third grade students identified with disruptive behavior problems. The students that received TAPP showed significant improvements on teacher reports of their adaptive functioning and social skills. Parents of students receiving TAPP reported significant reductions in the frequency of their children's arguing, defiance, noncompliance, and tantrums at home (Sheridan et al. 2013) and improvements in their social skills (Sheridan et al. 2012).

Findings from this research suggest the effects of TAPP extend beyond student outcomes. For example, Sheridan and colleagues (2013) found that parents who received TAPP reported greater improvements in their perceived competence to engage in educational problem solving compared to reports from parents in the control groups (Sheridan et al. 2013). In fact, TAPP consistently results in improvements in the quality of the relationship between parents and teachers (Sheridan et al. 2006, 2012). Recently, this relationship has been identified as critical to the success of TAPP. Sheridan et al. (2012) found the quality of parent-teacher relationship partially mediated the effects of TAPP on students' social skills (Sheridan et al. 2012).

7 TAPP in Rural Communities

Like other family-school partnership programs, TAPP theory and practice is undergirded by an ecological-systems perspective (Bronfenbrenner 1977). As such, emphasis is placed on the interactions and relationships within *and* among the primary environments (i.e., home, and school) and local contexts (e.g., community) that support students' development and shape their learning and functioning. This consideration of environmental, contextual, and relational conditions that influence students' development uniquely positions TAPP to bypass challenges faced by rural parents and teachers seeking to work together to address students' difficulties while building upon the inherent strengths of rural communities. The following sections discuss features of TAPP that address common challenges in rural communities associated with access to services, lack of privacy, and stigma associated with accessing specialized support services.

7.1 Availability of and Access to Acceptable Services

By definition, rural communities are geographically isolated and specialized services to address students' behavioral, emotional, and academic difficulties are often unavailable, inaccessible, or unacceptable in these communities (DeLeon et al. 2003). There is often a reliance on rural schools to provide specialized services; however, rural schools often lack the necessary infrastructure (e.g., professional development, onsite support) to effectively meet the needs of students with emotional and behavioral difficulties (Malhoit 2005; Monk 2007; Thornton et al. 2006). TAPP addresses challenges to partnerships in rural settings by providing access to evidence-based instructional and behavioral supports. Intentional emphasis is placed on building the capacity of parents and teachers to effectively work together to address students' behavioral, emotional, and academic concerns. Meaningful communication and cooperative, solutions-focused interactions between parents and teachers are planned, modeled, and reinforced throughout the process with the goal of promoting future partnering and problem-solving. Considerable efforts are made to provide parents and teachers with the skills and rationale to allow them to appropriately identify behavioral concerns, develop methods for monitoring students' behavior, set achievable and challenging behavioral goals for students, and implement and evaluate effective strategies to support students' development. Yet, the long-term impact of TAPP depends on the fit of TAPP within the daily activities of rural educators and families. Mutual input toward solutions and a consideration of contextual features that may facilitate or hinder the implementation of behavioral interventions is solicited to ensure services are acceptable to rural parents and teachers and feasible to implement within each child's unique home and school environment.

7.2 Establishment of Relational Supports and Partnerships

Fears about being judged, distrust, and lack of privacy may prevent rural parents and teachers from working together to address students' difficulties (Beloin and Peterson 2000; Owens et al. 2007). TAPP's strengths-based and goal-oriented approach may increase trust between parents and teachers and improve attitudes about partnering to improve students' behavior (Sheridan et al. 2015). Rather than placing blame on any individual or assuming the student's problems are the result of internal causes, focus is placed on identifying and modifying environmental conditions that contribute to students' difficulties. Efforts are made to build upon the existing strengths and competencies of students, parents, and educators to promote shared ownership and mutual accountability for developing solutions.

8 Research Support for TAPP in Rural Communities

Recent and ongoing research extends the empirical support for the efficacy of TAPP to rural communities. In this section, we report the preliminary results of a recently completed five-year large-scale randomized controlled trial evaluating the efficacy of TAPP for rural students with challenging behaviors. The purpose of the study was threefold: (a) to identify the effects of TAPP in rural communities on students' behavioral and social-emotional outcomes; (b) to determine TAPP's effects on rural teachers' and parents' use of effective behavioral strategies and problem-solving skills; and (c) to discern the effects of TAPP on parent and teacher partnership outcomes. The study involved 250 students and their parents, and 146 teachers across 45 rural schools in three Midwest states. Rural designation was defined using the National Center for Education Statistics (NCES) urban-centric locale designation system whereby schools fall into a locale category based on community population size and proximity to a densely settled urbanized area. Schools in NCES designated rural communities and towns were included. Participating students were identified by teachers as having disruptive behavior concerns (e.g., aggression, non-compliance). Teachers were randomly assigned to treatment and control groups and all students within a classroom were assigned accordingly. Measures of students' behavioral and academic outcomes, parent and teacher effects, and partnership quality were used to evaluate the efficacy of TAPP. Additionally, the degree to which TAPP "fits" into rural communities as a feasible and acceptable approach was assessed.

8.1 Preliminary Outcomes of TAPP in Rural Communities

Student outcomes. Initial analyses of parent and teacher reports of students' functioning and direct observations of student behavior indicate that TAPP is effective for reducing rural children's problem behaviors and improving their prosocial skills. Relative to a business-as-usual control group, students who received TAPP demonstrated a significant reduction in parent-reported externalizing problems and teacher-reported school problems (measured on the Behavior Assessment Scale for Children; Reynolds and Kamphaus 2004). Independent observations confirmed that compared to students in the control group, TAPP students showed significantly greater increases in appropriate social behavior and engagement in academic activities, as well as a significant decreases in off-task behavior, distracting peers (interference), and inappropriate motor movements (Sheridan et al. 2015).

    Parent and teacher outcomes. Consistent with objectives of TAPP, preliminary evidence suggests the effects extend beyond student outcomes to influence rural parents' and teachers' practices. Relative to the control group, teachers who received TAPP reported significant improvements in their use of effective teaching strategies and competence to use problem-solving to remediate students' difficulties in the classroom. Corroborating evidence from direct observations of teachers' behavior suggests teachers who participated in TAPP delivered significantly more positive attention and rewards than the teachers in the control group (Sheridan et al. 2015).

    Results for rural parents also suggest that TAPP helps parents develop the necessary skills to address problem behaviors at home. Relative to the control group, parents who received TAPP reported a significant improvement in parenting strategies (measured on the Alabama Parenting Questionnaire; Dadds et al. 2003) and competence in problem solving (Sheridan et al. 2014c). Given the paucity of services available to rural parents and teachers, TAPP appears to be a promising method to increase families' and schools' access to effective behavioral supports and build rural teachers' and parents' skills to address problem behaviors.

    Partnership outcomes. In addition to behavioral outcomes, TAPP has shown to overcome some of the challenges with establishing constructive family-school partnerships in rural communities. In particular, relative to the control group both parents and teachers who received TAPP reported significant improvements in their relationships with each other. Moreover, both rural parents and teachers reported improvements in engagement in consultation activities (Sheridan et al. 2014c, 2015).

8.2 "Fit" of TAPP in Rural Communities

Despite promising outcomes, TAPP's long-term impact on rural communities is dependent on how well it fits the daily realities faced by rural schools and families. Parents and teachers must find TAPP beneficial and feasible for it to meet the needs of rural students. Initial reports indicate that TAPP is indeed a viable intervention for rural communities. One father reported that TAPP was an efficient way to meet his son's needs saying, "The benefits far exceed any time or effort required of the parent." Similarly, a second-grade teacher explained that what she most enjoyed about TAPP was that "it has been very beneficial to the students and their families who participated." According to parents and teachers, TAPP is particularly beneficial to rural students. As one first-grade teacher stated, "TAPP provides access to resources and ideas that wouldn't otherwise be available in a small school." The father of three boys stated "I grew up in small schools and I appreciate them so much, but I think to bring TAPP to a smaller rural school is a huge benefit for the community because it brings in resources that might not be there otherwise." Furthermore quantitative survey data reveal that parents and teachers find TAPP highly acceptable. On a 15-item survey designed to capture the acceptability of TAPP, parents rated TAPP as 5.05 and teachers rated TAPP as 5.07 (1 = strongly disagree, 6 = strongly agree).

9 Rural Family-School Partnerships: Future Research Directions

Despite what is known about the empirical and practical benefits of family-school partnerships in rural settings, a significant number of elusive issues remain in need of careful and intentional empirical attention. Some areas for future research follow.

9.1 Access and Relationships

Rural schools are by definition distal and sometimes very small. As described previously, access to the availability of family-school partnerships is challenging for several reasons. Research addressing these logistic and interpersonal challenges to family-school partnerships in rural settings is sorely needed. The use of technology is being explored as a potential means to bridge families and schools. For example, digital video conferencing may provide a method by which personal interactions between teachers and parents can occur without the need for travel. Web-based distance meeting software (e.g., WebEx) can provide an inexpensive and convenient tool for parents and teachers to meet for purposes of creating and maintaining partnerships. The use of cellular or internet technology (e.g., text messages, email), social media (e.g., Facebook, Instagram, Twitter) and other platforms hold promise as potential sources for supporting partnerships. Very little research has been conducted on the utility and efficacy of these formats and represent significant directions for research investigations.

Beyond technology addressing logistical issues, the relational aspects involved in creating and sustaining family-school partnerships in rural communities are significant. Promoting partnerships in rural settings may benefit from intentional efforts to create climates that are positive, inviting, and rewarding for parents and teachers to work together in constructive ways. Processes described in previous sections may be particularly effective in rural schools, yet research has not identified evidence-based practices for establishing and sustaining rural family-school partnerships. Interventions that support family-school connections have the potential to positively impact students, parents, and teachers, and the connection between the school and the community may be a critical component of effective rural schools. It is likely that the practice of forming and sustaining family-school partnerships in rural schools may differ from other settings; however, too few studies have been conducted with research questions that investigate the unique and specific effects of the rural context on family-school connections and outcomes. Finally, additional unknown barriers to the development of family-school connections may be present in rural communities, warranting greater attention to the importance of uncovering specific and operational strategies fostering connections within rural school settings.

9.2   Implementation and Sustainability

The long-term benefit of interventions in rural schools is dependent upon the capacity of the system to sustain evidence-based programs within its typical structures. That is, it is necessary that interventions identified as efficacious through grant-supported research programs in highly controlled conditions be tested within the context of natural school practices. The effectiveness of family-school partnership interventions for promoting social and behavioral competence and positive, high-quality relationships between parents and teachers given a rural school's available internal resources (i.e., once an externally-supported program "goes away") requires research attention.

Research is needed to determine methods to deliver family-school partnership interventions in rural schools with greater efficiency, while maintaining integrity of the process and student-focused interventions. Small numbers of staff members in rural schools require the adoption of several responsibilities; thus, additional requirements associated with parental engagement and social-behavioral support may increase burden. On the other hand, school personnel in rural schools often have a "do what it takes" mentality and challenges are often usurped by individuals with the capacity to intervene early. Empirical attention toward the interaction of unique practice and personnel characteristics in rural schools and the delivery of family-school partnership programs is warranted.

9.3   Increased Rigor

There is currently a dearth of studies conducted on family-school connections in rural settings. Those available in the published literature tend to be largely descriptive and take advantage of qualitative methods that explore the unique nuances of rurality. Hence, literature on the distinctive role and efficacy of rural family-school partnerships and their role at producing generalizable outcomes is currently underdeveloped (Semke and Sheridan 2012). It is essential that research in the area of rural family-school connections increase, with particular emphasis on studies using sound quantitative, qualitative or mixed method designs.

Much more research is needed that is designed to draw clear and causal relationships associated with the efficacy of family-school partnerships within rural educational settings. When testing the efficacy of interventions to promote family-school partnerships, evidence of random assignment, reliable and valid measures, implementation fidelity, and statistical validity is necessary. Furthermore, highly rigorous qualitative and mixed methods research is needed to address certain questions about rural context and place-based education. Any one type of research is not sufficient to advance a rich and broad agenda, and the strength of conclusions one can draw is bound by the rigor of the design used. A general call for increased sophistication and rigor in research related to family-school partnerships in rural schools is made, irrespective of the methodological paradigm employed.

9.4   Unique Aspects of Family-School Partnerships in Rural Contexts

Within rural schools, the distinctions of what type of family-school paradigm works for which students in what contexts or under what conditions is of significant importance (Semke and Sheridan 2012). Questions about operative elements of rural family-school partnerships to achieve distinctive outcomes are relevant and in need of research attention. Arnold and colleagues (2005) called for research that addresses parent expectations for student achievement, asserting that schools can improve student achievement by encouraging parents and community members to recognize the potential of high academic aspirations and expectations. This is one aspect of family/parent involvement, but only a small component of what we envision as family-school partnerships to boost learning and achievement. Also necessary are broadened questions that begin to ask about relevant roles and novel practices for rural families and schools to work together to promote student achievement. Continued research on the efficacy of actions associated with joint decision making, collaborative problem-solving, complementary learning opportunities, and relevant out of school activities are ripe areas for research attention in rural schools.

Acknowledgments This research was supported by grants awarded to the first author by the U.S. Department of Education's Institute of Education Sciences (R324A100115; R305C090022).

References

Agbo, S. A. (2007). Addressing school–community relations in a cross-cultural context: A collaborative action to bridge the gap between First Nations and the school. *Journal of Research in Rural Education, 22*, 1–14.

Arnold, M., Newman, J., Gaddy, B., & Dean, C. (2005). A look at the condition of rural education research: Setting a difference for future research. *Journal of Research in Rural Education, 20*(6). Retrieved from http://www.umaine.edu/jrre/20-6.pdf

Barley, Z. A., & Beesley, A. D. (2007). Rural school success: What can we learn? *Journal of Research in Rural Education, 22*, 1–16.

Barnard, W. M. (2004). Parent involvement in elementary school and educational attainment. *Children and Youth Services Review, 26*, 39–62.

Bauch, P. A. (2001). School–community partnerships in rural schools: Leadership, renewal, and a sense of place. *Peabody Journal of Education, 76*, 204–221.

Beloin, K., & Peterson, M. (2000). For richer or poorer: Building inclusive schools in poor urban and rural communities. *International Journal of Disability, Development, and Education, 47*, 15–24.

Brody, G. H., Stoneman, Z., & Flor, D. (1995). Linking family processes and academic competence among rural African American youths. *Journal of Marriage and the Family, 57*, 567–579.

Bronfenbrenner, U. (1977). Toward an experimental ecology of human development. *American Psychologist, 32*, 513–531.

Bronfenbrenner, U. (1979). *The ecology of human development: Experiments by nature and design*. Cambridge, MA: Harvard University Press.

Bronfenbrenner, U. (1992). Ecological systems theory. In R. Vasta (Ed.), *Six theories of child development* (pp. 187–250). Philadelphia, PA: Jessica Kingsley.

Christenson, S. L., & Sheridan, S. M. (2001). *Schools and families: Creating essential connections for learning*. New York, NY: Guilford Press.

Dadds, M. R., Maujean, A., & Fraser, J. A. (2003). Parenting and conduct problems in children: Australian data and psychometric properties of the Alabama Parenting Questionnaire. *Australian Psychologist, 38*, 238–241.

DeLeon, P. H., Wakefield, M., & Hagglund, K. J. (2003). *The behavioral health care needs of rural communities*. Washington, DC: American Psychological Association.

Dornbusch, S. M., & Glasgow, K. L. (1996). The structural context of family–school relations. In A. Booth & J. F. Dunn (Eds.), *Family–school links: How do they affect educational outcomes* (pp. 35–44). Mahwah, NJ: Erlbaum.

Durlak, J. A., & DuPre, E. P. (2008). Implementation matters: A review of research on the influence of implementation on program outcomes and the factors affecting implementation. *American Journal of Community Psychology, 41*, 327–350.

Epstein, J. L. (1995). School/family/community partnerships: Caring for the children we share. *Phi Delta Kappan, 79*, 701–712.

Fan, X., & Chen, M. (2001). Parental involvement and students' academic achievement: A meta-analysis. *Educational Psychology Review, 13*, 1–22.

Fantuzzo, J., Tighe, E., & Childs, S. (2000). Family Involvement Questionnaire: A multivariate assessment of family participation in early childhood education. *Journal of Educational Psychology, 92*, 367–376.

Galindo, C., & Sheldon, S. (2012). School efforts to improve parental involvement and effects on students' achievement in kindergarten. *Early Childhood Research Quarterly, 27*, 90–103.

Galloway, J., & Sheridan, S. M. (1994). Implementing scientific practices through case studies: Examples using home-school interventions and consultation. *Journal of School Psychology, 32*, 385–413.

Grey, M. A. (1997). Secondary labor in the meatpacking industry: Demographic change and student mobility in rural Iowa schools. *Journal of Research in Rural Education, 13*, 153–164.

Henderson, A. T., & Mapp, K. L. (2002). *A new wave of evidence: The impact of school, family, and community connections on student achievement.* Austin, TX: Southwest Education Development Laboratory.

Henderson, A. T., Mapp, K. L., Johnson, V. R., & Davies, D. (2007). *Beyond the bake sale: The essential guide to family–school partnerships.* New York, NY: New Press.

Hoover-Dempsey, K. V., Walker, J. M. T., Sandler, H. M., Whetsel, D., Green, C. L., Wilkins, A. S., et al. (2005). Why do parents become involved? Research findings and implications. *Elementary School Journal, 106*, 105–130.

Howley, C. B., & Howley, A. A. (2004). School size and the influence of socioeconomic status on student achievement: Confronting the threat of size bias in national data sets. *Education Policy Analysis Archives, 12*, 1–35. doi:10.14507/epaa.v12n52.2004

Jerald, C. D. (2002). *All talk, no action: Putting an end to out-of-field teaching.* Retrieved from http://edtrust.org/wp-content/uploads/2013/10/AllTalk.pdf

King, S. B. (2012). Increasing college-going rate, parent involvement, and community participation in rural communities. *The Rural Educator, 33*(2), 20–26.

Kushman, J. W., & Barnhardt, R. (2001). Reforming education from the inside-out: A study of community engagement and educational reform in rural Alaska. *Journal of Research in Rural Education, 17*, 12–26.

Larson, J. E., & Corrigan, P. W. (2010). Psychotherapy for self-stigma among rural clients. *Journal of Clinical Psychology, 66*, 524–536. doi:10.1002/jclp.20679

Malhoit, G. C. (2005). *Providing rural students with a high quality education: The rural perspective on the concept of educational adequacy.* Washington, DC: The Rural School and Community Trust.

McBride, B. A., Bae, J., & Wright, M. S. (2002). An examination of family–school partnerships in rural prekindergarten programs. *Early Education and Development, 13*, 107–127.

McLeskey, J., Huebner, E. S., & Cummings, J. A. (1984). Issues in the delivery of psychological services in rural school settings. *Professional Psychology: Research and Practice, 15*, 579–589.

Miedel, W. T., & Reynolds, A. J. (1999). Parent involvement in early intervention for disadvantaged children: Does it matter? *Journal of School Psychology, 37*, 379–402.

Monk, D. (2007). Recruiting and retaining high-quality teachers in rural areas. *The Future of Children, 17*, 155–174.

National Education Association. (2008). *Rural education.* Washington, DC: Author.

Noell, G. H., Witt, J. C., Slider, N. J., Connell, J. E., Gatti, S. L., & Wi, K. L. (2005). Treatment implementation following behavioral consultation in schools: A comparison of three follow-up strategies. *School Psychology Review, 34*, 87–106.

Owens, J. S., Murphy, C. E., Richerson, L., Girio, E. L., & Himawan, L. K. (2008). Science to practice in underserved communities: The effectiveness of school mental health programming. *Journal of Clinical Child and Adolescent Psychology, 37*, 434–447.

Owens, J. S., Richerson, L., Murphy, C. E., Jageleweski, A., & Rossi, L. (2007). The parent perspective: Informing the cultural sensitivity of parenting programs in rural communities. *Child & Youth Care Forum, 36*, 179–194.

Pearce, L. R. (2009). Helping children with emotional difficulties: A response to intervention investigation. *The Rural Educator, 30*(2), 34–46.

Phillips, R., Harper, S., & Gamble, S. (2007). Summer programming in rural communities: Unique challenges. *New Directions for Youth Development, 114*, 65–73.

Ray, K. P., Skinner, C. H., & Watson, T. S. (1999). Transferring stimulus control via momentum to increase compliance in a student with autism: A demonstration of collaborative consultation. *The School Psychology Review, 28*, 622–628.

Reynolds, C. R., & Kamphaus, R. W. (2004). *Behavior assessment system for children* (2nd ed.). Circle Pines, MN: American Guidance Service.

Roeser, R. W., & Midgley, C. (1997). Teachers' views of issues involving students' mental health. *The Elementary School Journal, 98*, 115–133.

Schafft, K. A., Prins, E., & Movit, M. (2008). *Poverty, residential mobility, and persistence across urban and rural family literacy programs in Pennsylvania.* University Park, PA: Goodling Institute for Research in Family Literacy.

Semke, C. A., & Sheridan, S. M. (2012). Family-school connections in rural educational settings: A systematic review of the empirical literature. *School Community Journal, 22*(1), 21–48.

Sheldon, S. B., & Epstein, J. L. (2002). Improving student behavior and discipline with family and community involvement. *Education in Urban Society, 35*, 4–26.

Sheldon, S. B., & Van Voorhis, F. L. (2004). Partnership programs in U.S. schools: Their development and relationship to family involvement outcomes. *School Effectiveness and School Improvement, 15*, 125–145.

Sheridan, S. M., Bovaird, J. A., Glover, T. A., Garbacz, S. A., Witte, A., & Kwon, K. (2012). A randomized trial examining the effects of conjoint behavioral consultation and the mediating role of the parent-teacher relationship. *School Psychology Review, 41*, 23–46.

Sheridan, S. M., Clarke, B. L., & Christenson, S. L. (2014a). Best practices in promoting family engagement in education. In P. L. Harrison & A. Thomas (Eds.), *Best practices in school psychology: Systems-level services* (pp. 439–453). Bethesda, MD: National Association of School Psychologists.

Sheridan, S. M., Clarke, B. L., Knoche, L. L., & Edwards, C. P. (2006). The effects of conjoint behavioral consultation in early childhood settings. *Early Education and Development, 17*, 593–618.

Sheridan, S. M., Clarke, B. L., & Ransom, K. A. (2014b). The past, present, and future of conjoint behavioral consultation research. In W. P. Erchul & S. M. Sheridan (Eds.), *Handbook of research in school consultation: Empirical foundations for the field* (2nd ed., pp. 210–247). New York, NY: Taylor and Francis Group/Routledge.

Sheridan, S. M., Dee, C. C., Morgan, J., McCormick, M., & Walker, D. (1996). A multimethod intervention for social skills deficits in children with ADHD and their parents. *School Psychology Review, 25*, 57–76.

Sheridan, S. M., Eagle, J. W., Cowan, R. J., & Mickelson, W. (2001). The effects of conjoint behavioral consultation: Results of a four-year investigation. *Journal of School Psychology, 39*, 361–385.

Sheridan, S., Holmes, S., Witte, A., & Dent, A. (2015). CBC: Operationalizing a family–school partnership Tier III intervention. In S. A. Garbacz (Chair), *Family engagement across tiered mental health service delivery in schools.* Symposium conducted at the annual meeting of the National Association of School Psychologists, Orlando, FL.

Sheridan, S. M., & Kratochwill, T. R. (2008). *Conjoint behavioral consultation: Promoting family-school connections and interventions.* New York, NY: Springer.

Sheridan, S. M., Kratochwill, T. R., & Elliott, S. N. (1990). Behavioral consultation with parents and teachers: Delivering treatment for socially withdrawn children at home and school. *School Psychology Review, 19*, 33–52.

Sheridan, S. M., Kunz, G. M., Witte, A., Holmes, S., & Coutts, M. (2014c). *Rural parents and teachers as partners: Preliminary results of a randomized trial* (R²Ed working paper no. 2014-4). Retrieved from http://www.r2ed.unl.edu

Sheridan, S. M., Ryoo, J. H., Garbacz, S. A., Kunz, G. M., & Chumney, F. L. (2013). The efficacy of conjoint behavioral consultation on parents and children in the home setting: Results of a randomized controlled trial. *Journal of School Psychology, 51*, 717–733.

Sheridan, S. M., Witte, A., & Holmes, S. (in press). Case studies of randomized controlled trials in rural education settings. In J. Bovaird & S. M. Sheridan (Eds.), *Conducting education research in rural settings.* Washington, DC: U.S. Department of Education, Institute of Education Sciences.

Smith, J., Stern, K., & Shatrova, Z. (2008). Factors inhibiting Hispanic parents' school involvement. *The Rural Educator, 29*(2), 8–13.

St. Clair, L., Jackson, B., & Zweiback, R. (2012). Six years later: Effect of family involvement training on the language skills of children from migrant families. *The School Community Journal, 22,* 9–20.

Swanger-Gagne, M., Garbacz, S. A., & Sheridan, S. M. (2009). Intervention implementation integrity within conjoint behavioral consultation: Strategies for working with families. *School Mental Health, 1,* 131–142.

Thornton, B., Hill, G., & Usinger, J. (2006). An examination of a fissure within the implementation of the NCLB accountability process. *Education, 127,* 115–120.

Tompkins, R., & Deloney, P. (1994). *Rural students at risk in Arkansas, Louisiana, New Mexico, Oklahoma, and Texas.* Austin, TX: Southwest Educational Development Laboratory.

Weiner, R., Sheridan, S. M., & Jenson, W. R. (1998). The effects of conjoint behavioral consultation and a structured homework program on math completion and accuracy in junior high students. *School Psychology Quarterly, 13,* 281–309.

Witte, A. L., & Sheridan, S. M. (2011). Family engagement in rural schools. In S. Redding, M. Murphy, & P. Sheley (Eds.), *Handbook on family and community engagement* (pp. 153–156). Lincoln, IL: Academic Development Institute/Center on Innovation and Improvement.

Future Directions for Rural Education Research: A Commentary and Call to Action

Andrea D. Beesley and Susan M. Sheridan

Abstract Research in rural education is alive and well; the chapters in this book demonstrate that researchers are doing rural education work that is both rigorous and responsive to (and inclusive of) the communities in which it takes place. They are addressing a broad range of meaningful research questions and using multiple methods to approach the challenges inherent in rural research. In addition, these chapters call us to action to continuously improve our own research work and dissemination. In this final chapter we suggest some lessons for rural researchers taken from the work presented in the book, including the importance of explaining how rural is defined, describing the rural context of a study, addressing how the rural context affected the conduct of the research, considering multidimensional risk in rural environments, including a variety of stakeholders in research partnerships, trying rigorous designs even with small samples, being realistic about rural recruiting costs, and preparing for sustainability after studies end.

Keywords Rural education · Education research · Research design · Research partnerships · Small samples · Risk mitigation · Study recruiting · Dissemination

Research in rural education is alive and well. The chapters in this book demonstrate that rural education researchers are doing work that is both rigorous and responsive to (and inclusive of) the communities in which it takes place. They are addressing a broad range of meaningful research questions and using multiple methods to approach the challenges inherent in rural research. In addition, chapters in this volume call us to action to continuously improve our own research work and dissemination. What lessons do these chapters provide for those planning, conducting,

A.D. Beesley (✉)
IMPAQ International, Columbia, MD, USA
e-mail: abeesley@impaqint.com

S.M. Sheridan
Nebraska Center for Research on Children, Youth, Families, and Schools,
University of Nebraska–Lincoln, Lincoln, USA

© Springer International Publishing Switzerland 2017   291
G.C. Nugent et al. (eds.), *Rural Education Research in the United States*,
DOI 10.1007/978-3-319-42940-3_15

and reporting rural education research? Below we identify some suggestions based on the chapters that, if addressed routinely, could improve the state of rural education research significantly.

1 Explain How Rural Is Defined

Distance from urban areas and community size are usually part of rural definitions. As Hawley, Koziol, and Bovaird note in Chapter "Defining and Communicating Rural," however, the specific definitions of rural we choose matter a lot in determining a research problem and interpreting results. The definition chosen will provide the lens through which all subsequent aspects of the research study must be specified and interpreted. It will determine the sample being considered "rural" and the contextual features contained therein. Regardless of what approach to defining rural we choose, we must specify why we chose it, and articulate subsequent implications of the chosen definition for the study. It is also necessary to include our rural definitions in sensitivity analyses to determine the effect of the definitions on our results, and remain open to new developments in defining rural as our ability to bring together geospatial, economic, and demographic data improves.

2 Describe the Rural Context, Regardless of Definition

We know that rural communities in the same locale code or label can differ greatly. There is vast heterogeneity among rural contexts, communities, and regions. Economic, political, socio-cultural and spatial differences can be large. These factors will impact all aspects of the research enterprise—from collecting data (what kind, how much, and how) to analyzing and interpreting findings. In order for readers of rural research to understand where the work was conducted and how context may be influencing the results, we must describe the setting more completely. Chapters by Autio (Chapter "Recruiting Rural Schools for Education Research: Challenges and Strategies"), Deussen, Pfannenstiel and Gebhardt (Chapter "Improving Education Outcomes for American Indian Children: Community and Family Influences on Rural Student Academic Success"), and Sorensen and Price (Chapter "Accelerating the Mathematical Development of Young Navajo Children") provide excellent examples. When reporting results of studies conducted in rural contexts, information about the following will be helpful and informative to understanding the rural context being investigated:

- What do people do for a living in the communities or contexts studied?
- What access is there to community services like hospitals and libraries?

- How close is the community to transportation networks (e.g., bus stations, airports, interstate highways)?
- What are the socioeconomic circumstances of the community?
- What is the source of the community's economic base (e.g., agriculture, industry, recreation/tourism)?
- What type of work is available in the community (e.g., service, seasonal, factory) and how are work shifts defined?
- What are the demographic characteristics of the population or community (age, race, level of education, etc.)?
- What are the housing conditions of the community?
- How transient is the family and student population?

Reporting on variables such as these supports understanding of the rural research context, and may help build the body of literature around rural environmental factors that can impact educational outcomes. For example chapters in this volume describe research on reservations (Chapter "Accelerating the Mathematical Development of Young Navajo Children"), in the Deep South (Chapter "Rural Parenting: Cumulative Risk and Parenting Process"), in the Midwest (Chapters "The Effectiveness of E-Coaching in Rural Science Classrooms" and "Family-School Partnerships in Rural Communities: Benefits, Exemplars, and Future Research"), and at the national level (Chapter "The Effects of Rurality on Parents' Engagement in Children's Early Literacy"). Variables such as access to transportation, libraries, and social supports differ greatly within and across these regions, and their integration in the research design and analysis would go far in deepening our understanding of the diversity of rural context.

3 Explain How the Rural Context Affected Research Execution and Implementation

In rural research, the context can affect program selection and implementation as well as outcomes. When we report our studies, we need to address the effect of context at every stage of the work. If the program being studied was adapted or implemented differently than originally proposed because of some features of the rural context (as in Autio and Deussen in Chapter "Recruiting Rural Schools for Education Research: Challenges and Strategies"; and Sheridan, Kunz, Holmes, and Witte in Chapter "Family-School Partnerships in Rural Communities: Benefits, Exemplars, and Future Research"), readers will benefit from knowing the changes that were made and why. If there was something about the study that was especially appropriate to the rural setting, or unexpectedly difficult there, this information should be provided as well. Researchers need to unpack context as a mediator or moderator of outcomes within rural research studies, as Glover recommends in Chapter "Investigating Teacher Professional Development with Distance Coaching to Promote Students' Response to Reading Interventions in Rural Schools."

Rural researchers sometimes presume affective variables (e.g., sense of isolation, lack or presence of trust in researchers/outsiders, sense of community/relationships, value of education) to be present in the contexts we study. We can start to identify, define, and measure these variables within rural research settings in order to investigate and understand their presence, strength, and influence on educational practices and outcomes. For example, issues associated with the culture, socioeconomic status, educational background and workforce contribute uniquely to rural contexts. Along these lines, researchers have called for greater understanding of cultural and psychological constructs that may play into the rural definition (Koziol et al. 2015; Schafft and Brown 2000). We need to know more about which of these variables "matter" and which do not: whether they are predictive of outcomes and/or could moderate relationships between practices and outcomes.

4 Consider Multidimensional Risk in Rural Environments

While family socioeconomic status is the most influential factor in student outcomes in the U.S., Mokrova, Vernon-Feagans, and Garrett-Peters remind us in Chapter "Rural Parenting: Cumulative Risk and Parenting Process" to operationalize how risk in families affects children in rural-specific ways. To some extent, our work as rural education researchers focuses on mitigating risk to students: risk of low achievement or dropout, risk of students failing to achieve their full potential. Much of our research aims to solve problems, and student risk contributes to the presence of the identified problem. Identifying, analyzing and presenting descriptive data in the context of interventions is necessary. As Mokrova, Vernon-Feagans, and Garrett-Peters point out, changes in patterns of rural employment have negatively affected children because parents' non-standard work hours and multiple jobs interfere with parenting time. This is especially impactful on rural children because they have fewer resources for enrichment outside of family due to geographic isolation (for example, the lack of access to libraries as Clarke, Koziol, and Sheridan point out in Chapter "The Effects of Rurality on Parents' Engagement in Children's Early Literacy"). This issue connects to the need for high-quality early childhood programs that have been described by Knoche and Davis (Chapter "Rural Language and Literacy Connections: An Integrated Approach to Supporting Low-Income Preschool Children's Language and Literacy Development"), and Pfannenstiel and Gebhardt (Chapter "Improving Education Outcomes for American Indian Children: Community and Family Influences on Rural Student Academic Success"), and also points to the difficulty in delivering them in settings in which parents do not have access to reliable transportation or predictable schedules. These examples demonstrate that rural education researchers must develop and use our understanding of the research setting to fully appreciate how risk operates, and be open to the possibility that the risk is multidimensional.

5   Include a Variety of Stakeholders in Research Partnerships

Doing research in partnership with stakeholders promises to make rural education research more meaningful and successful. When the research matters to constituent groups, its findings are likely to have greater impact than research that is derived and executed devoid of situational or setting relevance. Sheridan, Kunz, Holmes, and Witte (Chapter "Family-School Partnerships in Rural Communities: Benefits, Exemplars, and Future Research") point out that there is theory to describe and support family-school partnerships, and this can be useful in framing partnership research in rural settings. Kunz et al. (Chapter "Partnership-Based Approaches in Rural Education Research") also make recommendations for partnership-based approaches based on researcher and practitioner input. Overall, collaborations and partnerships in rural research settings need to be multidirectional, moving from researcher to practitioner and practitioner to researcher. To be most responsive and beneficial, they should be concerned with issues identified within the field. Responsive researchers will work together with the practice community to advance the knowledge base across all stages of research (identifying needs, formulating questions, designing studies, proposing interventions/approach, collecting and interpreting data). This is necessary for not only the effective conduct of rural research, but also the efficient translation and sustainability of innovative practices gleaned from research. As researchers, we can place ourselves in the role of liaison or connector among participants in the partnership, and can help people explore issues broadly and on the basis of evidence.

This advice applies to any family and/or community partnerships with researchers. Fortunately in Chapter "Partnership-Based Approaches in Rural Education Research," Kunz et al. provide guidance regarding partnerships that is specific to rural education research. Rural partnerships are unique, and to be effective at bridging the two-way research-to-practice gap, partnerships should study interventions particularly suited for rural environments (such as the one Glover describes in Chapter "Investigating Teacher Professional Development with Distance Coaching to Promote Students' Response to Reading Interventions in Rural Schools" and Nugent et al. in Chapter "The Effectiveness of E-Coaching in Rural Science Classrooms"), grapple with the time needed to deal with geographical distance and the desire of people to connect face to face, use rural-appropriate methods (including those that Bovaird and Bash describe in Chapter "Methodology Challenges and Cutting Edge Designs for Rural Education Research"), and address any prior negative experiences that participants have had with education research. Rural research partnerships can also help researchers make sound decisions, such as those associated with adapting assessments and choosing appropriate interventions to minimize cultural intrusion, as so clearly described by Sorensen and Price (Chapter "Accelerating the Mathematical Development of Young Navajo Children") in their efforts to support families and schools and address achievement gaps.

6 Try Rigorous Designs

For policymakers, descriptive research is often useful to help understand how policies may play out in rural places. But when the concern is with determining the efficacy of programs, rural researchers struggle with small population size and low density. Bovaird and Bash (Chapter "Methodology Challenges and Cutting Edge Designs for Rural Education Research") provide help in the form of several methodological approaches that are especially suited for the rural environment. Multilevel modeling with cluster-randomized trials makes it possible to check for variance between sites, which is very characteristic of research in rural contexts. Stepped designs make the best use of the available samples and can be economically efficient when used with geographically-based cohorts. Usefulness of non-concurrent multiple baseline designs can work with both low-incidence populations and rolling recruitment and implementation. Planned missing data can be useful with smaller samples and limited measurement capacity. Sequential designs with sample size as a random variable can reduce cost and measurement burden. Finally, a wise choice of model fit measures can help with small samples. Adding to this, Glover addresses the possibilities in exploring certain factors within rural contexts as mediators (e.g., teacher knowledge or self-efficacy) to avoid one-size-fits-all approaches. Evaluations of variations in programs can help to determine optimal interventions.

Rural researchers who have been daunted by the problem of small samples with rigorous rural experimental and quasi-experimental approaches, and who have struggled with variations in the rural context, will no doubt be encouraged by these methodological advances. While these chapters may not prepare readers fully to determine when and how to use the approaches, they give hope that doing rigorous research in rural settings is feasible and practical—and should encourage us to develop meaningful partnerships with statisticians and research methodologists to help incorporate meaningful design and analytic elements into rural research.

7 Be Realistic About the Costs of Recruiting

Even if we use the latest techniques to conduct rigorous research in rural settings with small samples, there is a need to recruit research sites. Rural sites often have limited experience in conducting research, adding to the need to articulate clear guidelines and expectations, support rural school staff in participating, and respond to questions and issues promptly and effectively. In Chapter "Recruiting Rural Schools for Education Research: Challenges and Strategies," Autio and Deussen remind us of the need to be frank about the time and costs of recruiting and involving rural communities in research—but also encourage us keep pushing ourselves and colleagues to continue doing so. Rural places will never be particularly conveniently located. Recruiting will remain challenging, but research in nonrural areas has its own set of challenges too.

Autio and Deussen share several useful lessons in their research. For example, in recruiting for rural studies, we must elicit and understand the needs of rural education practitioners and students, and not assume that they are universal across all rural contexts. The choice of programs to study must also respond to the goals and needs of stakeholders, so that they feel a desire to participate. Rural researchers must respect any hierarchies present in their research contexts, and recognize that rural environments (where local control is prized) might be as top-down hierarchical as anywhere else. Finally, as they found, geographically isolated rural teachers may not agree to a classroom-based random assignment approach that further isolates them from their local professional community, so site-level assignment may be necessary.

Autio and Deussen's experience points out that it is unrealistic to think that high-quality recruitment can be completed without sufficient funds to carry out the work. This creates difficulties when research funders expect applicants to demonstrate full recruitment has been accomplished at the time of proposal submission. Indeed, there are clear differences in recruitment issues and their implications for researchers in rural versus urban and suburban settings. For example, in large urban or suburban environments, one large district may provide a sufficient sample; in that case, one letter may be all that is necessary to demonstrate full commitment. In a rural environment, a single district would rarely yield enough schools for a to sufficient study sample. Rural researchers often must spend time and money after a research award to firm up district commitments, recruit at the school level, and deal with turnover in district/school leadership. For the benefit of all educational researchers, and for rural researchers in particular, funders should support recruitment efforts to ensure successful program implementation.

8 Disseminate and Translate for Sustainability

Considering that so much has been done to improve the conduct of rural education research (as evident throughout this volume), we must also pay significant attention to understanding processes for translating and diffusing research findings into everyday practice. This is an issue in all of education research, but there are additional layers of the problem to consider in rural research. The long-term benefit of rural education research studies is dependent on how the findings will impact rural communities and stakeholders and change practice. What will be picked up and retained? How will those decisions be made by local policymakers and practitioners on the ground?

Efforts regarding translation are influenced by factors in the natural, immediate rural school setting. There is a need to determine how we move research-based elements into rural practices, classrooms, schools, and communities given all that we've learned about challenges associated with access, resources, and capacity for uptake in rural schools. Efforts regarding sustainability are influenced by decision-making processes that occur at the local level. The question for rural decision makers is: What research-based elements do we want to sustain? Characteristics of evidence-based interventions, the rural setting, school improvement goals, and expected outcomes likely influence these decisions, but we need to understand this better from a field-practitioner perspective in order to design and conduct research that will be beneficial in the long run.

The issue of dissemination and translation is a lens through which we can view the connections between all of the rural education research issues addressed in this book. To have the lessons of high-quality rural research understood and sustained in the field, we need to define and describe what rural is. We have to understand the complexities of the problem we are trying to solve (i.e., the risks we are trying to mitigate), and work in partnership with stakeholders to plan responsive action through research. We must adapt our programs, methods, and measures to the rural context, and explain how and why that occurred. We should choose the most rigorous methods that are available and feasible, and get a sufficient number of participants to enroll and engage in our studies. During and after our studies, we must share our results with our partners and with the wider field of rural education research. Only then will the increased demand for and execution of meaningful rural education research deliver on its promise to improve the educational experiences of millions of rural children across the U.S.

References

Koziol, N. A., Arthur, A. M., Hawley, L. R., Bovaird, J. A., Bash, K. L., McCormick, C., et al. (2015). Identifying, analyzing, and communicating rural: A quantitative perspective. *Journal of Research in Rural Education, 30*(4), 1–14.

Schafft, K. A., & Brown, D. L. (2000). Social capital and grassroots development: The case of Roma self-governance in Hungary. *Social Problems, 47*, 201–219. doi:10.1525/sp.2000.47.2. 03x0288b

CPSIA information can be obtained
at www.ICGtesting.com
Printed in the USA
BVOW07*0253140717

489339BV00004B/7/P